Literature & Nation

BRITAIN AND INDIA 1800–1990

edited by Richard Allen and Harish Trivedi

ROUTLEDGE

in association with

The Open
University

Published by Routledge
11 New Fetter Lane
London EC4P 4EE

Written and produced by The Open University
Walton Hall
Milton Keynes MK7 6AA

Simultaneously published in the USA and Canada by Routledge
29 West 35th Street
New York, NY 10001

First published 2000

Edited, designed and typeset by The Open University.

Printed and bound by Replika Press Pvt. Ltd., 100% EOU, Delhi 110 040.

A catalogue record for this book is available from the British Library

Library of Congress Cataloging-in-Publication Data

Literature and nation: Britain and India, 1800 to 1990 / edited by Harish Trivedi and Richard Allen.
　　p. cm.
　　Includes bibliographical references and index.
　　1. English literature – Indic influences. 2. English literature – 19th century – History and criticism. 3. English literature – 20th century – History and criticism. 4. Nationalism and literature – Great Britain – History. 5. Indic literature (English) – History and criticism. 6. Nationalism and literature – India – History. 7. Literature, Comparative – English and Indic. 8. Literature, Comparative – Indic and English. 9. Great Britain – Relations – India. 10. India – Relations – Great Britain. 11. Nationalism in literature. I. Trivedi, Harish. II. Allen, Richard, 1946 June 23–

PR129.I5 L58 2000
820.9'3254–dc21

00-042205

ISBN 0 415 21206 5 hardback

ISBN 0 415 21207 3 paperback

This book forms part of an Open University course A813 *Literature and Nation: Britain and India 1800–1990*. Details of this and other Open University courses can be obtained from the Course Reservations Centre, PO Box 724, The Open University, Milton Keynes MK7 6ZS, United Kingdom: tel. +44 (0)1908 653231.

For availability of this or other course components, contact Open University Worldwide Ltd, The Berrill Building, Walton Hall, Milton Keynes MK7 6AA, United Kingdom: tel. +44 (0)1908 858585, fax +44 (0)1908 858787, e-mail ouwenq@open.ac.uk

Alternatively, much useful course information can be obtained from the Open University's website: http://www.open.ac.uk

1.1

B010030/A813 Bk1i1.1

CONTENTS

CONTRIBUTORS

Dr Richard Allen is Dean of Arts at The Open University

Dr Vrinda Nabar writes on gender issues and was formerly Professor of English at the University of Bombay

Dr Lynda Prescott is Staff Tutor in Literature at The Open University

Dr Stephen Regan is Lecturer in English at Royal Holloway, University of London

Dr Harish Trivedi is Professor of English at the University of Delhi

PREFACE

Literature and Nation is in two parts. In the first part we aim to guide you into study of a series of major texts written in Britain or India from around 1800 to around 1990. The second part is an anthology of literary texts and historical documents from the same period, most of them now hard to find. Throughout, we focus on key themes – 'the White Man's Burden', 'liberal dilemmas', 'Gandhian nationalism', and so on – which we take to be vital to an understanding of colonial dominance and the struggle for independence. The period has many literary and historical moments that stand out: Thomas Babington Macaulay's arrogant dismissing of all Hindu literature in 1835; the insurrection of 1857, and its defeat; the apparent triumph of empire after 1876; the massacre at Amritsar in 1919; Independence and Partition in India in 1947; the development of a post-colonial state in both India and Britain. Our aim is to prompt you into thinking how these events and the social, economic and political processes that surround them interact with literature, and how literature is connected with empire- and nation-building in both Britain and India throughout this period.

Literature and Nation has itself been a work of British–Indian interaction. Discussions began on a bench in the gardens of the University of Delhi; planning and writing continued in Delhi, Kerala (where particular thanks are due to Dr T. Muraleedharan for help with the choice of several source texts), Chicago, Birmingham and Milton Keynes. Throughout, e-mail has enabled the constant mutual exchange of ideas. Thanks are also due to all involved with the book from The Open University, particularly Julie Dickens, and our ever helpful editors, Hazel Coleman and Alan Finch. Valuable comments on drafts came particularly from Dr Susheila Nasta, Dr W.R. Owens, Professor Judie Newman and Professor Dennis Walder.

Finally, the book is dedicated to our respective children, who have already moved on from literature to science, and from their own nation to one or two others, but who know that they bear in various ways an impress of the historical formations this book seeks to trace.

Richard Allen   *Milton Keynes/Delhi*
Harish Trivedi

HOW TO USE THIS BOOK

This book forms the basis of a module within the MA in Literature programme at The Open University. Those studying the course work through
the introductory chapters and write essays based on these themes and texts;
many go on to write a dissertation on a topic of their own devising. The
rationale and method of *Literature and Nation* relate to this context but also to
our own preoccupations. Thus, we focus on a series of specific texts rather
than construct a narrative overview because we want to insist that any
generalizations must stand up to the irreducible particularity and complexity of a novel, a poem or a play. The texts discussed in the opening
chapters are mostly canonical, because we wish even the most canonical of
texts to be read in a new and enquiring way, as appropriate to our theme
here. Through the anthology of texts that follows we aim to suggest the
richness of Indian writing in English and in the Indian languages in the
period, and to encourage a wide range of follow-up reading and research.

To provide you with the means to find out more for yourself, each introductory chapter begins with a section or two about basic sources relating to
the author and text. There follow interpretations and analyses with extensive references to critical materials, suggesting three or four different, often
competing, ways of reading the text. At the end of each chapter you will
find 'Questions and Exercises'. We hope you will find these interesting
enough to spend time on them, putting into practice some of the approaches
and ideas in the chapters, and thus helping fix them in your mind.
Occasionally you may suspect that we do have a particular 'take' on a text,
but our aim is to get you, the reader, to find your own way into the texts and
themes and ask your own questions to follow up the hypothesis set out in
Chapter 1: 'if generally there is always a link (of influence or determination)
between any literary text and "context" from which it emerges, and if the
particular text under discussion comes from a period of colonialism or
decolonization, then it follows that the particular text must be marked
in some way by colonialism or decolonization. The task is to find that
marking.'

1 LITERATURE AND HISTORY

by Richard Allen

Introduction

The chapters that follow are about 'literature', about 'nation', about 'Britain', about 'India', and about a particular period of history lasting two hundred years or so. They are also about the relationships between these separate terms, and so almost always focus on some permutation of literature *and* Britain *and* India *and* nation. Most of the chapters that follow concentrate on a single text or the work of a single author; each also addresses a particular theme that to us seems important for understanding Britain and India since around 1800. Concentrating on particular texts and events in this way is partly pragmatic – a way of dealing with a period rich in events and writings that have in turn inspired a wealth of commentary – but it also embodies a methodological principle that runs through the chapters, which we hope you will find stimulating. In abstract terms, we want to encourage you to adopt the position that the surest way of exploring large issues is one that involves the investigation of specific events and texts. To feel at all sure in our conclusions about what we might call 'macro' issues – such as nation, colonialism and identity – they must be anchored in the specifics of investigations at the 'micro' level.

At the 'macro' level we ask in effect what it means to say that for most of the nineteenth and twentieth centuries the relationship between Britain and India has been one of colonialism and empire. One response might be that during this time the relationships between Britain and India have been marked by a whole array of structures of power (involving inequality of one kind or another) which may be political, economic or – and this is the area that concerns us most here – cultural. How should we take the definition of 'colonial' and 'imperial' further? Should we, for example, confine our use of the terms just to relations *between* the countries? Might they not be as important *within* India – and *within* Britain? These power relationships may be relatively straightforward; for example, under colonial and imperial rule Indian soldiers did obey the orders of their British officers (orders that may well have had their origin in London). Often the process is more complicated. Historians regularly comment with surprise on the small numbers of British who were able apparently to control an almost immeasurably larger Indian population. One term that can help explain things here is 'hegemony'. This is a difficult word to define, but to say that the British established a hegemonic power in India is to say that there were particular elements in the system of colonial and imperial power of the British in India that made it work. First, the system of rule had a way of incorporating contradictions. In the colonial period the Indians and the British accepted that British values were superior and dominant in government and education, and yet they also accepted things that seemed to contradict this. Indian culture, for example, was acknowledged to have a strong spiritual and religious element and in this respect it was acknowledged as superior to British culture, which was dominated by materialist values. Furthermore, within the system of rule those who were 'subject' actually consented to being ruled; in cultural terms this means that Indians (particularly those in the classes more closely involved with the British in governing India) came somehow to accept that they should adopt some aspects of British culture and see it overall as superior. The value of literary study is that we can see these complexities worked out in particular examples.

At the 'micro' level we focus on a series of texts and periods that we take to be of particular significance. We use 1800 as a starting date for the period under review – suggesting that the same year heralded both the nineteenth century and the beginnings of the British colonial enterprise in India. Using the date 1800 does have some advantages as a kind of shorthand (indicating, for example, that nation and nationalism as we see them here are very much things that characterized the nineteenth century), but in fact there is considerable debate about the 'real' starting point for India as a British colonial entity. These issues are dealt with in Chapters 2 and 3, which in consequence cover texts from before and after 1800. We are in sympathy here with those historians who see 1800 as just too tidy a date for the end of one 'century' period and the beginning of the next – for us the period of 'the nineteenth century' is a long one, beginning around 1780. From there we move in Chapters 4 to 7 first to what might be described as the low point of British colonialism in 1857 and then to the period when the empire achieved its greatest extent – the years from 1890 to 1925. Finally, in Chapters 8 to 11 we focus on the period of the struggle for independence in India, and the loss of an imperial identity in Britain.

In these chapters we are drawing on what is known as 'post-colonial' literary study. We aim to engage your interest in the continuing debates in this new and developing area of study, and encourage you to develop your expertise further. (We hope you will not be satisfied just to be an observer in these debates, but will take up your own position.) Post-colonial criticism is both simple and complex; it contains certain common driving principles but also a wealth of debates, different positions, emphases and approaches. (Terry Eagleton's review of Gayatri Spivak's *A Critique of Post-Colonial Reason: Toward a History of the Vanishing Present*, in *London Review of Books*, 13 May 1999, vol.21, no.10, pp.3–6, provides a ready example of the fervour of those who debate ostensibly from the same general theoretical position.) It is underpinned by a belief that has informed literary studies for many years: that there is a connection between literary texts and the 'context'– social, political, economic, philosophical – from which they emerge.

Often the links made seem unproblematic – as when we conclude, for example, that the commercial and physical impact of railways in Britain in the mid-nineteenth century influenced Dickens's use of railways in *Dombey and Son* (1847–8), or that the cataclysmic events of war in Europe between 1914 and 1918 influenced the Modernist movement. The links become more problematic, however, when we push beyond the idea of influence to the idea of determination; when we assert that historical circumstances determine a particular literary text. As Raymond Williams has remarked, the idea of the 'individual autonomy' (or free will) of the author – and hence the individual text – has great power in Western culture, and people react sharply when it is challenged (see his *Marxism and Literature*, Oxford: Oxford University Press, 1977, pp.192–3). This is an issue at the heart of our project. Put baldly, the thesis to be argued and the task that follows from it are as follows:

> If generally there is always a link (of influence or determination) between any literary text and the 'context' from which it emerges, and if the particular text under discussion comes from a period of colonialism or decolonization, then it follows that the particular text must be marked in some way by colonialism or decolonization. The task is to find that marking.

It is only fair to add that the chapters that follow do more or less accept the validity of the thesis, and that lack of space limits us from referring to readings of the text that do not make the links we want to explore.

Each chapter provides details of historical and literary resources to prompt further thinking about the central text. We also set great store by comparative work: each chapter encourages study of the central text through comparisons with other texts, both literary and non-literary. From this it should be clear that we aim to encourage 'new historicist' readings of texts – readings, that is, which in Stephen Greenblatt's rather dense phrasing see them as 'complex symbolic and material articulations of the imaginative and ideological structures of the society that produced them' (quoted in *Modern Literary Theory: A Reader*, ed. by Philip Rice and Patricia Waugh, London: Arnold, 3rd edn, 1996; see also *A Handbook to Literary Research*, ed. by Simon Eliot and W.R. Owens (London: Routledge/The Open University, 1998, pp.150–58). Throughout we have sought a balance between well-known, canonical texts and those that are less familiar. In our choice of Indian texts we have also sought to avoid the assumption, too easily made in the West, that Indian writing consists largely of work by those writers who have an international publishing career. To carry these points home (particularly to make some element of comparative work available to all) and to complement the chapters that deal with our chosen texts, we are including here a collection of less well known and less easily accessible texts.

Understanding history: Britain and India

Throughout your study of individual texts you will find it useful to read as widely as possible in the history of India and Britain in the period since 1800 so as to gain a deeper knowledge of the political and social world from which the texts emerge. One of the books from the list below would make a good starting point. All the books have their own distinctive strengths and – as a matter of course – all have their own particular emphases. As you read, it is a good idea to try to work out what these emphases are; a useful exercise is to look at the way different historians treat the same events or the same people, asking yourself such questions as how they are described and what causes are said to lie behind the events. Initially you might find it best to examine major figures or events: Curzon or Gandhi, perhaps, or the events of 1857 or 1947.

Selected sources in modern Indian history

Sugata Bose and Ayesha Jalal, *Modern South Asia: History, Culture, Political Economy* (London: Routledge, 1998).

Judith Brown, *Modern India: The Origins of an Asian Democracy*, 2nd edn (Oxford: Oxford University Press, 1994).

Bipan Chandra, Mridula Mukherjee, Aditya Mukherjee, K.N. Panikkar and Sucheta Mahajan, *India's Struggle for Independence* (Delhi: Penguin, 1989).

A Cultural History of India, ed. by A.L. Barsham (Oxford: Clarendon Press, 1975).

Lawrence James, *Raj: The Making and Unmaking of British India* (London: Little, Brown, 1997).

Herman Kulke and Dietmar Rothermund, *A History of India*, 3rd edn (London: Routledge, 1998).

The Oxford History of India, ed. by Percival Spear (4th edn, Delhi: Oxford University Press, 1981).

Percival Spear, *India: A Modern History* (Ann Arbor: University of Michigan Press, 1971).

Burton Stein, *A History of India* (Oxford: Blackwell, 1998).

Stanley Wolpert, *A New History of India*, 2nd edn (Oxford: Oxford University Press, 1982).

Selected sources in modern British history

Linda Colley, *Britons: Forging the Nation 1707–1837* (London: Pimlico, 1994).

Peter Clarke, *Hope and Glory: Britain, 1900–1990* (London: Penguin, 1996).

George Dangerfield, *The Strange Death of Liberal England* (1936; London: Macgibbon and Kee, 1966).

Norman McCord, *British History, 1815–1906* (Oxford: Oxford University Press, 1991).

Keith Robbins, *The Eclipse of a Great Power, 1870–1975* (London: Longman, 1983; 2nd edn *The Eclipse of a Great Power, 1870–1992*, London: Longman, 1994).

Selected sources in the history of colonization and empire

P.J. Cain and A.G. Hopkins, *British Imperialism: Innovation and Expansion, 1688–1914* (London: Longman, 1993).

P.J. Cain and A.G. Hopkins, *British Imperialism: Crisis and Deconstruction, 1914–1990* (London: Longman, 1993).

E.J. Hobsbawm, *Industry and Empire* (London: Abacus Little, 1969).

Denis Judd, *Empire: The British Imperial Experience from 1765 to the Present* (London: Fontana, 1997).

The Oxford History of the British Empire: The Eighteenth Century, ed. by P.J. Marshall (Oxford: Oxford University Press, 1998).

Indian names in reference books and library catalogues

In the early period of British writing about India and the including of Indian books in British libraries, Indian names were transcribed phonetically according to the hearing and judgement of individual writers and cataloguers. Variations naturally occurred. Through the nineteenth century, especially as Anglicization meant that more Indians wrote their own names in English, these transcriptions became more standardized; variations still remain, though, which can make looking up writers in catalogues a bit of a hit and miss affair. Sometimes, a cataloguer may try to translate an Indian name to match the British 'second name, first name' format. Another might, on the other hand, aim for an authentic Indian version. Experience suggests that an unsuccessful search will succeed if one changes a vowel, or changes a single consonant to a double or vice versa. Puzzled by 'Mudrassa', for example, I eventually found an explanation under 'Madrasa'. Following up a passing reference in a book to 'Raja Ram Mohan Roy' in the British Library catalogues I found nothing until I searched for 'Raja Rammohun Roy'. Even more potentially frustrating, searching in the pre-1976 section of the same catalogue for the author 'Tagore' is quite ineffective as his works are catalogued under 'Ravindranatha Thakura'. Place-names can also require a little ingenuity. During British rule they became more or less standardized but since 1947 many have been changed to reflect more accurately the local pronunciation – 'Cawnpore' has become 'Kanpur', 'Poona' has become 'Pune' and 'Bombay' 'Mumbai'. In the chapters that follow we have mostly used modern versions although in extracts from other works and in quotations we have retained the spellings used in the source.

Understanding 'nation'

It is easy now to think of 'nation' and 'state' as being more or less one, and to think of almost all states being held together in differing degrees by feelings of national identity and nationalism. It is important to understand, however, that this has not always been so, just as it is important also to remember that forms of social organization (such as the nation and the state) vary in different cultures and continents across the world. In Europe, a series of changes affecting nation and state occurred around 1800. Through events such as the First Partition of Poland (1775), the American Declaration of Independence (1776) and the French Revolution (1789), and writings such as Fichte's *Addresses to the German Nation* (1807), nationalism became a genuinely potent force. In parallel, the idea that a state was formed on the basis of the rule of a great dynasty or ruling family lost its force. Revolution swept away the monarchy in France; in its place national identity and the idea of a more or less homogeneous French nation came to be the basis of the state. After 1800 this change spread across mainland Europe as Napoleon conquered country after country, deposing dynasty after dynasty and establishing members of his own family in their place. When Napoleon was defeated everything changed again, allowing further opportunities for nationalism and ethnic identity to become more powerful forces. Though Britain successfully resisted Napoleon and retained its ruling dynasty through all this, it was not immune to these changes, and the British state came increasingly to be understood as based on a national identity that was separate from its monarchs. The monarchy in turn learnt that its success depended on its being able to identify with this national spirit. Through the nineteenth century, nation states came into being across Europe, each centred in its own individual way on 'the possession in common of a rich legacy of remembrances' and 'the actual consent, the desire to live together, the will to continue to value the heritage which all hold in common' (Ernest Renan, 1882; quoted in *Nationalism*, ed. by John Hutchinson and Anthony D. Smith, Oxford: Oxford University Press, 1994, p.17). In turn, these were the principles which European states like Britain and France exported to inform their colonial ventures.

The briefest consideration of the history of Europe and colonialism since 1800 shows that nationalism has been pretty much the major source of civil war, persecutions and pogroms. Competition between nation states for power and resources has been an important cause of this rather depressing situation but there are other factors to take into account. In particular, although nation, ethnic identity and language are now more or less the only basis on which a state can be said to exist, paradoxically the number of modern states with anything like a homogeneous national identity that includes almost all the people is small. In contrast, in 30 per cent of modern states the 'nation' on whose identity the state is ostensibly built constitutes less than half the total population (see Walker Connor, 'A Nation is a Nation, is a State, is an Ethnic Group, is a ...', in *Nationalism*, pp.36–46 (p.39)). Such states are fertile ground for civil war, but in fact most do hold together because some potent but actually artificial idea of nation comes into play. Benedict Anderson in a seminal article coined the phrase 'imagined communities' to describe this process, while E.J. Hobsbawm in an equally important contribution to the debate wrote of states/nations 'inventing traditions' (extracts from both writers can be conveniently found in *Nationalism*, pp.89–96 (Anderson), and pp.76–83 (Hobsbawm)). The United States offers a clear example of all this in practice. Constantly in its institutions, practices and culture there are references to common 'American' values, yet geographically the overall nation state is vast, made up of a wide range of groups that might themselves claim to be nations – the whole entity mysteriously divided from the Canadian nation by a line on a map. In summary, the nation is as likely – if not more likely – to exist as an idea or aspiration, something that belongs in propaganda and sentiment, as it is to exist as a simple fact. The idea that the nation has a common language is almost always an important part of these ideas and aspirations, with that common language being seen as the basis of a common culture, and literature equally regularly plays a part. The existence of a national literary tradition signals that 'rich legacy of remembrances' to which Renan referred; translated into a school and university subject, literature becomes a valuable part of a nation-building education system.

Nation and nationalism can be part of decolonization in a quite straight-forward way. By reclaiming its traditions and sense of community the colonized group reclaims its standing as a nation and uses this identity as a strength in its struggle against the colonizing power. As I have already suggested, they have an important part to play also in the process of British colonization and empire-building. Thus, in India through the nineteenth century, education and other social institutions were recast so as to embody the principles underlying the British community and tradition and create a kind of 'super' English-speaking 'national' identity. (A survival of these ideas can be seen in the ambiguity of the title of Winston Churchill's *A History of the English-Speaking Peoples* (1956–8), which seems to make a claim for a unified and singular 'history' of an entity that it describes as plural.)

Two further examples relating to Britain and India may be helpful in under-standing how the idea of nation can be used in practice. The first comes from a Bill, proposed in the British Parliament in 1783, that was designed to limit corruption in the East India Company's activities in India. After cataloguing the possibilities for corruption, the Bill ends by saying that

> Parliament will give signal marks of its displeasure against any person or persons ... who shall wilfully adopt or countenance a system tending to inspire a reasonable distrust of the moderation, justice, and good faith of the British nation.

> (quoted in P.J. Marshall, *Problems of Empire: Britain and India 1757–1813*, London: George Allen and Unwin, 1968, p.161)

Rather vaguely, the 'victim' of this offence is the reputation of the British nation not the government or the Crown. The Bill thus intentionally keeps the offence at a distance from the British state. The second example is from *Hind Swaraj* by Gandhi, written in 1909 in the form of a dialogue between a 'Reader' and an 'Editor' (Gandhi himself):

READER: But I am impatient to hear your answer to my question. Has the introduction of Mahomedanism not unmade the nation?

EDITOR: India cannot cease to be one nation because people belonging to different religions live in it. The introduction of foreigners does not necessarily destroy the nation; they merge into it. A country is one nation only when such a condition obtains in it. That country must have a faculty for assimilation. India has ever been such a country.

(quoted in *The Penguin Gandhi Reader*, ed. by Rudrangshu Mukherjee, Delhi: Penguin, 1993, p.26)

In this passage Gandhi seems to be at the same time both evoking the power of the idea of nation and adapting it in a way that apparently contradicts aspects of its original formulation.

The ideas introduced briefly here are explored in much greater and more compelling detail in a number of the books listed below. Reading widely in these texts will help you develop your own position on the issues:

Benedict Anderson, *Imagined Communities: Reflections on the Origin and Spread of Nationalism* (London: Verso, 1991).

Partha Chatterjee, *The Nation and its Fragments: Colonial and Post-Colonial Histories* (Princeton: Princeton University Press, 1993).

Ernst Gellner, *Nations and Nationalism* (Oxford: Blackwell, 1983).

E.J. Hobsbawm, *Nations and Nationalism since 1780* (Cambridge: Cambridge University Press, 1990).

E. Kedourie, *Nationalism* (London: Hutchinson, 1967).

Mapping the Nation, ed. by Gopal Balakrishnan (London: Verso, 1996).

Nation and Narration, ed. by Homi Bhabha (London: Routledge, 1990).

Nationalism, ed. by John Hutchinson and Anthony D. Smith (Oxford: Oxford University Press, 1994).

In your reading you may also find discussions of how the development of English literary studies as an academic subject coincides with the development of national identity and the nation state. The issues are specifically explored in D.J. Palmer, *The Rise of English Studies* (Oxford: Oxford University Press, 1965), Chris Baldick, *The Social Mission of English Criticism, 1848–1932* (Oxford: Clarendon Press, 1983), and Gauri Viswanathan, *Masks of Conquest: Literary Study and British Rule in India* (London: Faber, 1989). This debate certainly seems an important one; as education spread and more schools and colleges were established, common syllabuses evolved, which formed the canon of English literature for many years. In passing, it is worth considering whether this process affected only English literary studies, or whether it had an effect on other subjects, such as archaeology and anthropology, which are also said to have originated in the latter part of the nineteenth century. Perhaps it is more useful to think about the development of English literary studies in the context of the development of other academic subjects in the same period, and relate all this in a broader interdisciplinary study to ideas of nation.

Literature, colonialism and post-colonialism

Alongside the reading of history suggested in the previous sections, it is useful to read more of what cultural and literary critics have said about the literary issues you will meet later. This means – as noted above – becoming more familiar with what is generally described as post-colonial criticism and theory. If you have not come across this work before, you can find a short general historical introduction in 'Post-Colonial Theory' by Dennis Walder, in *A Handbook to Literary Research*.

A good way into further understanding of the motivations and debates of post-colonial criticism is still via its classic texts: books such as Frantz Fanon, *The Wretched of the Earth* (1961; London: Penguin, 1967), Edward W. Said, *Orientalism* (1978; London: Penguin, 1985), or Bill Ashcroft, Gareth Griffiths and Helen Tiffin, *The Empire Writes Back* (London: Routledge, 1989). There are also now a number of general accounts of work in the area, for example Elleke Boehmer, *Colonial and Postcolonial Literature: Migrant Metaphors* (Oxford: Oxford University Press, 1995), Bart Moore-Gilbert, *Postcolonial Theory: Contexts, Practices, Politics* (London: Verso, 1997), and Dennis Walder, *Post-Colonial Literatures in English: History, Language, Theory* (Oxford: Blackwell, 1998). Another common route is via one of the anthologies of post-colonial writings that have been published – for example *Colonial Discourse and Post-Colonial Theory*, ed. by Patrick Williams and Laura Chrisman (London: Harvester Wheatsheaf, 1993), *Interrogating Post-Colonialism*, ed. by Harish Trivedi and Meenakshi Mukherjee (Shimla: Indian Institute of Advanced Study, 1996), or Padmini Monga, *Contemporary Postcolonial Theory: A Reader* (London: Arnold, 1996). Williams and Chrisman's anthology is useful in the present context because it explicitly covers both the colonial and the post-colonial and does so in a wide-ranging way. Moreover the introduction offers an account of the development of post-colonial criticism which parallels and complements that by Walder in *A Handbook to Literary Research*. Finally, Williams and Chrisman's editorial policy involves including a relatively smaller number of pieces at a relatively greater length than some others, which allows the reader to get a fuller sense of the ideas of the authors included.

In the rest of this section I want to tackle a particular aspect that many people, both beginners and readers more experienced in this subject area, find troubling: the peculiar and difficult language regularly encountered. Following our emphasis on reading texts in context, we might ask if there is something in the context of the period in which it is written that influences or causes this way of writing. Certainly post-colonial criticism came to the fore at a time when literary criticism in general was moving through a newly complex 'theoretical' phase, so perhaps we can find an explanation outside the post-colonial area itself. But it may be that the often complex nature of post-colonial writing does arise from inside the subject itself, from the fact that it requires new concepts and new structures of language and thinking. These are questions to think about further rather than to answer here. What I want to do instead – perhaps by way of groundwork for answering these questions – is to look in detail at two quite short passages (both from Williams and Chrisman's anthology). I have chosen extracts that seem to touch on important post-colonial issues, and I'll be trying to unpick the meaning, asking myself just why the language ends up in the way it does.

Cultural identity

The first extract is from a discussion of cinema in the Caribbean: 'Cultural Identity and Diaspora' by Stuart Hall (*Colonial Discourse and Post-Colonial Theory*, pp.392–403). The section I want to focus on comes early in the essay and shows Hall discussing two different ideas of cultural identity. Questions of cultural identity – 'Who am I?', 'Where do I belong?' – are of pressing concern for colonizers and colonized alike and are thus of great importance for thinking about the condition of living under colonialism; and since many stories, poems and plays present characters asking just these questions, they are of great importance in post-colonial literary study too. How, for example, might a young person growing up in India answer such a question? A person who lives within a traditional family structure at home and speaks an Indian language there, but who attends a school where the teaching is in English, wears an English-style school uniform, and is taught by an Indian teacher who seems to revere Shakespeare and Shelley? But equally, for example, how might a person in England, watching a film of British troops landing in Egypt in 1956, answer the same question?

For convenience I give some key extracts from the passage here; space constraints mean that I have had to edit things quite heavily – it is very much worth looking at the section (and the essay) in full.

> There are at least two different ways of thinking about 'cultural identity'. The first position defines 'cultural identity' in terms of one, shared culture, a sort of collective 'one true self', hiding inside the many other, more superficial or artificially imposed 'selves', which people with a shared history and ancestry hold in common. Within the terms of this definition, our cultural identities reflect the common historical experiences and shared cultural codes which provide us, as 'one people', with stable, unchanging and continuous frames of reference and meaning, beneath the shifting divisions and vicissitudes of our actual history. This 'oneness', underlying all the other, more superficial differences, is the truth, the essence, of 'Caribbeanness', of the black experience. It is this identity which a Caribbean or black diaspora must discover, excavate, bring to light and express through cinematic representation [...]

Crucially, such [rediscovered] images offer a way of imposing an imaginary coherence on the experience of dispersal and fragmentation, which is the history of all enforced diasporas. They do this by representing or 'figuring' Africa as the mother of these different civilizations. This Triangle is, after all, 'centred' in Africa. Africa is the name of the missing term, the great aporia, which lies at the centre of our cultural identity and gives it a meaning which, until recently, it lacked [...]

There is, however, a second, related but different view of cultural identity. The second position recognizes that, as well as the many points of similarity, there are also critical points of deep and significant *difference* which constitute 'what we really are'; or rather – since history has intervened – 'what we have become'. We cannot speak for very long, with any exactness, about 'one experience, one identity', without acknowledging its other side – the ruptures and discontinuities which constitute, precisely, the Caribbean's 'uniqueness'. Cultural identity, in this second sense, is a matter of 'becoming' as well as of 'being'. It belongs to the future as much as to the past [...] Far from being grounded in mere 'recovery' of the past, which is waiting to be found, and which when found, will secure our sense of ourselves into eternity, identities are the names we give to the different ways we are positioned by, and position ourselves within, the narratives of the past.

It is only from this second position that we can properly understand the traumatic character of 'the colonial experience'. The ways in which black people, black experiences, were positioned and subjected in the dominant regimes of representation were the effects of a critical exercise of cultural power and normalization [...] They had the power to make us see and experience *ourselves* as 'Other' [...]

[Adopting this second view of cultural identity means that] [t]he past [...] is always constructed through memory, fantasy, narrative and myth. Cultural identities are the points of identification, the unstable points of identification or suture, which are made, within the discourses of history and culture. Not an essence but a *positioning*. Hence, there is always a politics of identity, a politics of position, which has no absolute guarantee in an unproblematic, transcendental 'law of origin'. (pp.393–5)

Essentially, in this passage Hall seems to be contrasting two senses of identity: one that draws its strength from some deep-seated essential qualities (which may in the present be hidden or which people might be forbidden from expressing), and one that is much more shifting and changing – something existing in the present.

In a colonized or newly independent society, investigating identity in the first sense means searching for something real in the past – almost like an archaeologist searching for the remains of the original buildings that have been buried under more modern ones; in the second sense it needs some-thing like political activism, something involving planning, negotiation and struggle to achieve your aims and carry forward the interests of your social group. Stuart Hall's writing seems to me generally quite accessible but there are examples of that more difficult language which I want to explore. One that caught my eye was a matter of a single word in the following sentence: 'Africa is the name of the missing term, the great aporia, which lies at the centre of our cultural identity'. 'Aporia' was not a word I knew and was not in the first two dictionaries that I consulted. I eventually discovered that it means a doubt or a perplexing difficulty, so the point Hall is making is that, paradoxically, the essential identity that people seek does not lead to their becoming suddenly clear as to who they are and where they belong; rather it leads them to a state in which their original doubts are simply reiterated. Looking back on my struggle to work out what Hall meant here, I felt that:

1   If I had not found 'aporia' in the dictionary I could still have understood the gist of what Hall was saying from the other words, especially 'the missing term' – so I would have been well advised to press on and not get too caught up with this one individual difficulty.

2   Conversely, the word 'aporia' did actually add a particular meaning (that 'the missing term' was not straightforward but was to do with doubt and puzzle).

3   Finally, as someone familiar with poetic and literary language I could also see that here was something I might call a witty rhetorical device; how better to convey the idea of a puzzle than to use a word which is itself a puzzle, wrapping it in a phrase – 'the great aporia' – that makes it seem a grand and weighty concept?

The whole process seemed familiar in my experience of reading post-colonial criticism. If I stop to pick at every detail I do not understand, I lose the overall thread of the argument; therefore, I usually keep going, depending on my half-knowledge to carry me through. When I do stop, though, I usually find something that gives me a deeper sense of the argument and of the writer's own frame of reference and way of thinking.

When Hall comes to discuss the second view of cultural identity, the complexity of language spreads to occupy larger parts of his sentences. Look, for example, at the sentence in the second paragraph of the extract above beginning 'The ways in which black people ...'. What is needed, I think, is mostly just the time to tease apart the layers of meaning in the sentence. First, there is a doubling of phrases that almost seem to repeat each other – 'black people, black experiences' or 'power and normalization'. It seems almost as if two sentences have been knit together here. Perhaps Hall is intent on demonstrating a virtuoso way with sentence construction, but as likely he is making the point that these elements are all connected. In this respect they all rightly belong in the same sentence even if this does make it complicated. But why in the doubled phrase 'positioned and subject-ed' should he have put a hyphen in the word 'subject-ed'?

Without the hyphen, the word can easily be understood in the simple sense of black people being subjected to foreign domination under colonialism. Hall wants, it seems, to elaborate that notion, and the parallel word 'positioned' helps explain what is going on. The black person is 'positioned' and fixed mentally, just as members of a class can be physically positioned by a teacher telling them to pay attention, face the front and concentrate on the subject of their lesson – thus limiting their ability to talk among themselves about their own interests. 'Subject-ed' appears to be making the same kind of point; to be the subject of a ruler – to be subjected to his or her power – is to lose at least some part of your freedom and ability to act for yourself. But there is another meaning of 'subject' which is to do with the grammar of a sentence. The subject of a sentence is the active part: in the sentence 'She scored the highest mark in the class', 'She' is the subject. Stuart Hall seems to me to be pulling that second meaning into what he says, so that the black person is not just subjected in the sense of being dominated, but also subjected in the sense of being made the active part of the sentence. As when I sorted out 'aporia' for myself, I am finding myself in a situation where I could set out to read for the overall argument and not dwell on these details, or I could pause on the detail and find myself drawn into a more complicated meaning in the detail. Continuing on that latter route for a moment longer, I think Hall is engaging implicitly with a set of ideas that are to be found in the work of the French philosopher Louis Althusser (see, for example, *Lenin and Philosophy and Other Essays*, trans. by Ben Brewster, London: New Left Books, 1971). Althusser argues that we are all vulnerable to the dominant ideologies in society to the extent that these ideologies influence and even create our sense of our own individual identities. Thus, to use Hall's pun, even when we are 'subject-ed' (being like the active part of the sentence), we are 'subject-ed' in the sense of being dominated. I think Hall tries to limit this sense that the dominant ideologies are all-enclosing through his second idea of what identity is; through, that is, the idea that the subject can actively enter into 'the politics of identity', something that involves arguing, contesting and debating and – especially – shifting one's identity and position. (The example of the teacher positioning the pupils is perhaps susceptible to the ambiguity Hall wants to exploit. Maybe the pupils still talk behind the teacher's back about – say – a club only open to people of their age and from which the teacher is excluded. Maybe they talk, too, in a particular slang. They may still be positioned by the teacher and by the dominant values of the school, but they may also be setting up something almost like an enclave within these dominating forces.)

Interestingly, almost the only word or phrase without the kind of doubling I mention above is 'dominant regimes of representation'. The force of the phrase here is to suggest that in any culture the forces that dominate and repress are powerful because they embody representations (in simple terms, pictures) which in one way or another coerce us into behaving in particular ways. A simple example of this might be the way that we dress –

and this is not entirely an innocent example, because the British colonial regime exerted a powerful influence on how Indians dressed, both when they wore British clothes and when they wore Indian clothes. Advertisements, accepted conventions of dress codes and so on create pictures (representations) of how we should dress. These representations also work like mirrors – mirrors that are powerful but always false. When we see an advertisement, we may see clothes we want to buy so that we can become like the advertisement, but at the same time we also see an image of what we are. For many years the absence of black faces and bodies in advertisements meant that black people in Britain saw themselves in these false mirrors identified (perhaps, 'subject-ed' or made into subjects) as white.

A final word catches my eye in this sentence: 'critical' in the phrase 'critical exercise of cultural power'. On the face of it there is no reason why 'critical' should not have its simple meaning: 'important', 'the one that makes a difference', as in 'this is the critical match for this team'. But, perhaps because I have been thinking about the way that Hall suggests matters of power involve representations and because these are things that are regularly analysed through the methods of literary criticism or art history, I begin to think that perhaps the dominant regimes are exercising power through something like the same processes. In other words, power in society should not be thought of in terms of a simple and visible instruction from one person to another, but in a more subtle way; it is more like a writer or a critic using language – in the form of apparently innocent and impersonal words such as 'It is common sense that ...', 'Here we see ...', or 'It is plain that ...' – to organize the reader's response and secure their agreement.

The narrative of imperialism

The second example of the complex language found in post-colonial criticism and theory is from Gayatri Chakravorty Spivak, 'Can the Subaltern Speak?' (*Colonial Discourse and Post-Colonial Theory,* pp.66–111). Spivak has been seen as one of the key contributors to debates on post-colonialism; at the time of writing her most recent book is *A Critique of Post-Colonial Reason: Toward a History of the Vanishing Present*, London: Harvard University Press, 1999). Her topic in the extract here – whether and how someone living in an oppressed society can speak for themselves, as opposed to simply repeating the representations imposed upon them – is of great importance. It is a classic piece, often referred to and rewarding to read through as a whole; however, it is long, remarkably densely written and difficult, so the most I have space to do here is to pick my way through a single paragraph. Spivak is exploring the kinds of things that might have led to the condition whereby the Subaltern, or oppressed person or group, has been denied speech in the past:

The clearest available example of such epistemic violence is the remotely orchestrated, far flung, and heterogeneous project to constitute the colonial subject as Other. This project is also the asymmetrical obliteration of the trace of that Other in its precarious Subject-ivity. It is well known that Foucault locates epistemic violence, a complete overhaul of the episteme, in the redefinition of sanity at the end of the European eighteenth century. But what if that particular redefinition was only a part of the narrative of history in Europe as well as in the colonies? What if the two projects of epistemic overhaul worked as dislocated and unacknowledged parts of a vast two-handed engine? Perhaps it is no more than to ask that the subtext of the palimpsestic narrative of imperialism be recognized as 'subjugated knowledge', 'a whole set of knowledges that have been disqualified as inadequate to their task or insufficiently elaborated: naive knowledges, located low down on the hierarchy, beneath the required level of cognition or scientificity' (*PK*, p.82).

(p.76; '*PK*' indicates that Spivak is quoting from Michel Foucault, *Power/Knowledge: Selected Interviews and Writings 1972/1977*, ed. by Colin Gordon, trans. by Colin Gordon *et al.*, Brighton: Harvester, 1980)

I will take the first two sentences first. The 'problem' here is largely in the compacting of language, so the best way to approach things is by taking a closer look at difficult words and phrases. (Reading post-colonial criticism and theory is often best done with the aid of a good dictionary and a book such as *A Glossary of Literary Terms*, ed. by Michael H. Abrams, 7th edn, New York: Harcourt Brace, 1998.) 'Epistemic violence' was the first phrase at which I stopped. My dictionary gave me a good start, though I had to deduce the meaning of 'epistemic' from the word given, 'epistemology', meaning the study of knowledge. So 'epistemic violence' means violence – an assertion of power – which involves or even arises from knowledge. I hope you will already be making a connection with the ways of thinking in Stuart Hall's article – or even the catchphrase 'knowledge is power'. It is a central tenet of post-colonial theory and criticism that those who control knowledge – through the control of education, publishing, the fixing of the official language and so on – control power. Spivak is addressing that issue directly in this passage. Less puzzling but again typical is the use of a string of adjectives – 'remotely orchestrated', 'far flung', 'heterogeneous' – all qualifying 'project'. The meaning of each needs to be registered separately and put beside the issue of the epistemic violence that is involved with knowledge, which Spivak is raising. Together they suggest that power works from afar in a complicated way (like an orchestra playing in tune but with different sections, rather than a single instrument, playing different notes), and that power works in many countries and places. The word 'heterogeneous' seems particularly important here, prompting us again to avoid any simple lumping together of people and situations. Finally in this sentence we are given more details of the specific case of knowledge/ violence to be explored: the 'project to constitute the colonial subject as Other'. The use of 'Other' in this context is particularly associated with the work of Edward W. Said in *Orientalism* (1978; London: Penguin, 1985), though the term was used before this by Simone de Beauvoir, writing in 1949 about gender difference in *The Second Sex* (Harmondsworth: Penguin, 1972, p.16, and elsewhere), and by Jacques Lacan in his writings on psycho-analysis in the 1950s and 1960s (see Elizabeth Grosz, *Jacques Lacan: A Feminist Introduction*, London: Routledge, 1990, p.63 and elsewhere). You will need to read *Orientalism* to get a fuller sense of the meaning of the term in the post-colonial context, but here it is perhaps sufficient to register that it involves seeing the colonized as defined in terms of 'not': as the colonial subject is 'Other' so he or she is 'not-Self', 'not-Western' and not a whole range of other things the West associates with itself – 'not-civilized', 'not-scientific' and so on.

With the next sentence Spivak takes this process a stage further. It might be helpful to start at the end, with 'that Other in its precarious Subject-ivity'. What is captured here is the notion that though the Other is primarily defined by what it is not, even this negative provides a kind of identity. (An example from a quite different context comes to my mind here: the way that characters in Samuel Beckett's plays and novels seem entirely drained of rationality and individualism and yet, paradoxically, even in that state retain identity.) So in this sentence Spivak is suggesting a further act of violence and oppression – involving knowledge and culture rather than guns – aimed at obliterating even this 'Subject-ivity'. Why is this process described as 'asymmetrical'? To understand this I had to remind myself that the process of constituting the colonial subject requires someone who con-stitutes themselves as a colonizer as well as someone constituted as colonized; or as one might say a 'Self' as well as an 'Other'. The process seemed to me then 'asymmetrical' (not even) – because the 'Subject-ivity' of the oppressing Self is not precarious and faces nothing of the further process of 'obliteration' which faces the Other.

The next two sentences refer back to the discussions of the first section of 'Can the Subaltern Speak?' (not reproduced here), and I will just summarize these in order to focus more on the last two sentences of the paragraph. Foucault's interest was in the way that knowledge (scientific knowledge, medical knowledge, philosophical knowledge and so on) was used in the nineteenth century as a way of categorizing people and behav-iour; society became increasingly structured on the bases of these categories (rather than in the past on the basis of the power of the king, or the church, or some other authority figure). This involved the hardening of categories of behaviour and personality; qualities and behaviour that had been a *part* of a person's identity became instead the *only* way that their identity could be defined. Thus anyone behaving in a way that did not fit the expectations of society might become identified as insane: this insanity became the essence of their identity and quite fixed, the only possible course being either to change this identity through medical interventions or to incarcerate them in an asylum. Foucault also wrote extensively on sexuality and particularly homosexuality. He argued that the nineteenth century saw a change whereby society constructed sexual activity between men not just as a kind of sexual behaviour but as the principle of a person's identity, again so fixed in society's view that the only appropriate response was medical intervention – or incarceration.

The 'two projects of epistemic overhaul' to which Spivak refers are the one she refers to in the second sentence of this paragraph, whereby the colonial subject is constituted as Other, and the one she alludes to in Foucault's work, where the 'insane' become equally constituted as Other. The force of the penultimate sentence is to bring graphically to our minds the notion that these processes of Other-ing are related and bound together. This is then imagined through the metaphor of the 'vast two-handed engine', something that sounds to me like a great old fashioned weapon but that is in fact a literary allusion. In his poem 'Lycidas' Milton describes the fate that awaits a corrupt world: 'But that two-handed engine at the door, / Stands ready to smite once, and smite no more' (ll.130–31). The image is echoed also in *Paradise Lost*, where the archangel Michael attacks the army of fallen angels led by Satan 'and felld / Squadrons at once, with huge two-handed sway' (VI. 250–51). By almost silent implication the canon of Western literature – that collection of dead white males – is complicit in the 'epistemic overhaul'.

Coming then to the last sentence, let us put the puzzle of 'subtext' and 'palimpsestic' to one side for a moment. Spivak uses Foucault's words to define how the Subaltern's words have been seen and valued to date; the words of the colonized subject (and this might be taken to apply to literary writings as well as other more intellectual writings) were taken to be 'inadequate ... naïve ... beneath the required level of cognition [understanding] or scientificity'. Returning to the puzzle of 'subtext' and 'palimpsestic', perhaps we are dealing with the same kind of possibilities of rhetoric or wit as I referred to in discussing Stuart Hall's use of 'aporia'. Certainly, again I had to get out my dictionary to discover that a 'palimpsest' is 'twice-used writing material, where partly erased early writing can be seen below more recent writing'. Putting the whole thing together, I think Spivak is saying that the knowledge that flows from the oppressed has in the past been defined into something Other, something not valued, something 'subjugated', something that is under the rule of others. But in the 'narrative of imperialism', this valuing of the knowledge has become the 'subtext' in a new 'palimpsest' story. From this point of view the narrative of imperialism that we read now is quite different from that old version; we cannot ignore that 'erased early writing' which tells us how the oppressed were subjugated by knowledge and power, but the only way to recover it now is through an act of archaeology.

I hope that you have found it valuable to look at these extracts at this level of detail, and that you will be encouraged to subject other critical and theoretical writings to this level of scrutiny at least on occasion. Reading for the fullest meaning at first seems an intimidatingly slow process, but with practice comes a familiarity with the discourse and the possibility of much faster progress.

'The beginning ...'

In the opening section of this chapter I refer to 1800 as a date that can mark the beginning of the period of British colonialism in India; I describe it as a convenient shorthand but in the end something altogether too tidy. In this last section of the chapter I want to return in a little more detail to this issue. By starting at a particular point, any historical narrative almost inevitably constructs some event or some individual as 'the beginning'. Another way of putting this is to say that the choice of a starting point necessarily creates a 'myth of origin'. Each of these terms has a value in itself and each has implications. Each can also be understood as embodying a retrospective prospect, a making sense of the past from the present. And as with any story told with hindsight, the beginning is already inextricably – though often quite obliquely – involved in the ending that ensues.

The phrase 'myth of origin' seems to highlight the value of the narrative to those who look back from the present – 'myth' here is used in the modern sense of a story about the past that we tell in the present and that makes sense of that present world. (As Freud, for example, uses the myth of Oedipus to describe and make sense of the structures and emotional patterns of growing up in a modern middle-class family.) The phrase 'the beginning' appears perhaps more straightforward, carrying an implicit assumption that the past will be truly open to real knowledge untainted by our own point of view. In either case the story that follows is likely to be a story of change. The 'change' may appear to us in retrospect to be blatant and obvious: for example, to the reader in the twenty-first century it may seem self-evident that there was a decisive event in Indian history in 1858 – the East India Company was abolished and rule was transferred from the company to the government; however, at the time it may have appeared as something altogether different. This question is important when studying the relationship between literature and nation because we will often wish to juxtapose a literary text written at a particular time and embodying a particular perspective with history texts written and constructed later and in retrospect.

Three short extracts from three standard histories of India – all informative and worth reading – will illustrate the issues here. Each deals with the period around 1740. The first is from Michael Edwardes, *A History of India from the Earliest Times to the Present Day* (London: Thames and Hudson, 1961). The chapter and section headings show Edwardes conceptualizing this period in India as to do with 'The Foundations of British Power' in India but also in quite European terms – that is, 'English and French Conflict in the Carnatic'. He is also quite happy to put his own viewpoint prominently into the first sentence, diagnosing the period as 'curious' – not, one might imagine, a diagnosis that British or Indian people would have made at the time:

> The period we are about to enter is a curious one. It is a time of conflict not only between France and England but between trade and politics. For the first time on a major scale, military and political events in Europe penetrate the lives of the Indian people in no uncertain manner. (p.207)

The historian's view is also evident in the next extract, from Percival Spear, *India: A Modern History* (Ann Arbor: University of Michigan Press, 1971), as he constructs 'an air of expectancy in south India'. Again, also, the period is conceptualized in European terms – these sentences are from a chapter headed simply 'British and French':

> In consequence of these conditions there was an air of expectancy in south India by 1740. The north could no longer control the events in the south; the balance of power was known to be precarious, and there was no obvious empire-builder in sight. (p.186)

The final extract is the most recent; it is from Burton Stein, *A History of India* (Oxford: Blackwell, 1998). Signs of a desire to recognize that India was not a blank sheet on which the British wrote their empire can be seen in the reference to 'existing ... mercantilist institutions', but there is still a strong European emphasis in the history. The sentences come from a section dealing with the East India Company and titled 'The Joint Trajectory of Development'. Furthermore, the historian is again to be seen quietly using metaphors to place particular ways of seeing in the reader's mind; here we have the notion of a 'relational web' joining Britain and India. Few readers would perhaps pause to consider just how stretched and irregular that web was, given the scale of the geographical and economic links between Britain and India at the time:

> By the middle of the 18th century, the East India Company had become one of the great mercantilist enterprises in the world as well as the east, and, in asserting its dominion over ever-larger parts of the subcontinent, it thrust existing, weaker mercantilist institutions to higher levels of development. The relational web between Britain and India was woven quite early, well before actual British dominion was formalised. (p.207)

I am obviously taking these extracts out of context here, but to make a particular point about how history is told and how stories are begun – they describe what one might call a 'prologue' to our main 1800–1990 period. The next chapter tells our own version of the beginning of the story of how colonized and colonizer saw themselves and each other by looking at the cultural products of the Britain and India, and the shifting effect that colonialism has had on both nations. As you read we hope you will be alert to our ways of generalizing and colouring our version of the narrative, and to the assumptions we are making – to be, in other words, as attentive a reader of narratives in history as you are of narratives in literature.

Questions and exercises

1   Look carefully at the three paragraphs beginning 'Here it seems to me ...' in the introduction to Edward W. Said, *Orientalism* (London: Penguin, 1985, pp.14–15). Rewrite Said's argument in your own words.

2   Consider the significance for the British colonization of India of one of the following Governor Generals: Lord Cornwallis, the Marquess of Dalhousie, Lord Curzon.

3   Analyse the paragraph from Spivak's 'Can the Subaltern Speak?' beginning 'Can the Subaltern Speak?' (*Colonial Discourse and Post-Colonial Theory*, p.90) in the detailed way demonstrated in the preceding chapter.

4   Find a copy of Jane Robinson, *Angels of Albion* (London: Viking, 1996). What are the key points she makes in Chapters 1 and 2? How can they help in our investigation of 'Literature and Nation'?

5   Read the discussion of nationalism in India by Partha Chatterjee, *The Nation and its Fragments* (London: Princeton University Press, 1993, pp.110–15; repr. in *Nationalism*, pp.209–14). Write down what you see as the key points of Chatterjee's argument.

2 FIRST ENCOUNTERS: WORKS BY SIR WILLIAM JONES AND OTHERS

by Richard Allen

Introduction

Strictly speaking, the first official encounters between Britons and Indians in South Asia date from around 1600 – the year in which the British East India Company was awarded a Royal Charter. For the first hundred years or so, however, the activities of the company were more or less confined to the coastal regions and to simple trading transactions. Some time after 1700 things changed. Some of the key changes were ones of scale. These can be exemplified in the introduction into the English language of the word 'nabob'. This was derived from the Urdu title *nawab*, used to indicate the governor of a district in India under the Mughal Empire; from 1764 it came into common use in English as 'nabob', which the *Oxford English Dictionary* defines as 'a person of great wealth, especially one who has returned from India with a large fortune'. Essentially, wealth arising from trade between Britain and the East was overtaken by wealth accumulated from dealings within India. A more colourful summing up is provided in an exchange in Act 2 of Samuel Foote's play *The Nabob* (1772) – we can perhaps presume that the audience would share the attitudes conveyed in this apparently innocent description:

> MAYOR: ... I have often been minded to ask you what sort of things them there settlements are; because why, as you know, I have never been beyond sea.
>
> TOUCHIT: Oh, Mr Mayor, I will explain that in a moment. Why here are a body of merchants that beg to be admitted as friends, and take possession of a small spot in a country, and carry on a beneficial commerce with the inoffensive and innocent people, to which they kindly give consent.
>
> MAYOR: Don't you think that is very civil of them?
>
> TOUCHIT: Doubtless. Upon which, Mr Mayor, we cunningly encroach and fortify by little and by little, till at length, we growing too strong for the natives, we turn them out of their lands, and take possession of their money and jewels.
>
> MAYOR: And don't you think, Mr Touchit, that is a little uncivil in us?
>
> TOUCHIT: Oh, nothing at all, these people are but a little better than Tartars or Turks.

MAYOR: No, no, Mr Touchit; just the reverse; it is *they* who have caught the Tartars in us.

(quoted in P.J. Marshall, *Problems of Empire: Britain and India 1757–1813*, London: George Allen and Unwin, 1968, pp.147–8)

How might this process of 'growing too strong for the natives' and taking 'possession of their money and jewels' be related to the apparently more political matter of the forming of a nation – by the British and by the Indians alike – in India? How, that is to say, can it be related in the history of the years that follow to the development of ever more elaborate processes of British colonial rule in India and the creation eventually of what Judith Brown calls 'modern India' (*Modern India: The Origins of an Asian Democracy*, Oxford: Oxford University Press, 1994)? As the discussion at the end of Chapter 1 indicates, such questions raise further questions about how we create a narrative of the past. Clearly, we had to choose a point at which to begin that would have some historical logic and some practical value. In the end we opted for 1783 as the symbolic point at which British involvement in India, and the political structure of India itself, changed in such a way that first a colonial nation – British India – came into existence and then an independent modern state – India as we know it today. Putting our starting point alongside two other possibilities – 1757 and 1818 – shows something of what lies behind that choice.

1757 – This is the date of the Battle of Plassey, at which, in a kind of civil war for control of the kingdom of Bengal, British forces under Robert Clive intervened and defeated its current ruler. Clive was in the service of the East India Company; hitherto, Bengal had been ruled by viceroys of the Mughal emperor, and it was under their protection that the English East India Company carried on its trade. With Clive's support, Mir Jaffar, an elderly general, was installed as the new ruler, to ensure conditions favourable to the company's trade. Established as Jaffar's protector, Clive became more and more involved in the actual ruling of Bengal until in 1765 the East India Company was appointed as the official tax collector. In many historical accounts the Battle of Plassey is the key event, not only because it enabled the British to establish themselves in India but because it established the model for their takeover – a mixture of military conquest and insinuating themselves into the local Indian governments.

1818 – The process that we can describe as beginning in 1757 can also be described as complete by 1818. We might therefore have seized upon this later date as the 'real' beginning of the British colonization of India: as Percival Spear puts it, in *India: A Modern History* (Ann Arbor: University of Michigan Press, 1971, p.225), by 1818 'the British dominion *in* India [had become] the British dominion *of* India'. Taking this date as a starting point does put more emphasis on culture and government; however, again it strongly prompts us to see the narrative as originating from a military event. The year 1818 marks the surrender of the Maratha princes to East India Company troops led by Lord Francis Rawdon-Hastings. Their territories were annexed and British sovereignty was established over most of

India. There is a further 'military' aspect to this beginning: some historians argue that Hastings's victories were only possible because the defeat of Napoleon in Europe in 1815 allowed the British to attend to military matters further afield. The defeat of France in Europe also summarily ended the conflicts between the two powers over colonial spoils in India.

1783 – This is our chosen starting point for the colonial relationship between Britain and India: the year in which Sir William Jones was appointed as a judge of the Supreme Court in Bengal. Choosing this date emphasizes the cultural over the military and the more purely political, but it is only fair to begin by allowing that there is still an important military dimension – albeit one that is very different from the victories associated with 1757 and 1818. This involves making a link between British actions in India and those in North America. Before 1750, to speak of the British colonies was almost invariably to speak of North America where Britain had had significant possessions since the sixteenth century. All this changed in the twenty-five years after 1750, when the North American colonies rebelled and fought for their independence. The War of Independence formally ended in 1783, but essentially the die was cast with the defeat of the British under Lord Cornwallis at the Battle of Yorktown in 1781. Remarkably, five years later Cornwallis was appointed governor-general of India. Cornwallis's move seems sufficiently symbolic to create a 'beginning' or a 'myth of origin' in its own right; defeated in the West by the energy of the white North American settlers, the British turned to the East where they in turn could overcome the natives, perceived as the products of a now decadent civilization. Equal to this in importance we can put the appointment of Sir William Jones as a judge of the Supreme Court. Later sections of this chapter suggest how his career may be followed up in more detail, but we might summarize his importance here by suggesting that Jones stands at the beginning of a hegemony exerted by British culture which runs in India through the nineteenth century to 1947 – and arguably beyond.

A starting point based on events important for the history of the culture of India seems apt given that the focus of *Literature and Nation* is on literature. But beyond that, the choice of starting point also throws into relief the question of just what creates a nation and a national identity. Is it a matter of war and the marking out of boundaries? Or is it a matter of culture? Prudently, we might argue that a whole range of factors including these are involved, and it would be rash to claim that literature has a dominant role in forming and perpetuating an idea of nation. But if it is wise not to overplay the role of literature in *Literature and Nation*, we should also be careful not to underplay it. The ideas and values that – in our narrative – have their beginning in the work of Sir William Jones have a vital import-ance in enabling the imperial structures to work. And, looking boldly forward, we might even hazard that the narrative did not quite reach its end with independence. We could say, that is, that the ideas of shared culture and of nation fostered in English literature have outlasted the colonial and imperial political structures within which they were born, and continue to play a part in enabling the notion of India as a single nation with a single overall national identity to persist against the pressures of regionalism and communalism.

Where to begin? Sources

The three standard histories of India cited in the last section of Chapter 1 (Michael Edwardes, *A History of India from the Earliest Times to the Present Day*, London: Thames and Hudson, 1961; Percival Spear, *India: A Modern History*, Ann Arbor: University of Michigan Press, 1971; Burton Stein, *A History of India*, Oxford: Blackwell, 1998) all provide the kind of information necessary to form an opinion on what constitutes an appropriate starting point for an account of the British involvement in India, as do Brown, *Modern India*, and Stanley Wolpert, *A New History of India* (2nd edn, Oxford: Oxford University Press, 1982). D.K. Fieldhouse, *The Colonial Empires: A Comparative Survey from the Eighteenth Century* (London: Macmillan, 1966), provides a general comparative account – useful if you want to make connections between British activity in different parts of the world. To consider the issue in more depth in India you will need to turn to more specialist studies. All of C.A. Bayly's works are authoritative; particularly apt here is his *Indian Society and the Making of the British Empire* (Cambridge: Cambridge University Press, 1987). Marshall, *Problems of Empire*, combines a series of helpful commentaries with reprints of documents of the time which are useful for study of some of the people discussed later in this chapter. At the risk of complicating matters, mention might also be made of H.V. Bowen, *Revenue and Reform: The Indian Problem in British Politics 1757–1773* (Cambridge: Cambridge University Press, 1991). Bowen comes close to claiming a different 'beginning', namely 'the parliamentary session of 1772–3', which 'represented a watershed in the development of the relationship between the state and the East India Company' (p.187), and which resulted in the passing of Lord North's Regulating Act. By this Act, and to a considerable degree prompted by the stories of corruption in Bengal after 1765, the government took responsibility for 'regulating' – at least to some degree – the activities of the East India Company. The British government increasingly felt it had no alternative but to become involved directly in Indian affairs, though it was very reluctant to take on an open-ended commitment; the result was a kind of halfway house (some might say a mish-mash), whereby the company retained its 'private' status and continued to serve its shareholders but the governor-general and the governing council of the company were appointed by the Crown on the advice of the British government. Once begun, this gradual shift from a trading relationship to a governing relationship was unstoppable; the climate was created for the work of those like Sir William Jones and Thomas Babington Macaulay who began the design of what was in effect a new kind of civil state in British India. The rather cumbersome term 'British India' emphasizes that, formally, British rule in India was only ever partial – it was ostensibly shared with the Indian princes.

The texts

Later chapters all focus on particular literary texts; by contrast, in this chapter our 'text' is the work and ideas of a man – Sir William Jones (1746–94) – as represented in certain key writings. For many years Jones's work was not widely published or read, but a revival of interest means that wider selections of his work are now available for those who wish to explore his writings further; they are: *Sir William Jones: Discourses and Essays*, compiled and ed. by M. Bagchee (Delhi: People's Publishing House, 1984), *Sir William Jones: A Reader*, ed. by S.S. Pachori (Delhi: Oxford University Press, 1993), and *Sir William Jones: Selected Poetical and Prose Works*, ed. by M.J. Franklin (Cardiff: University of Wales Press, 1995). Those who wish to see how he appeared to his contemporaries might also hunt out the collected edition of his works published soon after his death: *The Works of Sir William Jones* (1807), which contains *Memoirs of the Life, Writings, and Correspondence of Sir William Jones* by Lord Teignmouth (then himself newly retired from serving as governor-general of India).

Investigating the case of Warren Hastings (1732–1818), and the later example of Thomas Babington Macaulay (1800–59), will give some idea of how things evolved after 1783 and suggest the kind of narrative of ideas about India that can develop from Sir William Jones's work and ideas. Hastings was governor-general from 1773 to 1784. Macaulay served as a member of the Supreme Council of India from 1834 to 1838, and during that time presided over a commission for composing a criminal code for India. You may be able to find *The Benares Diary of Warren Hastings*, ed. by C.C. Davies (London: Camden Society, 1948), but for an extended sense of Hastings in his own words you will need to go back to the original editions of 1800, as no full later edition exists. There are several monumental editions of Macaulay's large and varied output, for example *The Works of Lord Macaulay* (12 vols, London: Longman, 1898).

Biographical and bibliographical information

As well as the original account of his life by Lord Teignmouth (a former governor-general of India), published as part of the first collected edition (see above), two modern biographies of Sir William Jones exist: Garland Cannon, *Oriental Jones: A Biography of Sir William Jones 1746–1794* (Cambridge: Cambridge University Press, 1990), and S.N. Mukherjee, *Sir William Jones: A Study in Eighteenth-Century Attitudes to India* (Cambridge: Cambridge University Press, 1968; 2nd edn, London: Sangam Books, 1987). Cannon has also published two bibliographical reference volumes: *Sir William Jones, Orientalist: An Annotated Bibliography of His Works* (Honolulu:

University of Hawaii Press, 1952), and *Sir William Jones: A Bibliography of Primary and Secondary Sources* (Amsterdam: Benjamins, 1979).

Biographical accounts of Hastings and Macaulay provide useful contextual material not only for their own ideas but also for the life and work of Sir William Jones. Perhaps because of the complex contemporary attitudes to Hastings and his impeachment (see below) no biography appeared immediately after his death, but his name continued to provoke interest through the nineteenth century; a biography by the eminent historian of the events in India of 1857 – G.B. Malleson, *Life of Warren Hastings* (London: Chapman & Hall) – eventually appeared in 1894. There are two twentieth-century biographies: A.M. Davies, *Warren Hastings: Maker of British India* (London: Ivor Nicholson & Watson, 1935), and K.G. Feiling, *Warren Hastings* (London: Macmillan, 1966). Macaulay's reputation (gained perhaps more from his work after he left India in 1838, including his *History of England* and his *Lays of Ancient Rome*) was more sure. His biography was first written in 1876 by his nephew, G.O. Trevelyan (*The Life and Letters of Lord Macaulay*, London: Harper, 1876; rev. edn, with preface by G.M. Trevelyan, Oxford: Oxford University Press, 1978). A more recent account is that of O.D. Edwards, *Macaulay* (London: Weidenfeld, 1988). Macaulay's letters are also available in *T.B. Macaulay: Selected Letters*, ed. by T. Pinney (Cambridge: Cambridge University Press, 1982).

Sir William Jones

Languages and 'Orientalism'

Sir William Jones is an important figure in a number of fields. Currently available discussions of his work tend to occur within accounts of those separate fields, but M.J. Franklin, *Sir William Jones* (Cardiff: University of Wales Press, 1995), does offer a useful general account. So far as his work on languages and 'Orientalism' are concerned, the achievements which concern us here come from the ten years of his life when he served in the judiciary in Calcutta, but his interest in the languages and cultures of Asia were much more long standing – his first publication in 1770 was a translation from Persian into French. Jones eventually went to India to serve as a judge in Calcutta but almost immediately on arrival he was instrumental in the founding of the Asiatic Society of Bengal; many of his writings on literature and language were published as part of the proceedings of that society. Further details of this society, which was extremely important in the history of study of India, can be found in M. Bagchee, *The Asiatic Society: A Brief History* (Delhi: People's Publishing House, 1984), and O.P. Kerval, *The Asiatic Society of Bengal and the Discovery of India's Past 1784–1838* (Oxford: Oxford University Press, 1988). Jones's interests and enthusiasms here qualify him to be described as one of the first Orientalists. The words 'Orientalist' and 'Orientalism' need to be treated with some care. In their original senses and up until the publication of Edward W. Said's *Orientalism*

(1978; London: Penguin, 1985) they were used in a relatively innocent – even benevolent – sense to signify an academic or cultural interest in the cultures of Asia. Said argued that all kinds of writing about Asia needed to be read in a new way, and in so doing effectively redefined the ideological overtones of the word 'Orientalism'. Instead of being generally positive and to do with the commendable search for knowledge and enlightenment, they became almost entirely negative and to do with the abuse of power. It is hardly fair to say that Said has been alone in his discoveries – Orientalism is for example also the subject of Raymond Schwab, *The Oriental Renaissance: Europe's Rediscovery of India and the East 1680–1880* (trans. by G. Patterson-Black and V. Reinking, New York: Columbia University Press, 1984) – but Said has become so much the centre of the debate that it is worth spending a moment looking at how he works with the term. To my mind, the key intellectual move is Said's linking of the knowledge accumulated by Orientalists (in the 'older' usage) with the power that characterizes any national or colonial government. Said expresses these ideas in the passage quoted below. He is referring to 'The Government of Subject Races', a piece written by Lord Cromer. (Evelyn Baring, 1841–1917, created Earl of Cromer in 1892, had an extraordinary career including a stint as private secretary to the viceroy of India from 1872 to 1877, and appointment as British agent and consul-general in Egypt in 1883, during the crucial period of the major British imperial expansion in Africa.) Said writes that

> Cromer envisions a seat of power in the West, and radiating out from it towards the East a great embracing machine, sustaining the central authority yet commanded by it. What the machine's branches feed into it in the East – human material [e.g. Indian labourers to work in the sugar plantations in the Caribbean], material wealth [profit from British companies operating in India], knowledge [from the work of, e.g., academics and government servants], what have you – is processed by the machine, then converted into more power. The [local] specialist does the immediate translation of mere Oriental matter into useful substance: the Oriental [e.g. the Indian] becomes, for example, a subject race, an example of an 'Oriental' mentality [which is inevitably different from the Western 'Occidental' mentality so far as work and energy are concerned], all for the enhancement of the 'authority' at home ... What Cromer quite accurately sees is the management of knowledge by society, the fact that knowledge ... is regulated ... by the general concerns of a ... system of authority.

> (Said, pp.44–5)

(These few sentences can hardly do justice to the wealth of Said's knowledge and the richness of his ideas; see in particular the introduction and Chapter 1 of *Orientalism*.)

Turning back to Sir William Jones, we return to a period long before the Cromer 'system' was at all well developed. So what was the nature of

Jones's Orientalist knowledge? Jones's education in Britain left him with a knowledge of Latin, Greek and a number of modern languages. In India he is said to have been the first European fully to have mastered Sanskrit, and his translations of Jayadeva's *Gita Govinda* and Kalidasa's *Sakuntala* in 1789 gave the first wider European circulation to the riches of writings in that language (see Text 2.2). Other translations and other original verses by him in Indian languages can be found in the modern editions of Jones's work referred to above. The paper 'On the Origin and Families of Nations', which Jones delivered to the Asiatic Society, summed up the ideas for which he is perhaps best known today (see Text 2.3). He put his new knowledge of Indian languages and Sanskrit together with his wide knowledge of European languages and concluded that all the Indian and European languages were related to each other. The paper not only provides an excellent summary of Jones's ideas but also shows the frameworks of thinking in which he felt the ideas of language belonged; he particularly aimed to link evidence from language to the more historical interpretation of the Bible. Stripped of this framework, Jones's idea of a family of languages was eventually taken up by historians of language in the nineteenth century and developed more fully into theories of the origin of languages and the suggestion of a now lost single original proto-Indo-European language; a good general reference book covering all these topics is D. Crystal, *The Cambridge Encyclopedia of Language* (Cambridge: Cambridge University Press, 1997).

The law and British ideas of India

Jones's profession of the law in England before 1784 had also been touched by his interest in languages; in 1782 he translated from Arabic *The Mahomedan Law of Succession to the Property of Intestates*. In Calcutta his practice of law and his work for the government on the codification of Indian law (which culminated in his translation of the *Institutes of Hindu Law; or the Ordinances of Menu* in 1794) put him at the centre of key debates as to how the British should act as a governing power in India; this in turn set the stage for the development of ideas of nation in Britain and in India through the nineteenth century. To understand these debates it is necessary to understand the nature of the apparatus of British 'government' after the Battle of Plassey in 1757. Useful general accounts are to be found in C.H. Philips, *The East India Company 1784–1834* (Manchester: University of Manchester Press, 1940), and in P.J. Marshall, *Bengal: The British Bridgehead. Eastern India 1740–1828* (Cambridge: Cambridge University Press, 1976). The particular period before Jones arrived in India and the debates about the limits of responsibility of the East India Company and British government are discussed in Bowen, *Revenue and Reform*. Essentially, the company's activities had progressed from trading to tax gathering to – in 1772 when Hastings was governor of Bengal – taking responsibility for the administration of civil justice in Bengal.

Jones's legal work is discussed along with other aspects of his career in Javed Majeed, *Ungoverned Imaginings: James Mill's 'The History of British India' and Orientalism* (Oxford: Clarendon Press, 1992). To be able to implement justice in Bengal the British needed to understand the law as it had been practised in the existing Indian traditions. Majeed quotes the following passage from the preface to the *Institutes of Hindu Law* as a key indicator of Jones's attitudes as he translated and codified existing practice and thought about how the British should proceed in the future:

> the best intended legislative provisions would have no beneficial effect ... unless they were congenial to the dispositions and habits, to the religious prejudices, and approved immemorial usages, of the people, for whom they are enacted.

(Majeed, p.19)

In the next section, I suggest ways of exploring the significance of this work and these ideas within a wider framework, but here you might immediately notice an apparent contradiction in Jones's thinking which warrants a moment's pause. In his legal work and in his enthusiasm for Sanskrit literature Jones is an Orientalist – a believer in the value of a true and original Indian culture and tradition quite separate from that of the European world; yet at the same time, in his studies on the development of languages, which many now regard as the most important area of his work, his thinking is shot through with the notion of interconnections between Indian and European culture. How is it possible to reconcile these two positions?

Orientalism or Anglicization? Warren Hastings and Edmund Burke

While Jones pursued his work in India, in Britain the questions about the relationship of Britain and India – which in his work are about law, language and culture – became entangled in one of the determining events in this debate: the impeachment of Warren Hastings, then Governor-General of Bengal. The case came to trial in the House of Lords in 1794, the year of Jones's death; the prosecuting speech, which lasted for nine days, was given by Edmund Burke.

Studying Hastings's life and work (particularly in the period up to 1800) is particularly valuable for the way it represents intellectual dilemmas about government, about colonial relations and about ideas of racial difference (and was seen to do so at the time). This was particularly the case during his impeachment and trial before the House of Lords, which began in 1788 and continued intermittently until 1797. The impeachment charges constructed Hastings as a criminal who had exploited and abused his power over the Indian people in Bengal. Hastings was in the end acquitted, but the publicity surrounding the trial, the great speeches made against

Hastings by Edmund Burke and Richard Brinsley Sheridan, and the publication of the proceedings of the impeachment hearings themselves had
two powerful effects. Most obviously, people became convinced that corruption was endemic in the workings of the East India Company; its moral
right to rule in India was thus fatally damaged. Less obviously, but with
hindsight more importantly, the whole affair seemed to define India as a
place of barbarism; such a definition worked rapidly to authorize a new
kind of colonialism that was geared to a notion of British culture as more
'advanced' and 'superior'. This was a considerable contradiction of
Hastings's own position; as his 1784 preface to Charles Wilkins's translation of *The Bhagavad-Gita* shows, he admired Indian culture and
encouraged those in the service of the company to get to know more
about it (see Text 2.1). Similarly, as governor-general he began the policy
which suggested that the British should learn more about established
Hindu and Muslim codes of law – the kind of work in which Sir William
Jones became involved – rather than simply importing their own legal
codes and assumptions.

The issues we aim to open out here are perhaps most easily pursued in the
historical detail of the period 1780 to 1830, but they can also be construed
within the framework of more theoretical thinking about post-colonialism.
The question at issue here relates to the notion – almost commonplace since
the publication of Said's *Orientalism* with its redefinition of the term – that a
colonial power inevitably exerts a strong hegemonic force, simultaneously
incorporating and reducing the colonized culture. Jones and Hastings may
potentially offer an example of ways of thinking and behaving which
complicate this matter. There is a danger of overstating the case, but
certainly, to a considerable degree, both felt that the colonized society had a
separate and autonomous tradition which was to be valued alongside that
of the European colonizers rather than simply cast aside. Perhaps this is just
an accident of history – Jones and Hastings were part of an early period of
colonialism whose ideas were superseded. But perhaps also, Said's
interpretation of Orientalism is too all-determining; perhaps elements
survive of Orientalism in the earlier sense, of being sympathetic to native
traditions. Looking forward for a moment to the texts discussed in later
chapters, this is certainly an issue that can be raised in relation to both *Kim*
and *A Passage to India*.

There are a number of sources of information about Hastings's life and
attitudes, and particularly his impeachment, beyond the biographical
material cited above. These include M.E.M. Jones, *Warren Hastings in Bengal*
(Oxford: Clarendon Press, 1918), E.P. Moon, *Warren Hastings and British
India* (London: Hodder, 1947), and P.J. Marshall, *The Impeachment of Warren
Hastings* (Oxford: Oxford University Press, 1965). Note the spread of publication dates of these books: Hastings continues to be a weather-vane of
attitudes to India and empire across the years. From this point of view, one
of the most recent treatments – 'Reading the Trial of Warren Hastings', in
Sara Suleri, *The Rhetoric of English India* (Chicago: Chicago University Press,

1992) – is particularly interesting and distinctive. Suleri concentrates not on the rights and wrongs of the occasion but on seeing the trial as a kind of spectacle which in fact was geared to concealing the truth it was ostensibly designed to reveal. She writes:

> To read the impeachment proceedings is thus to confront less a trial than a documentation of the anxieties of oppression, where both the prisoner and the prosecutors are equally implicated in the inscribability [sic] of colonial guilt. For eighteenth century England, however, the theatricality of the event overshadowed the historical and political questions that it raised, causing the popular imagination to believe that it observed a spectacle with a definite end. (p.53)

Hastings's most famous prosecutor in the impeachment trial was Edmund Burke (1729–97). Conor Cruise O'Brien, *Edmund Burke*, abridged by J. McCue (London: Sinclair-Stevenson, 1997), provides useful and easily accessible source material for enquiries about Burke's attitudes to Hastings and to India. The original version of the book (C.C. O'Brien, *The Great Melody: A Thematic Biography and Commented Anthology of Edmund Burke*, London: Sinclair-Stevenson, 1992) also contains extracts from Burke's writings. A complete text, giving in detail the charges faced by Hastings, can be found in *The Writings and Speeches of Edmund Burke* (Oxford: Clarendon Press, 1981– ; VI: *India: The Launching of the Hastings Impeachment, 1786–1788*, ed. by P.J. Marshall, 1991).

It is interesting to compare the ideas of Jones, Hastings and Burke, both as a useful activity in itself and for the contrast it offers with the later thinking of Macaulay, discussed in the last section of this chapter. There seem, at least on the face of it, to be resonances between Jones's respect and admiration for the existing culture of India, Hastings's admiration for Indian culture (and the way in which, although he used force ruthlessly to conquer territory, he then was inclined to leave local laws and practices in place), and finally Burke's notion of the value of continuity and tradition in society.

The pattern set: Indo-Anglian poetry

The 'contest' between Anglicization and Orientalism so far described has involved a Welshman (Jones – strictly, a man born in London to Welsh parents), an Englishman (Hastings) and an Irishman (Burke); the outcome was to determine British policy and practice in India for the following century or more. But Indian people were not merely spectators of the process. British valuations of Indian culture could hardly not have an impact, most obviously perhaps in defining the education of the wealthy and the elite of Indian society. A pattern was rapidly set, favouring Anglicization and British models, which governed ideas of what was acceptable for the kind of poetry that was to be publicly valued and that persisted until well into the twentieth century. Some earlier examples of this work can be found in *The Golden Treasury of Indo-Anglian Poetry* (see Text 2.4). The poem 'To the Pupils of the Hindu College', for example, immediately demonstrates the links between literature and education which are so important. Its author, Henry Louis Vivian Derozio (1809–31), was half Indian and half Portuguese. He began writing verse in English at the age of fourteen and through this became a teacher of English and eventually Master of English Literature and History in the Hindu College (now the Presidency College) in Calcutta in 1828. Reading the poem, one can hardly avoid being struck simultaneously by the apparently absolute valuing of English literature it embodies and the now evident irony of such lines as 'I watch the gentle opening of your minds', and 'how you worship truth's omnipotence'. A similar double message arises in the poem 'King Porus – A Legend of Old', by Michael Madhusudan Dutt (1824–73). Dutt was born a Hindu; he married an Englishwoman and in the earlier part of his life wrote a good deal of poetry in English following English conventions. 'King Porus' celebrates an Indian legend, an Indian hero and bewails the country's present lack of freedom. Yet it does so in English, in an English metre and evoking English ideals of freedom – Shakespeare and Byron. (Later in life Dutt wrote more in Bengali and is regarded by some as the most important poet in Bengali before Rabindranath Tagore.) Further information on these poets and on the developing tradition of Indo-Anglian writing is to be found in K.R. Srinivasa Iyengar, *Indian Writing in English* (5th edn, Delhi: Sterling Publishers, 1985).

As you read further in this area, you will come across the phrases 'Indo-Anglian' and 'Anglo-Indian'. 'Indo-Anglian' is a relatively recent word used to describe writings by Indians (particularly those writing in India) in English. 'Anglo-Indian' is older and more complicated. It can refer to something that has been part of the period of British rule in India – for example, we speak of Anglo-Indian cookery. Or it can refer to someone of mixed Indian/British race; in 1911 the Government of India adopted the term 'Anglo-Indian' for official use in preference to 'Eurasian'.

The pattern set: the example of Macaulay

The last section of this chapter focuses on Thomas Babington Macaulay. Macaulay's claim to attention here rests not just on the iconic status he has acquired in accounts of British India but also on the similar standing he has had in British culture. If his 'Minute on Education' of 1835 (see Text 2.7) can be said to be instrumental in defining the nature of British Indian culture, so too his *Lays of Ancient Rome* (1842), and his *History of England* (1848–55) were important contributions to the developing imperial ethos in Britain itself. To get an understanding of his life as a whole alongside the biographical works cited above, consult J. Clive, *Thomas Babington Macaulay: The Shaping of a Historian* (London: Secker & Warburg, 1973), or K. Young, *Macaulay*, ed. by Ian Scott-Kilvert (Writers and Their Work, 225, Harlow: Longman, 1976). For the purposes of the present discussion the classic account of the significance of his work is contained in E. Stokes, *The English Utilitarians and India* (Oxford: Clarendon Press, 1959). A more recent account is Gauri Viswanathan, *Masks of Conquest: Literary Study and British Rule in India* (London: Faber, 1989).

The process in which Macaulay played perhaps the crowning part, as described by Stokes, began almost at the same time as the impeachment of Warren Hastings. Alongside ideas arising from the trial came ideas emerging from evangelical Christianity which were intensely Anglocentric. As a flavour, here is a passage Stokes quotes from Charles Grant, written in 1792: 'the people of Hindustan [are] ... obstinate in their disregard of what they know to be right, governed by the malevolent and licentious passions, strongly exemplifying the effects produced on society by a great and general corruption of manners, and sunk in misery by their vices' (p.31). Stokes is then able to weave a seamless continuity between these words and such as the following from a speech by Macaulay in the Houses of Parliament in 1832:

> To have found a great people sunk in the lowest depths of slavery and superstition, to have ruled them so as to have made them desirous and capable of all the privileges of citizenship, would indeed be a title to glory all our own ... The sceptre may pass away from us ... But there are triumphs which are followed by no reverse. There is an empire exempt from all natural courses of decay. Those triumphs are the pacific triumphs of reason over barbarism; that empire is the imperishable empire of our own arts and our morals, our literature and our laws. (p.45)

Within this kind of general frame Viswanathan focuses particularly on the way the ideology and the institutions of education in British India put into action the ideas of 'arts', 'morals' and 'literature' there, and on the central role literature has in creating an empire that is 'imperishable' and yet free of political structures and force of arms. As her work illustrates, this kind of enquiry takes us into the heart of an increasing emphasis on Anglicization at any point in Indian society where it touched the British governing structures (see, for example, the extracts from the writings of Raja Rammohan Roy reprinted as Texts 2.5 and 2.6). It also carries us into a similar Anglicization within Indian culture, leading eventually to the pro- duction of Indian novels written in the English realist tradition and to poetry written particularly in the English romantic tradition.

But to conclude this chapter we should note that enquiries which trace the shifts and conflicts of ideas between Orientalism and Anglocentrism in India need also to be turned back onto culture in Britain. This would lead to exploration of the different ways in which the Orient was presented and the different role it performed in English society. Less obviously, but perhaps ultimately more importantly, it might lead us to think in terms of the function of literature and education in Britain. If 'our arts', 'our morals' and 'our literature' were to make British colonialism 'imperishable' – or at least if the ideology of the time were to proclaim this as truth – then should we not see writings after 1800 as likely to be geared to reinforcing this sense of 'our'selves? These are questions to bear in mind as you read subsequent chapters.

Questions and exercises

1   Review the references to Sir William Jones in Said's *Orientalism*, particularly the discussion in Chapter 1.3 'Projects' (pp.77–9). What importance does Said see Jones as having in the context of more modern figures, such as Balfour?

2   Given the ferocity and scale of the battles fought in India between 1750 and 1820 that involved British forces or where armies were led by British leaders, can it really be said that such matters as the formulation of law had a more important role in the establishing of British dominion?

3   'Orientalism' is said to be a word with two historically separate meanings: one current from the eighteenth century to the early twentieth century, the other a more recent construction. Is this the case? Is it best to see 'Orientalism' as if it were two words, or are there links between the two which make this inadvisable?

4   In *Masks of Conquest* Gauri Viswanathan refers to there being 'a relationship between the institutionalization of English in India and the exercise of colonial power, between the processes of curricular selection and the impulse to dominate and control' (p.3). What implications does such a view have so far as the critical practice of reading and analysing individual texts is concerned?

5   From the evidence of the texts in our selection, to what extent can it be said that a poet such as Derozio or Dutt has fully absorbed the conventions of English poetry? (You might wish to test this by comparing a particular poem by Derozio or Dutt with one by Keats or another English writer.)

3 THE BRITISH NATION AND THE COLONIES: MANSFIELD PARK

by Richard Allen

Introduction

With this chapter we begin the second strand of *Literature and Nation*, focusing squarely now on the process of the constructing of ideas of nation in literary texts in Britain. As we begin it is right to raise the same kind of issues as are raised at the end of Chapter 1 and the beginning of Chapter 2. Put simply, we must ask: why begin here? Or, in more complex terms, why is it appropriate to make *Mansfield Park* and the period around 1815 the centre of a 'myth of origin'? In response, historians and literary critics might say that there are certainly earlier texts and earlier dates that could stand as the beginning. So far as the idea of the nation is concerned, it is certainly the case that discussion of what it was to be British – and particularly the value that rested in being British – was an important topic at various times during the eighteenth century, particularly during periods of war with France (see Linda Colley, *Britons: Forging the Nation 1707–1837*, London: Pimlico, 1994). So far as literature, and particularly the novel, is concerned it has been a commonplace – albeit a regularly challenged one – that the novel began in the eighteenth century (the *locus classicus* for this view remains Ian Watt, *The Rise of the Novel*, Harmondsworth: Penguin, 1963). A third reason for thinking of an earlier date – related to the concern with colonialism – would be that literature and art in the eighteenth century regularly featured representations of the East, particularly of China. Raymond Schwab, *The Oriental Renaissance: Europe's Rediscovery of India and the East 1680–1880*, trans. by G. Patterson-Black and V. Reinking (New York: Columbia University Press, 1984), provides the most thoroughgoing exploration of this earlier period.

For all this, however, the choice of the period around 1815 is not arbitrary. In terms again of the nation, 1815 marks the end of a period of war and upheaval which began in 1789 with the French Revolution and ended with the defeat and exile of Napoleon. After 1815, dominance in Europe and dominance as a colonial power could become central parts of the British identity. The example set by Britain in abolishing the slave trade (though not slavery) within its own jurisdiction in 1807 gave an additional moral gloss to this new identity. But we should also look to less tangible factors. The year 1815 stands more or less midway through the writing career of Jeremy Bentham, and is close to the beginning of the writing career of James Mill – his *History of India* was published in 1817. The work of these two men can be taken as a sign of the development of a new ethical and value system which had perhaps the most important impact of any through the nineteenth century. Turning to literature, it would be wrong to say that Jane Austen wholly invented the realist style of writing or that the values she endorsed had never been seen before in fiction, but most critics would argue that Austen shows a completeness of commitment to the style that makes it seem as if her novels represent something new. It can also be argued that with the style comes not an admiring depiction of an existing world that is to be preserved but a radical prescription for change, a desire for a world that needs to be brought into existence based on a system of values that intercuts all matters of class with matters of ethics. Without such powerful and persuasive representations of the values that should lie at the heart of the nation, colonization and dominion based on ethical and cultural values – something appropriate to peacetime rather than wartime – could not be sustained. Triumphalism is not the keynote; the note struck at the conclusion of *Mansfield Park* is much more fitting for the ethos of a developing nation as it rebuilds its colonial structures:

> In *her* [i.e. Susan's] usefulness, in Fanny's excellence, in William's continued good conduct, and rising fame, and in the general well-doing and success of the other members of the family, all assisting to advance each other, and doing credit to his countenance and aid, Sir Thomas saw repeated, and for ever repeated reason to rejoice in what he had done for them all, and acknowledge the advantages of early hardship and discipline, and the consciousness of being born to struggle and endure.

> (Jane Austen, *Mansfield Park*, ed. by Claudia L. Johnson, New York and London: Norton, 1998, p.321)

This, perhaps, is a particular manifestation of one aspect of the general process described by Linda Colley as follows:

> In the half century after the American War, there would emerge in Great Britain a far more consciously and officially constructed patriotism which stressed attachment to the monarchy, the importance of empire, the value of military and naval achievement, and the desirability of strong stable government by a virtuous, able and authentically British elite.

> (Colley, p.145)

But if *Mansfield Park* can be said to represent the beginning of a new order in fiction and society, it is only fair to refer again to the possibility of debate. Take, for example, Firdouz Azim's *The Colonial Rise of the Novel* (London: Routledge, 1993). Azim's book covers the period discussed so far, and her introduction signals that the issues of colonialism and literature that pre-occupy us here are her central concern – 'The focus in this book is on the place of the English text in colonial and post-colonial practices, and the connections between the subject/s of literature and the formation of colonial subjectivities ... I have tried to trace an imperialist background for the novel, and to show how the world of the novel is tied to the historical tasks of colonial, commercial and cultural expansion' (pp.5–7). Given these parallels it is interesting that Azim's way of seeing things appears entirely different from that set out in this chapter. Jane Austen figures only as a passing reference in Azim's book, which focuses instead on writers who lie to either side; she deals with Aphra Behn's *Oroonoko* and Daniel Defoe's *Roxana* as a prelude to an extended discussion of the work of Charlotte Brontë. Azim sets her project out in the following way:

> I would like ... to show that [Charlotte Brontë] inherited and worked within a form of writing that had been set up around the notion of a coherent, consistent narrating subject, often female, who was constructed by the effacement of *Other* subjects. That many of these narrative voices were female has detracted critical attention from the imperialistic and oppressive factors within the genre. The novel does not work in a simple way: female-narrated or authored, speaking to other women. It is part of the discursive terrain in which the ideal, unified Enlightenment subject is placed, where a fantasy of unity is created by the invocation and subsequent obliteration of the Other subject, differentiated by class, race and gender. (p.88)

The text

Mansfield Park was first published in 1814; a second edition from a different publisher appeared in 1816. As with Austen's other best-known novels it was reprinted regularly throughout the nineteenth century, but there was no significant attempt to establish an authentic text until the publication of the edition prepared by R.W. Chapman in 1923. The reputation of this text remains high; it is the basis, for example, of the Oxford World's Classics edition first published in 1970. There are, however, reasons to question it as the best choice for study. The original versions of eighteenth- and early nineteenth-century novels can be difficult for modern readers because of conventions of sentence structure, punctuation and presentational style – the whole thing appears rough to the modern eye and ear. After 1900 any editor had to work out how to balance producing a text which was access-ible to a modern reader's eye and ear against truth to the original. Austen's style is perhaps as accessible as any but still it seems that Chapman's edition, published at a time when English as an academic subject was relatively undeveloped and aimed if anything at a 'collector's' market, did involve some of the characteristic smoothing. With these things in mind we prefer to cite the much more recent edition of *Mansfield Park* which appears in the Norton Critical Edition series (New York and London: Norton, 1998) and is described by its editor, Claudia L. Johnson, in her introduction as 'rawer and less lapidary than Chapman's' (p.xxi). The differences are relatively small but the style of the differences can be significant; a 'smoother' text such as Chapman offers carries Austen closer to her successors, George Eliot and Anthony Trollope, whereas a 'rougher' text would carry her closer to her eighteenth-century predecessors. (Johnson's edition also contains a very useful set of documents drawing together material from Austen's own time and more recent criticism.)

Biographical and bibliographical information

Any attempt to draw Austen closer to matters of colonialism of the time is likely to depend upon – or at least take into account – the events of Austen's life, the circumstances and social relations of her family and friends. In this respect it is likely to draw on biographical writing about her. Such biographical accounts are easily available, the most recent are Claire Tomalin, *Jane Austen: A Life* (London: Viking, 1997), and David Nokes, *Jane Austen: A Life* (London: Fourth Estate, 1997). But this approach is not unproblematic: the essential elements have been subject to a kind of filtering process which may or may not have been objective. Because she remained within her own family circle throughout her life we are dependent on evidence from members of her own family for information – you could say she remained family 'property' for most of the nineteenth century. The first major source was the *Memoir of Jane Austen* published in 1870 by J.E. Austen-Leigh and this was followed in 1913 by William Austen-Leigh and Richard Arthur Austen-Leigh, *Jane Austen Her Life and Letters: A Family Record*, revised and enlarged edition ed. by Dierdre Le Faye (London: British Library, 1989). The most up to date collection of the letters that have survived is to be found in *Jane Austen's Letters*, collected and edited by Dierdre Le Faye (Oxford: Oxford University Press, 1995). Slightly out of this pattern, Jan Fergus, *Jane Austen: A Literary Life* (London: Macmillan, 1991), offers an account of Austen which focuses more strongly on her as a writer.

The Norton Critical Edition of *Mansfield Park* contains a useful bibliography of recent work on the novel, but a much more comprehensive listing is to be found in David Gilson, *A Bibliography of Jane Austen* (Winchester: St Paul's Bibliographies, new edn 1997). A more selective and descriptive account of work before 1970 can be found in F.B. Pinion, *A Jane Austen Companion: A Critical Survey and Reference Book* (London: Macmillan, 1973). Examples of the way Austen's work has been approached and valued over the years are also to be found in the two volumes of *Jane Austen: The Critical Heritage*, ed. by B.C. Southam (London: Routledge & Kegan Paul, 1968 and 1987).

Approaching Mansfield Park

Anyone wanting to know how literary study has approached Jane Austen as part of the canon of the English novel could usefully begin with, for example, Tony Tanner, *Jane Austen* (London: Macmillan, 1986), or Meenakshi Mukherjee, *Jane Austen* (London: Macmillan, 1991), or Barbara Hardy, *A Reading of Jane Austen* (London: Owen, 1975). Focusing more on *Mansfield Park* we are fortunate now in having a group of excellent collections of critical writings on the novel which between them include extracts from many of the works cited in the next sections. These include *Mansfield Park*, ed. by Isabel Armstrong in the Penguin Critical Studies series (London: Penguin, 1988); *'Mansfield Park' and 'Persuasion': A New Casebook*,

ed. by Judy Symons (London: Macmillan, 1997), and *Mansfield Park*, ed. by
Nigel Wood in the Theory in Practice series (Buckingham: Open University
Press, 1993).

Mansfield Park, *history and politics*

For many years there was a tendency to compartmentalize the English
novel at the beginning of the nineteenth century. For fiction dealing with
politics one turned to the philosopher and political writer William Godwin;
Jane Austen offered fiction dealing with ethics and choices within a
domestic sphere and within the family; while for fantasy and more purely
imaginative writing one turned to the Gothic novelists such as M.G. 'Monk'
Lewis. No single critical work has played a more important part in the
revision of this view so far as Jane Austen is concerned than Marilyn Butler,
Jane Austen and the War of Ideas (Oxford: Clarendon Press, 1975; new edn
1987), and any exploration of Jane Austen in terms of literature and nation
could very usefully start here. Butler's technique is to read Austen in the
literary, historical and political context of her time rather, for example, than
in the context of a history of the development of the English novel in the
nineteenth century. Instead of being represented as an isolated figure and
the founder of this new literary form, 'Realism', Austen is implicated in a
larger history and in a dialectical argument about ideologies which can be
seen to be conditioning the form of her writing.

Jane Austen and the War of Ideas provides an excellent stimulus to the pursuit
of very specifically located historical study, and in this respect the date of
first publication might be important. One approach might be to explore just
how the particular messages, problems and choices contained in *Mansfield
Park* relate to 1814. Before going down this avenue, however, you need to
bear in mind that the novel was most probably written between the
February of 1811 and the summer of 1813. By 1813 in most people's eyes
victory over Napoleon seemed more likely, but any sense of imminent
triumph might perhaps have been offset by feelings of financial responsibilities to come. (By borrowing heavily to finance the war the government
was more in debt than it had ever been before and these debts would have
to be repaid through taxation.) Might we see Austen as a kind of sensitive
antenna allowing us to hear the reality of the time, catching public events
not in terms of great men and government politics but in terms of a particular social class? Once again our interest in colonial matters should make
us particularly attentive to the signals picked up in that area; the character
of William Price then becomes interesting not just as Fanny's brother but as
a kind of carrier of historical resonances which can inform our reading of
the novel. To be a sailor – it could be suggested – was to have something in
common with Austen's brothers, for whom the sea meant the opportunity
to rise to high naval rank at a time of naval warfare and to be involved not
just in service in European and North American waters but in the naval
escorts of the East India Company ships trading with China.

Roger Sales, *Jane Austen and Representations of Regency England* (London: Routledge, 1996), pursues just these kinds of issues in depth, offering a detailed account of the history of the period from 1811 to 1820 and Austen's novels at this time, particularly *Mansfield Park*. His eminently reasonable assumption is that writers react to contemporary events, making judge-ments about what is important that may not be the same as those made later by historians of the period. Events such as the French Revolution and the abolition of the slave trade in Britain seem all important to us now but maybe this is because we can see the later ramifications of these events. In connecting up writings of the time we need to be at least as alert to events then seen as important but which now seem to us insignificant in the narrative of history. Sales finds *Mansfield Park* 'intriguingly contradictory', particularly because of the way Henry Crawford is 'both hero and villain', while the questions surrounding the acceptability of the theatricals are 'equally complicated' (p.131).

Finally, it is interesting to note the time gap between the availability of essential details about Austen's life and critics beginning to see her as a writer with a political agenda as opposed to 'just' a writer of family comedy. Information on the public rank of Austen's relatives was available from 1870 onwards and was fully explored in, for example, J.H. and E.C. Hubbach, *Jane Austen's Sailor Brothers: Being the Adventures of Sir Francis Austen, G.C.B., Admiral of the Fleet and Rear Admiral Charles Austen* (London: John Lane, 1906). 'Political' readings did not appear until the 1960s and 1970s in, for example, Avrom Fleischman, *A Reading of 'Mansfield Park'* (Minneapolis: University of Minnesota Press, 1967), and Marilyn Butler, *Jane Austen and the War of Ideas* (1975).

The political connections critics have now recognized are just as evident as those which link a writer such as William Godwin, for example, with the world of politics. Exploring why these links were not made earlier or more prominently provides an interesting way into the politics of English literary studies.

Gentry and nation

It could well be argued that understanding the politics of *Mansfield Park is* a matter of seeing three things in relation to each other, namely (a) the novel, (b) the landed gentry estate and (c) the nation. The characters of the novel live in fiction but – through the techniques of Realism – their fictional lives collect resonances from a wider world. In writing about the Bertrams and their estate Austen is entering into a literary tradition that goes back at least a century; it is explored in John Barrell, *English Literature in History 1730–80: An Equal, Wide Survey* (London: Hutchinson, 1983). By way of a clear earlier example of this tradition one might cite Fielding's *Tom Jones* (1749), where a good deal of the debate about values in which the reader becomes engaged is epitomized through the relative merits (and faults) of Mr Allworthy and Squire Western, each on his own estate. Alongside Austen's own novels, set primarily in the families of the English rural gentry, we may place the beginnings of the Irish 'big house' novel with works such as Maria Edgeworth's *Castle Rackrent* (1800). To exemplify the later development of this tradition one might then cite the depiction of rural life in the novels of George Eliot, particularly in *Adam Bede* and in the Garth subplots of *Middlemarch*. Putting these novels side by side with *Mansfield Park* shows how ideas of the rural and of rural value had changed over the first half of the nineteenth century. The changes in the representation of the rural gentry are particularly striking, with Austen perhaps seeming to have more in common with Fielding's novels than with the portrayal of a differently structured world in George Eliot.

The particular value of the rural estate and of the English gentry in Austen's work is explored in Alistair M. Duckworth, *The Improvement of the Estate* (London: Johns Hopkins University Press, 1994). An earlier pioneering work emphasizing that Austen's novels deal with larger political issues – as opposed simply to family comedies of manners – was Mary Evans, *Jane Austen and the State* (London: Tavistock, 1987). In a sense one might take the contrast between these two titles as emblematic of the test faced when attempting to relate a novel like *Mansfield Park* to matters of colonialism. Taking the view that the novel has a moral and political dimension might be to say only that it is to do with the improvement of the 'estate' for the benefit of the Bertram heirs, an aim that runs to the park boundary and perhaps hardly beyond. To say that the outcome of the novel is to do with the 'state' is dramatically to push out the areas of concern and the potential influence. Making a case for the latter position can often involve almost subliminal elements, for example the way the Mansfield estate with its Portsmouth relations and its Caribbean estates 'stands' for (or is a metaphor for) a nation dependent on its navy and its colonies. Eric Stokes's classic *The English Utilitarians and India* (Oxford: Oxford University Press, 1959) and Javed Majeed, *Ungoverned Imaginings: James Mill's 'The History of British India' and Orientalism* (Oxford: Clarendon Press, 1992), both offer a way into these issues. Stokes's account describes the changes in the government of British India in the period after 1810 whereby – under the 'Bengal' system – the citizen was ruled 'with a paternal and simple government' (p.13) which was both local and fair. (Fairness was assured through the creation of district magistrates who were appointed in parallel to, but separate from, collectors responsible for tax gathering.) Majeed in his book traces the background and ideas of James Mill's influential *History of British India* published in 1817. Of particular interest here is Mill's emphasis on the middle classes 'whom he hoped would take the lead in reforming society, since it was their interests which were identical with society as a whole. It was the "middle rank" of society which was "the most wise and the most virtuous part of the community"' (pp.126–7).

Discussions of British ideological positions such as those of Stokes and Majeed tend to take place with reference to the actions of individuals whose behaviour can then be 'generalized' in an expanding series of circles. For

example, a religious belief and practice seen in individuals carries resonances for the estate, the nation and the whole ethos and ideology of the
colonial enterprise. But we should never accept that the way a novel is
written is irrelevant or neutral so far as ideological messages are concerned.
Tara Goshal Wallace, *Jane Austen and Narrative Authority* (London:
Macmillan, 1995), gives an indication of how 'form' can be involved in
carrying ideology generally in Jane Austen's work. So far as *Mansfield Park*
itself is concerned, of relevance are the way the focus on the estate itself
more or less precludes the lower or upper classes having a part in the
'message' of the novel, and the way the last chapters are used finally to
bring home that same 'message'. How, for example, are we to read the
curious sentence 'Let other pens dwell on guilt and misery' (p.312) that
precedes the careful disposing of the characters in the dénouement of the
final chapter? Are we to take this as indeed a resounding and authoritative
endorsement of the now morally revived Bertram/gentry household, or is
there perhaps an irony – a fictional conclusion blocking our sight of a less
securely captured 'real-world' conclusion? Understanding the particular
inflection which Austen gives to this ideological tradition in *Mansfield Park*
involves generally thinking about the way the plot works to include and to
exclude certain positions. The message of Fanny Price is clearly something
which is included: eventually, Edmund and even Sir Thomas are allowed a
similar presence. By contrast other characters – such as Julia, Maria or
Henry Crawford – are in the end summarily silenced by being dismissed
from the plot or are confined within the narrator's controlling voice.

Having come to conclusions about these kinds of moral messages in the
novel and their possible 'sources' in the national events of 1811–14, one
might wish also to ask whether we can know the impact the message had on
its readers and the time. Research into this question might soon come up
against the problem that we know Austen's novels had only small sales
when they first appeared (see Francis, *Jane Austen*). We certainly cannot
claim that here is a Byron catching the mood of the moment with publications that tens of thousands bought. Two possibilities might be explored.
First, there is the notion that great writers – as Austen certainly is – possess
certain gifts which leave them 'ahead of their time', influencing future
generations more than they do their own. An alternative view – more in
tune with the kind of investigation pursued here – is to see Austen as a
writer working in and for a particular class of society which was relatively
small in numbers but particularly large in importance so far as the development of colonial Britain was concerned. The nature of that class and the
processes that sustained it are explored in Raymond Williams, *The Country
and the City* (London: Chatto & Windus, 1973); he writes neatly of Austen
being concerned with the 'conversion of good income into good conduct'
(p.116). More elaborately, P.J. Cain and A.G. Hopkins, *British Imperialism:
Innovation and Expansion 1688–1914* (London: Longman, 1993), describe the
class interests as follows:

Britain's strength and stability relied on continuing capitalist development, which was held to be in the interest of the poor, the 'middling orders' and the rich alike. The brand of capitalism in question was thought to rest upon a foundation of law and custom which the gentlemanly elite could fairly claim to have created and sustained. As the French Wars drew to a close, the central issue was not whether the gentlemanly order would have to yield to a rising industrial bourgeoisie, but what direction policy would have to take to carry that order into the nineteenth century. (p.78)

Foreign parts

Pursuing still what one might describe as a broadly political reading of the novel, let us now look at how the world abroad is referred to and represented. It is worth remembering here that the meaning of the word 'foreign' is historically specific, just as when we refer to the British colonial world we are referring to something that shifts. (In 1820 anyone hearing the world 'colony' might think, not of North America and the West Indies but of India and the East Indies.) Arguably – as the use of the name 'Indies' for territories to the West and to the East indicates – notions of the differences between territories overseas are also historically constructed and not the same as those that prevail today. At the end of a protracted war against France, it might be argued that for the British the 'foreign' began in Europe. Perhaps the most common imaginings of the 'foreign' in the period before 1820 are to be found in the Catholic, Italian landscapes of the Gothic novel. Literary historians may claim that this way of writing had run its course by 1820 and was ripe for the treatment meted out by Austen in *Northanger Abbey*, but the evidence of later years suggests that the genre was far from losing its grip on the imagination of readers. Almost contemporary with *Mansfield Park*, for example, is Mary Shelley's *Frankenstein* (1818). What could be more foreign and strange than the story of the 'manufacture' of a creature? Yet this takes place not in some invented or far-off land such as China but in Austria and (almost) in the Orkneys. Ice is the natural habitat of the creature for parts of the novel but this ice world is, again, in Europe before the final dénouement in the Arctic. (For further discussion of these possibilities see Richard Allen, 'Reading *Frankenstein*', in *The Realist Novel*, ed. by Dennis Walder (London: Routledge, 1995).

The foreign world that appears briefly but importantly in *Mansfield Park* is more distant and appears to reflect more rationally based economic realities than the Gothic novel or *Frankenstein*, but it is worth bearing this context in mind as one explores it further. Edward W. Said, *Culture and Imperialism* (London: Chatto & Windus, 1993), contains one of the most well known explications of the role of the references to Antigua in the novel. For him it is a crucial element in locating the Bertram family:

The Bertrams could not have been possible without the slave trade, sugar, and the colonial planter class ... As the old system of protected monopoly gradually disappeared and as a new class of settler-planters displaced the old absentee system, the West Indian interest lost dominance: cotton manufacture, an even more open system of trade, and the abolition of the slave trade reduced the power and prestige of people like the Bertrams, whose frequency of sojourn in the Caribbean then decreased. (pp.112–13)

A similar point is made by Joseph Lew in '"That Abominable Traffic": *Mansfield Park* and the Dynamics of Slavery' (reprinted in the Norton Critical Edition of the novel). He writes that, 'having accustomed himself to exerting *de facto* absolute power over his Negro chattel ... Sir Thomas expects an identical submission from the inhabitants of Mansfield, females especially' (p.507).

Such views as these have been influential in setting the novel in a wider social framework but they should not stand entirely beyond scrutiny. Might they – curiously perhaps – be seen as embodying a construction of the 'foreign' as a place necessarily of evil which is akin to that of the Gothic novel? Are we also naturally to assume that Sir Thomas falls necessarily on the 'wrong' side in the matter of slavery? Just what kind of estate owner was Sir Thomas Bertram? In fictional terms you might say the question is meaningless; the events in Antigua happen outside the narrative and simply allow the plot to proceed. But the space they make is troubling to an enquiry involving colonialism because of that. Without more information we cannot 'read' whether this is a representation of a cruel slave owner or one caught up in the problems facing those plantation owners who were trying to make the best world for their slaves – slaves who with the ending of the slave trade in 1807 could not simply be replaced but had to be nurtured to maintain the workforce. This is not the place to press this argument to a conclusion – if indeed that is possible. My aim is rather to suggest possible ways of reading this novel, which has at its core a colonial Britain that increasingly was intent on a moral justification for its overseas rule.

Further foreign parts

Finally in this chapter I want to suggest other comparative possibilities which might through contrast prompt our thinking about *Mansfield Park*. The other texts to which I refer are mostly poetry and this in itself is interesting since most critics now would say that the decision by a writer to write in a particular way – in poetry or prose, for example – is seldom a matter of accident but is part of finding a form appropriate to the subject matter. Nigel Leask, *British Romantic Writers and the East: Anxieties of Empire* (Cambridge: Cambridge University Press, 1992), provides an excellent point of departure here. Discussions of canonical writers are interspersed with a wealth of references to writers who are hardly known or read nowadays. Amongst the many possibilities are Lady Morgan's novel *The Missionary* (1811), and two poems, Robert Southey, *The Curse of Kehama* (1810; see Text 3.1), and Thomas Moore, *Lalla Rookh* (1817; see Text 3.2). Moore's poem achieved a success well beyond that of Austen; *Lalla Rookh* went through twenty editions between 1817 and 1840. *The Curse of Kehama* was less popular, but is of interest not least because of the insight the preface gives us into the way Indian religion and culture were seen at the time. Southey's work is discussed in Majeed, *Ungoverned Imaginings*. A comment in Majeed's discussion potentially allows the development of ways of thinking about this period that draw together the representations of India in Southey's poetry, the developing colonial ideology as expressed in the work of Sir William Jones and the ethical and moral values of Britishness implicit in *Mansfield Park*:

> This rhetoric of authenticity and fidelity in Southey's epics [seen in the preface to *The Curse of Kehama*] was in part indicative of the anxiety in the oriental renaissance in this period to draw 'orient knowledge from its fountains pure', for purposes of legal codification [as in the work of Sir William Jones, see Chapter 2 above] and works of fiction [as evident in the emphasis on the need for truthfulness and honesty in Austen], purposes which were simultaneously diverse and intimately related. (p.52)

These comparisons allow us to understand what Austen is, as it were, avoiding writing in *Mansfield Park* when she refers to places overseas. But even though she only refers to India once in the novel, it was part of the same colonial world as Antigua. And at that time, to pick up Leask's subtitle, the 'anxieties of Empire' were not confined to the Caribbean, so that the emphasis on the value of the estate and the landed gentry is just as important in relation to India as to the Caribbean. If in the final chapters the disruptive elements seem just too quickly despatched and the marriage of Fanny and Edmund just too tidily concluded, then maybe that is a sign of the strength of those anxieties and the difficulty Austen finds in imagining the establishing of her new order.

Questions and exercises

1   Consider the ways in which gender is (or is not) important to the ethical message of *Mansfield Park* (for example in the presentation of Fanny or Mrs Norris). How might these aspects of the message be relevant to the conduct of British colonial rule?

2   'Improvement' of the estate (as advocated by Mr Rushworth or actually brought about through Fanny Price) is a theme in *Mansfield Park*. What implications might there be in this theme which could be applied also in British colonial rule?

3   Read Elizabeth Inchbald's *Lover's Vows* (reprinted in the Norton edition). From the evidence of the play what can we conclude (a) about how we

should understand the events of Austen's novel, and (b) what we can deduce about a society which would find Inchbald's play generally morally objectionable?

4   Explore further the campaigns against the slave trade and against slavery itself. In particular consider if there are links to be made between the religious affiliations of the campaigners and the religious themes of *Mansfield Park*.

5   Take another text – perhaps *the Curse of Kehama*, *Lalla Rookh* or *The Missionary* listed in the 'Further foreign parts' section above – and work out what elements are brought together in the representation of the foreign world.

4 LITERATURE, NATION AND REVOLUTION: A TALE OF TWO CITIES

by Richard Allen

Introduction

A Tale of Two Cities is a story of the mob in the French Revolution and of English and French people caught up – sometimes willingly, sometimes unwillingly – in those events. Or to put it in a more abstract way, imaginings of violent revolution – internal to one nation but also involving another nation – become narrative, plot and character. The reader is drawn into these three elements and hence into the violence, ideas and emotions of the novel. It seems easy to track a source for the story – Thomas Carlyle's *History of the French Revolution*, published in 1837. Carlyle's *History* was one of the most fêted publications of the day, but in addition there are very evident connections between Dickens and Carlyle. They met first in 1840 and soon became friends; at his death Dickens's library contained both the original 1837 edition of the *History* and the reprint of 1857; Dickens read and reread Carlyle's work – there is a specific mention of his rereading it in a letter of 1851; finally on 30 October 1859 Dickens wrote to Carlyle sending him some advance copy from the novel and explaining his plan for a preface recording his debt to the *History*. (The correspondences of novel and historical events can be followed up in Andrew Sanders, *The Companion to 'A Tale of Two Cities'*, London: Unwin Hyman, 1988, and G. Newlin, *Understanding 'A Tale of Two Cities'*, London: Greenwood Press, 1998.) None of this should be discounted but it is also possible to see a further set of 'influences' and 'sources' cross-cutting Carlyle and the French Revolution. This involves reading the novel more as a mirror of its own time – the 1850s – than of fifty years past.

A Tale of Two Cities was probably originally conceived late in 1857; it was eventually published in 1859. As such it quite specifically coincides with what is often described simply as 'the Indian Mutiny'. This insurrection, which began on 10 May 1857 and ended officially on 8 July 1859, was the most major rebellion against British rule overseas since the North American colonies had inflicted a military defeat on Britain and gained independence in 1783. It was evident at the time – as it is now – that if the Indian uprising had succeeded it would have had as momentous an impact on Britain as the defeat in North America.

There were a number of unsuccessful local uprisings in the months up to May 1857, but 10 May 1857 – when three Native Infantry regiments rose against their officers at Meerut and marched on Delhi – is taken conventionally as the start of the rising. The capture of Delhi and its recapture by the British on 20 September 1857 took on a symbolic significance for the events as a whole, but this should not obscure the fact that in real terms the rising took the form of a number of separate incidents across India. Beyond Delhi, accounts of the time focused on events at Lucknow between June and November 1857, and at Kanpur where there were mass-acres of Europeans on 27 June and 15 July 1857 – on the latter occasion it was women and children who were killed. Gradually, as reinforcements arrived from Britain, the British began to regain control; considerable unofficial and judicially sanctioned violence against Indians ensued, of which the blowing of Indians from cannons is the most notorious.

The classic British account of the rebellion remains Christopher Hibbert, *The Great Mutiny, India 1857* (London: Allen Lane, 1978), but the period is still very much the subject of debate, particularly so far as the causes are concerned. Did everything spring from the issue of a new type of cartridge or were there more complex underlying causes? (For an overview of the debates see Judith Brown, *Modern India: The Origins of an Asian Democracy*, Oxford: Oxford University Press, 1994, pp.85ff., and Bipan Chandra, Mridula Mukherjee, Aditya Mukherjee, K.N. Panikkar and Sucheta Mahajan, *India's Struggle for Independence 1857–1947*, Delhi: Penguin, 1989, pp.31ff.) Just how the events should be named is also an issue. For many years 'the Indian Mutiny of 1857' was the generally accepted form. After 1947, nationalists in India and those sympathetic to India's new independence could be found referring to the events as 'the First War of Indian Independence' or 'the Uprising of 1857'. More recently, and with an eye to the disparate events and disparate causes, reference has been made to 'the military mutiny and the civil insurrection of 1857'.

The years 1857–8 are important also because they provoked further reflection in Britain on the appropriateness of the formal political links between Britain and India. As Chapter 1 signals, the British government had reluctantly involved itself more and more in the governing of India, yet in 1857 formally India was still governed 'privately' by the East India Company – officials were servants of the Company and only indirectly of the British state. This changed in November 1858 when an Act took effect which decreed that all the East India Company's territories were vested in Queen Victoria; from then on all British power in India was to be exercised directly in her name. Although this seemed only to regularize a situation which had been more or less fact for some time, it did give a further impetus to the British government regulation of Indian life (see Thomas R. Metcalf, *Ideologies of the Raj*, Cambridge: Cambridge University Press, 1995, especially Chapter 2).

The text

A Tale of Two Cities was published between April and November 1859 as the weekly serial in the initial numbers of Dickens's magazine *All the Year Round*. It also appeared on its own in monthly form published by Chapman & Hall between June and December of the same year, appearing in book form in November 1859. Enormous numbers of copies of Dickens's novels have been published and sold since then but it is only relatively recently that a new critical and authoritative edition has begun to appear under the Clarendon Press imprint. At the time of writing, however, no edition of *A Tale of Two Cities* has appeared in this series. The most commonly available versions are that edited by George Woodcock for Penguin (1970), and that with an introduction and notes by Andrew Sanders for the Oxford World's Classics series (1988). The latter can be recommended particularly for the information it gives about links between the events of the novel and those of the French Revolution (based on Sanders's own *Companion*).

Biographical and bibliographical information

Dickens's life has been the subject of considerable study. Later writers have always to a considerable extent relied on the original biography by Dickens's friend John Forster, *The Life of Charles Dickens* (1872–4; repr. London: Dent, 1966). Among later biographies, perhaps the most extensive – and still authoritative – is Edgar Johnson, *Charles Dickens: His Tragedy and Triumph* (2 vols, London: Gollancz, 1953). More recent versions include Norman and Jean Mackenzie, *Dickens: A Life* (Oxford: Oxford University Press, 1979), Fred Kaplan, *Dickens: A Biography* (London: Hodder & Stoughton, 1988), and Peter Ackroyd, *Dickens* (London: Sinclair-Stevenson, 1990). Dickens was an energetic letter writer, and a wonderful impression of the hectic rush of his life can be gained from volumes of *The Pilgrim Edition of The Letters of Charles Dickens*. This is still incomplete but the period of the composition and publication of *A Tale of Two Cities* is covered in volumes 8 and 9 (ed. by Graham Storey and Kathleen Tillotson, Oxford: Clarendon Press, 1995 and 1997).

Dickens has been the object of so much literary criticism that it is difficult to offer suggestions for works which summarize the field, and there is no available bibliography of the critical work as a whole. Some sense of what has been produced over the years can be gathered from *Charles Dickens: Critical Assessments*, ed. by Michael Hollington (4 vols, Robertsbridge: Croom Information, 1995). Recent approaches to Dickens's work in general can be sampled in *Charles Dickens*, ed. by Steven O'Connor (London: Longman, 1996), which has a useful 'Further Reading' section. Finally, although at the time of writing there is no collection of essays devoted just to *A Tale of Two Cities*, those that exist for other novels can give a sense of how Dickens's work is now approached; *Bleak House: A New Casebook*, ed. by Jeremy Tambling (London: Macmillan, 1998), is a good example.

Approaching A Tale of Two Cities

The remainder of this chapter suggests four ways in which *A Tale of Two Cities* can be read in the context of literature and nation. The first two in their different ways both suggest making links between the literary text and the history of which it is a part. The other two suggest more obviously literary comparative approaches, putting Dickens's novel alongside first the work of Edward Fitzgerald and then detective novels.

A Tale of Two Cities *in the context of the 'mutiny' of 1857*

Thinking about how to understand Dickens writing in 1858–9 about the French Revolution as relevant to events in India at the time is likely to prompt research into the facts of his life. Here the details of his son Walter Landor Dickens catch the eye. Dickens had successfully enlisted the interest of his friend and patron Miss Burdett Coutts to get Walter into the service of the East India Company; Walter sailed from Southampton for India on 20 July 1857, barely two weeks before the first reports of the rebellion reached England. Letters reached Dickens recording his son's steady progress to India just as increasingly sensational reports appeared in British newspapers describing, for example, the massacre at Kanpur. (In his *Dickens and the New Historicism*, London: Macmillan, 1997, W.J. Palmer comments on the importance of the shipwreck metaphor in Chapters 21 to 24 of Book 2 of *A Tale of Two Cities*.) After he arrived in India Walter fought with a regiment that was involved in the relief of both Kanpur and Lucknow. Through all this Dickens's own letters – including the now infamous ones of 4 and 23 October 1857 in which he looked forward to the extermination of all Indians – show how close he was to the agitated public mood. He was, moreover, acquainted with William Howard Russell of *The Times*, whose reports from India began to appear from January 1858, and corresponded directly with him in India. The piece Dickens and Wilkie Collins contributed to the *Household Words* Christmas Number of 1857, 'The Perils of Certain English Prisoners' (the chapters by Dickens are reprinted in Charles Dickens, *Christmas Stories*, with an introduction by Margaret Lane, Oxford: Oxford University Press, 1956, pp.161–208), might be brought forward by way of further evidence here. The story is set in an imaginary place on the north-east coast of South America adjacent to the Caribbean islands but it deals with a capture and escape and with interracial violence, presenting on a small scale events parallel to the larger-scale events in India at the time. In its telling, too, the story embodies racist attitudes that are quite consistent with Dickens's private comments about India. The conclusion from this evidence is that Dickens shared not only the personal feelings of those whose loved ones were fighting in India but also the popular opinion that the Indian mutiny was a direct threat to British colonial power and to the supremacy of the white nations.

Darnay, Dr Manette, his daughter, Sydney Carton and the other English characters in *A Tale of Two Cities* who are victims of foreign treachery and mob violence are in a situation exactly analogous to those British who were attacked by violent mobs in India. The idea that a novel can in this way be related directly to public events even when it makes no direct reference to them may seem strange, but we can take strength, perhaps, from the fact that just this same suggestion has been made in relation to *Little Dorritt*, the novel preceding *A Tale of Two Cities*, which Dickens wrote between 1855 and 1857. Apart from an excursion some of the characters take to Italy, *Little Dorritt* deals with family events in London, but critics have associated it with reactions to the Crimean War (1853–6). At one stage Dickens contemplated using the title 'Nobody's Fault' for *Little Dorritt*, a title which would have signalled more explicitly both the way that in the end individuals are exonerated from blame in the events of the novel and the way the Dorritt family events mirror the wider world with a similar mood of exoneration in public responses to losses in the Crimea. *Little Dorritt* links directly to *A Tale of Two Cities* in that both novels feature a hero who is remarkably unheroic. Dickens seems intent on building a sense of the impossibility of action into the centre of the character of Arthur Clennam in *Little Dorritt* just as he is intent on making Carton an ironic and laconic hero almost until the end. Both are far from the model of the military hero of events in India as exemplified by Sir Henry Havelock. (For a discussion of literary representations of this latter type of hero see G. Dawson, *Soldier Heroes: British Adventure, Empire and the Imagining of Masculinities*, London: Routledge, 1995.)

Comparison with other texts of the time dealing with India is a fruitful way, meanwhile, into understanding and situating Dickens's representations of violent insurrection against Britain and the British response to it that is mirrored in *A Tale of Two Cities* (see Text 4.1). Such accounts can be found in newspapers and periodicals selling alongside *Household Words* – *The Times*, *The Spectator* and *Blackwood's Magazine* – but also in books, for example, Charles Ball, *History of the Indian Mutiny* (2 vols, London: London Printing and Publishing Company, 1858–9). Supposedly direct representations of events in India are excellently discussed in the chapter 'The Well at Cawnpore: Literary Representations of the Indian Mutiny of 1857', in Patrick Brantlinger, *Rule of Darkness: British Literature and Imperialism, 1830–1914* (London: Cornell University Press, 1988). Other comparative work is rewarding, particularly that which compares *A Tale of Two Cities* with British works looking back on the events of 1857–9 from a later imperial vantage point. The years up to 1856 had genuinely seemed to carry forward British ideas for the modernization of Indian society conceived in the 1820s and 1830s. Eric Stokes, *The English Utilitarians and India* (Oxford: Oxford University Press, 1959), offers an excellent overall account of these developments, while Judith Brown gives the following revealing vignette of the particular example of the development of railways:

> In 1848, for example, the East India Railway Company urged the Prime Minister that railway building could deeply influence for good the lives of all Indians. 'This is a matter of extreme importance in India, where the energy of individual thought has long been cramped by submission to despotic governments, to irresponsible and venal subordinates, to the ceremonies and priesthood of an irrational religion, and to a public opinion founded not on investigation, but on traditional usages and observances.'
>
> (*Modern India*, p.83)

The incorporation of India within British values based on land, trade and religion was massively disrupted by the events of 1857; after what in British eyes seemed a massive betrayal of trust, a new way forward was necessary. This might involve an even greater emphasis on the need for modernization, a belief that India should be transformed by Western values of rationality, industry, progress and improvement. But as Metcalf explains in *Ideologies of the Raj*, it was commonly accepted that quite un-modern methods were appropriate to achieve these ends. For much of the nineteenth century Romantic ideas of the East such as can be seen in Robert Southey's *The Curse of Kehama* (1810) continued to hold an important place amongst British attitudes; it was an essentially despotic, almost barbaric world. To expect such people to progress rationally of their own accord into the modern world seemed unrealistic and it seemed entirely acceptable for the British in turn to employ despotic rule to achieve their progressive ends. The forty years after the Act for the Better Government of India of 1858 focused on consolidating and securing British rule, culminating in Queen Victoria's Diamond Jubilee celebrations of 1897. Perhaps because of this the 1890s seem to have seen a period of renewed interest in the events of 1857–9. One account based on his own experience is *Mariam: A Story of the Indian Mutiny of 1857* by J.F.F[anthorne] – 'one of the survivors' (see Text 4.3). Another account – perhaps better known and this time based on reports collected later in India – is Flora Annie Steel, *On the Face of the Waters* (London: Heinemann, 1896). These later fictional accounts of the violence of the 1850s – and perhaps even *A Tale of Two Cities* itself – can also be compared with historical accounts of the rebellion.

A key source for comparison would be the work of Sir John Kaye and G.B. Malleson, whose six-volume history was published between 1864 and 1880 (see *Kaye's and Malleson's 'History of the Indian Mutiny of 1857–58'*, ed. by G.B. Malleson, London: W.H. Allen, 1888; see Text 4.2). As time passed alternative readings of events began to appear; one example of this more sceptical kind of account is *The Other Side of the Medal* (London: L. & V. Woolf, 1925) by the novelist and 'India hand' Edward Thompson. Examples of popular novels which used the events of 1857–8 are given and discussed in 'And to think that Henrietta Guise was in the hands of such Human Demons', in *Shades of Empire in Colonial and Post-Colonial Literatures*, ed. by C.C. Barfoot and T. D'Haen (Amsterdam: Rodopi, 1993). Another more recent novel which might be allowed to offer a more serious version of events is J.G. Farrell, *The Siege of Krishnapur* (London: Weidenfeld & Nicolson, 1973). Entirely different results arise from comparison of *A Tale of Two Cities* with twentieth-century novels that describe rebellion in India.

Writing nation

I want now to move to a different kind of approach, one that involves seeing texts as working within 'discourse'. 'Discourse' – a notion conceived by the French writer Michel Foucault – may be defined as the systems of seeing, writing and knowing which imbue the language we use and within which our experience of living within society is formed; in any society many parallel, overlapping, sometimes even contradictory discourses will be in play at the same time. Crucially, these systems also embody the power structures that determine our values and how we see ourselves and our experience within society. You will perhaps already have encountered the idea in your reading since discourse is explicitly fundamental to Edward W. Said's methodology in *Orientalism* (London: Penguin, 1985). When he refers to the Orient as being managed and produced 'politically, sociologically, militarily, ideologically, scientifically, and imaginatively during the post-Enlightenment period' (p.3), he is making a point of running together very different things so that his readers do not form easy notions about the way certain discourses – political, military, legal – are to do with action whereas others – sociological, ideological, imaginative – are to do with thought. But there might be a value in adopting the idea of a spectrum where things can be considered a little more separately. 'Imaginative' discourse (exemplified by novels such as *A Tale of Two Cities*) could then be placed at one end of this spectrum, while at the other end most prominently would sit military discourse. Military power – brute force – often decides the outcome of colonial matters, but advocates of the power of discourse would say that the system of discipline, loyalty and obedience embodied in military language or discourse is just as powerful. On the other hand, while literature may be pure fantasy, its narrative structures and conventions even then carry messages which powerfully organize and sustain social life – through the notions of order restored, of the hero, of the value of nature, of cause and effect which have been part of European literature since the Enlightenment. Midway, perhaps, on the spectrum are other discourses: the scientific knowledge that organizes the relations between races, the geographical discourse that means that to map is to control the land, and so on. There is also congruity between these ideas and those embodied in the ideas of nation put forward by Homi Bhabha in his seminal collection, *Nation and Narration* (London: Routledge, 1990). In his introduction, for example, Bhabha describes something he calls the political 'rationality' of 'the nation' (i.e. its political organizing principle) as akin to 'a form of narrative'. He then goes on to cite 'Benedict Anderson's view of the space and time of the modern nation as embodied in the narrative culture of the realist novel' (p.2); in other words, people live everyday life in the modern nation in discourses which are quintessentially embodied in the realist novel.

A Tale of Two Cities provides opportunities for exploring these ideas in relation to a particular text. One of the essays in *Nation and Narration* – Bruce Robbins, 'Telescopic Philanthropy: Professionalism and Responsibility in *Bleak House*' – can provide a starting point even though it deals with a different Dickens novel. Robbins aims to highlight the way Dickens's writing in the 1840s focuses on the developing discourse of 'professionalism' which – Robbins suggests – represents the modern state in embryo. Examples of that discourse in the novel are the sections relating to the Circumlocution Office – professionalism in government –

and to Mrs Jellyby's efforts for Africa – professionalism in charity. When professionalism and the modern world are represented as in these two examples, our reading of *Bleak House* shows that Dickens's view of them is plainly critical. Robbins goes on to suggest, however, that things are more complicated than this. For Mr Bucket, the detective who 'solves' the mystery in *Bleak House*, is also represented within this 'modern-world' 'professional' discourse. Our reading tells us that while we may not warm to Mr Bucket as we do to Esther Summerson, we do need his assistance if the narrative of the novel is to be completed – and thus by plain implication 'professionalism' is also essential to the narrative of the modern world. Robbins draws from this that here Dickens is in some way 'complicit in the inhumanity he attacks' elsewhere (p.225).

Building on Robbins's point and thinking of both *Bleak House* and *A Tale of Two Cities* one might identify a quite different discourse that is also characteristic of the modern world in the character of Skimpole and, at times, in John Jarndyce. This is something that could be described as a discourse of 'autonomy'. The idea of the autonomous individual – and thus also the discourse of autonomy – is at the heart of Dickens's vision. Whatever general social forces are in play the effects are constructed in his novels in terms of the individual, and it is as individuals that his heroes and heroines rise and fall in the world and achieve a final reconciliation with their societies. As imagined in Skimpole, however, this individualism is carried to a logical conclusion which involves a denial of responsibility for anything beyond the self. Dickens wants to make the reader critical of this (through devices such as making Skimpole careless of the suffering of the dying crossing sweeper, Joe). And yet it seems too as if Dickens is also complicit with something he condemns, for this 'denial-of-responsibility' aspect of autonomy is also built into characters who have a much more positive role in their respective novels, such as John Jarndyce in *Bleak House*, Sydney Carton in *A Tale of Two Cities* and Eugene Wrayburn in *Our Mutual Friend*. In *A Tale of Two Cities* particularly, through Sydney Carton, this discourse of autonomy is allowed an important concluding and conclusive power in the novel.

Examination of the representation of violence in *A Tale of Two Cities* can lead to a similar conclusion. The depiction of the French revolutionaries imagines a modern world which is violent but also significantly beyond the reach of reason (see, for example, the later chapters of Book 2); it had, in other words, all the qualities that characterized the insurrection in India in British eyes. Military discourses of discipline and obedience were available to incorporate and nullify the threat of this violence. Equally potent were scientific discourses embodying ideas of racial superiority which can be seen in the depiction of individual characters and in the narrative of *A Tale of Two Cities*, and even more prominently in 'The Perils of Certain English Prisoners' (the narrator at one point urges the white people around him 'for the love of all who are dear to him, to trust no Sambo', p.184). But the narrative conclusion of *A Tale of Two Cities* depends on a different kind of discourse which by implication is also important to the modern state. In the final resolution it is an individual who thwarts the power of violence, but an individual who can be said also to be complicit in the irrationality that he attacks. To put things more crudely than the book really allows, the narrative reaches conclusion through a cavalier and sentimental act – the almost magical translation of Carton into Darnay/Evrémonde.

To sum up, then, in *A Tale of Two Cities* Dickens appears to take on the mantle of Carlyle, the historian looking back and fixing the truth of events of violence, and we might surmise that this offered something highly attractive to readers amidst the violence and uncertainty of the Indian rebellion. The novel is bracketed, as it were, with words that assert this; in the preface we find 'trustworthy' and 'philosophy' while at the end the onlookers notice that Carton is 'sublime and prophetic' (p.464). Yet it also validates Darnay as Evrémonde, an ambiguous choice for one to be saved to live into the modern world that exists beyond the novel. It seems that all the discourses that work to enable power structures and values in what for Dickens was the modern world are marked by contradiction and ambiguity.

History that 'clears to-day of past regrets and future fears'

The third approach to *A Tale of Two Cities* which I want to introduce here involves a comparative method, and one that puts the novel next to a very different piece of writing – Edward Fitzgerald's *The Rubáiyát of Omar Khayyám*. (A readily accessible modern edition of this work is that edited by Dick Davis, Harmondsworth: Penguin, 1989.) This is parallel to the way I suggested *Mansfield Park* be put next to the very different *Lalla Rookh* or *The Curse of Kehama* in Chapter 2. (At the very least such comparisons demonstrate the need to see the links between literature and history in any period as something almost intrinsically diverse.)

Though *A Tale of Two Cities* and *The Rubáiyát* seem worlds apart, there are factors which might go some way to suggesting the appropriateness of a comparison. Both were, for example, written around the same time and published in 1859, although *The Rubáiyát* has an altogether more complicated publishing history than *A Tale of Two Cities*. (For full details see Edward Fitzgerald, *The Rubáiyát of Omar Khayyám: A Critical Edition*, ed. by Christopher Decker, London: University of Virginia Press, 1997.) Like Dickens, Fitzgerald had no direct experience of India but did have particular personal links: Fitzgerald learnt Persian from Sir William Jones's *Grammar* with Edward Byles Cowell as tutor. The two were very close friends but were parted in 1856 when Cowell left England to take up a post as Professor of Modern History and Political Economy in Calcutta. Cowell arrived in India only months before the insurrection; Calcutta was a comparatively safe place but the anxieties of the insurrection period run like a thread through Fitzgerald's letters to his friend. There is a further connection as one of the key manuscripts used by Fitzgerald came, via Cowell, from Calcutta. The subject matter of *The Rubáiyát*, finally, provides a prime link between the poem and India. British rule succeeded the rule of the Mughal emperors, whose culture was strongly marked by Persian influences (though the actual ruling dynasty seems more likely to have come from Afghanistan). Fitzgerald's poem is thus at the same time plainly not directly about British India of the 1850s, and yet precisely a representation of that world. *The Rubáiyát* offered a refracting lens through which the British reader in 1859 could imagine India – an older, somehow more essentially Eastern world – just as *A Tale of Two Cities* offered a refracting lens through which that same reader could imagine the violence of India.

Implicit in what I say here is the notion that although *The Rubáiyát* is a translation it should be considered as part of British culture. Certainly Fitzgerald never visited Persia or India and did not aim for an exact literal translation. It seems quite appropriate to turn the comparison back from looking East and see it as indirectly allowing the imagining of an idea of Britishness. The Persian world of the poem – like the world of the French mob – is most definitely not British, but both worlds act as shadowy mirrors in which we see Britishness. Most prominent is the image of a nation which is active, energetic and rational, not content just to 'fill the cup', and certainly not inclined to act as a mob. And yet lurking in the shadows of this official construction is the desire for just those qualities embodied in these other worlds. (Nigel Leask, *British Romantic Writers and the East: Anxieties of Empire*, Cambridge: Cambridge University Press, 1992, and Raymond Schwab, *The Oriental Renaissance: Europe's Rediscovery of India and the East 1680–1880*, New York: Columbia University Press, 1984, provide many more examples of texts that can be discussed in this way.)

Solving the problem of evil

Finally, I want to suggest another comparative possibility, this time putting *A Tale of Two Cities* alongside earlier examples of the detective novel genre. This seems appropriate not least because of the way suspense – integral to the detective novel genre – is so important in *A Tale of Two Cities*. Another factor is that detective novels, like Dickens's novel, regularly show characters confronting and attempting to 'solve' problems of evil.

Wilkie Collins's *The Moonstone* (1868) offers an interesting example of a text one can put beside *A Tale of Two Cities*, not least because Dickens and Collins worked together on Dickens's magazines *Household Words* and *All the Year Round* (they co-wrote 'The Perils of Certain English Prisoners'; see above). On the surface the books seem quite different but in each there is an element clearly associated with something external which is a source of violence and disruption linked somehow to events in the past. *The Moonstone* is often identified as the first detective novel; this genre is far from uniform but Collins's novel sets a pattern not only in the way the resolution of the novel involves the solving of a mystery and the removing of a crime but also in its implicit assertion of the superiority of British rationalism, as represented by Sergeant Cuff. A comparison of *A Tale of Two Cities* and *The Moonstone* can also be interesting as a test of the notion that the relation of a literary text and its history needs to be considered in very specific terms given that one of the novels belongs to 1857 and the other to 1868. Attitudes to Britishness and to India, for example, seem different in the later novel. The Indians who threaten the peace and sanctity of English family life in search of the moonstone seem very much the villains of the novel. But Collins balances this from the start, showing the taking of the diamond in the Battle of Seringapatam (1799) as straightforward looting, making an Englishman share in the villainy of the book and presenting the return of the moonstone to India as almost the proper thing.

This time difference would again be an important point of interest if comparing the way the problem of evil is solved in *A Tale of Two Cities* with the way it is solved in the later detective stories of Sir Arthur Conan Doyle. *The Sign of Four* (1890) provides an example of a mystery in which evil is distinctly associated with the East, while the British have the power to understand and overcome this evil. By this time the nature of British colonialism had changed – Victoria was formally named Empress of India in 1876 bringing the British Empire into formal existence, and the Anglicization of India had progressed significantly. Just as importantly, however, 'the scramble for Africa' had led to a major colonial expansion elsewhere and opened up new avenues for the civilizing mission. C.C. Eldridge, *The Imperial Experience: From Carlyle to Forster* (London: Macmillan, 1996), provides a good overall account of the new developments and is particularly useful for its citing of original material. So far as British colonial expansion in Africa is concerned, Thomas Pakenham, *The Scramble for Africa* (London: Weidenfeld & Nicolson, 1991), offers a highly reliable and readable account of the major historical developments; discussion of literary representations can be found in, for example, *Literature and Imperialism*, ed. by Robert Giddings (London: Macmillan, 1991), or in more specialized studies such as W.R. Katz, *Rider Haggard and the Fiction of Empire* (Cambridge: Cambridge University Press, 1987).

To suggest some of the continuities and differences that can be found, here are sentences taken from the final chapters of *A Tale of Two Cities* and three other novels:

> If he had given any utterance to his [thoughts], and they were prophetic, they would have been these ... I see a beautiful city and a brilliant people rising from this abyss ... I see the evil of this time and of the previous time of which this is a natural birth, gradually making expiation for itself and wearing out. I see the lives of those for which I lay down my life, peaceful, useful, prosperous and happy, in that England which I shall see no more ...
>
> (*A Tale of Two Cities*, 1859; pp.464–5)

> I turned and saw on the rocky platform the figures of three [Indian] men. In the central figure I recognised the man to whom I had spoken in England ... Yes! after the lapse of eight centuries, the Moonstone looks forth once more, over the walls of the sacred city

in which its story first began ... So the years pass, and repeat each other; so the same events revolve in the cycles of time. What will be the next adventures of the Moonstone? Who can tell?

(Wilkie Collins, *The Moonstone*, 1868; Oxford: Oxford University Press, 1982, pp.520–22)

Often I sit alone at night, staring with the eyes of the mind into the blackness of unborn time, and wondering in what shape and form the great drama will be finally developed, and where the scene of its next act will be laid. [For certain] that final development ... as I have no doubt ... must and will occur, in obedience to a fate that never swerves and a purpose that cannot be altered ...

(Henry Rider Haggard, *She*, 1887; Oxford: Oxford University Press, 1991, pp.316–17)

Marlow ceased, and sat apart, indistinct and silent, in the pose of a meditating Buddha. Nobody moved for a time. 'We have lost the first ebb,' said the Director, suddenly. I raised my head. The offing was barred by a black bank of clouds, and the tranquil waterway leading to the uttermost ends of the earth flowed sombre under an overcast sky – seemed to lead into the heart of an immense darkness.

(Joseph Conrad, *Heart of Darkness*, 1902; London: Penguin, 1973, p.111)

In each of these novels violence of one kind or another has been transcended by a wider colonial or imperial view, but in each perhaps the undertows of anxiety and uncertainty still draw hard.

Questions and exercises

1   Look carefully at the chapters of *A Tale of Two Cities* describing Evrémonde's past; how does Dickens want us to see the 'old' world represented there which the Revolution will sweep away?

2   How are ideas of nation and race constructed in 'The Perils of Certain English Prisoners'? What would you say is the overall ideological message?

3   Consider the character of Dr Manette, or Mr Lorry, in *A Tale of Two Cities*; how might they be seen in terms of discourses operating in British culture in the 1850s?

4   Find out as much as you can about the reception of Fitzgerald's *The Rubáiyát of Omar Khayyám;* what explains the place it came to have in British culture?

5   Taking a specific event from *A Tale of Two Cities* and one from *Mariam* or *The Siege of Krishnapur*, compare the presentation of the reality and the causes of violence in India at the time of the mutiny and insurrection.

5 THE WHITE MAN'S BURDEN: KIM

by Lynda Prescott

Introduction

Any reading of Rudyard Kipling's *Kim* is likely to be coloured, initially at least, by two background factors. The first is Kipling's reputation as an unofficial laureate of empire, a reputation that lingers persistently around his writings about India, and that provoked political rather than literary responses during Kipling's own lifetime as well as after his death in 1936. The second concerns the status of *Kim* itself, which, partly because of its boy-hero, has often been grouped with Kipling's writings for children, such as *The Jungle Books* and *Just-So Stories*. Even when it managed to slip out of the 'written-for-children' corral, *Kim* was frequently labelled an 'adventure' or 'romance'. Edmund Wilson, who in his long and memorably titled essay of 1941, 'The Kipling that Nobody Read' (collected in *Kipling's Mind and Art*, ed. by Andrew Rutherford, Stanford: Stanford University Press, 1964, pp.17–69), offered an important reappraisal of Kipling's 'broken career' (p.18), describes *Kim* as 'Kipling's only successful long story: an enchanting, almost a first-rate book' (p.29), implying something more limited in critical valuations than 'novel'.

These two sets of considerations about *Kim* can be transcended in a single stroke, according to some later critics, by recognizing that *Kim* is unique. Mark Kinkead-Weekes's essay 'Vision in Kipling's Novels' (1963) claimed that '*Kim* is the answer to nine-tenths of the charges levelled against Kipling and the refutation of most of the generalizations about him ... It is an artistic triumph that occurs only by virtue of its own conditions, and it never happened again' (in *Kipling's Mind and Art*, pp.197–234 (pp.233–4)). *Kim* was Kipling's last work set in India; it is usually seen as the most benevolent, written with an 'insider's' insight, though it was completed more than ten years after Kipling had left India for good and had settled in England after several years spent living in the United States. It appeared at a fragile moment in the history of empire, when England's own sense of national cohesiveness depended on a belief in her imperial destiny that was almost a secular religion in itself; this faith, however, was underscored by anxiety. The anxiety arose partly from actual and feared reversals in what was seen as the onward march of civilization across the globe, and the prolonged strain of bearing 'The White Man's Burden', in the words of Kipling's poem of 1899. The subtitle of 'The White Man's Burden' is 'The United States and the Philippine Islands', which suggests another aspect of England's anxiety: although imperial rivalry is not a theme of this particular poem, the fact that America, Britain's former colony, had just wrested an important Far Eastern colony from Spain is a reminder that Britain's was not the only empire that was expanding at this period. (Kipling was concerned, in *Kim*, with the pressure that was being felt on India's northern border from the powerful Russian Empire.) The dynamic of Britain's imperial progress was also threatened in another way: the very sense of nationalism that sustained the vast enterprise of building and maintaining an empire that spread into every continent of the world was a force that could ultimately fracture that empire from within, as subject peoples developed their own sense of national identity. The setting up of the Congress Party in India in 1885 is just one indicator of emergent nationalism that would eventually lead to outright resistance to British rule. All these tensions can be felt in *Kim*, so the relationship of the novel to its complex moment in imperial history is never as simple as the 'imperialist adventure' label would suggest.

The text

Kim was a long time in the writing. It was published in 1901 in Britain and the USA, having appeared in almost concurrent magazine instalments on both sides of the Atlantic (the American serialization began first, in *McClure's Magazine*, where the story ran from December 1900 to October 1901, with the British publication beginning a month later in *Cassell's Magazine*). However, Kipling had been working on the novel intermittently for at least eight years and maybe twice as long as that if we trace its origins back to an earlier, unrealized novel called *Mother Maturin*. This was begun when Kipling was only twenty, and it was also concerned with the collisions and interactions of East and West, as British government secrets were traded in Lahore's bazaar. In an essay called 'The *Kim* that Nobody Reads' (*Studies in the Novel*, Fall, 1981, 266–81), Margaret Peller Feeley conjectures that when Kipling sometimes flagged in his sporadic composition of *Kim* he would insert sections from *Mother Maturin* into the draft, in order to keep some forward momentum. Whether this was so or not, the essay traces interesting patterns in Kipling's painstaking revisions to his manuscript, revisions that add depth and complexity to the Eastern characters and reduce the prominence of the English ones.

Kipling destroyed the manuscript of *Mother Maturin*, but presented the manuscript of *Kim*, under its original title 'Kim O' the Rishti', to the British Museum in 1925, on condition that it should not be made public until after his death and that it should not then be reproduced photographically. (As well as this Additional Manuscript no.44840, the British Library also holds a glossary to *Kim* prepared by Kipling but never apparently used in any edition of the novel – see Thomas C. Pinney, 'The Canon and the Kipling Papers', in *Kipling 86*, ed. by Angus Ross, [Brighton]: University of Sussex Library, 1987, pp.5–23 (p.11).) Kipling's revisions to his story did not stop with the numerous changes and insertions in the 'Kim O' the Rishti' manuscript, but continued after the magazine publication of *Kim*, so that the English edition published by Macmillan in October 1901 represents a further stage in the novel's evolution. Kipling made yet more revisions towards the end of his life when preparing *Kim* and some other texts for publication in the special Sussex and Burwash editions of his works – the latter an American edition following the Sussex text – both of which appeared after his death, in 1937–9 and 1941 respectively.

The Macmillan text of 1901, soon and frequently reprinted, is particularly interesting for its illustrations. These are by Kipling's father, John Lockwood Kipling, with whom he had discussed his plans for the book extensively, and they take the form of photographs of low-relief plaques. Like the white-bearded Englishman in the first chapter of *Kim* who delights in showing the lama the precious Buddhist sculptures now in the custody of European scholarship, John Lockwood Kipling was the curator of the museum at Lahore. The plaques he made to illustrate *Kim* recall artefacts more usually seen in museums; when they represent actual relics, such as the cannon Kim bestrides in the opening scene of the novel, it seems almost as if the plaques predate the narrative that threads them together. Lockwood Kipling's illustrations of 1901 thus reinforce the retrospective nature of the text, whose main action, judging from internal evidence, seems to belong to the late 1870s and early 1880s – Kipling's own teenage years.

Like *The Jungle Books* and the *Just-So Stories* (which Kipling illustrated himself), *Kim* is an immensely popular work that has remained in print, in numerous editions, ever since its first appearance. Fifty years after Kipling's death, when his work went out of copyright, there was a flurry of new paperback editions, notably those published by Penguin Books and by Oxford University Press in 1987, with introductions by Edward W. Said and Alan Sandison respectively. Now that European Union legislation has extended the copyright period to seventy years following an author's death, we are unlikely to see further new, cheap editions of *Kim* for a little while, but the Said and Sandison editions remain in print (now in the series Penguin Twentieth-Century Classics and Oxford World's Classics respectively). Sandison's text is based on the revised English text of October 1901, with recourse to the Sussex Edition of 1937–9 to clarify suspected inaccuracies, and Said's is taken directly from the Burwash Edition. Both paperback editions are well annotated, drawing on the relevant volume of *The Reader's Guide to Kipling* (see below), and Said's long introductory essay is especially impressive. Sandison supplies a useful Select Bibliography after his rather shorter introduction.

Biographical and bibliographical information

From a literary point of view, Kipling's life was perfectly rounded off. Not only did he spend part of his final years preparing his works for publication in the definitive thirty-five-volume Sussex Edition, but his last work of all was an autobiography, *Something of Myself*, published posthumously in 1937. In fact this autobiography does not cover the whole of Kipling's life (it does not go much beyond his receipt of the Nobel prize in 1907), and it is notably reticent about important aspects of his personal history. Its real subject is his 'working life', and his reflections on the process of writing, particularly when he feels himself to be the channel of his inspiring 'daemon', are compelling. *Something of Myself* can be read alongside four other shorter autobiographical pieces in an edition with introduction and notes by Thomas Pinney (Cambridge: Cambridge University Press, 1990). There are also several biographies, beginning with Charles Carrington, *Rudyard Kipling: His Life and Work* (London: Macmillan, 1955; rev. edn 1978); this was the official biography, authorized by Kipling's daughter Elsie, and making use of family documents, some of which were subsequently destroyed. Several further biographical and critical studies were published in the 1970s, including Angus Wilson, *The Strange Ride of Rudyard Kipling: His Life and Works* (London: Pimlico, 1977). Most recently, Harry Ricketts's *The Unforgiving Minute: A Life of Rudyard Kipling* (London: Chatto & Windus, 1999) gives a balanced account of the relationship between Kipling's life, writings and reputation. Ricketts has been able to draw on the first three volumes of Thomas Pinney's edition of *The Letters of Rudyard Kipling*, covering the years 1872–1910 (London: Macmillan, 1990– , I–II (1990), III (1996), IV (1999)). There is also an interesting recent compilation of extracts from Kipling's letters, speeches and other pieces – some well known, some previously unpublished – entitled *Writings on Writing*, ed. by Sandra Kemp and Lisa Lewis (Cambridge: Cambridge University Press, 1996), that illustrates Kipling's views on, for example, the commerce of literature and art as a social force.

In spite of much recent biographical and critical activity in Kipling studies, there has not yet been a new bibliography to supersede the several North American listings that have long formed the foundation for Kipling scholarship. The extensive bibliography compiled by a Canadian lawyer, J.M. Stewart, on the basis of his own massive Kipling collection, is still the standard work: *Rudyard Kipling: A Bibliographical Catalogue* was edited for publication after Stewart's death by A.W. Yeats and published by the University of Toronto Press in 1959. A rather different kind of bibliographical enterprise was undertaken in Britain in the years following publication of Stewart's *Catalogue*: under the editorship of R.E. Harbord, a large team of scholars and enthusiasts, mostly from the Kipling Society, contributed to *The Reader's Guide to Kipling*, which annotated the works listed in Stewart's bibliography and also included some previously uncollected works. The eight volumes of *The Reader's Guide* appeared between 1961 and 1972 in a limited edition of 100 sets printed by Gibbs & Sons, Canterbury, Kent; although produced privately, sets of the *Guide* can be found in some libraries.

Kipling's poetry

From the very beginning of his career, Kipling was known equally as a writer of poetry and of prose, and, moreover, he was always interested in linking poetry and prose together. In fact, T.S. Eliot, in his influential essay prefacing *A Choice of Kipling's Verse* (London: Faber & Faber, 1941), claimed that Kipling's verse – Eliot has much to say about the use of the term 'verse' rather than 'poetry' – and his prose are inseparable, and that he should be judged not as either a poet or a writer of prose fiction, 'but as the inventor of a mixed form'. The short pieces of verse that stand as headings to each of the chapters in *Kim* are good examples of Kipling's experiments in this direction (especially striking are the verses from 'The Two-Sided Man' that preface Chapter 8).

In both his prose stories and his verse Kipling is a great ventriloquist, and this quality, along with his brilliant manipulation of rhythm, is most evident in *Barrack-Room Ballads* (1892). His vigorous use of the vernacular in soldier-ballads such as 'Danny Deever' and 'Gunga Din' delighted his British readership, and the echo of music-hall songs in his verse helped to confirm his populist appeal during the 1890s. This appeal, which was partly based on the novelty of his work – in prose as well as verse – modulated into contempt in some critical quarters: Robert Buchanan, in an article of 1899 called 'The Voice of the Hooligan' (included in *Kipling: The Critical Heritage*, ed. by Roger Lancelyn Green, London: Routledge & Kegan Paul, 1971, pp.233–49), condemned the *Ballads*, and much more of Kipling's work, as presenting a picture of 'unmitigated barbarism'. T.S. Eliot's 1941 selection of Kipling's verse was the first serious attempt to rehabilitate Kipling's reputation as a poet, and its timing, during the early years of the Second World War, is perhaps significant. A good selection of Kipling's poetry covering the whole of his writing life and arranged chronologically is available in *Rudyard Kipling: Selected Poems*, ed. by Peter Keating (London: Penguin, 1993).

After *Barrack-Room Ballads* and the earlier collection *Departmental Ditties* (1886), India tended to fade from Kipling's poetry. Although in his prose writing he was drawing on Indian themes and memories long after his departure from the country, he seems to have adopted a more Anglocentric stance in his poetry. His poems about public issues and international events seem to be written from the 'heart' of empire, even though they might be complicated by Kipling's unusual perspective as a 'two-sided man'. An example of this is 'Recessional', published in *The Times* a few weeks after the celebrations marking Queen Victoria's Diamond Jubilee in 1897. Kipling was by now a prominent public figure, associated with expansionist politicians such as Cecil Rhodes and widely regarded as the unofficial poet laureate of the empire, so on the occasion of the Diamond Jubilee something celebratory, even triumphalist, might have been expected. However, the solemn, hymn-like 'Recessional' strikes an entirely different note: the poem certainly exults in a sense of Britain's imperial power ('Dominion over palm and pine') but it does so amidst ostensible calls for humility and appeals to God's mercy ('Judge of the nations, spare us yet'). 'Recessional' suggests a complex view of empire, which is even more interesting when set alongside an earlier poem, 'What the People Said', written in India to mark Queen Victoria's Golden Jubilee in 1887. In his biographical study *Kipling the Poet*

(London: Secker & Warburg, 1994), Peter Keating discusses this poem, which calls on the Indian people to rejoice in the Great Queen's dominion over them, but at the same time recognizes that British rule makes little difference to ordinary Indians: 'the Indian ploughman is not impressed, or even interested. He simply goes on trying to turn the dusty earth, for "the wheat and the cattle are all my care / And the rest is the will of God"' (Keating, p.22). Arguably this double view of empire can also be felt in *Kim*.

Approaching Kim

Boys' games

A thriller element in the novel is provided by Kim's participation in the 'Great Game' of espionage. The phrase was not Kipling's invention: it was coined by a cavalry officer named Arthur Conolly in the mid-nineteenth century in relation to Anglo-Russian conflicts in Asia, and is generally thought to allude to chess-like diplomatic manoeuvres (a compliment to Russian prowess at this game); however, since Conolly had been a school-boy at Rugby in the 1820s, when the new version of football evolved, he might have had a much more physical game in mind. Certainly, Kipling's treatment of the Great Game as sport evokes images of India as a playing-field rather than a chessboard. It was Kipling's enthusiastic use of the phrase in *Kim* that popularized the idea of the Great Game, but by 1901 the game was nearly played out, at least as far as the troubled North-West Frontier of India was concerned. There is no recognition in *Kim* of the fact that the border-disputes involving Russia, India and Afghanistan were settled by the mid-1890s, for the novel is set around the time of the second Afghan War (1878–80). *Kim's* long gestation period may be a relevant factor here, but doubtless the invasion scare that underpins the Great Game is also partly a means of displacing Indian politics as an issue in the novel (there are only glancing references to the 1857 uprising and subsequent internal events).

Since Kim is in fact a child when he is recruited into the secret service, Kipling is able to manipulate the 'game' idea very productively. Martin Green in *Dreams of Adventure, Deeds of Empire* (New York: Basic Books, 1979) discusses the way that 'the Game metaphor is always being demetaphorized by its context in the book – Kim is literally only playing games; though of course it is remetaphorized by the matters of life and death involved' (p.267). Green sees connections between *Kim* and Mark Twain's *Huckleberry Finn* (1884), another adventure novel that straddles the boundary between children's and adult literature: both novels are centred on Irish orphan heroes who develop important relationships with rather unlikely older men (the lama in Kim's case, Jim the runaway slave in Finn's). Green's perspective on the adventure novel and imperial history is a long one, spanning three centuries, and he posits Defoe's *Robinson Crusoe* as an antecedent for both *Huckleberry Finn* and *Kim*; this enables us to look at the relationship between the white adventurer and his native subordinate as part of a long literary tradition associated with empire, or, in the case of *Huckleberry Finn*, frontier.

In *Kim* the exclusively masculine flavour of these central relationships is given a extra dimension through the novel's allusions to freemasonry. Kipling became a (slightly underage) freemason in 1886 when he was admitted to the Order at the Lahore Masonic Lodge; he refers to this, the 'Magic House', in the first chapter of *Kim*, but the topic of freemasonry does not receive a great deal of critical attention in most discussions of the novel. One attempt to integrate Kipling's faith in the fraternity of mankind via freemasonry with other aspects of religious belief is Shamsul Islam's study, *Kipling's 'Law'* (London: Macmillan, 1975). Shamsul Islam, himself a Punjabi Muslim, attempts to define Kipling's philosophy of life, often fluidly expressed in the term 'Law', as incorporating a conception of a universal moral order that embraced most of the major orthodox religions. Freemasonry takes its place alongside the Judaeo-Christian, Islamic, Hindu and Buddhist traditions in Kipling's heterodox outlook as a further buttress against 'the nameless, shapeless Powers of Darkness, Disorder and Chaos' that lurk in every corner of Kipling's often bleak universe (Islam, p.5). But perhaps it is also relevant to Kipling's purposes in *Kim* that freemasonry has certain features in common with the secret, oath-bound and exclusively masculine Great Game.

Another way of looking at the boy-centred structure of *Kim* is to see the novel as a maturation story combined with 'a lost dream of possibility for an eternal childhood in an imagined India'. This kind of reading emerges in Zohreh T. Sullivan, *Narratives of Empire: The Fiction of Rudyard Kipling* (Cambridge: Cambridge University Press, 1993, p.148), through a productive blending of psychoanalytic, formal and historicist approaches. Sullivan traces Kipling's often troubled negotiations between England and India as homes and suggests that he uses the trope of the family (a familiar imperial metaphor) as a way of trying to contain his disturbed relationship with India. So in *Kim* we find the search for a father complicated by the cultural fragmentation of Kim's world. In choosing the unworldly lama for Kim's father-figure, Kipling attempts to transcend, through private emotion, the boundary between colonizer and colonized, and also to resolve tensions between different systems of values: so

> what appears to be a boy's adventure story is also a complex
> fantasy of idealized imperialism and colonialism, and the friendship
> between Kim and his lama is Kipling's fable of the ideal relationship
> between the Englishman (ever a boy at heart) and the Indian –
> eternally passive, unworldly and childlike.
>
> (Sullivan, p.150)

Comparing *Kim* with other works by Kipling that embody different fantasies of a boy's growing up, for example *The Jungle Books*, can yield valuable insights. Also interesting is to compare *Kim* with an Indian novel written at about the same time, which also puts the 'maturation' of a boy in India at its centre: Rabindranath Tagore's *Gora*, originally written in Bengali (1908; see Text 5.1). There are multilayered possibilities in such an approach, ranging from a direct comparison between the heroes of the two novels, to questions concerning the relationship between Kipling's work and that of an Indian writer such as Tagore, who came under the influence of British culture but was an advocate of Indian nationalism. (The relationship between Tagore's work and that of W.B. Yeats is discussed in Chapter 6.)

Orientalism

In *Something of Myself* Kipling expresses outrage at Britain's lack of interest in its empire. This point of view was not unique to Kipling: in a speech at London's Guildhall in 1904 Lord Curzon, viceroy of India, commented: 'The most remarkable thing about British rule in India is the general ignorance that prevails about it in England' (*Lord Curzon in India, 1898–1905: A Selection from His Speeches*, ed. by Sir Thomas Raleigh, London: Macmillan, 1906, p.33). Kipling claimed that one of his purposes in writing was to tell the English something of the world outside England, and *Kim* can be seen as, among other things, a vehicle for transmitting knowledge about India to a British and American reading public. But as was pointed out in Chapter 2, since Edward W. Said's redefinition of the term 'Orientalism' in his book of 1978, it is difficult now to see any promotion of interest in the cultures of Asia as ideologically neutral; it is, rather, a way of 'dominating, restructuring and having authority over the Orient' (*Orientalism*, Harmondsworth: Penguin, 1985, p.3). The concept of (European) knowledge as a form of control is evident in *Kim*, represented in the character of Colonel Creighton and the Survey of India. The Survey, which Kim is destined to join as a 'chain-man', was just one aspect of the charting of India that was conducted through a variety of topographical and statistical means during the later years of the nineteenth century, supported by august British institutions such as the Royal Geographical Society and the Royal Society (to which Hurree Babu hopes to be elected). But this apparently neutral knowledge-gathering activity is overlaid with the Survey's secret purpose as a spy-network, and Kim's movements through the novel are dictated by this clandestine mechanism of imperial control just as surely as the lama's movements are driven by his search for the River of Life.

However, Said's redefinition of Orientalism has not gone unchallenged by Kipling scholars. B.J. Moore-Gilbert, in *Kipling and 'Orientalism'* (London: Croom Helm, 1986), argues that India doesn't altogether fit Said's somewhat monolithic model, and he offers instead a specifically Anglo-Indian context for the reading of Kipling's fiction. Moore-Gilbert is in turn taken to task by Patrick Williams in an essay called '*Kim* and Orientalism' (in *Kipling Reconsidered*, ed. by Philip Mallett, Basingstoke: Macmillan, 1989, pp.33–55). Williams rebuts Moore-Gilbert's treatment of Said as unnecessarily reductive, and answers his rather scanty comments on *Kim* with a sharp analysis of the novel. Williams sees *Kim* as 'both registering and participating in an important historical development ... [the novel] is a refracted image of political realignment, the ruling class in the process of transition, but manoeuvring to strengthen its hold rather than bidding farewell to its power' (Williams, p.53). When Said returns to the subject of Kipling in *Culture and Imperialism* (London: Chatto & Windus, 1993) he steers a slightly different course from Williams in his long discussion of *Kim* (on pp.159–96): at the end of the novel, says Said, 'the conflict between Kim's colonial service and loyalty to his Indian companions is unresolved not because Kipling could not face it, but because for Kipling *there was no conflict*; ... for him it was India's best destiny to be ruled by England' (Said, p.176).

Before leaving the subject of Orientalism, it is worth mentioning Sandra Kemp's book *Kipling's Hidden Narratives* (Oxford: Basil Blackwell, 1988). Kemp starts from the position that Kipling, like other Modernist writers, explored the way narrative makes and unmakes identity, but in his case this exploration is informed by an immersion in Eastern thought. She suggests that political readings of Kipling were encouraged initially by reviewers 'supervising' encounters between Kipling's readers and the texts, and over-emphasizing the extent to which his writings asserted European ideas and values; the 'hidden' element in his narratives, she argues, concerns 'the ways in which identity is created by faith and superstition, by psychic and paranormal experience, by trauma, and by a pre-occupation with art and the agency of inspiration' (Kemp, p.2). Sara Suleri, in *The Rhetoric of English India* (Chicago and London: University of Chicago Press, 1992), views Kipling's account of Eastern transcendentalism (in the shape of the lama's quest) less positively: 'the lama and Kim represent two opposite poles of cultural adolescence: Teshoo Lama's naivety suggests an atrophied absence of adulthood that is mirrored by the aggressive exuberance of his ostensible disciple' (Suleri, p.117). The idea of adolescence gives the key to Suleri's interpretation of Kipling, with whom 'the story of empire learns how to atrophy in its own prematurity' (p. 111). The argument of *The Rhetoric of English India*, which is traced through from Edmund Burke to Salman Rushdie, is sometimes obscured by Suleri's own perverse rhetoric, but her central point about Kipling is that he intuitively apprehends the futility of empire, and that *Kim* is 'the colonial voice on the brink of aphasia'. Kim's collapse and loss of language just before the end of the novel are symptomatic of a more general breakdown of communicative ability that disturbs coherent chronological development, in Suleri's dark reading of the novel.

The White Man's Burden

Kipling's poem of 1899 exhorting America (like Britain) to 'Take up the White Man's Burden' is an expression of the 'service' ethos of empire. But, as I suggested earlier, by the closing years of the nineteenth century this was not an ideology that could be maintained with unquestioned confidence.

Patrick Brantlinger's wide-ranging *Rule of Darkness: British Literature and Imperialism, 1830–1914* (Ithaca, NY: Cornell University Press, 1988) traces the literary expressions of imperialist anxieties in the upsurge of romance writing towards the end of the century; his category of 'popular romance' includes 'imperial Gothic, Wellsian science fiction, invasion fantasies, spy stories' – even the upbeat *Kim* presenting a treacherous world (p.236).

One text Brantlinger mentions briefly, which can provide an interesting context for a reading of Kim – especially given the long gestation period of the novel to which I refer above – is J.R. Seeley, *The Expansion of England* (see Text 5.2). Eighty thousand copies of Seeley's book were sold in its first two years, and on his death in 1895 he was lauded as one of the greatest opinion-formers of the day. It is difficult to believe that Kipling's imagining of the empire in India was not in some way affected by Seeley's account and his arguments as to how, almost by accident, Britain had created the most powerful entity since the Roman Empire.

Alongside these literary and historical perspectives Brantlinger discusses socioeconomic theories of the period relating to imperialism, in which, as with the popular romances, ideas of progress are conspicuously absent. For example, in the writings of J.A. Hobson imperialism is presented as a direct result of capitalist expansion into overseas markets, bolstered by coarse patriotism and ultimately descending to barbarism (Brantlinger, pp.236–8). This is a view of empire that corresponds much more closely with that of Joseph Conrad than with Kipling's, and comparisons between these near-contemporaries can be instructive. John McClure, in *Kipling and Conrad: The Colonial Fiction* (Cambridge, MA: Harvard University Press, 1981), brings out Conrad's awareness of the economic basis of imperialism as one major difference between the two writers. He also argues that with *Kim* Kipling abandons his complaints in earlier Indian stories about the bureaucratic imperial hierarchy and settles instead for an ahistorical fantasy. It is possible to see, up to a certain point in Kipling's colonial fiction, a critical perspective that matches Conrad's. Ricketts even suggests, in *The Unforgiving Minute*, that 'We can, with an effort, imagine him not as the ardent imperialist he actually became, but as a forerunner of George Orwell, arriving in England to expose the impracticability of the system of which he had been a part' (p.116). By the time of *Kim*, however, these remote possibilities have quite vanished. At one level, Kipling's overt acceptance of the 'civilizing mission' reflects a sense of responsibility that is long-standing in the case of Britain and India, but it may also be the case that shouldering the White Man's Burden is less troubling, in the end, than confronting the more fearful possibilities of inward disintegration.

In some ways Kipling's writings on India can be seen as a culmination of a particular view of empire, embodying tensions that would become increasingly marked with the passing of Victorianism. But Kipling is also seen by some critics as standing at or near the beginning of a modern literary tradition dealing with British/Indian encounters. It is worth mentioning two quite different studies by academics who are neither

British nor Indian: in *Images of the Raj: South Asia in the Literature of Empire* (Basingstoke: Macmillan, 1988) the Sri Lankan D.C.R.A. Goonetilleke traces the tradition of Raj literature from Kipling through Leonard Woolf, E.M. Forster and George Orwell to Paul Scott; the Canadian Teresa Hubel's book *Whose India? The Independence Struggle in British and Indian Fiction and History* (London: Leicester University Press, 1996) focuses on the Indian nationalist movement to provide a framework that includes Kipling and Forster as well as Mulk Raj Anand and Bhabani Bhattacharya.

Questions and exercises

1   Do Kim's relationships with the main Indian characters in the novel conform to the standard pattern for colonizers and colonized?

2   How far does the interweaving of the lama's and Kim's quests enable Kipling to maintain the 'inclusiveness' that many readers have claimed for the novel? Is this claim justified?

3   Consider the relationship between the verse-heading and themes of the ensuing chapter in one or more of *Kim's* chapters. Do you agree with T.S. Eliot's claim that the prose and the verse are inseparable?

4   Does *Kim* express a general yearning towards pre-industrial society as well as conveying Kipling's specific affection for India?

5   How is Kim's search for identity connected with the novel's wider representation of the British in India? (You may like to consider the effect of the 'cog-wheel' image in Chapter 15 of the novel.)

6 POETRY AND NATION: W.B. YEATS

by Stephen Regan

Introduction

Throughout the period covered in the chapters so far, the British government exerted a fresh colonizing power in a number of places other than India; each of these countries had its own specific pre-colonial history, each had colonial elements in common and at variance with the others. The history of British involvement in Ireland stands slightly apart from all this in most accounts of British colonialism, not least because there is considerable debate as to whether after 1801 the relationship between Britain and Ireland can be either accurately or usefully defined as 'colonial'. Some would argue that from the Act of Union in 1801 until independence in 1921 Ireland was formally and politically directly part of the United Kingdom and in this respect cannot be described as a colony. But it was also very much *sui generis* since its structure of government was partly akin to an English county with, for example, a lord lieutenant representing the Crown and partly quite different, for example, in having a chief secretary. Adopting this kind of approach and seeing Ireland as not being a colony might lead one into an exploration of cultural and economic divisions within Britain itself at the heart of the empire (a project analogous to that pursued by Cain and Hopkins in their analysis of the different ways in which 'gentlemanly capitalists' in the south of England and industrialists in the midlands and the north of England were involved in colonialism and empire, see P.J. Cain and A.G. Hopkins, *British Imperialism: Innovation and Expansion 1688–1914*, London: Longman, 1993). From a less formal point of view, others would argue that the cultural and linguistic situation within Ireland and between Ireland and Britain was marked by so many of the patterns of power which are associated with Britain's colonial rule that it is perverse not to use the term colonial. Irish nationalism contested British/English cultural hegemony in the nineteenth century just as much as Indian nationalism was later to contest the dominance of those same forces in India.

This chapter steps a little way on to this ground through an exploration of certain aspects of the work of W.B. Yeats. Following the 'Ireland cannot be seen as a colony' line of argument might lead us to consider Yeats as giving a voice in his poetry to ideas of nation in Britain – for all his Irish allegiances, Yeats was committed to Britain. Following the 'Ireland can be seen as a colony' approach leads to something different. In this context, comparison of Ireland and India – two cultures in parallel but different stages of colonial development, crisis and decolonization – is of great interest. In focusing such comparisons on the work of Yeats we risk the charge that we are making an idiosyncratic – even downright peculiar – figure stand as 'typical' of Ireland. However, this seems a risk worth taking because through Yeats – and particularly through Yeats and Tagore – we can see ideas of nationalism that resonate in both India and Ireland. To include Yeats here may also offer useful challenges to the desire to generalize about writing in English from the heart of the empire during the period 1890– 1925; Yeats's career overlaps with those of both Kipling and Forster and yet the three hardly overlapped in their lives or in their work.

So far as Yeats is concerned, in any event, the 'literature and nation' issue seems clear and unequivocal: 'there is no great literature without national- ity, no great nationality without literature'.This is W.B. Yeats making what seems like a clear and unequivocal statement about the relationship between literature and national identity. As the author of poems and plays in which 'Ireland' is the palpable subject, Yeats is commonly regarded as a nationalist poet. The nature of his nationalist commitment, however, is not easy to establish, since Yeats's own pronouncements vary considerably according to context, and his volatile politics are complicated by particular linguistic, religious and class allegiances. What Yeats himself says about nationality should be regarded with caution, and this applies to many of his best-known essays in books such as *Autobiographies* (London: Macmillan, 1955) and *Essays and Introductions* (London: Macmillan, 1961). The lines quoted above appear in a collection of articles and reviews written mainly for American journals and magazines (see *Letters to the New Island*, ed. by George Bornstein and Hugh Witemeyer, London: Macmillan, 1989, p.30). Although Yeats was fond of these lines and used them with slight variation elsewhere, the opportunity of playing 'The Celt in London' to an American audience seems to have encouraged him to be more outspoken than usual. In the same collection, Yeats insists that 'Ireland is the true subject for the Irish' and that 'an Irish magazine should give us Irish subjects'. In a short piece written in November 1892 he refers to London as 'the capital of the enemy' (pp.21, 163, 64).

The text

The availability of Yeats's work was for many years determined by copy- right. Most of his works remained in copyright under the fifty-year rule until 1989; the copyright of other works, particularly prose, belonged to his wife and runs until much later. The most commonly available editions were the authorized editions published by Macmillan and later editions derived from them. After 1989, out-of-copyright editions of most works were poss- ible but these works have now returned to copyright under the more recent seventy-year rule. The Macmillan-authorized volumes are a phenomenon worthy of study in their own right for the image of the poet late in life that they construct. As this chapter suggests, it is perhaps even more interesting to study Yeats's writings in their original context, both as individual poems or plays, and in the original volumes in which they were published. A scholarly account of the textual variants that resulted from Yeats's authorial revisions can be found in *The Variorum Edition of the Poems of W.B. Yeats*, ed. by Peter Allt and Russel K. Alspach (New York: Macmillan, 1957). Of the many available editions of the poems in paperback, Daniel Albright's Everyman edition can be recommended for its detailed, comprehensive notes (*W.B. Yeats: The Poems*, London: Dent, 1994). For our purposes, however, the modern Oxford Authors edition has been chosen, particularly because it amply represents both the occult speculation and the nationalist ambition in Yeats's writings. It includes plays and prose selections, as well as a comprehensive choice of poems. All quotations from Yeats's poems and plays are from this edition unless otherwise stated. As the editor, Edward Larrissy, points out, 'the topic of magic and the occult sciences' is 'interwoven with Yeats's profoundest thoughts throughout his life' and needs to be understood in relation to his political aspirations rather than as a quaint and eccentric preoccupation (see the introduction to *W.B. Yeats*, Oxford: Oxford University Press, Oxford Authors critical edition, 1997, p.xxiii).

Biographical and bibliographical information

It is hardly surprising that there has been a strong interest in Yeats's life, especially in view of his prominent involvement in key periods of the Irish struggle for independence and his own fostering of a myth of himself through autobiographical poems and prose. The first full-length biography, Joseph Hone, *W.B. Yeats 1865–1939* (London: Macmillan, 1942), appeared shortly after Yeats's death, and there have been numerous biographies since. One of the most popular for many years was A. Norman Jeffares, *W.B. Yeats: Man and Poet* (London: Routledge & Kegan Paul, 1949; rev. edn 1962). Jeffares also wrote *W.B. Yeats: A New Biography* (London: Hutchinson, 1988). However, the first volume of the authorized biography, R.F. Foster, *W.B Yeats: A Life* (Oxford: Oxford University Press, 1997), is now available, and so, too, is a new biography (with the same title) by Stephen Coote (London: Hodder & Stoughton, 1997).

Some excellent bio-critical information can be found in the early writings of Richard Ellmann (see especially *The Identity of Yeats*, London: Faber, 1954, and *Yeats: The Man and the Masks*, London: Faber, 1961). A more recent and accessible bio-critical study is Alasdair D.F. Macrae, *W.B. Yeats: A Literary Life* (London: Macmillan, 1995). A selection of letters was published in *The Letters of W.B. Yeats*, ed. by Allan Wade (London: Rupert Hart-Davis, 1954), and a valuable selection of the correspondence with Maud Gonne can be found in *The Gonne–Yeats Letters 1893–1938*, ed. by Anna MacBride White and A. Norman Jeffares (London: Hutchinson, 1992). John Kelly is the general editor of *The Collected Letters of W.B. Yeats*, the third volume of which covers the period from 1901 to 1904 (Oxford: Clarendon Press, 1994). Further volumes of the collected letters are currently being prepared for publication.

The standard bibliography is *A Bibliography of the Writings of W.B. Yeats*, ed. by Allan Wade (London: Rupert Hart-Davis, 1968). A bibliography of critical writings up to 1978 was edited by K.P.S. Jochum in *W.B. Yeats: A Classified Bibliography of Criticism* (Illinois: University of Champaign-Urbana, 1978). Useful critical materials can also be found in *W.B. Yeats: The Critical Heritage*, ed. by A. Norman Jeffares (London: Routledge & Kegan Paul, 1977). These sources should be supplemented with listings and reviews that regularly appear in the *Yeats Annual*, ed. by Warwick Gould (London: Macmillan, 1982–) and *Yeats: An Annual of Critical and Textual Studies*, ed. by Richard Finneran (Ann Arbor: UMI Research Press, 1983–).

Approaching Yeats, poetry and nation

There are several books which offer a good general and contextual approach to Yeats and his work. One of the best is David Pierce's superbly illustrated *Yeats's Worlds: Ireland, England and the Poetic Imagination* (New Haven and London: Yale University Press, 1995). Alternatively, a clear and thoughtful guide can be found in *A Preface to Yeats*, ed. by Edward Malins and updated by John Purkis (London: Longman, 1994). It is helpful to consult some of the available guides to the poems, even though many of them were published several decades ago. Of these, the most interesting are John Unterecker, *A Reader's Guide to William Butler Yeats* (London: Thames and Hudson, 1959), T.R. Henn, *The Lonely Tower: Studies in the Poetry of W.B. Yeats* (London: Methuen, 1950; rev. edn 1965), and A. Norman Jeffares, *A New Commentary on the Poems of W.B. Yeats* (London: Macmillan, 1984). Among more recent introductory studies, Stan Smith, *W.B. Yeats: A Critical Introduction* (London: Macmillan, 1990), is highly recommended.

Strongly contrasting approaches to the poetry can be found in the available critical sources. Several critics insist on placing the poetry in the context of late Romanticism, aestheticism and decadence, stressing Yeats's allegiances with Blake, Shelley, Morris, Rossetti and the poets of the 1890s. In this respect, it is still well worth considering the arguments proposed by Graham Hough in *The Last Romantics* (London: Duckworth, 1949) and by Frank Kermode in *Romantic Image* (London: Routledge & Kegan Paul, 1957). On the other hand, there are those critics who argue strongly for the Modernist Yeats, and one of the most influential arguments was put forward by C.K. Stead in *The New Poetic: Yeats to Eliot* (London: Hutchinson, 1964; new edn London: Athlone Press, 1998). Stead's emphasis on Modernism also shapes his *Pound, Yeats, Eliot and the Modernist Movement* (London: Macmillan, 1986), which should be read alongside Cairns Craig, *Yeats, Eliot, Pound and the Politics of Poetry* (London: Croom Helm, 1982). There are two Macmillan Casebooks worth perusing: *Yeats: Last Poems*, ed. by Jon Stallworthy (London: Macmillan, 1968), and *Yeats: Poems, 1919–1935*, ed. by Elizabeth Cullingford (London: Macmillan, 1984).

Yeats's fascination with the occult continues to attract a good deal of interest. Among the main critical sources here are George Mills Harper, *Yeats's Golden Dawn* (London: Macmillan, 1974), *Yeats and the Occult*, ed. by

George Mills Harper ([Toronto]: Macmillan of Canada, 1975), and Graham Hough, *The Mystery Religion of W.B. Yeats* (Brighton: Harvester, 1984). As Edward Larrissy has argued, however, the attempt to separate Yeats's occult interests from his political interests is likely to produce a distorted account of the poet's complex imaginative world. Larrissy has endeavoured to give a more balanced account of Yeats's ideas in both his Oxford Authors edition of the writings and in his critical study, *Yeats the Poet: The Measures of Difference* (London: Harvester Wheatsheaf, 1994).

Turning more particularly to the relation between Yeats's poetry and ideas of nationality, it is advisable to read the poems alongside a reliable general history of modern Ireland. The closing three chapters of *The Oxford Illustrated History of Ireland*, ed. by R.F. Foster (Oxford: Oxford University Press, 1989), are valuably informative, and Declan Kiberd's chapter, 'Irish Literature and Irish History', is especially illuminating. Declan Kiberd, *Inventing Ireland: The Literature of the Modern Nation* (London: Jonathan Cape, 1995), is strongly recommended for its thoroughgoing concern with colonial and nationalist politics, as is David Cairns and Shaun Richards, *Writing Ireland: Colonialism, Nationalism and Culture* (Manchester: Manchester University Press, 1988). Terence Brown, *Ireland: A Social and Cultural History 1922–79* (London: Fontana, 1981), is also recommended, though – as the title indicates – its scope omits the early, formative years of Yeats's career. What is needed is a careful assessment of the work of W.B. Yeats in relation to the complex ferment of Irish cultural politics, especially in the period from roughly 1890 to 1920. We need to understand how the writing gathers momentum and power from the intense political and cultural friction between Britain and Ireland at a critical turning point in modern history, but we also need to understand how Yeats's ideals of national unity were informed by the contact he had with other emerging nations, especially India.

Yeats and the 1890s

The 1890s are crucially important, since these were the years of the so-called Irish Literary Revival or Celtic Twilight when Yeats and his compatriots were intent on achieving national unity through shared cultural endeavour, and they were also the years when the struggle for Home Rule reached a critical phase. Yeats's own mythologizing of history is apt to overstate the national importance and political consequences of the Irish 'renaissance', but the 1890s is nevertheless one of the most significant decades in modern Irish culture.

The Irish Literary Society was founded in London in 1891, the National Literary Society in Dublin in 1892, the Gaelic League in 1893 and the Irish Literary Theatre in 1897. Yeats was a tireless and committed agitator on behalf of such organizations. The most significant event of the decade in Yeats's estimation, though, was undoubtedly the fall from power and subsequent death of Charles Stewart Parnell in 1891. Looking back on the event from 1923, Yeats saw the death of Parnell as precipitating a new mood and attitude in Irish intellectual life:

> The modern literature of Ireland, and indeed all that stir of thought which prepared for the Anglo-Irish war, began when Parnell fell from power in 1891. A disillusioned and embittered Ireland turned from parliamentary politics; an event was conceived; and the race began, as I think, to be troubled by that event's long gestation.
>
> (*Autobiographies*, p.559)

Yeats acknowledges here a decisive turning from political nationalism to cultural nationalism, but this stirring account of the dawn of modern Irish culture has been seriously questioned by both historians and literary critics. Terry Eagleton, for instance, argues that 'The Yeats-sponsored view that politics yielded ground to culture after the fall of Parnell, while one sees what it means, betrays a narrowly parliamentarian view of politics and a curiously depoliticized notion of culture' (*Heathcliff and the Great Hunger: Studies in Irish Culture*, London: Verso, 1995, p.232). There is no doubt, however, that the 1890s witnessed the most powerful burst of cultural nationalism in Irish history, even though the ground had been well prepared by Thomas Davis and the Young Ireland Movement some fifty years earlier.

The key volumes which Yeats produced in the early years of his career are *Crossways* (1889), *The Rose* (1893) and *The Wind Among the Reeds* (1899). It is well worth studying these *fin-de-siècle* books as a group, as they provide a highly revealing impression of the unusual convergence of aesthetic and nationalist commitments in Yeats's work at this time.

John O'Leary and Maud Gonne

Two friendships, well documented in biographical studies, were extremely influential in shaping Yeats's ideas of the nation. In the late 1880s Yeats had met John O'Leary, a renowned supporter and member of the Fenians (the name derives from the *Fianna* (warriors) of Irish legend). Foster gives a detailed account of the friendship in the first volume of his biography, (*W.B. Yeats: A Life*, pp.43–4). O'Leary had enjoyed some notoriety after serving a prison sentence for founding the *Irish People*, a nationalist newspaper, but at the time Yeats knew him it would seem that his colleagues in the Republican movement regarded him as a spent force. Yeats could commune with his mentor without fearing any actual revolutionary involvement. Michael North even doubts whether O'Leary could be called a republican, since he nourished 'an aristocratic dream' that Ireland would one day have its own king (Michael North, *The Political Aesthetic of Yeats, Eliot, and Pound*, Cambridge: Cambridge University Press, 1991, p.28). If the Fenian connection was for Yeats a romantic attachment (a way of tapping into heroic legends and stories), it was also perhaps a pragmatic one. O'Leary had told the Protestant Yeats: 'In this country a man must have upon his side the Church or the Fenians and you will never have the Church' (quoted by R.F. Foster in 'Anglo-Irish Literature, Gaelic Nationalism and Irish Politics in the 1890s', in *Ireland After the Union* (Oxford: Oxford University Press, 1989, p.63).

The other crucially important influence in Yeats's evolving career was his love for the militant nationalist Maud Gonne. Yeats and Maud Gonne differ in their accounts of how and when they met, but the impact on Yeats's work was powerful and prolonged. Foster claims that Yeats's intellectual position on nationalist issues was probably 'radicalized' so that the poet could present himself as 'an appropriate suitor' (*W.B. Yeats: A Life*, p.114). The intensity of the relationship certainly helps to explain why Yeats occasionally veers from what seems to be republican fervour to the most vague and non-committal sentiments. It is well worth consulting *The Collected Letters of W.B. Yeats*, the first three volumes of which have been published under the general editorship of John Kelly (Oxford: Clarendon Press, 1986–), for information about Yeats's involvement with prominent nationalists, but the letters only confirm the lack of a clearly defined political stance in Yeats's early thinking about national unity. Yeats's shifting and uncertain political allegiances are clearly evident in the poems published in *The Green Helmet and Other Poems* (1910) and *Responsibilities* (1914). The mood veers from the bewilderment of 'No Second Troy' in the earlier book to the bitterness and disillusionment of 'September 1913' and 'To a Shade' in the later book.

Yeats, the occult and spiritualism

To espouse a belief in esoteric forms of knowledge was an implicit criticism of English materialism and utilitarianism. Yeats did not need to emulate the Catholic mysticism of some of his Irish contemporaries, since he was able to draw on a long tradition of occultism and supernaturalism inherent in his own specifically Protestant background. R.F. Foster has written persuasively of 'the supernatural dimension of the Protestant subculture', stressing the extent to which Yeats's lifetime interest in the occult was an essential part of his social and cultural identity. Especially striking is his contention that occultism and magic provided a refuge for a Protestant class that was becoming increasingly marginalized in modern Ireland. Yeats, in this context, belongs to a line of writers 'whose occult preoccupations surely mirror a sense of displacement, a loss of social and psychological integration, and an escapism motivated by the threat of a takeover by the Catholic middle classes' (R.F. Foster, 'Protestant Magic: W.B. Yeats and the Spell of Irish History', *Proceedings of the British Academy*, 75 (1989), 243–66 (pp.251, 254)).

The kind of nationalism Yeats espouses in the 1890s is the product of a complex set of allegiances and identities; it emerges from a deep sense of colonial insecurity and a deep sense of anxiety about the future of his own embattled class. Yeats's concern about the increasing dislocation of the class

he identified with – the so-called 'Anglo-Irish Ascendancy' – provides the
psychological impulse and motivation behind such early works as 'The
Crucifixion of the Outcast' and 'The Wanderings of Oisin'. What Yeats was
seeking in the 1890s was a way of re-establishing his own cultural identity
and that of his class in a country that was witnessing a strongly emerging
Catholic nationalism. Behind the changing balance of power lay the
Catholic Emancipation Act of 1829, the Disestablishment of the Church
of Ireland in 1869, the Land Wars in the 1880s and the Home Rule Crisis in
1886. Given this historical context, it is difficult to ignore Seamus Deane's
opinion that the story of the Literary Revival is 'the story of the spiritual
heroics of a fading class – the Ascendancy in the face of a transformed
Catholic "nation"'. Put more bluntly, 'Irish culture became the new property of those who were losing their grip on Irish land ... It was in essence a
strategic retreat from political to cultural supremacy' (Seamus Deane,
'Heroic Styles: The Tradition of an Idea', in *Ireland's Field Day*, London:
Hutchinson, 1985, pp.47–8).

Romanticism and spiritualism

Yeats's early idealization of Ireland was fed, in part, by the undisguised
hostility to English industrial and utilitarian society he encountered in
Romantic poetry, especially that of Blake and Shelley. The Ireland Yeats
imagined in the 1890s was conceived in opposition to a philistine, commercial, urban England, and in this respect Yeats also owes much to a
tradition of cultural criticism exemplified by Matthew Arnold, John Ruskin,
Walter Pater, William Morris and Oscar Wilde. The affiliation is immediately evident in Yeats's remark that 'I had dreamed of enlarging Irish hate,
till we had come to hate with a passion of patriotism what Morris and
Ruskin hated' (quoted in Foster, 'Anglo-Irish Literature', p.73). Ironically,
then, Yeats draws upon a mode of criticism already at work within English
culture, and one that was directed at reforming England rather than ensur-
ing its divorce from Ireland. We might be forgiven for identifying such a
tendency as 'literary unionism' rather than revolutionary nationalism (as
Seamus Deane has argued in several essays; see Chapters 2 and 3 of his
Celtic Revivals, London: Faber & Faber, 1985). At the very least we need to
recognize the deep ambivalence in Yeats's nationalist ideals. If the cultural
nationalism of the Literary Revival served to justify and support the more
overt political struggle for freedom, might it not also serve as a diversion
and a distraction from that political struggle?

'To Ireland in the Coming Times' and Cathleen ni Houlihan

I have suggested already the value of following Yeats's ideas of himself and
of Ireland into the detail of his poems and other works. In this section I want
to exemplify this by looking in a little more detail at two particular works,
the poem 'To Ireland in the Coming Times' and the play *Cathleen ni
Houlihan*. 'To Ireland in the Coming Times' (1892) is perhaps the most

revealing statement of Yeats's uncertain nationalist sentiments. As Seamus Heaney has argued, the poem is 'full of imperatives and peremptory claims' which create a sense of authority and control (Seamus Heaney, 'A Tale of Two Islands: Reflections on the Irish Literary Revival', *Irish Studies*, 1 (1980), 1–20 (p.4)). The poem's declarative mood, however, conceals an anxiety about the writer's relationship with Irish national culture:

> Know, that I would accounted be
> True brother of a company
> That sang, to sweeten Ireland's wrong,
> Ballad and story, rann and song.

The pursuit of the red rose of spiritual beauty co-exists with a desire to 'Sing of old Eire and the ancient ways'. Each stanza involves both a commitment to an established national tradition and a declaration of difference:

> Nor may I less be counted one
> With Davis, Mangan, Ferguson,
> Because, to him who ponders well,
> My rhymes more than their rhyming tell
> Of things discovered in the deep,
> Where only body's laid asleep.
>
> (p.25)

At the time of composing this poem, Yeats had already signalled his departure from Thomas Davis and James Clarence Mangan and his growing preference for the work of the Unionist Sir Samuel Ferguson. Ferguson's rewriting of Celtic legends in English showed Yeats a way of remaining true to the Protestant middle class while helping to shape and inform a new sense of nationhood in Ireland. This is not to deny that there are images and gestures in Yeats's early work that might aptly be described as 'revolutionary', but these are relatively few and require careful qualification. There are those poems like 'The Valley of the Black Pig' (1896) which anticipate a violent, apocalyptic transformation of Ireland:

> The dews drop slowly and dreams gather: unknown spears
> Suddenly hurtle before my dream-awakened eyes,
> And then the clash of fallen horsemen and the cries
> Of unknown perishing armies beat about my ears.
> We who still labour by the cromlech on the shore,
> The grey cairn on the hill, when day sinks drowned in dew,
> Being weary of the world's empires, bow down to you,
> Master of the still stars and of the flaming door.
>
> (p.32)

As George Watson points out, Yeats had absorbed this prophetic heralding of a new epoch from Madame Blavatsky's *Secret Doctrine*, but 'the messianic belief; the sense of imminent upheaval, the eager anticipation of apocalypse, was also a part of the emotional make-up of the revolutionary patriots in the Fenian movement' (George Watson, *Irish Identity and the Literary Revival*, London: Croom Helm, 1978, p.92). Yeats himself comments on the poem that 'All over Ireland there are prophecies of the coming rout of the enemies of Ireland, in a certain Valley of the Black Pig, and these prophecies are, no doubt, now, as they were in the Fenian days, a political force' (p.477). The insertion of 'no doubt' has a distancing effect which ironically casts doubt on Yeats's own commitment to the 'political force' of the prophecy. Much of his commentary on the poem is concerned with the Celtic origin of the legend, and with pointing out that the battle is a mythological one in which the pig serves as an emblem of winter battling with summer or death battling with life. In private correspondence Yeats appears to pursue a much more moderate nationalist line than poems like 'The Valley of the Black Pig' might suggest.

On the stage, the nationalist stirrings which Yeats experienced in the early years of his career found their most powerful embodiment in *Cathleen ni Houlihan*. The play was first performed in 1902 and was dedicated to the memory of William Rooney, a proto-Sinn Féiner. The Old Woman who persuades Michael Gillane to serve his country rather than be married speaks eloquently of her suffering and dispossession. The dialogue functions naturalistically and yet acquires a tremendous mythological and allegorical charge. The Old Woman, later transformed into a young girl with the walk 'of a queen', inspires her listeners with 'the hope of getting my beautiful fields back again; the hope of putting the strangers out of my house' (p.217). The sacrifice she calls for is the blood sacrifice of militant republicanism: 'It is a hard service they take that help me. Many that are red-cheeked now will be pale-cheeked: many that have been free to walk the hills and the bogs and the rushes will be sent to walk hard streets in far countries ...' (p.219). At the same time it is significant that Yeats sets the play in 1798, at the time of the French landings at Killala. In doing so, Yeats appeals to the spirit of United Ireland – to a broad-based secular republicanism – and cautiously distances himself from the specifically Catholic republicanism of his own day. As Watson argues, the play is very much 'an attempt to assert a sense of identity with an uncompromised "Irishness"' (p.89). It is also a work that identifies with a strong romantic element in republican nationalism, and even if *Cathleen ni Houlihan* appears to promote a Fenian view of Ireland there remain severe doubts about its political intention and effect. In asking 'Did that play of mine send out / Certain men the English shot?' (p.179) was Yeats perhaps not so much congratulating himself as regarding with some misgiving and surprise the idea that *Cathleen ni Houlihan* might have contributed to the mobilization of revolutionary patriots in the Easter Rising of 1916?

The myth of 'Mother Ireland' in *Cathleen ni Houlihan* and elsewhere in Yeats's writings has given rise to some important and revealing studies of gender and its role in the formation of ideas about nationhood. Among the most impressive and illuminating accounts of this aspect of Yeats's work are Marjorie Howes, *Yeats's Nations: Gender, Class, and Irishness*

(Cambridge: Cambridge University Press, 1996), and Elizabeth Butler Cullingford, *Gender and History in Yeats's Love Poetry* (Cambridge: Cambridge University Press, 1993). There is also a good deal of valuable material, including a chapter on 'The School of O'Leary' and a thoughtful assessment of *Cathleen ni Houlihan*, in Cullingford's earlier book, *Yeats, Ireland and Fascism* (London: Macmillan, 1981). Howes argues that gender and sexuality are 'intimate elements of Irish national discourses' and that Yeats's political thinking is 'profoundly irrational and deeply eroticized' (p.12). Her book provides a comprehensive and deftly theorized study of the ways in which women in Yeats's writings represent a range of national ideals.

Yeats and post-colonial theory

I want now briefly to shift the emphasis from looking at Yeats's own ideas and works in the years after 1890 to exploring how all this might be seen in relation to post-colonial theory. In so doing I return implicitly to the questions posed in the introduction to the chapter concerning the appropriateness of seeing Ireland as a colonized nation. For myself I would begin here with a note of caution. It is all too easy to envisage some single, uniform nationalism being pitted against an equally generalized and global colonialism, without proper consideration of the complexities and contradictions inherent in the version of nationalism that Yeats espoused.

One of the most striking and engaging studies of Yeats as an anti-imperialist writer is Edward W. Said's essay 'Yeats and Decolonization', which first appeared in the Field Day series of pamphlets on 'Nationalism, Colonialism and Literature' in 1988. Said places Yeats's early poetry in a phase of anti-imperialist resistance (generated mainly by poets and visionaries) which preceded the more openly liberationist movements of the mid-twentieth century. He rests his claim on those poems such as 'The Lake Isle of Innisfree' which are concerned with the recovery and repossession of colonized land through the act of imagination. Yeats, in Said's estimation, belongs with 'the great nationalist artists of decolonization and revolutionary nationalism, like Tagore, Senghor, Neruda, Vallejo, Cesaire, Faiz, Darwish'. In the revised version of this essay which appears in *Culture and Imperialism*, Said offers two important qualifications which serve to complicate any assessment of Yeats's nationalism. As well as writing in English, not Irish, Yeats had a strong affiliation with the Anglo-Irish or Protestant 'ascendancy' and was therefore an unlikely militant. Said chooses not to explore these seeming contradictions in Yeats's nationalism, and instead repeats his original claim that the early poetry embodies 'liberationist and Utopian revolutionism'. In a powerful and provocative way, Said enables a reconsideration of both the alleged wilful mysticism of Yeats's poetry and its later drift into reactionary politics (Edward W. Said, *Culture and Imperialism*, London: Chatto & Windus, 1993, p.283). When Yeats's nationalism is measured against other forms of nationalist sentiment and activity in Ireland, however, the word 'revolutionary' is likely to appear exaggerated and unjustified.

Said rests his defence of Yeats's early nationalist writings largely on the poet's imaginative recovery of the land:

> One of the first tasks of the culture of resistance was to reclaim, rename, and reinhabit the land ... The search for authenticity, for a more congenial national origin than that provided by colonial history, for a new pantheon of heroes and occasionally heroines, myths, and religions – these too are made possible by a sense of land reappropriated by its people.
>
> (*Culture and Imperialism*, p.273)

The geographic or cartographic impulse that Said identifies is powerfully at play in Yeats's early poetry, the most celebrated instance being the opening stanza of 'The Lake Isle of Innisfree', written and published in 1890:

> I will arise and go now, and go to Innisfree,
> And a small cabin build there, of clay and wattles made:
> Nine bean-rows will I have there, a hive for the honey-bee,
> And live alone in the bee-loud glade.
>
> (p.19)

W.J. McCormack, however, regards Yeats's poetic landscapes with a degree of scepticism and warns against any easy acceptance of him as a local celebrant. There is, at first reading, a profound sense of intimacy with the landscape of Sligo underpinned with concrete references to the names of mountains, lakes and villages. But, as McCormack points out, 'we underestimate the subtle reservations of Yeats's poetic perception if we mistake the *possibility* of intimacy for the thing itself, if we mistake the accessibility of those place-names on the map for the integration of a poet in a known and comprehensive culture' (W.J. McCormack, *Ascendancy and Tradition in Anglo-Irish Literary History from 1789 to 1939*, Oxford: Clarendon Press, 1985, p.295). North agrees with McCormack that the poem's linguistic, as well as geographical, contours require careful scrutiny, and that what they reveal has more to do with separation than with intimacy. The title of the poem, based on 'Inis Fraoigh' (meaning 'heather island'), conveniently embodies for Yeats the English word 'free', but at the same time betrays a deep anxiety about the poet's relationship to the place: 'The only remnant of Irish in the otherwise thoroughly English speech of the poem, the place name acts to connect the poem linguistically to its subject, but just by virtue of its difference, the name also advertises the distance of that subject' (North, p.25). Yeats's relationship to the land then seems more complex and ambiguous than Said's anti-colonial label would suggest. Some critics would go so far as to claim that Yeats's longing for the landscape of his youth and his preoccupation with childhood in such poems as 'The Stolen Child' are evidence of 'infantile regression' rather than progressive nationalism (see, for instance, Kiberd's account of 'Childhood and Ireland', Chapter 6 of *Inventing Ireland*, pp.101–14).

The same critical problems attend Yeats's treatment of the people who inhabit the land. There are many early poems such as 'The Fisherman', in which Yeats romanticizes the Irish peasantry (p.68). At one level it seems valid enough to claim that 'Yeats's unique contribution to Irish thought [was] the proposition that Ireland's purest essence was located in the peasant's primitive belief in holy wells and fairy thorns' (Malcolm Brown, *The Politics of Irish Literature from Thomas Davis to W.B. Yeats*, London: George Allen and Unwin, 1972, p.317). The stereotype of the savage, ignorant peasant is replaced with a more dignified and appealing image. At another level, however, it might be claimed that Yeats's rehabilitation of the peasantry as the source of Irish wisdom and value is so idealistic and exclusive as to hinder rather than promote the cause of national identity and national unity. Although Yeats seems to have regarded Home Rule as inevitable, there are moments in his poetry when, as Heaney has pointed out, he succeeds in creating a version of Irish life untouched by contemporary political realities such as Home Rule: 'the very elements of this life are impeccably aesthetic' (Heaney, p.8). Heaney suggests that Yeats's version of Irish peasant life effectively predates contemporary sectarian conflict. What the peasant appears to practice is not Catholicism but a form of occult spirituality close to Yeats's own. The response Yeats makes to the land and the people cannot, then, be considered as a direct act of 'decolonization', since the account of English–Irish relations on which it is based is both ambivalent and evasive. Such a response issues from the insecurity and marginalization of the Anglo-Irish Ascendancy in the face of growing Catholic nationalist aspiration, and not simply from some shared or unified resistance to English colonial power.

Yeats and politics after 1902

In what remains one of the most provocative and influential accounts of Yeats's politics, Conor Cruise O'Brien claims that after the impact of *Cathleen ni Houlihan* in 1902 Yeats 'turned aside from Irish politics'. His contention is not that Yeats ceased to be an Irish nationalist but that his nationalism became conservative and aristocratic rather than populist and active. He believes that throughout the 1890s Yeats had been emphasizing his 'Irishness' while minimizing the Protestant tradition to which he belonged. After 1902, Yeats was no longer able to disguise his contempt for the rising Catholic middle class and 'the Protestant now re-emerged with an audible sigh of relief' (Conor Cruise O'Brien, 'Passion and Cunning: An Essay on the Politics of W.B. Yeats', *In Excited Reverie: A Centenary Tribute to William Butler Yeats 1865–1939*, ed. by A. Norman Jeffares and K.G.W. Cross, London: Macmillan, 1965, p.222). A similar line of thinking is adopted by Edward Said, who believes that the 'revolutionism' of Yeats's early poetry is 'belied and even cancelled out by his later reactionary politics' (*Culture and Imperialism*, p.283). Both arguments emphasize a sharp distinction between the youthful radical and the elder statesman. As we have seen, however, there is a good deal of evidence to suggest that Yeats's nationalism in the 1890s was not as advanced or as radical as is sometimes implied.

Nevertheless, there is a growing disenchantment in Yeats's view of Ireland, especially after the death of John O'Leary in 1907. Yeats wrote of O'Leary's funeral, 'I shrank from seeing about his grave so many whose Nationalism was different from anything he had taught or that I could share. He belonged ... to the romantic conception of Irish Nationality' (Foster, *Yeats: A Life*, p.367). The mood of disillusionment is captured most memorably in 'September 1913', with its insistent refrain, 'Romantic Ireland's dead and gone, / It's with O'Leary in the grave' (p.51). A note of bitterness and sarcasm enters into poems like 'To a Shade' (an elegiac poem for Parnell), 'To a Wealthy Man ...' and 'On Those that Hated "The Playboy of the Western World", 1907' (pp.53, 50, 54). From this time onwards, Yeats was careful to distance himself from the militant republicanism of Sinn Féin, and began to declare an overt allegiance with the Anglo-Irish aristocratic culture of Lady Gregory and her class. The distance travelled is evident in the poem 'Upon a House Shaken by the Land Agitation', an indication of Yeats's increasingly sympathetic identification with the landowners in Ireland (p.44). While some critics have responded with distaste and discomfort to Yeats's right-wing overtures, including his flirtation with fascism, Eagleton reminds us that 'Yeats is the supremely fine poet he is, not despite his politics but in some measure because of them – a truth which offers little comfort to either liberal aesthete or reductive leftist' (p.301).

Many of the poems Yeats wrote and published in the 1920s, especially those in the volume *Michael Robartes and the Dancer* (1921) and *The Tower* (1928), are characterized by a haughty disdain for modern democracy and an impending catastrophic violence. 'Easter, 1916' is one of the best-known poems of this period, but its attitude to the Easter Rising is not easy to gauge (p.85). In a seminal essay, 'History and Myth in Yeats's "Easter 1916"', Eagleton has pointed out how, at one level, the poem seems confidently affirmative and rhetorically assured, but at another level functions as a candid confession of unresolved doubts and dilemmas. The ballad-like refrain, 'A terrible beauty is born', both celebrates heroic achievement and recognizes desultory failure (see *The Eagleton Reader*, ed. by Stephen Regan, Oxford: Blackwell, 1998, pp.350–58). Similarly, 'The Second Coming' is a poem that generations of critics have struggled to elucidate (p.91). In a brilliant analysis, Seamus Deane argues that 'The Second Coming' is 'a poem that clearly responds to and participates in the pan-European militarization of politics that put an end to nineteenth-century liberalism' (Seamus Deane, *Strange Country: Modernity and Nationhood in Irish Writing since 1790*, Oxford: Clarendon Press, 1997, p.172).

'The Second Coming' is undoubtedly concerned with revolution, and was probably written in response to the Russian Revolution of 1917. But was Yeats committed to violent political revolution in Ireland? The nationalist politics to which Yeats gave his tentative allegiance should not be confused with revolutionary separatism. According to Foster, Yeats had little enthusiasm for political separation from England: 'at his most committed there was always the congenital ambivalence of the Protestant bourgeois ... For all his identification with the Gaelic ethos, a wistful hope remained for leadership from a regenerated landlord class' (Foster, 'Anglo-Irish Literature', pp.66, 74). Foster reminds us that Coole Park, where Yeats was a frequent visitor after 1897, was 'an imperial house memorializing generations of service to the Empire' (Foster, 'Protestant Magic', p.257). To regard Irish nationalism in Yeats's time as wholeheartedly 'anti-colonial' is to overlook many of its cultural and political complexities. The nationalist sentiments Yeats espouses are essentially those of *déclassé* Irish Protestantism.

Yeats and India: Tagore and nationalism

Earlier sections of this chapter have referred to the possible parallels to be drawn between the struggle for independence in Ireland and in India, and to Yeats's long-running interest in the occult and the spiritual. This last section introduces a way of approaching these interactions further through consideration of the specific links between Yeats and the Bengali writer Rabindranath Tagore (1861–1941). These interactions should not in any way be taken as somehow 'representative' of the parallels between Ireland and India – if such representative parallels exist they would lie much more centrally within the nationalist movements in the two countries – but they are of great interest because of the way both writers weave together a number of parallel elements in constructing their ideas of nationalism. Both wrote extensively on nation and nationalist issues. Early examples of Yeats's linking of nationalism and culture are to be found in journalistic writings such as 'Irish Writers Who Are Winning Fame' contributed to the Boston *Pilot* in 1889 (see Text 6.1). A more mature example, which Yeats felt was important enough to revise himself, is 'Ireland and the Arts', contributed to the *United Irishman* in 1901 (see Text 6.2). So far as Tagore is concerned perhaps the most interesting longer piece is his *Nationalism* of 1917 (see Text 6.5), which includes sections on 'Nationalism in the West' and 'Nationalism in India'.

Yeats's unusual mingling of nationalist and spiritual ideals found congenial support and encouragement in the works of contemporary Indian writers and mystics. In April 1886, through his association with Madame Blavatsky and the Dublin Theosophical Society, Yeats met Mohini Chatterjee, a lawyer and philosopher who greatly strengthened his interest in ancient India and Indian traditions. From Chatterjee, Yeats learned about Hindu mystical thought and the Vedantic forms of meditation and asceticism. Two early poems, 'The Indian upon God' and 'The Indian to his Love', were written about this time, while a later poem, 'Mohini Chatterjee', was written in 1928 (pp.5, 6, 130).

Of even greater importance was Yeats's meeting in June 1912 with Tagore. Yeats helped revise Tagore's own translations of a selection of his Bengali songs, *Gitanjali* (1912), and contributed an ecstatic 'Introduction' when it was reprinted in a limited edition by the India Society in London in 1913 (see Texts 6.3 and 6.4). He had a decisive influence, too, in establishing Tagore's reputation in the West and in providing the groundswell which led to Tagore's winning the Nobel prize in 1913 on the basis of a book that was only seventy-two pages in length. The award, Yeats said, was also 'a piece of wise imperialism from the English point of view' (quoted in Buddhadev Bose, *Tagore: Portrait of a Poet*, Bombay: University of Bombay, 1962, p.101); his own Nobel was not to come until 1923.

Yeats appears to have valued Tagore not only for his supreme lyricism but equally for revealing a civilization he inferred to be still organically integrated as the West no longer was. But ultimately, Tagore was to be valued, Yeats said, for being mysterious, religious and spiritual: 'we fight and make money and fill our heads with politics – all dull things in the doing – while Mr. Tagore, like the Indian civilization itself, has been content to discover the soul and surrender himself to its spontaneity' ('Introduction,' p.xiv). But Tagore was not so quintessentially mysterious and spiritual as Yeats imagined in his orientalist way. He came from an Anglicized and privileged background, in some respects comparable to the Anglo-Irish Ascendancy. His grandfather was called a prince and had been sympathetic to the establishment of British rule in India, his eldest brother had been the first Indian to be admitted to the Indian Civil Service, and Tagore himself had been sent to England at the age of seventeen to study and try to get into the ICS. Altogether, in Edward Thompson's words, 'he faced both East and West, filial to both, deeply indebted to both' (*Rabindranath Tagore: Poet and Dramatist*, 1926; repr. Delhi: Oxford University Press, 1991, p.311).

Tagore's head had been full of politics too, though on occasion he found such matters vexatious – the stances he adopted seem to us now also somewhat ambiguous. He had participated vigorously in the nationalist campaign against Lord Curzon's decision in 1905 to partition Bengal, but then had withdrawn abruptly at the height of that movement. In protest against the massacre of Jallianwala Bagh in 1919, he had resigned the knighthood conferred on him in 1915. Yet even then he said he retained throughout a deep respect for the British individually and as a race, blaming the evils of imperialism on a different entity – the British or Western 'nation'. Tagore's linking of nation and imperialism together in this way – to the extent that he often used 'nationalism' and 'imperialism' almost synonymously – led to somewhat paradoxical consequences. Just how could one square passionately debunking the idea of nation and nationalism everywhere and anywhere with support for greater freedom and autonomy for India?

Thus, when Gandhi launched his first major nationalist movement in 1920–21, Tagore not only stood aloof but engaged directly in a public controversy with him. He was now, with his worldwide reputation as a prophet from the East, a champion of internationalism and universalism. The Sanskrit motto of a university he founded in 1921 described it as a place 'where the world becomes as one nest'. Later, courteously accommodating his uncompromising transcendent indifference to the nationalist movement, Gandhi declared that Tagore was 'international because he is truly national' (quoted in Krishna Kripalani, *Rabindranath Tagore: A Biography*, rev. edn, Calcutta: Visvabharati, 1986, p.457). In an ironical reversal, Tagore himself in a lecture delivered at the end of his life finally expressed utter disenchantment with British rule and wished it would end.

Yeats, of course, had lost all interest in Tagore long before this. In fact, exasperated with persistent invitations to contribute to the adulatory *Golden Book of Tagore* projected for his seventieth birthday, he had in 1935 begun a letter to a common friend with the words, 'Damn Tagore'! (*The Letters of W.B. Yeats*, p.835). His enthusiasm for Tagore had once been unbounded; his disillusionment now was no less complete.

Questions and exercises

1   Yeats was instrumental in creating an ideal of national unity and in mobilizing support for that ideal. Using two or three specific pieces of writing (poetry, prose or drama) consider how radical or revolutionary his nationalism was.

2   Consider Yeats's representation of Maud Gonne in the poems said specifically to refer to his relationship with her.

3   Is Yeats's interest in spiritualism and the occult entirely idiosyncratic or can it be said to be part of a wider interest in such matters at the time (as seen, for example, in the work of Fiona Macleod, or the writers listed as involved in these matters in Peter Keating, *The Haunted Study*, London: Fontana, 1991, pp.360–63)?

4   'Romantic Ireland's dead and gone, / It's with O'Leary in the grave' ('September 1913'). Discuss Yeats's changing view of Ireland with reference to two or three poems from different phases of his writing career.

5   Is the apparent closeness of Yeats and Tagore around 1912 evidence for a real congruity between Ireland and India, or for the fact that they both helped create a gap between culture and nationalist politics in the two countries?

7 LIBERAL DILEMMAS IN ENGLAND AND INDIA: A PASSAGE TO INDIA

by Richard Allen

Introduction

E.M. Forster began *A Passage to India* in 1913; he then laid it aside in 1914, and did not complete it until 1924, the year of its first publication. Written in a style at first sight akin to that of a nineteenth-century realist novel, the book's third-person narration seems to give a sense of objectivity to this portrait of the British in India just after the 1914–18 war. That the novel can be, and has been, read in different ways, however, suggests that within it there are considerable ideological tensions. Consideration of the history of the British Empire in the period 1913–24 – as outlined in the books cited in Chapter 1, in the section 'Understanding history: Britain and India', or in an older study such as A.P. Thornton, *The Imperial Idea and Its Enemies* (London: Macmillan, 1959) – suggests perhaps that this is only to be expected. A more 'local' study, of great relevance to *A Passage to India*, is A. Draper, *Amritsar: The Massacre That Ended the Raj* (London: Cassell, 1981). From these accounts you might conclude, for example, that by 1924 the high point of British imperialism had passed. Ireland had achieved independence from Britain; in India, Britain's chief remaining imperial possession, the Indian National Congress was well established. The increase both in nationalist violence and in the ferocity of the British response (especially in the Amritsar Massacre of 1919) signalled tensions in the empire that Britain was finding more difficult to manage. Something of this can be seen in the decision taken in 1911 to move the Indian imperial capital to Delhi, to be housed in what was effectively a new city. On the face of it, this was an act of grandiloquent self-confidence. But it can be seen in quite different terms, particularly against decisions first in 1905 to partition and then in 1911 to reunite Bengal; 'the British decided to remove their capital from the troublesome province of Bengal. As viceroy Hardinge made a ceremonial entry on an elephant into New Delhi in 1912, he was greeted with a Bengali revolutionary's bomb' (S. Bose and A. Jalal, *Modern South Asia: History, Culture, Political Economy*, London: Routledge, 1998, p.122). These things said, it remains the case that the British Empire was still expanding; in 1924 it had only just achieved its greatest extent, with its takeover of the German imperial possessions in South-West Africa (now Namibia) and East Africa (part of what is now Tanzania). In parallel fashion, *A Passage to India* simultaneously offers a trenchant critique of imperial practices and the prospect of a value structure that just might allow the pan-Anglian project to be reinvented.

The text

The textual history of *A Passage to India* is relatively straightforward. After the first publication in 1924, the same text formed the basis of all editions until it was replaced after Forster's death by the Abinger Edition text (E.M. Forster, *A Passage to India*, ed. by Oliver Stallybrass, London: Arnold, 1978). A modified version of the Abinger Edition, with less textual commentary and more explicatory notes, became the basis of a new edition of the Penguin text in 1979. Alongside the definitive text, Stallybrass also edited a further volume for the Abinger Edition, *The Manuscripts of 'A Passage to India', Correlated with Forster's Final Version* (London: Arnold, 1978). This enables us to understand the compositional history of the novel and to study Forster's shifting conception of it. There is an earlier and slightly less technical discussion of these matters in J.P. Levine, *Criticism and Creation: 'A Passage to India'* (London: Chatto, 1971).

The novel's reputation and status is evident from the fact that it became part of two ventures that changed the face of British intellectual life and brought serious reading to a wider audience. *A Passage to India* was one of the first volumes in the Penguin series (no.48, published in 1937), and in 1942 (with an introduction by Peter Burra and notes by Forster himself) it became part of the Everyman's Library series.

Biographical and bibliographic information

You will find a full listing of Forster's works in B.J. Kirkpatrick, *Bibliography of E.M. Forster* (2nd edn, Oxford: Clarendon Press, 1985). By 1924 his literary reputation was well established and critical discussions of his novels soon began to appear, gaining impetus after the 1940s. Details of critical works to date are in F.P.W. McDowell, *E.M. Forster: An Annotated Bibliography of Writings About Him* (De Kalb: Northern Illinois University Press, 1976), and in C.T. Summers, *E.M. Forster: A Guide to Research* (London: Garland, 1991). Since Forster's death, exemplary work has been done by his literary executors, so that alongside the Abinger Edition of the novels and stories we now have *E.M. Forster: A Commonplace Book*, ed. by P. Gardner (London: Scholar, 1985), and *E.M. Forster: Interviews and Recollections*, ed. by J.H. Stape (London: Macmillan, 1993).

Indispensable to anyone wishing to understand Forster's work is P.N. Furbank, *E.M. Forster: A Life* (2 vols, London: Secker, 1977–8). Furbank rigorously maintains a barrier between literary criticism and his work as a biographer: facts in Forster's life that parallel the moments in the novels are mentioned but the novels are not allowed to act as a means of filling in details of Forster's own feelings, and the biography contains no critical accounts of texts. With Mary Lago, P.N. Furbank has also edited *Selected Letters of E.M. Forster* (2 vols, London: Collins, 1983–5). More recently, another biography has appeared: N. Beauman, *A Biography of E.M. Forster* (London: Hodder, 1993). Beauman is happier to use the kind of conjecture that Furbank rejects, and offers much more of an interpretation of Forster's character and work.

Approaching A Passage to India

General

Two useful collections of criticism give a general sense of how critics have approached Forster's work as a whole and *A Passage to India* in particular. *E.M. Forster, 'A Passage to India': A Casebook*, ed. by M. Bradbury (London: Macmillan, 1970), has the advantage of focusing just on this one novel; it brings together a number of classic accounts by, for example, Leonard Woolf, Lionel Trilling and John Beer, but is inevitably a little dated. A collection that was written at about the same time, but that focuses on more modern critical essays and on Indian criticism is: *Perspectives on E.M. Forster's 'A Passage to India': A Collection of Critical Essays*, ed. by V.A. Shahane (New York: Barnes and Noble, 1968); of particular interest are the essays by Nirad C. Chaudhuri and Benita Parry.

More recent thinking about Forster can be found in *E.M. Forster: Contemporary Critical Essays*, ed. by J. Tambling (London: Macmillan, 1995); more than half of this collection is devoted directly and indirectly to discussion of *A Passage to India*. Exploring the way that Forster's work has been interpreted and valued by critics is a rewarding study in itself and tells us much about the changing ideologies of the twentieth century; anyone interested in this might move from Bradbury's and Tambling's selections to J.H. Stape, *E.M. Forster: Critical Assessments* (4 vols, London: Helm Information, 1998).

Book-length general studies of Forster's work as a whole have been less common than might perhaps be expected. The way *A Passage to India* fits (or does not fit) with the earlier novels and his non-fiction writing is discussed in, for example, D. Shusterman, *The Quest for Certitude in E.M. Forster's Fiction* (Bloomington: Indiana University Press, 1965), and J. Colmer, *E.M. Forster: The Personal Voice* (London: Routledge, 1975). Discussions of Forster as a writer to be read within the context of the Bloomsbury Group are also regularly to be found; for example, D. Dowling, *Bloomsbury Aesthetics and the Novels of E.M. Forster and Virginia Woolf* (London: Macmillan, 1985).

Finally, of course, Forster's own writings will offer you one of the most pleasant ways into understanding his ideas about writing and about culture. *Aspects of the Novel* (1927) shows Forster at his most disarming and engaging; after commenting that 'Yes – oh dear yes – the novel tells a story', he goes on: 'the more we look at the story ... the more we disentangle it from the finer growths that it supports, the less we shall find to admire. It runs like a backbone – or may I say a tapeworm, for its beginning and end are arbitrary' (E.M. Forster, *Aspects of the Novel and Related Writings*, Abinger Edition, London: Edward Arnold, 1974, p.34). A similarly personal style fills the essays collected in *Abinger Harvest* (1936; Abinger Edition, London: Deutsch, 1997) and *Two Cheers for Democracy* (1951; Abinger Edition, London: Edward Arnold, 1972).

An analysis of India?

For all that in later sections I shall suggest different ways of approaching the text, the realist interpretation should not be entirely displaced. The interest in this approach lies in two related questions: how accurate and fair ('how real') is Forster's depiction of the Indian nation? And how accurate and fair (again 'how real') is his depiction of the English nation abroad? When Forster was in India he wrote regularly to his mother, describing his experiences in a quite factual way; he wrote so that she could read his letters aloud to other members of the family. A good deal of the substance of these letters was then incorporated into *A Passage to India* – evidence surely that he wanted the novel to appear authentic. This material plainly continued to have an authentic feel to it, for he later incorporated details from the novel into the explicitly autobiographical *The Hill of Devi* (1953; Abinger Edition, London: Edward Arnold, 1983). A realist reading of the novel might begin from such material and continue to, for example, R.J. Lewis, *E.M. Forster's Passages to India* (New York: Columbia University Press, 1979); the fullest and best guide in such research is, however, G.K. Das, *E.M. Forster's India* (London: Macmillan, 1977). You might then wish to 'test' Forster's accounts and his knowledge – taking into account how and where it was gained – against other accounts. P. Gardner, *E.M. Forster: The Critical Heritage* (London: Routledge & Kegan Paul, 1973), gives examples of comments from the 1920s doubting Forster's knowledge and understanding of India. Of particular interest perhaps are the different accounts by Forster's friend Sir Malcolm Darling – for example *Apprentice to Power 1904–1908* (London: Hogarth Press, 1966). The values of those in this official world are discussed in C. Dewey, *Anglo-Indian Attitudes: The Mind of the Indian Civil Service* (London: Hambledon Press, 1993). Two rather less formal and academic accounts of the British encounter with India are Charles Allen, *Plain Tales from the Raj* (London: Deutsch/BBC, 1975), and an account by a close friend of Forster, J.R. Ackerley, *Hindoo Holiday: An Indian Journal* (London: Chatto & Windus, 1932).

Comparing *A Passage to India* with other accounts raises further questions, which relate to two main areas. One group relates to the extent to which Forster's novel is – or should be – inclusive in its representation of India. Comparing it with almost any account of the years around 1920 in the histories of India cited in Chapter 1 will reveal Forster's selectivity. Take as an example the chapter titles that cover this period in Bose and Jalal, *Modern South Asia*: the message of *A Passage to India* seems quite in keeping with the main part of the title of Chapter 12, 'Colonialism Under Siege', but the subtitle, 'State and Political Economy After World War 1', suggests areas of British and Indian life Forster leaves untouched. Equally, Bose and Jalal's next chapter title, 'Gandhian Nationalism and Mass Politics in the 1920s', finds hardly an echo in the novel. Indeed, it might be argued that Forster's novel was out of date in adhering to the older colonial issues of friendship and good, and in remaining oblivious to the changing situation brought about by Gandhi's mass movement. Another English writer, almost a contemporary of Forster, offers a contrast here, namely Edward Thompson (1886–1946), father of the historian E.P. Thompson. His works are not well known now and are not generally in print, but they are worth hunting down. His play *Atonement* (London: Ernest Benn, 1924) registers fully the impact of Gandhi, who appears only lightly disguised as Mahatma Ranade. Thompson's novels – *An Indian Day* (London: A.A. Knopf, 1927) and its sequel, *A Farewell to India* (London: Ernest Benn, 1931) – also discuss Gandhi and the liberal British response to his movement. Thompson also wrote non-fiction dealing with the history and politics of India and set out his ideas for the future. *The Reconstruction of India* (see Text 7.4), for example, again shows him fully cognisant of the Indian nationalist movement but still coming to a conclusion that seems to show him adopting a stance not dissimilar to that of Forster at the end of *A Passage to India*:

> I believe that by remaining in the Empire India can most effectively use her own qualities. East and West are by no means as apart as many represent. The historical and cultural contact of Great Britain and India has laid down a causeway, which should be used.

> (Text 7.4, p.299)

So is the absence of any representation of the Indian nationalism movement simply a sign of Forster's having begun writing *A Passage to India* in 1913, before – for example – the events at Amritsar, which heightened tensions so much more? Perhaps, but it can be seen just as appropriately as a sign of Forster silently but self-consciously positioning his message on a spectrum of Indian nationalist opinion and belief. At one extreme stood the example of Bal Gangadhar Tilak (1856–1920), who had urged the Indian National Congress of 1907 thus:

> The remedy is not petitioning but boycott. We say prepare your forces, organise your power, and then go to work so that they cannot refuse you what you demand ... The point is to have the entire control in our hands ... If you mean to be free, you can be free; if you do not mean to be free, you will fall and be for ever fallen.

> (Text 7.1, pp.288–9)

At the other extreme, much more congenial to Forster, stood the example of Gopal Krishna Gokhale (1866–1915). In his view, Indians must

> recognize that the new self-government has to be on Western lines, and therefore the steps by which the goal is reached must necessarily be slow, as, for the advance to be real, it must be from experiment to experiment only. But there is all the difference in the world between such cautious progress and no progress at all.

> (Text 7.2, p.289)

The second set of questions raised about Forster's representation of India cuts across these issues of accuracy by declaring that as a matter of intellectual principle *A Passage to India* can tell us nothing about life in India as experienced by Indians. These questions assume that Forster's view is so marked by a sometimes conscious, sometimes unconscious filtering that it can tell us only about the West and the India that it creates as the 'other' to itself. If there is authenticity in the novel it lies not in the depiction of India but in the depiction of the Western observing consciousness – not only as dramatized in Fielding or Heaslop, but also, and just as importantly, as embodied in the narrator's eye and voice. What is at issue here is 'Orientalism' in Edward W. Said's use of the word. Said makes barely a mention of *A Passage to India* in *Orientalism* (Harmondsworth: Penguin, 1985), though he does deal with it in a little detail in *Culture and Imperialism* (London: Chatto & Windus, 1993). For many critics, an earlier account of *A Passage to India* in this light – that in B. Parry, *Delusions and Discoveries: Studies on India in the British Imagination 1880–1930* (London: Allen Lane, 1972) – remains equally if not more illuminating. I return to these issues in the section on 'Difference and desire' below.

Modernism and liberalism

To read *A Passage to India* in the way outlined in the previous section is to see it as very much a novel of India, and in this respect something rather separate from Forster's earlier novels. In contrast, seeing it in the context of novels such as *A Room With a View* (1908; Abinger Edition, London: Edward Arnold, 1977) or *Howards End* (1910; Abinger Edition, London: Edward Arnold, 1973) can lead to a different emphasis, and to the idea that this is more a novel about England and Englishness. If, that is to say, Forster aimed to reform any group of people, then his concern was with the English rather than with the Indians. Just what his aims were in this respect may be deduced from his novels but can also be seen in his personal writings, such as those collected in *Two Cheers for Democracy*. Forster's earlier association with the Bloomsbury Group was also based on a shared political agenda; political issues based on class, for example, were later clearly involved in his decision to become President of the National Council for Civil Liberties in 1934.

Seeing *A Passage to India* as a novel about Englishness perhaps also prompts us to see it within a European literary frame, and particularly within that of Modernism. Forster's work is not characterized by the obvious experimental Modernism of, say, James Joyce's *Ulysses* (1922), but for Virginia Woolf (in her essays 'Mr Bennett and Mrs Brown' and 'The Novels of E.M. Forster', in *Virginia Woolf: Collected Essays*, ed. by Leonard Woolf, 4 vols, London: Hogarth Press, 1966–7) there was no question but that Forster was one of those who were challenging worn-out Victorian realism and finding new ways to write.

Following Woolf, and starting from the assumption that *A Passage to India* is an experimental novel rather than a realist novel, is valuable. Equally interesting is to see *A Passage to India* in the cultural context that critics see as having given rise to Modernism. *Modernism*, ed. by M. Bradbury and J. McFarlane (Harmondsworth: Penguin, 1976), offers a valuable and wide-ranging account (interestingly, *A Passage to India* provides thē epigraph for one of the contributions; see *Modernism*, p.443). In their introductory chapter Bradbury and McFarlane identify Modernism as a movement that faces two ways, towards disaster and towards fulfilment: the artist is simultaneously set free *and* has a premonition of disaster, or conversely just as he or she faces disaster there is a moment of hope. In this context, it is useful to compare T.S. Eliot's seminal text of Modernism, *The Waste Land* (1922), with *A Passage to India*. The common elements in the two texts (albeit differently expressed) are a sense of a disastrous emptiness at the heart of the present and a sense that Eastern religion might offer some salve. But Eliot looks also to cultural values; Forster's preoccupation is more political, adhering determinedly to what in shorthand might be called 'liberal values'.

Forster's political significance is identified in one of the earliest critical accounts, L. Trilling, *E.M. Forster: A Study* (London: Hogarth Press, 1944). More recently, his attitudes are discussed in J. Raskin, *The Mythology of Imperialism: Rudyard Kipling, Joseph Conrad, E.M. Forster, D.H. Lawrence and Joyce Cary* (New York: Random House, 1971) – where the now almost forgotten novelist L.H. Myers (1881–1944), author of the tetralogy *The Near and the Far* (1929–40), is put forward as a more sure critic of imperialism than is Forster – and in P.J.M. Scott, *E.M. Forster: Our Permanent Contemporary* (London: Vision, 1984). To understand the roots of liberal thinking in the nineteenth century it is useful to consult standard reference books in philosophy – particularly the entries on John Stuart Mill, whose ideas were still very influential when Forster was at Cambridge in the 1890s. B. May, *The Modernist as Pragmatist: E.M. Forster and the Fate of Liberalism* (London: University of Missouri Press, 1997), for example, offers an opportunity to explore how Forster put his own particular spin on this tradition of ideas. All this provides, perhaps, a means of understanding a key criticism that has been advanced concerning Forster's critique of imperialism in *A Passage to India*: that he makes no reference to the Indian nationalist cause beyond the comments in the scene in the Club in Chapter 20. Forster's project is not to develop Aziz as a proto-Jinnah figure ready to lead the Muslim League and India into the future. Rather it is to allow the reader to imagine that – in a suitably tentative but assuredly political way – we can be 'friends again' (Chapter 37).

To end this section, I want to refer to two further books, neither of which refers extensively to *A Passage to India* but both of which offer useful models for thinking about the novel in relation to liberalism and Modernism. M. Whitebrook, *Real Toads in Imaginary Gardens: Narrative Accounts of Liberalism* (Lanham: Rowman & Littlefield, 1995), does not talk about

Forster at all, but does deal with writers of roughly the same period, such as Henry James and Joseph Conrad. In a wide-ranging account that begins with Dickens, D. Born, *The Birth of Liberal Guilt in the English Novel: Charles Dickens to H.G. Wells* (Chapel Hill: University of Carolina Press, 1995), includes a chapter on *Howards End*. As his title indicates, Born sees liberalism and guilt as necessary companions, taking Arthur Clennam in Charles Dickens's *Little Dorritt* (1855–7) as the classic example of liberal guilt. Clennam is a broken hero – someone who feels guilt about things for which he has only indirect responsibility, drawing that sense of guilt away from characters who are directly responsible. Though *Little Dorritt* and *A Passage to India* seem very different novels, there does seem scope for a comparison in that Fielding too seems to carry a sense of guilt for the English in India even though he is as little involved as anyone in their actions.

Difference and desire

At the heart of *A Passage to India* is an undoubtedly sexual (and heterosexual) event; the paradox is that study of the development of the text shows Forster moving to mystify rather than to clarify what happens. One explanation might be, of course, that even in 1924 descriptions of sexual activity were still rare in a consciously literary text. This is not to say, however, that readers would not supply details of events or possibilities that are – as it were – written between the lines or simply alluded to. In the initial narration of Adela's experiences in the cave, for example, Forster is carefully vague about what goes on, but the passage works precisely because readers can call on images of what the sexual attack might involve. Similarly, the text provides only asexual elements to the relationship of Fielding and Aziz, but readers can import elements of desire which, if carried to any conclusion, would involve ways of behaving that were still punishable by imprisonment and, if written down, would turn the novel from serious realist text to pornography. The problem is that it is difficult to be sure just how readers can or could read between the lines in this way. Two books that might allow you to begin to construct hypotheses in this area are M. Mason, *The Making of Victorian Sexual Attitudes* (Oxford: Oxford University Press, 1994), and J. Weeks, *Sex, Politics and Society: The Regulation of Sexuality Since 1800* (London: Longman, 1981); S. Szreter, *Fertility, Class and Gender in Britain, 1860–1940* (Cambridge: Cambridge University Press, 1996), is also useful. Extending these hypotheses to cover events occurring far from England increases the difficulty; the most important collection of information as to what went on is probably R. Hyam, *Empire and Sexuality: The British Experience* (Manchester: Manchester University Press, 1990). For many the question is, however, not so much what went on – which can to a degree be taken for granted – but how such sexual activities were overwritten by, and involved in, power structures based on gender, race and empire. These issues are dealt with in relation to *A Passage to India* in J. Sharpe, 'The Unspeakable Limits of Rape: Colonial Violence and Counter-Insurgency', in *Colonial Discourse and Post-*

Colonial Theory, ed. by Patrick Williams and Laura Chrisman (London: Harvester Wheatsheaf, 1993), and Christopher Lane, 'Volatile Desire: Ambivalence and Distress in Forster's Colonial Narratives', in *Writing India 1757–1990: The Literature of British India,* ed. by Bart Moore-Gilbert (Manchester: Manchester University Press, 1996).

Alongside the (possibly mutual) heterosexual interracial desire in the novel, critics have wanted to put homosexual desires. This cannot be done without what might be described as 'interpretation' of both the text and its author, and you will need to ask yourself whether you find these interpretations legitimate or not. At the risk of appearing to digress, I want to begin this discussion with a comment on the title of the novel. Forster might be seen as choosing an entirely 'realistic' or 'descriptive' title for *A Passage to India*; he can appear also to be borrowing his title from that of a poem by Walt Whitman written in 1870 to celebrate equally the completion of the Pacific Railroad and the Suez Canal. Not surprisingly, the poem celebrates the romantic adventuring spirit: Stanza 9 contains the lines 'Sail forth – steer for the deep waters only / ... we will risk the ship, ourselves and all / ... O farther farther sail!' (Walt Whitman, *Complete Poems*, ed. by Francis Murphy, Harmondsworth: Penguin Education, 1975, p.437). Forster was perhaps drawn to the poem because Whitman's optimism about the future is not just a matter of technology but is also about people; in Stanza 2 Whitman writes:

> Lo, soul, seest thou not God's purpose from the first?
> The earth to be spanned, connected by network,
> The races, neighbours, to marry and be given in marriage,
> The oceans to be cross'd, the distant brought near,
> The lands to be welded together.

> (p.429)

One can imagine Forster murmuring, 'No, not yet' as he read. Reading Whitman he might also have had in mind another barrier that in the future might be 'spanned', which has a relevance to his own life and to *A Passage to India*: the barrier against sexual relations between men. Whitman was assumed by many to be homosexual – that was part of the atmosphere of risk and the exotic which hung around his name; he was not the kind of author from whom one could innocently or accidentally draw a title. It is difficult, however, to get behind the borrowing, since so far as one can tell Forster made hardly any reference elsewhere in letters or other writings to Whitman. There is, however, a reference in a letter written in 1915. Forster had sent the publisher Edward Dent a copy of *Maurice*, the homosexual fantasy story he had written in 1914–15 after putting aside *A Passage to India*. Although he did not believe *Maurice* could be published, he did circulate it among selected friends such as Dent to get their opinions. In the accompanying letter to Dent, he writes:

I am much dependent on criticism, and now, backed by you and some others, do feel that I have created something absolutely new, even to the Greeks. Whitman nearly anticipated me but he didn't really know what he was after, or only half knew – shirked, even to himself, the statement.

(*Selected Letters*, I, 222)

What interpretations might an awareness of such facts encourage? One approach might be to take Forster's own homosexuality as a starting point. His first full sexual affair probably dates from 1917, when he was in Alexandria; it is possible to see *A Passage to India* as part of the pattern of feeling and consciousness revealed in *Maurice* and in Forster's comment on Whitman, and therefore to conclude that the novel must have a homo-sexual theme. Another approach might make more of the fact that Forster specifically put aside *A Passage to India* from 1914 until after the writing of *Maurice*, and that he was easily able to sustain a distance between his personal life and writings – which were to remain private until after the death of his mother – and his more public writings. A third approach (perhaps a compromise) might be to accept that the focus of the novel is indeed on men rather than women, but to explore how Forster constructs different kinds of masculinity rather than to focus on the sexual relations between men. A model for this last approach can be found in G. Dawson, *Soldier Heroes: British Adventure, Empire and the Imagining of Masculinities* (London: Routledge, 1995), which discusses such figures as Henry Have-lock and T.E. Lawrence, seen at the time as heroes of the empire. The most prominent discussions of homosexuality and homoeroticism in *A Passage to India* occur in two pieces by Sara Suleri: 'The Geography of *A Passage to India*', in *Literature in the Modern World*, ed. by D. Walder (Oxford: Oxford University Press, 1990), and the chapter 'Forster's Imperial Erotic' in her book *The Rhetoric of English India* (Chicago: Chicago University Press, 1992). Both are highly coloured by Orientalism (in Said's sense), seeing interracial sexual relationships in empire as inevitably overlain with the power struc-tures of empire. In the earlier of these pieces in particular Suleri takes a strongly moral and condemnatory tone (encapsulated, for example, in her reference to 'the lovely, half-realized slave-boys of Forster's will to power'; Suleri, 'The Geography of *A Passage to India*', p.249). Discussion and reinterpretation of *A Passage to India* in the contexts of Orientalism and of sexuality have contributed to keeping interest in the novel alive. From Suleri's comments, however, plainly there has been a reversal of reputation; the novel has lost its liberal progressive reputation, to become associated with the imperialism that it had been seen to condemn.

The argument can perhaps be taken forward by referring to the criticisms that have been made of Said's idea of Orientalism. Javed Majeed, for example, in *Ungoverned Imaginings: James Mill's 'The History of British India' and Orientalism* (Oxford: Clarendon Press, 1992), refers to Said as an 'indispensable starting point' but then asserts that those he writes about have 'a much more sophisticated awareness of the issues' (pp.4–5).

The same might be said of Forster in *A Passage to India*, both in terms of the kinds of characters he creates and the styles of writing he uses. As a Modernist writer he might be allowed to share with Virginia Woolf a sense that character is something shifting and evanescent rather than solid and fixed. Equally, as a Modernist he might be allowed to share with T.S. Eliot the notion that literature could offer answers in a world that was otherwise empty of meaning. Similar points might be made if he is seen as a realist writer. Realism does not preclude sophistication. In many nineteenth-century novels – such as those of Jane Austen or George Eliot – objective social analysis is combined with the luxury (or even fantasy) of a fictional happy ending. Forster's understanding and awareness of sexual and erotic relationships may also be more sophisticated than the monolithic valuations imposed by a moral point of view. Two scenes between Fielding and Aziz in the novel are perhaps crucial to these investigations: the scene involving the shower and the collar stud (Chapter 7), and the scene that takes place on the roof at night (Chapter 27). The notion that Forster is a Modernist because he uses symbolic methods to convey meaning carries some into seeing the first scene as having a sexual meaning which can be decoded; the business with the stud is read as phallic play. The second scene might prompt a different idea: that the text has much in common with the Modernism of Virginia Woolf. In both scenes an evanescent reality is conjured up, which requires from the reader a sophistication of feeling and imagination rather than a simple political or ideological response.

Those who follow Suleri's approach might doubt that such sophistication can neutralize the moral reprehensibleness of Orientalism. But one of the fascinations of *A Passage to India* is that it dramatizes the tension between the two senses of Orientalism, the one (going back to Sir William Jones) that contains a genuine desire for the Oriental, and the other, more modern, construction that sees such desire as almost akin to rape. Forster transposes this polarity into an ambiguity of fantasy and desire; the reader is left to supply the answer – as in the last scene, where physical intimacy is apparently banished just as the two men engage in an activity that is physical (Forster has Fielding directly feel 'passionately physical again'; *A Passage to India*, p.312).

Point of view

The various possibilities suggested here for a reading of *A Passage to India* can quite neatly be turned into one question: what point of view does the reader feel encouraged to take up by Forster (or by the novel)? Is it that of the third-person narrator? And if so, is his style confident or uncertain in his pronouncements about India or about the characters? Or does the reader see through the eyes of one of the women in the novel, joining Adela or Mrs Moore in a desire for the real India? Is it Fielding's point of view that attracts? Or a racially or nationally hybrid point of view, such as is imagined through Aziz? Or is the dominant point of view the oblique, and only briefly mentioned, silent but very Indian gaze of the punkah-wallah?

Or is it that in the end we have adopted the point of view of Ralph Moore – the description of whom is curiously reminiscent of that of Forster himself – 'a strange-looking youth, tall, prematurely aged, the big blue eyes faded with anxiety, the hair impoverished and tousled' (p.303)?

Questions and exercises

1   Look carefully at the scenes involving Professor Godbole. Is Forster creating a figure in a social comedy, or a figure who is representative of India, or a figure who is part of a political message, or all three?

2   In most respects the story in *A Passage to India* is complete at the end of the second section, 'Caves'. What is the effect of including the final section, 'Temple'?

3   Find out as much as you can about the specifics of British rule in India around 1924. How much is embodied in the representation of British officialdom in *A Passage to India*?

4   Compare and contrast Forster's *A Passage to India* with Edward Thompson's *A Farewell to India* as novels that address the political situation in India.

5   In his depiction of what happens during the expedition to the Marabar Caves and/or the depiction of the relationship between Fielding and Aziz, would you say that Forster was using fiction to analyse a sexual fantasy commonly held in British culture, or using fiction to pursue his own dreams and fantasies?

8 GANDHIAN NATIONALISM: KANTHAPURA

by Harish Trivedi

Introduction

This is the first of three chapters here (together with Chapters 9 and 11) dealing with works by Indian writers. Reading them will raise a new set of questions and probably also require a different set of approaches. To ease the way, however, these chapters will contain more exposition of the historical context of each work than the preceding chapters have given; you may wish to supplement this by going back to read more of the works cited in Chapter 1. One way to explore these texts may be to adopt a comparative approach, studying them in juxtaposition not only with each other and with similar works cited in these 'Indian' chapters but also with English texts where you see there are links. Another way may be to cast a wider interdisciplinary net, extending your range of study to include the history, politics and ideology of the British Empire, on which a considerable body of material is available, and even philosophy and (inter)cultural studies. Many aspects of the content and form of these texts will similarly be illuminated by works of post-colonial theory.

The text

Kanthapura was first published in London in 1938, with an author's 'Foreword' which began: 'My publishers have asked me to say a word of explanation.' Curiously, this sentence has been omitted from most reprints by subsequent publishers, thus compromising from the start the quietly sturdy confidence with which Rao narrates his tale of rural India from deep inside the culture, without making many concessions to the English-language reader. The first edition also contained several footnotes (perhaps again at the publisher's suggestion?) which too have been omitted or substantially reduced in subsequent reprints in India, and a two-page note at the end summarizing the story of the *Ramayana* to which constant allusion is made in the novel, which also has disappeared from all subsequent editions.

The novel was first published in India only in 1947, by Oxford University Press, Bombay, and then primarily to be used as a textbook, with an introduction by the eminent Indian academic C.D. Narasimhaiah. It is now one of the most widely read texts in Indian college classrooms: by 1996, the Orient Paperbacks edition, first published in 1970, had been reprinted fourteen times; the 'second edition', first published in 1974, has been reprinted eight times in the Oxford India Paperbacks series (Delhi: Oxford University Press, 1989). This is the edition cited here.

Interestingly, the American edition of *Kanthapura* (New York: New Directions, 1963) includes extensive notes on 'Indian myths, religion, social customs, and the Independence movement', which, as the blurb explains, 'fill out the background for the American reader's more complete understanding and enjoyment'. These notes were provided by Rao himself, who seems to have risen to the occasion with a vengeance, supplying sixty pages of notes to the 182 pages of text, though some of the details in them may perhaps only plunge the non-Indian reader into deeper waters.

The main text in all the editions has remained the same, except that some later editions are printed without chapter numbers (though with each of the nineteen chapters still beginning on a new page). This omission is interpreted by some critics as embodying the unbroken flow of the oral narrative.

Biographical and bibliographical information

Kanthapura, Raja Rao's first novel, is also one of the first major Indian novels written in English. Though there had been some sporadic Indian writing in English in the nineteenth century, it was in the 1930s that the Indian novel in English emerged as a sustained and significant genre; the three 'founding fathers' of this form of writing, R.K. Narayan, Mulk Raj Anand and Raja Rao, all published their first novels within a few years of each other – and each novel registered in a different way and to a different degree the contemporary impress of Gandhi. In *Swami and Friends* (1935) by R.K. Narayan (b.1907), the eponymous boy-protagonist hears a supporter of Gandhi make in a public speech the distinctly un-Gandhian suggestion: 'Let every Indian spit on England, and the quantity of saliva will be enough to drown England', upon which he 'involuntarily' shouts *'Gandhi ki Jai'* ('Victory to Mahatma Gandhi'); but for all this Swami remains more interested in cricket than in nationalism. *Untouchable* (1935) by Mulk Raj Anand (b.1905) has for its theme one of the burning issues of the time, and one with which Gandhi was engaged: the liberation and uplifting of the lowest of the Hindu castes. Anand had shown Gandhi the manuscript and benefited from his advice on how to represent such characters stylistically, even though Anand's Marxist treatment of the subject is distinctly critical of Gandhi himself.

But it is *Kanthapura* which remains the most comprehensively and intimately Gandhian of all the Indian novels written in English. It is also one of the earliest novels in any language to register extensively the impact of Gandhi. In the Indian languages, an early novel that is thoroughly imbued with the spirit of Gandhi, though it represents him indirectly, is the epic *Rangabhumi* by Premchand (1880–1936), still widely regarded as the greatest Hindi novelist. Here, the Gandhi figure is a blind, meek and devout beggar, who stands up against British brute force and is in the end shot dead by the British collector (district officer). Premchand himself answered the call when, after listening to one of Gandhi's speeches in February 1921, he resigned his government job. Shortly afterwards, he celebrated the sense of liberation he felt by writing the carnivalesque short story 'A Special Holi' (see Texts 8.2 and 8.3).

Rao too had published a few Gandhian nationalist short stories before *Kanthapura*. One of these, 'The Cow of the Barricades' (later collected in a volume with the same title, 1947), has for its central figure a cow that comes to stand on the barricades between the nationalist freedom fighters and the police, and is shot dead by a 'Red-man' (a Britisher). (Incidentally, both cows and blind beggars are invested with a certain holiness in Hindu symbology.) *Kanthapura* was written, according to Rao, between the years 1929 and 1933, right in the thick of Gandhi's Civil Disobedience movement. The movement began in March 1930, with Gandhi's march to the sea at Dandi, as a protest against the British Government's tax on salt. The march is reported in the novel as it progresses from day to day, but Rao himself was not directly involved in what he describes – indeed, he was remarkably distant from the scene of action. As he has recounted, 'I wrote *Kanthapura* in a thirteenth century castle in the French Alps belonging to the Dauphins of France and I slept and worked on the novel in the room of the Queen' (letter quoted in M.K. Naik, *Raja Rao*, New York: Twayne, 1972, p.60).

It was an extraordinary journey that had taken Rao to such an exotic workplace. He was born in 1909 (or in 1908 – see Naik, p.16) in Hassan, a small town in south India, and brought up there and in the village of Harihalli (the model for Kanthapura) by his grandfather, a man of spiritual inclinations. He went to college at the Aligarh Muslim University where one of his teachers was Eric Dickinson, an Englishman, 'who taught me to love France. He impressed me very much. I have been made by him. My literary sensibilities were formed by him' (quoted in Naik, p.17). Such crucial colonial–cosmopolitan formation led Rao at the age of twenty-one to go to France to study on a scholarship; he went first to Montpellier and then to the Sorbonne, where for three years he studied the Indian influence on Irish literature.

He began writing fiction in conventional English (which he later described as 'Macaulayan English') until his wife called it 'rubbish' (Naik, p.19). He reverted to writing in his native language, Kannada, only to find that he had virtually lost it: 'my Kannada was a babble. I tried and failed writing in it' (quoted in *Word as Mantra: The Art of Raja Rao*, ed. by Robert L. Hardgrave, Jr, Delhi: Katha, 1998, p.174). He went back to writing in English, but with the intention of forging a distinctive Indian variety of the language, which would be a more apt medium for his purpose. As he was to say in the foreword to *Kanthapura*, in a statement which has come to be seen as an early manifesto for all Indian writers in English: 'The telling has not been easy. One has to convey in a language that is not one's own the spirit that is one's own ... We cannot write like the English. We should not' (p.v).

In more recent years post-colonial theory has described this way of avoiding dependence on literary models of the colonial masters, at the same time as one adopts and adapts their language for one's own ends, as a strategy of 'appropriation'. It might even be seen as an attempt to reverse past processes and in Rao's case to 'counter-colonize' English. The extent to which the strategy has proved effective, and the question of whether writing in English by Indians really is an act of defiance and resistance rather than one of complicity and collaboration, remains open to debate; the questions are pertinent not only in the case of a writer such as Rao, who grew up in colonial times, but equally if not more so in the case of a self-consciously post-colonial writer such as Salman Rushdie (see Chapter 11).

After *Kanthapura*, Rao published no more fiction until *The Serpent and the Rope* in 1960. This story of an Indian student in Paris with a French wife is certainly the most metaphysical of all Indian novels in English, depending as it does on an elaborate and intricate exposition of the vedantic duality of illusion and reality. Similar preoccupations characterize Rao's most recent novel, *The Chessmaster and His Moves* (1988), a long work to which one or more sequels appear to be in progress. Meanwhile, in a fastidiously sparse career, Rao had published two novellas, one, cryptically titled *The Cat and Shakespeare* (1965), in which the protagonist constantly expounds the virtues of surrendering to divine providence, and another, published first in French translation as *La Camarade Kirillov* (1966) and later in English as *Comrade Kirillov* (Delhi: Vision Books, 1976), which has for its hero an Indian intellectual who has turned communist; he offers, *inter alia*, a harsh critique of Gandhi and is himself satirically treated by the author. After publishing *Kanthapura*, Rao had in fact gone to live in Gandhi's ashram for 'several months' in 1941–2; he has evoked a brief meeting between them in his volume of essays and memoirs, *The Meaning of India* (Delhi: Vision Books, 1976, pp.78–81). Rao's most recent published work is a 480-page biography, *The Great Indian Way: A Life of Mahatma Gandhi* (Delhi: Vision Books, 1998), in which he is concerned not so much with the political as with the spiritual dimensions of his subject.

Having divided the early part of his life between India and France, Rao has since 1966 lived in Austin, Texas, where he taught Indian philosophy at the University of Texas until 1980. (His first wife was French, his second and third have been Americans.) In March 1997, in his acceptance speech on being made a Fellow of the Sahitya Akademi (the Indian Academy of Literature), Rao began: 'I am a proud Indian. It is my karma that has destined me to live more than half my life outside the punyabhumi [sacred land]. India indeed is the land of ultimate value. The Truth.' And he went on to say: 'to have been born in India and not to have written in Sanskrit, or at least in Kannada, is, believe me, an acute humiliation. But I still dream of writing in Sanskrit – one day!' (*Word as Mantra*, pp.175–6).

Rao's life and career are thus an acute instance of what in post-colonial discourse is variously termed as exile, diaspora, migrancy and hybridity. At the same time, his case is widely characteristic of a large number of other Indian writers in English, such as Mulk Raj Anand, Attia Hosain, Kamala Markandaya, Salman Rushdie, Anita Desai, Bharati Mukherjee and Amitav

Ghosh, all of whom have lived for significant parts of their lives or continue to live in the UK or the USA. While all of them have continued to write largely if not exclusively about India or about Indian characters in England and America, the question is often asked, at least in India, just how Indian, or 'authentically' Indian, their writing is, especially when compared with that of writers living in India and writing in the Indian languages. The issue is complicated by the fact that because of the global reach of English, these expatriate writers, many of whom are now officially citizens of the countries of their residence, are often regarded in the West as 'representing' India, in the sense both of depicting it and speaking for it.

There exist two book-length studies of Rao published in the West which should be relatively easy to obtain; interestingly, these also represent widely different approaches. M.K. Naik, *Raja Rao*, gives an extensive and largely sympathetic account of Rao's life and career up to the date of its publication, 1972. Besides taking note of earlier criticism, it uses important personal information communicated to Naik by Rao himself, and is probably still the most helpful introduction to the author and his works. On the other hand, Rumina Sethi, *Myths of the Nation: National Identity and Literary Representation* (Oxford: Clarendon Press, 1999), which does not even mention Rao in its title, deals almost exclusively with *Kanthapura*, claiming to situate it within 'the history of the period'. Sethi finds it wanting on various counts as a historical novel, and 'exposes' many ideological 'biases' and 'contradictions' in Rao's writing, especially in his representation of Gandhi, peasants and women. Both Naik and Sethi offer detailed discussions of Rao's use of English and his narrative technique. *Word as Mantra*, ed. by Robert L. Hardgrave, Jr, is a recent collection of memoirs of and largely appreciative articles on Rao; it includes a 'chronology' of Rao's life and a twelve-page 'Selected Bibliography (1931–1998)' of works by as well as about him (both compiled by R. Parthasarathy).

More generally useful is an authoritative and comprehensive literary history, *Indian Writing in English* by K.R. Srinivasa Iyengar (1962; 5th rev. edn, Delhi: Sterling, 1985); Meenakshi Mukherjee's early study of the Indian novel in English, *The Twice-Born Fiction* (Delhi: Heinemann, 1971), is still valuable. Those interested in studying Gandhi further may turn to his autobiography, M.K. Gandhi, *An Autobiography, or, The Story of My Experiments with Truth*, translated from the original Gujarati by Mahadev Desai (Harmondsworth: Penguin, 1983), and to Judith Brown's *Gandhi and Civil Disobedience: The Mahatma in Indian Politics, 1928–34* (Cambridge: Cambridge University Press, 1977), which covers the phase of Gandhian nationalism depicted in *Kanthapura*. A good short introduction to Gandhi's own writings is *The Penguin Gandhi Reader* (see Text 8.1); his *Collected Works* have appeared in 90 volumes (Ahmedabad: Navajivan Press, 1958–84).

Some Western journals in which Indian novelists in English are regularly discussed are the *Journal of Commonwealth Literature*, *Wasafiri* and *Ariel*. *Interventions* is a journal of post-colonial studies that was launched in 1998.

Approaching Kanthapura

Gandhi as God: religion and politics

Perhaps the most fruitful approach to *Kanthapura* is to explore the novel's treatment of Gandhi and of the nationalist movement led and inspired by him. Gandhi is almost universally acknowledged as one of the iconic great men of the modern age; one of his greatest achievements was that the radically different political idiom he inaugurated had a moral, an ethical and even a spiritual core to it, as embodied especially in the practice of non-violent resistance. The ideal of *ahimsa* (non-violence) had been common to Hinduism, Jainism and Buddhism through the ages, but for Gandhi its adoption was also a matter of good strategy, given the enormity of the task of forcibly driving out Britain – the mightiest imperial power the world had ever seen. As he said in a public speech on 10 March 1930, just before launching the Civil Disobedience movement, 'Can you show me an example in history ... where the State has tolerated violent defiance of authority for a single day? But here you know that the Government is puzzled and perplexed' (quoted in Bipan Chandra, Mridula Mukherjee, Aditya Mukherjee, K.N. Panikkar and Sucheta Mahajan, *India's Struggle for Independence*, Delhi: Penguin, 1989, p.272). This was not only making a virtue of necessity; it also showed how Gandhi could be a shrewd and effective leader and a venerated holy man at the same time.

If non-violent, civil resistance to the Raj was the spearhead of Gandhi's nationalist strategy, its self-professed objective was a goal he saw as higher than freedom: that is, Truth. In his autobiography, Gandhi wrote: 'for me, truth is the sovereign principle ... This truth is ... the Absolute Truth, the Essential Principle, that is God ... I worship God as Truth only ... He alone is real and all else is unreal' (quoted in Judith Brown, *Modern India: The Origins of an Asian Democracy*, 2nd edn, Oxford: Oxford University Press, 1994, p.211). This belief of Gandhi's finds resonance in *Kanthapura* in the worship of the abstract *Satyanarayana* – that is, God as Truth (pp.166–72). It is in this sense that a demand for political freedom became a demand for (or insistence on obtaining) the Truth, which is the literal meaning of *satyagraha* (see Text 8.1, pp.300–04).

Such conflation of God with Truth (and of Truth with freedom) is an abstraction and belongs to what scholars have called 'higher' or *Upanishadic* Hinduism. To appeal to the masses, however, Gandhi had to deploy symbols and practices that belonged to popular Hinduism. *Swarajya* or *swaraj* (self-rule), Gandhi said, would ideally be like *Ramarajya*, the rule of Lord Rama, the divine hero of the epic-scripture *Ramayana* (see Text 8.1, pp.305–06). Some recent historians have seen this trope as indicative that Gandhi conceived of independence in communal (that is, sectarian) Hindu terms, but the term *Ramarajya* also carries an idiomatic secular meaning of 'utopia' or 'golden age'. For example, in his idealized description in the Hindi *Ramayana* (properly titled the *Ramacharitamanas*), the sixteenth-century Hindi saint-poet Tulsi Das says, 'In Ramarajya, no one suffered from any bodily, material, or spiritual affliction.' At least rhetorically, this was the kind of utopia Gandhi wished independent India to be.

As the leader who would help India attain that dream, Gandhi sought to achieve a personal purity and spirituality in his own life through various traditional Hindu modes of renunciation: by wearing only a loin-cloth (when asked if he was wearing enough when he went up to meet King George V at Buckingham Palace in 1931, Gandhi is reported to have replied: 'But the King will be wearing enough for both of us'); by abstaining from sex (*brahmacharya*); and by having recourse to long fasts – sometimes announced as 'fasts unto death' – at the height of political crises. These practices were seen as hypocritical ploys by many of his critics, and as contradictions even by some of his admirers, but it was Gandhi's spirituality and even sanctity that led, quite early in his career, to his being popularly called a 'Mahatma' (etymologically 'one with a great soul', and idiomatically 'a holy man'). '*Mahatma Gandhi ki Jai*' ('Victory to Mahatma Gandhi') became a national slogan quite as much as '*Vandè Mataram*' ('I Salute the Motherland'); both are heard to resound equally throughout *Kanthapura*.

The novel goes further when, during a *harikatha* (tales of God) discourse, Gandhi is identified with Lord Krishna, God himself. The epigraph on the title-page of the first edition, omitted from most subsequent editions, quotes (loosely) Lord Krishna's assurance from *The Bhagavad-Gita*: 'Whenever there is misery and ignorance, I come.' In a religion where all creatures are to be reborn endlessly, and in which God is supposed to incarnate himself ten times at various moments of crisis in human history (there have been nine incarnations to date), the supposition that Gandhi is God/a god (Hinduism is polytheistic and there are no capital letters in the Indian languages) is not as unique and superstitious as it may seem. Outside the novel, Gandhi (whose first name, Mohandas, means 'a devotee of Krishna') was already being represented as Krishna as early as 1921 (see Brown, p.230). Within the novel, oddly enough, a Hindu holy man, who is in favour of the British and against Gandhi, actually says in the course of a long public speech that, as promised in the *Gita*, it was 'the British' who had come, like Krishna, to save the Hindus, and that, like Krishna, 'the great queen Victoria' too was a saviour (p.92). Thus, in Gandhi's use of the term *Ramarajya* and Rao's (and the public's) use of the figure of the God Krishna, religion is being used not strictly as religion but as a cultural metaphor.

Moreover, several key tenets of Gandhian nationalism were not religious at all, such as the use of the *charkha* (spinning wheel) for the production of cloth, which would replace the huge exploitative imports of cloth from the mills of Manchester, and the choice of salt, that most common of commodities, as the emblem of a nationwide movement. Both were economic planks of nationalism; no sanctity was attached to them. Similarly unsanctified was Gandhi's advocacy of the adoption of Hindi as a common 'national' language to bind together the country; in *Kanthapura* the lawyer Sankar 'began to talk Hindi to his mother, who understood not a word of it', and punished himself whenever he let slip a word of English by paying a self-imposed fine (p.103). Again, the 'Hinduism' of Gandhi's nationalist project was further modified by his reiterated tolerance of all religions, including Islam and Christianity; he was in the end assassinated in 1948 by a *Hindu* fanatic who thought he was being too liberal to Pakistan.

In *Kanthapura*, though Gandhi is reverentially regarded by most villagers, he remains a distant and even somewhat blurred presence. He never appears in the novel, except in a dream or 'vision' to Moorthy, and he irradiates the village by refraction, through Moorthy, who is proclaimed to be 'our Gandhi'. Not many of the illiterate villagers really understand the details and nuances of his political philosophy, but they nevertheless act out faithfully and bravely his essential message, which is that the oppressive British must be opposed non-violently. The gap between what Gandhi preached and sought to achieve and how the masses who followed him actually viewed him has recently been highlighted by an influential collective of Marxist historians of India who have published a series of volumes titled *Subaltern Studies* (Delhi: Oxford University Press). Shahid Amin, for example, has documented how the rural masses took Gandhi to be a holy miracle-worker rather than a political leader, and were swayed by his religious charisma rather than by his nationalist agenda (see Shahid Amin, 'Gandhi as Mahatma', first published 1984 in *Subaltern Studies* III; repr. in *Selected Subaltern Studies*, ed. by Ranajit Guha and Gayatri Chakravorty Spivak, New York: Oxford University Press, 1988, pp.288–348). It is true that the mobilization of the masses achieved by Gandhi was not as ideologically coherent or correct a phenomenon as Marxist theory might expect revolutions to be. By the same token, the power of his influence on the villagers of Kanthapura and the workers of the Skeffington Coffee Estate offers a distinctly non-Marxist model of organizing mass movements, which serves to critique in its turn the Marxist project as the only possible or desirable model for revolution.

And yet, for all their devout Gandhism, even the villagers of Kanthapura are shown by Rao to be faced finally not by any triumph but by a crushing defeat and flight. Though the *satyagrahis* are still 'all for the Mahatma', it turns out that their leader Moorthy, their own Gandhi, is so no longer. As he says on coming out of prison:

> things must change ... Jawaharlal [Nehru] will change it. You know Jawaharlal is like a Bharatha [younger brother] to the Mahatma [seen as Rama], and he, too, is for non-violence and he, too, is a Satyagrahi, but he says in Swaraj there shall be neither the rich nor the poor. And he calls himself an 'equal-distributionist,' and I am with him and his men. (p.189)

Nehru remained the foremost and favourite disciple of Gandhi throughout his life, but he differed from him on economic matters. In his own auto-biography he spoke candidly and poignantly of his temperamental and ideological differences with Gandhi, even calling him 'delightfully vague' (see Jawaharlal Nehru, *Autobiography*, London: John Lane, 1936; rev. 1942 and reprinted many times thereafter, Chapter 61 'Desolation'). Having Moorthy turn to him at the end is a climactic indication of Rao's view. He shows that at the simplest level Gandhi was regarded as God (or at least as Mahatma) by the people of Kanthapura, just as he also qualifies and circumscribes Gandhi's divinity in many complex and historically plausible ways. The ending of *Kanthapura* is unwittingly prophetic of attitudes to Gandhi up to his death in 1948 and beyond. These are reflected in Nehru's own writings as well as anywhere (see Text 8.4). Writing in prison in 1943 on topics such as imperialism, philosophy and religion, and industrialization in India, and speaking on Independence Day in 1947, Nehru powerfully advocates just those modern and socialist desiderata of which Moorthy speaks. Meantime, that profound veneration for Gandhi continues to be heard, never more powerfully than in the speech Nehru delivered as the Mahatma's ashes were immersed in the Ganges in 1948.

Community and nation: the local and the imaginary

Kanthapura begins with the unapologetic expectation on the part of the narrator that the reader would not have heard of her village. No one could have heard of a fictional village, of course, but the point being made is that the place is especially obscure and remote. And yet, by the end of the short first paragraph, it is seen as not so remote as to be out of the ambit of empire: the local 'cardamoms and coffee get into the ships the Redmen [i.e. the British] bring, and, so they say, they go across the seven oceans into the countries where our rulers live' (p.1). The various modes of connection and communication between the little village and the wider world are seen in the novel to be tenuous and yet real. Gandhian influence percolates into the village through interaction with the town and through the 'Blue newspaper' that some of the villagers get and read, and what the villagers do is clearly affected by what people are doing elsewhere:

> and when somebody said in Bombay and Lahore did people gather at dawn to go singing through the streets, women in Rampur said, 'We, too, shall do it,' and they, too, rose up at dawn and ... went singing through the twilit streets ... O Mahatma, Mahatma, you're our king. (p.147)

But these developments are all new. We have the impression that before the change described in the novel, nothing in the village had changed for centuries. It had gone on with its traditional ways and customs: with its Brahmin's quarter set apart from its Pariah quarters and the Potters', the Weavers' and the Sudra quarters; with the priest and the patel and the *harikatha*-tellers performing their hallowed functions; and with the local mythical deity, Kenchamma, presiding over all. Significantly, when the change comes, it is brought about not by an outsider, but by Moorthy, a member of the village, who has left and then come back, transformed and transforming. The village has not been caught up in some external turmoil; it has gradually converted itself from within. When Moorthy crosses caste boundaries to enter a pariah house it causes offence to the extent of his being excommunicated, and when he enlists supporters for Gandhian *satyagraha*, not everyone comes forward with equal alacrity. A complex dynamism rather than any simple idealized homogeneity marks the process through which this small isolated community affiliates itself to the nation.

Recently, the whole idea of 'the nation' has been subjected to some rigorous rethinking by theorists such as Benedict Anderson, Fredric Jameson and Partha Chatterjee, and it may be useful to look at the dynamic between the village of Kanthapura and the Indian nation in the light of their views. Benedict Anderson in his *Imagined Communities: Reflections on the Origin and Spread of Nationalism* (London: Verso, 1991) seeks to explore the paradox that though people's feelings for their nation often run deeper than their feelings for their neighbours, 'the nation' is a concept too vast to be directly grasped: it must be 'imagined' into existence rather than seen and felt to be there. He writes, 'All communities larger than primordial villages of face to face contact ... are imagined' (p.6). In *Kanthapura* we may seem to have a pristine example of a traditional (if not quite primordial!) village and organic community in which everyone knows everyone else. The community then undergoes a process through which it not only politicizes but also 'nationalizes' itself. However, it may be argued that the village does so not by projecting and imagining itself as a particle of a larger unseen entity but by enacting the national within its local events and local space. In *Kanthapura* the nation is thus not an 'imagined' entity but a felt reality which invades the village. This apparent lack of fit between the village in *Kanthapura* and now orthodox ideas of nation can be argued as again evident if we place it in the context of some of the ideas of another influential theoretician of nation – Fredric Jameson suggests that every 'Third World' text should be read as if it were a 'national allegory' (see Fredric Jameson, 'Third World Literature in the Era of Multi-national Capital', *Social Text*, 15 (Fall 1986), pp.65–88). Leaving aside the question of whether all third world texts are national/-ist, it may be argued that a novel like *Kanthapura*, with its constant evocation of its physical specificity and its insistence on its cultural locality, is too realistically rendered for it to be read 'necessarily' as allegorical. In fact, to interrogate Jameson's essay (and possibly also Aijaz Ahmed's impassioned rejoinder to it to the effect that both the 'nation' and the 'First World/Third World' polarity are untenable in Marxist theory; see his *In Theory*, London: Verso, 1992, pp.95–122) would be to confront in more general terms the way texts from any one culture or nation are often read in another as encapsulating that 'Other'. There is a general sense, for example, in which notions of England that many educated Indian readers hold have come from what they happen to have read of Jane Austen, Dickens and even Conan Doyle or P.G. Wodehouse; that is not to say, though, that any of these authors must be said to present an 'allegorical' view of England. A text from one culture, when read by readers from another culture who may have only a partial knowledge of that alien culture and nation, may seem to them to be wholly or widely representative of it – which it may or may not be to any significant extent. But it is more likely to carry a truly 'allegorical' meaning – that is, to contain a dynamic and sustained metaphorical subtext within it – to readers from the same culture as the text rather than to outsiders (even if they come, as in Jameson's argument, from the first world).

Finally, from quite another point of view, critics attempting a historicist and ideological reading of Rao have asked if his village community offers a verifiably adequate or fair representation of the Indian nation, especially with regard to its depiction of minorities and the underprivileged. Rumina Sethi has charged Rao with an 'implicit bias towards brahminism which can be seen as a feature of chauvinist Hinduism employed by revivalist nationalists'. She points out that the villain of the piece is a Muslim (Badè Khan, the policeman), and claims that in the novel women are 'marginalized in the essentialist representations of nationalist discourse' (Sethi, pp.73, 97, 131). But one may ask if Sethi has reached these conclusions as a result of adopting the politically 'correct' practice of reading the novel 'against the grain' – that is, against the evidence of what the text itself seeks or seems to say. For example, while many of the major characters in the novel are indeed brahmins, their brahminism is shown as coming seriously into conflict with their newly adopted Gandhism and is not upheld except by a character such as the Swami, the excommunicating priest who is presented satirically. Badè Khan is, indeed, the villain of the piece, but it is probably more because he is a policeman than because he is a Muslim, and equally villainous if not more so is the aptly named Hunter Sahib, who started at the Skeffington Coffee Estate. Hunter Sahib promises evenhandedness – 'if you work well you will get sweets and if you work badly you will get beaten' – but the smallness of the reward and the detail that he 'grew so furious again that he beat them on the back and drove them to their huts' (pp.50–51) suggests the truth of the matter. In any case, the novel also features a 'good' Muslim, Imam Khan, who 'gun in hand and fire in his eyes' (p.138) escorts the women *satyagrahis* safely back to Kanthapura after the police have by brute force broken up their march on Boranna's toddy grove. And as for the women being marginalized, they are in fact, with Moorthy, the chief *satyagrahis* in the novel, which is indeed narrated by one of them, Achakka. Their prominence in the novel aptly reflects historical fact: a new development which marked the Civil Disobedience movement of Gandhi in 1930–32 was that 'women were a further new and unexpected source of support' (Brown, p.279), and that 'the women of India certainly demonstrated in 1930 that they were second to none in strength and tenacity of purpose' (Chandra *et al.*, p.276).

Of the several recent ways of reading the 'nation' and 'community' outlined above, not all may seem to be equally relevant to *Kanthapura* or to illuminate it equally. There is perhaps always something of a problem in fitting any one theory or ideology neatly to a particular literary text; this is especially the case with novels, which, as the influential literary theorist Bakhtin argued, are by their very form 'dialogic' and 'polysemic' (that is, they are designed to represent different and contrary views without having to strive towards a single resolution). *Kanthapura* is such a rewarding text to read precisely because it is so dynamic. It embodies a sense of traditions that show continuity and communality (though by no means unanimity) while it also explores the imagined as well as the only too real ties which bind together diverse communities as a nation.

'The telling has not been easy': style and form

Besides the thematic aspects of the novel discussed above, its style and form too represent a deliberate and original innovation. The personal circumstances which led to Rao paradoxically growing more fluent and competent in English than in his native language, Kannada, have already been touched on. One of the chief distinctions of *Kanthapura*, however, is that it attempts to fashion an un-British English, by representing in it 'various shades and omissions of a certain thought-movement [of an Indian language] that looks maltreated in an alien language' (*Kanthapura*, p.v). Rao sets himself a challenging task: his characters were not educated urban middle-class Indians like himself, who as he claimed 'are all instinctively bilingual' (p.v), but in contrast largely rural illiterates, as deeply recessed in their own indigenous language and cultures as presumably any characters ever depicted in an Indian novel in English. And he made things even more difficult for himself by choosing a grandmother as his novel's oral narrator.

Some of the main devices Rao uses to convey a 'vernacular' speech-rhythm and resonance are syntactical dislocations ('our village – ... Kanthapura is its name', p.1), and long but simple (that is, not compound) sentences, often extended breathlessly over many lines with the help of many 'and's and repetition of phrases ('we tell one interminable tale', p.vi). He also uses many Indian words, idioms, collocations and allusions, and suggests that some phrases may even be translations from Kannada, as Janet Power Gemmill has shown in her article 'The Transcreation of Spoken Kannada in Raja Rao's *Kanthapura*' (1974; cited and discussed in Sethi, pp.45–50). Interestingly, in Rao's collection of short stories *The Cow of the Barricades* (published in 1947, though written mostly in the 1930s), the publisher's note – possibly drafted by Rao – says: 'One of the stories ... is translated from the Kannada, and all the rest, although first written in English, are translations too' (quoted in Naik, p.45).

This is an early suggestion of a development in recent translation theory, through which (post-)colonial writing itself is seen as a kind of translation (see, for example, the essays by Maria Tymoczko on James Joyce and by G.J.V. Prasad on Indian novelists in English, in *Post-Colonial Translation: Theory and Practice*, ed. by Susan Bassnett and Harish Trivedi, London: Routledge, 1999). Other innovative Indian novelists, whose varied practices in this respect may be studied in comparison, are Mulk Raj Anand (see p.108 above); G.V. Desani, *All About H. Hatterr* (1948; repr. Harmondsworth: Penguin, 1972); Khushwant Singh's novel about Partition, *Train to Pakistan* (New York: Grove Press, 1956); and Salman Rushdie, *Midnight's Children* (1981; see Chapter 11 below).

Apart from the novel's experimental use of English, the whole form of *Kanthapura* may be viewed as embodying a literary tradition quite distinct from that of a Western realist novel. Novels by Indian writers such as Attia Hosain, Anita Desai, Arun Joshi and Nayantara Sahgal can perhaps be seen largely to conform to the Western model, at least in formal terms. It may seem to some readers that there is a lot more description in *Kanthapura* than action; for long stretches nothing really seems to happen, and when eventually something does happen, the action seems cocooned in, and even smothered by, the elaborate telling. The novel has a large number of characters but they are not easily distinguishable from each other; the novel thus seems to be not so much one individual's story (not even Moorthy's) as the saga of a community, or even the legend of a place – a *sthala-purana*, to use a term Rao himself evokes at the beginning of the foreword. (A novel with which *Kanthapura* can usefully be compared, which also names the place in its title, is Ahmed Ali, *Twilight in Delhi*, 1941; 2nd edn, Delhi: Oxford University Press, 1966.) Finally, in both their compliance with some outside force and the passivity or equanimity (even resignation) with which they accept the sad outcome of their actions, the villagers seem to lack subjectivity and agency: unlike characters in much Western literature, they do not seem to shape their own destiny. These are major differences not only in terms of literary form but more widely in terms of culture; they bring to mind V.S. Naipaul's controversial observation (with reference to R.K. Narayan) that, given the fatalistic lack of social concern in the Indian world-view (which regards the world as an illusion), 'the *aimlessness* of Indian fiction ... comes from a profound doubt about the purpose and value of fiction' (*An Area of Darkness*, 1964; repr. Harmondsworth: Penguin, 1968, p.216).

Questions and exercises

1   Identify the main features of Gandhian nationalism and compare and contrast them with models of nationalism from some other contexts (e.g. from the USA, from Ireland and from other third world countries).

2   Compare Rao's representation of Gandhi with that of some other Indian novelists, including R.K. Narayan (*Waiting for the Mahatma*, 1955) and Mulk Raj Anand (*The Sword and the Sickle*, 1942).

3   Read Chapter 8 'The Nation and its Peasants' in Partha Chatterjee, *The Nation and its Fragments: Colonial and Post-Colonial Histories* (Princeton: Princeton University Press, 1993). How far might *Kanthapura* be used to support or to critique Chatterjee's arguments?

4   Select a chapter from *Kanthapura*. Analyse Rao's style particularly so as to identify his ways of making the language sound Indian – if you wish, compare Rao's methods here with those of Anand and Rushdie.

5   Are the sections of *Kanthapura* dealing with the Skeffington Coffee Estate included simply to enable the reader better to understand the values of the villagers or does Rao use them to offer a complementary analysis of another aspect of colonial India?

9 FRAGMENTING NATIONS AND LIVES: SUNLIGHT ON A BROKEN COLUMN

by Vrinda Nabar

Introduction

Attia Hosain's *Sunlight on a Broken Column* appeared in 1961, long after India and Pakistan became independent countries in 1947. It is thus a historical novel, grounded in the issues of nation and identity that had always simmered beneath the surface during colonial rule and even earlier. The history of India has always been one of localized loyalties and regional kingdoms or fiefdoms. Even the much-touted unification of India, attributed to the British, can seem no more than a whitewash effected through the dubious, self-promoting policies of conquest and annexation. Divisive forces arising from economic, religious, class and land-ownership issues were at work even during the British presence in India, but their disruptive potential was by and large kept under control. The British were forceful enough when these threatened to disturb the administrative peace. They were less assiduous, however, about interfering in issues once they were able to convince themselves that Indians were following their own religious practices. Thus, for example, British decisions about sati (or widow-burning) were motivated not by notions of gender injustice but by discriminations as to what was or was not proper according to Hindu law. An East India Company circular of 1813 declared sati prohibited if it infringed Hindu law because, for example, the widow was less than sixteen, pregnant or coerced into immolating herself (see L. Mani, *Contentious Traditions: The Debate on Sati in Colonial India*, Berkeley: University of California Press, 1998, pp.18ff.). The guise of political expediency or respect for other religions made it possible to be selective about which issues needed the tempering influence of British fair play. In this introductory section I want to touch briefly on four aspects of this social and historic context for a reading of *Sunlight on a Broken Column:* the struggle for independence; communalism and the partition of colonial India into independent India and East and West Pakistan; the social structure of India; and the specific situation of women.

Following on from the unsuccessful revolt of 1857 in which rulers from different parts of India, in a rare and unprecedented show of solidarity, tried to overthrow British dominion, power was transferred from the East India Company to the Crown. As we have seen in earlier chapters, the 1850s also saw the initiation of moves to 'educate' the natives through the setting up of universities and the introduction of Western systems of thought into the syllabuses (see Gauri Viswanathan, *Masks of Conquest: Literary Study and British Rule in India*, London: Faber, 1989).

Meanwhile, the struggle for freedom proceeded in a series of phases. The most significant among these was the launching of the Indian National Congress in 1885. This was perhaps the first organized effort to bring together people from all over India and prepare an agenda that would seek to focus the government's attention on various social and national problems.

The freedom struggle was far from homogeneous. Fairly early on, it was embroiled in tussles between the so-called 'extremists' and the 'moderates' (see the references to Tilak and Gokhale in the section 'An analysis of India?' in Chapter 7 above). Another factor was the setting up of the Muslim League in 1905. This began as a reaction to the Partition of Bengal by the British but soon became a national body aiming to protect the future of Indian Muslims in a free India. From soon after 1900, then, the independence movement was marked, turn and turn about, by attempts to create a united front and by schisms between conservative Hindus demanding a truly Hindu state and those in the Muslim League insisting on a protected status for India's largest minority group. The annual Congress of 1928 was marked by particularly fierce division which meant that most organized Muslims stood aloof from the Civil Disobedience campaign begun in 1930 (see Judith Brown, *Modern India: The Origins of an Asian Democracy*, 2nd edn, Oxford: Oxford University Press, 1994, Chapter 5). Attia Hosain's novel, set mostly in the 1930s, draws on the ways in which these various splits eventually had friends and even families divided along very bitter lines.

In spite of these tensions, the freedom movement gathered momentum. The growing discontent with what the moderates had called the 'economic drain' of the country under colonial rule was buttressed by the extremist effort to translate this discontent into political form. The First World War brought home to Indian leaders the near impossibility of a fair and equitable solution on the part of the British towards India and her people. This hardened the attitude of those who had agreed to support Britain's war efforts in the belief that this would lead in turn to Britain giving greater autonomy to India. Even Indian industrialists, disillusioned with Britain's post-war prioritizing of British industries, threw themselves behind the call for *swaraj*, or self-rule.

From there to non-cooperation and, eventually, the demand that the British 'Quit India' was a progression that took a more or less predictable course. That it took so long to reach a point when independence was more or less certain (1920–42) perhaps in part reflects the fact that both British colonialists and Indians demanding independence realized the complexities of the situation. It also bears witness to the fact that the terms of independence were negotiated with extreme tenacity by both sides. However that is, with Gandhi's growing appeal the British juggernaut became increasingly aware of the impossibility of administering India as merely another colony, or as an extension of its dominions. The economic problems experienced back home in Britain after the Second World War made independence for India a more or less natural corollary – as P.J. Cain and A.G. Hopkins remark, 'from being one of Britain's major debtors, India emerged in 1945 as her largest single sterling creditor' (*British Imperialism: Crisis and Deconstruction, 1914–1990*, London: Longman, 1993, p.16). To gain a full sense of the context of Indian writing after 1940 you would need to explore the situation in more detail than space allows here, beginning for example with the account by Judith Brown or that given in Chapters 15–17 of Sugata Bose and Ayesha Jalal, *Modern South Asia: History, Culture, Political Economy* (London: Routledge, 1998).

What is unambiguous is that Independence was a milestone that has always been remembered with mixed emotions in the Indian subcontinent. Independence meant not just freedom from colonial rule but the division of British India into India and Pakistan (the latter comprised West Pakistan, now Pakistan, and East Pakistan, now Bangladesh). It also meant communal violence, bloodshed and, for vast numbers of people, a permanent rootlessness arising out of their forced migration from places where they had spent entire lives to new homes in a different country. In the weeks preceding and following 15 August 1947, bands of refugees crossed over the new borders: some accounts suggest that as many as ten million people were displaced from where they had lived before Partition. Some people had the luxury of freely and willingly settling anew according to their religion, but for the vast majority it was an exile – a choice without alternatives that simply took them to a refugee camp.

Implicit also in the history of this period were the several socioeconomic changes that became part of free India's move towards what was called a 'socialistic' pattern of development. New laws made the old feudal structures impotent, though more than fifty years of freedom have not wiped out the more insidious operations of feudal power, especially in the countryside. The more tangible changes were the new land laws, the curbing of landlord and princely privileges, and the gradual emergence of other hegemonic forces in the socioeconomic and sociocultural structure. The beginnings of these changes can be seen in *Sunlight on a Broken Column*. In the novel, they affect the way power groups aligned themselves even before Independence.

In India, family and the community have always played a central role. In spite of the changing life-patterns in urban India, lifestyles remain moulded by traditional notions of social roles. Individualism as a way of life has not yet penetrated Indian mores. Individual choices are often conditioned by the demands of family loyalty and 'honour' (*izzat*). Added to these constraints are those of caste, religion, region and class. These are particularly manifest in matters of marriage, arranged marriages still being the accepted norm. *Sunlight on a Broken Column* can only be properly understood against such a background.

Readers today, particularly non-Indian readers who see the 1990s in India described as a period of economic and social reform, might assume that the representation of women in *Sunlight on a Broken Column* can be considered now as safely historical and that 'modern' India has moved away from these traditional notions. To my mind this would be wrong; I would emphasize rather the need to look at the Indian women's movement in a sociocultural context that remains by and large conservative and ortho-dox, and in which tradition has been consistently and variously used to oppose individual freedom. You can follow up these arguments in more detail in Vrinda Nabar, *Caste as Woman* (Delhi: Penguin, 1995), especially in the introductory chapter, 'Our Women, their Women'. While the focus of my study has been Indian womanhood, I argue there that this constraint on individual freedom also applies to men.

It would be far more accurate to describe contemporary Indian social life (again, to most non-Indians this would mean its urban manifestations) as superficially Westernized but fundamentally loyal to traditional indigen-ous priorities. Awareness of the importance of such loyalty and rootedness was particularly strident in the most recent national elections (1999), which had Sonia Gandhi contending for membership of the Lok Sabha (the Lower House of Parliament). Throughout her campaign, Ms Gandhi's primary electoral message had been that she was a loyal wife (*patni*), widow (*vidhawa*) and daughter-in-law (*bahu*) of the Gandhi family.

The author and the text

Sunlight on a Broken Column was first published in 1961. As its title (borrowed from T.S. Eliot's *The Hollow Men*) indicates, the novel is heavy with memories. Attia Hosain's life, by all accounts, closely paralleled that of the protagonist. Like Laila, Hosain belonged to an orthodox Muslim feudal class, that of the Taluqdars, who enjoyed near princely privileges. Anita Desai's introduction to the Virago Modern Classics edition of Hosain's novel tells us the little we know about Hosain's life (Attia Hosain, *Sunlight on a Broken Column*, London: Virago, 1988; all page references are to this edition, but the Penguin India edition of 1994, which also includes Desai's introduction, uses a similar pagination).

Hosain was born in 1913, and migrated to England in 1947, the year India became independent. The years in between were largely spent in Lucknow, a city which even today retains some of the old nawabi ambience of the Mughal period. Lucknow has always been associated with the culture and mannered patterns of behaviour that marked a life lived in courts and feudal Muslim households. In keeping with this lifestyle, Hosain was taught Persian, Urdu and Arabic at home. As the daughter of the Taluqdar of Oudh she was a person of some status. (A sense of the nuances of feudal life in that once princely state can be had from Satyajit Ray's film *Shatranj ke Khiladi* ('The Chess-Players') based on a short story by Premchand.) Her father died when Hosain was eleven, and she and her siblings were brought up by her mother according to a curious mix of orthodoxy and liberalism. At home she experienced life more or less in purdah. The women's quarters were separate, the way they are in *Sunlight on a Broken Column*, and though she and her sisters did not observe the practice of purdah when they went out, we are told that their car had silk curtains at the windows, which was in fact a form of purdah (p.viii and cf. also p.88; the literal meaning of purdah is 'curtain'). Outside the home, however, Hosain studied in the elite La Martiniere school and, later, at the Isabella Thoburn College. She was also influenced by the nationalist movement and the Progressive Writers' Group in the 1930s. Although after 1947 she lived abroad, Hosain continued to be associated with India, dividing her time between her country of birth and her country of residence, and anchoring her own women's programme on the BBC Eastern Service.

Approaching Sunlight on a Broken Column

Hosain's early life coincided with the years of the freedom struggle. Virtually all educated middle-class Indian homes were affected by the ideological issues contouring this struggle. The call for *swaraj* and *swadeshi* goods (goods manufactured in India) had an especially emotive appeal to large numbers of people, and Gandhi's efforts to mobilize people into spinning their own cloth had also captured the imagination of patriotic Indians. Hosain's novel describes how Laila and her friends took to wearing coarse hand-spun cotton saris – a symbolic gesture of protest, which offended the sensibilities of women like her aunt Saira and the hawk-nosed Begum Sahiba (p.130). Laila's idealism is balanced by her ability to look at those around her objectively and not be swayed by rhetoric and jingoism. She survives the terrible years of Partition, when the family is divided much the way the country was, so that in retrospect Hosain is able to offer a hope for sanity that is particularly relevant to the troubled relations between India and Pakistan today.

Writing women's lives

The autobiographical nature of *Sunlight on a Broken Column* makes it very appropriate to pursue further discussion of it within the context of women's writing about their own situation in India. While the compositions of early Indian women writers were known and read through the ages, recent feminist scholarship has attempted to organize these in a more disciplined manner and to show how women in India have, for a long time, documented their lives and experiences. A valuable source here is *Women Writing in India*, ed. by Susie Tharu and K. Lalita (2 vols, Delhi: Oxford University Press, 1993). This groups these women according to historical period and the prevalent social mores and movements of the time. In my own *Caste as Woman*, I use some of these texts to highlight the fact that revolt against the traditional roles of Indian womanhood is not a new thing. At the same time, however, my case is that these accounts and these rebellions were sporadic rather than indicative of any sustained ideological conviction or struggle.

Such writing took varied forms, from the the early bhakti poets who wrote popular verse in various regional languages from the eighth to the sixteenth century, to the autobiographical and fictive efforts of women – again in regional (bhasa) languages – in the nineteenth and early twentieth centuries. In spite of the occasional presence of poets such as Toru Dutt (1856–77) and Sarojini Naidu (1879–1949), it was only in the 1950s and 1960s that Indian women writers in English began to gain any real reputation. Nayantara Sahgal's *Prison and Chocolate Cake* (London: Gollancz, 1954) is autobiographical, and her novels have frequently drawn on her life. Other more contemporary women writers – Anita Desai, Shashi Deshpande, Rama Mehta (whose autobiographical novel *Inside the Haveli*, London: Women's Press, 1994, is an interesting example of life in purdah in an orthodox Hindu household) and, most recently, even Arundhati Roy – have written fiction where the personal is central to the main issues and conflicts.

It could of course be argued that this is true of all writing and that auto-biographical fiction cuts across cultures. Why it becomes a point of interest in women writers in India is because conventionally women have not been given to public displays of their private lives. If one looks at the work of the early bhakti poets in India, what is significant is the unambiguous presence of the 'I' factor and the sense it gives of communities of women. The compositions narrate, with remarkable irreverence, the minutiae and trivia of their daily lives and their personal conflicts (Bahinabai, for instance, talks of how her fame and renown have made her husband jealous, see *Women Writing in India*, I, 107ff.).

In later autobiographical writing, while home and family continue to play an important part, writers will still talk of learning to read and write in secret. The Bengali writer Rassundari Devi (1810–?), author of *Amar Jiban*, describes how she wrote out the characters of the alphabet on the charcoal-blackened walls of the kitchen. Women such as Binodini Dasi (1863–1941, author of the Bengali work *Amar Katha*), and Hamsa Wadkar (1923–72, author of the Marathi work *Sangatye Aika*), both performing artists, are explicit about the way women like them were manipulated by men.

Other writers have written of their lives and, indirectly, of women's lives. The Bengali novel *Nabankur* by Sulekha Sanyal (1928–63) describes how the little girl Chobi was censured and discriminated against for being a daughter, but shows Chobi leaving home. All these writers feature in Volume 1 of *Women Writing in India*. Also included there is a story by Lalithambika Antharjanam (b.1909). Her account of her determined bid for an independent existence as a writer is told in 'Childhood Memories' (see Text 9.1). The poet Indira Sant (b.1914), writing in Marathi, uses the personal to project a politics very similar to that of feminism. Finally in these examples, writing in Bengali, Mahasweta Devi (b.1926) puts the lives of tribal women into her fiction, often using the all-pervasive influence of Hindi cinema and its insidiously exploitative lyrics to highlight sexual atrocities and oppression as in her novel *Stanyadayani* ('The Wet-Nurse/Breast Giver') of 1980. Three stories by Devi can be found in translation in *Imaginary Maps* (translated and introduced by Gayatri Chakravorty Spivak, London: Routledge, 1995). Another, 'Shishu', appears in Volume 2 of *Women Writing in India* along with three poems by Indira Sant (see pp.236–51, 123–6).

The personal and the political

In this section I want to focus specifically on the way fiction is a means of telling women's lives, and a means of autobiography, in relation to *Sunlight on Broken Column*. For me, Anita Desai's introduction offers an interesting way into such questions. It is tempting to see this introduction as a relatively innocent affair. The presence of any kind of introduction is of a piece with the fact that the novel is published as a 'Modern Classic', but the publishers are keen to avoid too scholarly an appearance: the introduction is more like a recommendation from a friend than the kind of thing one finds in an edition of Jane Austen. Students might see a consonance between this and the 'personal' nature of the fiction. That said, the opening sentences do touch on an important aspect of the political nature of the novel; Desai writes,

> In India, the past never disappears. It does not even become
> transformed into a ghost. Concrete, physical, palpable – it is present
> everywhere. Ruins, monuments, litter the streets, hold up the traffic,
> create strange islands in the modernity of the cities. No one fears or
> avoids them – goats and cows graze around them, the poor string
> up ropes and rags and turn them into dwellings, election
> campaigners and cinema distributors plaster them with pamphlets –
> and so they remain a part of the here and now, of today. (p.v)

The opening lines of Desai's introduction to *Sunlight on a Broken Column* are almost an echo of what Naipaul had attempted to convey in *An Area of Darkness* nearly thirty years earlier, when he spoke of the remnants of Indian relics in the Trinidad home of his boyhood: string cots, brass vessels, images of deities, one ruined harmonium, wooden printing blocks which were never used, all brought from India by his grandparents (V.S. Naipaul, *An Area of Darkness*, Harmondsworth: Penguin, 1979, p.29). Naipaul had been amazed at the tendency to cling to this dilapidated past, symbolized by objects, rituals and customs, and, as he grew up, had become obsessed enough with what he did not understand to travel to India and attempt to decipher the mysteries of this area of darkness.

Desai's introduction uses the observations about the past quoted above to comment on Hosain's writing. Hosain's novel and her collection of short stories 'are monuments to that past', Desai suggests, but while monuments are often 'grey, cold and immutable', Hosain's books are 'delicate and tender, like new grass, and they stir with life and the play of sunlight and rain ... To read them is like wrapping oneself up in one's mother's wedding sari, lifting the family jewels out of a faded box and admiring the glitter, inhaling the musky perfume of old silks in a camphor chest' (p.vi).

These remarks are obviously meant to be complimentary, but I think they are revealing in ways that perhaps Desai did not intend. It is true that the past is very central to Indian life, but if cattle and goats graze around monuments it is not a peculiarly Indian attribute of that past that makes them do so. Rather, it is because in a country overrun with so many living creatures, their presence in the most unlikely places is almost natural. The seeming harmony between man and beast is not so much mystical as part of a larger, and very real, chaos of poverty and deprivation, of contradictions and irrationalities that coexist with pragmatism, making India the kind of enigma that defies simplistic description.

However, Desai's romanticized assessment of Hosain's writing (the comparisons to old saris and family jewels) does not just risk merely trivializing the past but also, perhaps unwittingly, colours it with shades of Orientalism. Developments in post-colonial criticism and literature make *Sunlight on a Broken Column* a difficult novel to talk about, and my reservations about Desai's statements arise out of the overtly exotic ambience they give to a novel already replete with it. (I return to this theme in the last section of this chapter.)

A simple way into the issue is through the very beginning of the novel:

> The day my Aunt Abida moved from the zenana into the guest-room off the corridor that led to the men's wing of the house, within call of her father's room, we knew Baba Jan had not much longer to live. (p.14)

Death, the zenana and the men's wing. In just one sentence, Hosain brings in three elements that make for the dramatic. From this point onwards, the filling in of exotic details never stops: the quarrelling maid-servants, the men-servants, the sweepers, the gardeners, the washerman and the old faithful family retainer Hakiman Bua, with her quaint and colourful turn of phrase – 'Your books will eat you. They will dim the light of your lovely eyes, my moon princess, and then who will marry you, owl-eyed, peering through glasses?' (p.14). But as the story develops, these exotic details often carry political resonances. The exotic details do not form a comfortable shell because Independence and its aftermath are overriding concerns in the novel. The decision to stay on in India or migrate to Pakistan becomes a major subject of conflict in the family, with opinions and personalities sharply polarized on the issue.

Within these political resonances, the nature of the family and the stranglehold it can have on individual lives are at the centre of the novel. In India, the family is at once the source of much strength and of the near-total loss of individual freedom. It can make issues like loyalty, honour, respect for one's elders, and for the tried power of tradition override all concerns of individual happiness. Laila's grandfather Baba Jan is important to the novel because he holds the old feudal family together. This becomes clear from the conversation Laila has with her cousin Zahra, the one who 'said her prayers five times a day, read the Quran for an hour every morning, sewed and knitted and wrote the accounts' (p.14). Zahra is worried that Baba Jan's death will change the old ways, that their Uncle Hamid with his 'English ideas' may not want them all to stay together.

The role of the zenana is stronger in the first part of the novel, but diminishes once Baba Jan dies. Hosain's description conveys the sense of female bonding that is endemic to Indian life and constitutes so much of its strengths and weaknesses. It is through the zenana that the lives of women like Hakiman Bua, Saliman Bua and Nandi are also incorporated into the novel's canvas, but though Hosain touches on their exploitation, they remain shadowy appendages to a household defined by class privilege.

Though segregated, the women of the household form interesting contrasts: the fiery and sensitive Aunt Abida who had been rebel enough to spurn Uncle Mohsin's interest in her; her more subservient sister Aunt Majida, a quiet if somewhat whiny woman given to preying on people's sympathies and making a fetish of her religious absorption; and Aunt Majida's daughter Zahra, who fits the role of the dutiful young girl described in the passage quoted above. Interestingly, through the conventional Zahra, Hosain seems to allow the reader at least to think about the idea that liberation might mean a range of things depending on social class and education. Once married, Zahra seems to Laila a quite different – and physically assertive – person: 'Another year', she tells Laila, 'and you will have finished your studies, you will be taken everywhere, you will probably be married. Don't shake your head, you cannot always live an unnatural life.' Listening to her Laila observes how, as Zahra stretched her arms above her head, 'her blouse was tight across her breasts. No more loose, shapeless clothes, no more stooping and hunching of shoulders to conceal and deny one's body' (p.141).

Zahra even takes the differently rebellious Laila under her wing, bringing her out of purdah and dressing her up, dragging her to public events in defiance of their Aunt Saira's reservations. The orphaned Laila had been brought up by Aunt Abida in a relatively less constrained manner. But in contrast to Zahra, Aunt Abida, once married, is totally robbed of the spark she had always possessed. When she visits, Laila notices that she looks withdrawn, and that 'The two days her husband had stayed she had centred all attention on his care and comfort, as if everyone and everything else was secondary' (p.138). Much later, paying her a visit, Laila experiences the tensions and jealousies of a zenana very different from the one she had grown up in. There is no bonding here, only ingrowing pettiness and spite:

> In the days that followed I grew to sense the extent of their antagonism against Aunt Abida. They resented the sensitiveness of a character beyond their reach and understanding. They attacked what was bigger than their comprehension with petty thrusts.
>
> The jealousies and frustrations in that household of women were intangible like invisible webs spun by monstrous, unseen spiders.
>
> And yet without each other they had no existence. Physically and mentally their lives crushed each other. (p.251)

When the time comes for Laila to leave, Aunt Abida breaks down and weeps, something she had also done the night before she was married. This is the only real display of emotion she allows herself, and she is dry-eyed when she says goodbye in front of the other women. Yet, even in these moments of intimacy, complete intellectual honesty is impossible. Laila knows that she would not be able to tell her about her love for Ameer because of the distance of tradition.

Her fears are not unfounded, for Aunt Abida is consistent throughout the novel in her insistence on the rightness of the elders. The woman who had argued that Zahra and Laila needed to be present when Zahra's future is discussed had, even in that unusual moment, held on to the inviolability of duty and obedience. In reply to Uncle Mohsin's sarcastic query as to whether she would have Zahra choose her life partner, she admits that this would be unwise since the girl had had neither the upbringing nor the opportunity for such a choice. She could, however, 'be present while we make the choice, hear our arguments, know our reasons, so that later on she will not doubt our capabilities and question our decisions. That is the least I can do' (p.21).

Marriages had to be arranged because individual choice suggested a preference for love which is equated with sin over a love oriented to one's family and duty: 'love between man and woman was associated with sex, and sex was sin' (p.312). To Aunt Abida's way of thinking, Laila's decision to marry Ameer was unforgivable: 'You have been defiant and disobedient. You have put yourself above your duty to your family ... You have let your family's name be bandied about by scandal-mongers and gossips. You have soiled its honour on their vulgar tongues' (ibid.).

The notion of family honour, or *izzat*, and its hold on social behaviour remains strong even today. It informs the cinema of Bollywood as much as it does day-to-day life. As I emphasize in *Caste as Woman*, while *izzat* in many instances is particularly circumscribing of women's lives, it also makes individual action difficult for both men and women, particularly in relation to marriage and codes of behaviour. It was these considerations that had made marriage between Laila's cousin Kemal and her childhood friend Sita unthinkable. Though Laila rejects the old pressures of class and background when she marries Ameer, the past remains important to her, and it is to exorcize the ghosts of the past that she eventually returns to the old family home in Hosanpur in Part Four of the novel. The reflective tone here surely prompts the reader beyond a romanticized view of the past into the same kind of concerned feeling and thinking about its meaning and values.

Nationalism and the politics of Partition

Attia Hosain's novel describes the middle-class dilemma as many of her Muslim characters debate whether to stay on in India or move to Pakistan. The trauma of Partition haunts the Indian subcontinent even today and has found expression in literature both in English and in the regional languages. Among the better-known novels representing the humanitarian crisis of the time are Khushwant Singh, *Train to Pakistan* (London: Chatto & Windus, 1956); Amitav Ghosh, *The Shadow Lines* (London: Bloomsbury, 1988); and Bapsy Sidhwa's *Ice Candy Man* (London: Heinemann, 1988, but republished as *Cracking India*, Minneapolis: Milkweed Editions, 1991). There is also a large number of short stories about Partition. Bhisham Sahni, 'The Train Has Reached Amritsar', and Ajneya [S.H. Vatsayan], 'Getting Even', convey the feelings of those on the evacuee trains that have become a symbol of the horror of the time (see Texts 9.3 and 9.4). Lalithambika Antharjanam's story 'A Leaf in the Storm' (see Text 9.2) is particularly interesting because although it graphically depicts the reality of events it was written in Kerala by a woman who had never been to the areas of India most affected by the violent events of Partition; in this respect it shows the power of these events in the Indian consciousness. Saadat Hasan Manto, on the other hand, was born in the Punjab, the area most affected. Perhaps his best-known story, 'Toba Tek Singh' is, however, distinct among those I refer to here in taking a more oblique stance in relation to the violence – it begins 'A couple of years after the Partition of the country, it occurred to the respective governments of India and Pakistan that inmates of lunatic asylums, like prisoners, should also be exchanged' (see Text 9.5, p.351). Another collection is *Writings on India's Partition*, ed. by Ramesh Mathur and Mahendra Kulasrestha (Calcutta: Simant Publications, 1976). Writings on Partition are not confined to prose, however. In India poems depicting the feelings and mood of the time, such as Amrita Pritam's 'Ai Akan Waris Shah Nu' ('To Waris Shah I Say'), are regularly anthologized; Anju Makhija and Menka Shivdasani have recently edited an anthology of Sindhi poetry on Partition.

Partition has also become an important theme in Indian cinema with a number of films being based on novels and stories, including *Train to Pakistan* based on Kushwant Singh's novel and *1947-Earth* based on *Ice Candy Man*. Mention might also be made here of the film *Garam Hava*, which has a script by the well-known writer Ismat Chugtai based on an unpublished short story of her own, and the influential television serial *Tamas* (based on Bhisham Sahni's novel first translated as *Kites Will Fly*, Delhi: Vikas Publishing House, 1981, and now as *Tamas*, Delhi: Penguin, 1988).

Comparison of *Sunlight on a Broken Column* with any of these texts would be valuable not least because it is likely to highlight the way that although the 'family' – with its varied connotations, of love, belonging, duty, loyalty and *izzat* – forms the centre of the novel, it is the politics of the time that gives the book its flavour. Much of the novel is set in the years preceding Independence. It ends with the way Independence affected Laila's family and mirrors the complex events that shaped the nationalist struggle.

Laila's family, which represents the Taluqdars, or the landed gentry, is rooted in the mannered courtesies of a class that was to become socially redundant very soon. There is a period touch to Hosain's descriptions of Baba Jan and his three loyal friends (pp.33–4). As Laila observes,

> Baba Jan had ostensibly little in common with his three friends ...
> Yet they had in common a strange arrogance and a will to exercise
> power – always to be in a position which forced men to reach up to
> them; and if they ever stepped down themselves, it was an act of
> grace. In varying degrees they had been helped by birth, privilege
> and wealth to assume such a position; but without some intrinsic
> quality they could not have maintained it. (p.34)

This feudalism, intrinsic to Indian society since at least 1200, still survives
though in a less assertive form. It may be seen in the insistence on division
of labour as being a sign of social and caste status, because certain tasks are
perceived as demeaning.

Laila also hints at the growing nexus between men like these and political
power. The Raja of Amirpur, a patron of the arts and of philanthropic
causes, was 'politically powerful, able to influence the elections of coun-
cillors and the decisions of ministers'. In spite of the privileges that the four
men enjoyed, their commitment to their little world was complete. They
'loved the city to which they belonged, and they lived and behaved as if the
city belonged to them' (p.35). Implicit here is the old feudal notion of *mai-
baap* (the paternalistic face of feudalism, in which the feudal lord was seen
as father and mother) that was also cleverly used by the British in India to
manipulate the loyalty of the 'natives'.

The freedom struggle and its milestones affect individual lives in much the
same way that family loyalties do. Laila's cousins Asad and Zahid had lost
their father in the cause of the Khilafat movement. This movement was
triggered off by the British betrayal of their promise made to Indian
Muslims during the First World War, that the position of the Sultan of
Turkey (who was the Khilafa, or religious head of Muslims the world
over) would remain unaffected by the outcome of the war. Gandhi was
associated with the leaders of the movement almost from the beginning,
helping them devise a Khilafat Day and encouraging them to share in the
idea of non-cooperation. Not surprisingly, Asad and Zahid had been
brought up to wear hand-spun cloth and to hate all things that were foreign.
A firebrand idealist, Asad is repeatedly in trouble and is the first to defy
Uncle Hamid, who succeeds Baba Jan as the family patriarch, and leave
home. It is interesting – as Hosain allows Laila to be more liberated – to
compare how she presents the possibility of a relationship with Asad as
somehow still impossible as compared to the relationship that develops
with Ameer. How, for example, are we to understand the fact that the man
Laila loves joins the British Army, while the man held at a distance is the one
involved in Indian politics?

While Zahid leaves for Pakistan only hours before Independence, on the
ill-fated train that arrives at its destination filled with corpses, Asad stays
on in India. He grows increasingly involved in the freedom struggle, but
then the tone of the narration shifts after Ameer's death when he gets to
be Laila's source of comfort and hope:

We had dreamed when we were young of Independence; he was now part of it with all its undreamt-of reality – its triumphs and defeats, its violent aftermath, the breaking-up of our social order, and the slow emergence of another. (p.318)

Laila's student days are peppered with protests, black-flag demonstrations against the Viceregal visit, and riots in which her young cousins are repeatedly injured, but from which Hosain keeps Laila herself aloof. The Civil Disobedience movement initiated by Gandhi meets with a mixed response from members of the family. The uncle of Laila's childhood friend Sita has been a freedom fighter, but Sita herself is shown as disillusioned with idealism (pp.186–7). Her college friend Nita is rusticated for her involvement in what was to be a non-violent protest. She dies two days after reaching home as a result of head injuries received during a police lathi-charge.

Laila, Asad and Kemal are important in the context of Independence and the period following because they debunk fundamentalist distortions about the Hindu–Muslim divide. While it would be simplistic to pretend that irrational suspicion and hatred do not colour attitudes on either side of the border, significantly large numbers of Indian Muslims think of India as 'home', a choice made without any apparent mental conflict.

The period covered by the novel sees the freedom movement reach maturity, and ends with the creation of India and Pakistan. The communal political divide had begun as far back as 1905 with the setting up of the Muslim League and the division of Bengal along communal lines. (Lord Curzon, then Viceroy, had hoped this would undermine the strong nationalist movement in the province but in fact it had almost the opposite effect.) Relations between Hindu and Muslim nationalists, however, became more tense and heated as freedom came to seem a less nebulous goal. *Sunlight on a Broken Column* has characters repeatedly questioning the possibility of Hindus and Muslims being able to coexist in a free India. As students, Laila's college friends Nita and Nadira had argued fiercely about their differing ideologies and political convictions, but these had been arguments between two individuals belonging to different faiths. As Partition becomes an imminent event, such divisions become bitter as even members within families find themselves aligned differently.

Uncle Hamid represents the interests of the feudal Taluqdars, but his basic loyalty is specifically to the values of an India formed under British rule. He feels betrayed when Saleem confesses his love for Nadira and campaigns for the Muslim League which she and her mother are wholly committed to. Laila talks of the courteous city of Lucknow being invaded by harsh voices raised in dissent. At home, Saleem's demagoguery accuses the Congress of 'a strong anti-Muslim' bias which would surface once the British had left: 'The majority of Hindus have not forgotten or forgiven the Muslims for having ruled over them for hundreds of years. Now they can democratically take revenge', says Saleem during an argument about the creation of Pakistan. His father, Uncle Hamid, and later his brother Kemal, do not subscribe to Saleem's paranoia. 'I always found it was possible for Hindus and Muslims to work together on a political level', Uncle Hamid says in reply to Saleem, 'and live together in personal friendship' (p.234). You might like to take a passage like this and try to see whether Hosain aims to press the reader to take one side or another.

The harsher realities of the political arena are present in the way friends betray one another. Uncle Hamid finds himself let down by his old friend Waliuddin, who joins the Muslim League and actually agrees to contest the election against him. He is even supported in this move by Agarwal, Sita's father, a staunch Congress supporter, because the Congress and the Muslim League momentarily agree to sink their differences to fight the bigger enemy, the British. Uncle Hamid is compelled to withdraw his political nomination and represent the Taluqdars.

Though caught up in their own private dilemmas of love, freedom and individual choices, Laila and her cousins and friends find the larger world of national politics affecting their lives. Zahra more or less ignores the freedom movement, while Sita is caught up within it. Eventually, and in her own way, Laila allies herself with the nationalist cause, and at the end of the novel finds her freedom through Asad, the cousin she had been close to while she was growing up.

The final showdown of the main period of the story takes place a month before Independence. At the family reunion, the intended rational discussion to decide the future ends in anger, reaching a point of no return despite Kemal's plea for peace. Saleem and Nadira migrate to Pakistan with the fervour of new converts. As Laila observes, 'it was easier for them thereafter to visit the whole wide world than the home which had once been theirs' (p.289). On a first reading it perhaps comes as a surprise that the story does not stop here; certainly if it had done so the political messages of the book would have been different. As it is, Part Four takes the reader even closer to Laila's less politically involved point of view. The effect is heightened by the fact that many of the characters are absent from the physical location in which the story now takes place. In this last part, back home, those who elect to stay on find that the changed order and political choices have far-reaching implications. Besides the loss of the privileges of taluqdari, Laila's Aunt Saira has to come to terms with the fact that Saleem's share of the family property will be treated as evacuee property, and that it will be given over to complete strangers. Laila's retreat into the hills has not protected her from the terrible violence before and after Partition, and she reacts sharply to Zahra's accusation that that she had chosen the softer option:

'Where were you, Zahra, when I sat up through the nights, watching village after village set on fire, each day nearer and nearer? ... Do you know who saved me and my child? Sita, who took us to her house, in spite of putting her own life in danger with ours. And Ranjit, who came from his village, because he had heard of what was happening in the foothills and was afraid for us. He drove us back, pretending we were his family, risking discovery and death.' (p.304)

Purdah; the past and the future

Attia Hosain's place in the canon of Indian writing in English appears assured. She cannot be said to have star quality, the way Nayantara Sahgal, Salman Rushdie, Vikram Seth, Amitav Ghosh, Arundhati Roy or even Anita Desai do, but she has been studied, talked about, included in overviews and, more recently, rehabilitated within the genre of gender studies. She figures sporadically in anthologies that deal with women's writing and focus on themes such as purdah. *Margins of Erasure: Purdah in the Subcontinental Novel in English*, ed. by Jasbir Jain and Amina Amin (Delhi: Sterling Publishers, 1995) contains two articles on *Sunlight on a Broken Column*.

In the first, 'Beyond Purdah: *Sunlight on a Broken Column*', Sarla Palkar speaks of the novel's 'empathy and compassion for all the marginalised groups ... it seeks to go beyond the boundaries or purdahs created by the considerations of gender, race, religion, class, and also nation' (p.118). According to Amina Amin, the second essayist, 'The novel rests on a tightly controlled balance between a life within the household, ordained, enclosed, warm and secure but restricted by demands of modesty, and a life outside, free but insecure and confusing' ('Tension Between Restriction and Freedom: The Purdah Motif in Attia Hosain's *Sunlight on a Broken Column*', p.119).

In both these essays, the emphasis is on the element of purdah as a metaphor for women's lives. The men do not figure in the analyses except in passing, as appendages to Laila's ups and downs in her zenana-contoured life. It is tempting to dismiss these omissions as an overemphasis on women's concerns by women, except that my own reading of the novel also suggests that it is the women that hold the story together and are, to a greater or less extent, 'characterized'. It is in the world of the zenana that Hosain is most at ease, and though a large part of the story deals with perhaps the most tumultuous period of Indian history, it never really absorbs our interest as much as the other little world within which Laila and her aunts live.

This can take us back, but in a more qualified way, to the issue of the exotic raised above (see p.128). For all Laila's idealism and strength I would argue that the exotic element threatens to overwhelm our sense of this political side to her character. This is perhaps natural at one level, since these details define Laila's world. It is when they seem chosen for effect that it becomes difficult not to remember that this novel was first published in Great Britain and that it was perhaps an early post-Independence effort by a 'native' at capturing the nuances of those years. Part of the problem may be the novelist's own weakness for local colour of the more exotic kind, relevant enough in the normal scheme of things but just a little too laid on in the overall context of the novel. Whether it is the lush description of festivals (pp.40–41), or the cries and colours of the vendors of sweets, vegetables and bangles (pp.58–9), or the way cows, buffaloes, curds, ghee and the smell of acrid dung are all present in one amazing paragraph on page 98, the predilection for the 'Indian' detail is obvious. There is nothing fundamentally wrong in an Indian novel being obviously filled with the sights and sounds of India. My reservations have to do with a sense that a certain past is, overall, selectively presented in a way that is nostalgic and even sentimental. The larger, and more violent, reality which at times seems really important in the novel thus risks, ironically, appearing irrelevant.

Meenakshi Mukherjee comes closest to my own sense of unease. For Mukherjee, the trouble, particularly with the last section of the novel,

> lies in the confusion of purpose. Does the novelist intend to present from Laila's point of view a picture of men and manners in a particular period of Indian history, or does she intend to present one individual's groping towards self-realisation? If it is the former, then the case history method of the past has some validity; but if the novel is taken as a personal document the last chapter becomes extraneous.

> (*The Twice-Born Fiction: Themes and Techniques of the Indian Novel in English,* Delhi: Heinemann India, 1971, p.53)

Mukherjee in fact sees the end as an 'orgy of sentimentalism' (p.81), whereas I would suggest that sentimentalism is intrinsic in the whole depiction. Where it works (as in the intricate descriptions of women's lives in that household), such sentimentalism is camouflaged by the fictive strength of personal emotion at its best. It is less successful when the canvas expands to take in the larger world of political uncertainty and the way it affects the lives and careers of the men in the family.

While the rhetoric of political debate weaves its way through the novel, the personal and the political interconnect in a loosely knit, somewhat unsatisfactory manner. As already stated, the issues with which the novel is concerned appear rather differently in the post-colonial context. There is virtually no attempt at anything more than a mere narration of details, hardly any criticism, explicit or implicit, of the old ways or of the politics of the freedom movement. None of the actual violence preceding Independence touches the lives of the characters. Neither do the harsher paradoxes of displacement affect Hosain's characters as they do the characters of Amitav Ghosh's more recent *The Shadow Lines.*

In spite of Asad's occasional bloody clothes and wounds, the sweat and gore of the freedom struggle or the nightmare of Partition do not really find a place in the story. The men fail to become much more than a forum for intellectual debate. The novel's chief interest lies in its women, particularly Laila, who struggles against her class background and conditioning. Having said that, one should be wary of seeing the picture in too black and white terms. A good many novels and stories which do attempt to depict the actual violence of Partition seem to be shot through with a kind of melodrama which equally fails to engage the reader with the complexity of the situation. Comparison of the novel with the Partition texts referred to in the section 'Nationalism and the politics of Partition' above would be interesting here: for example, setting a 'direct' account of events such as is contained in one of the train stories against Manto's 'Toba Tek Singh' and against Part Four of *Sunlight on a Broken Column*.

I would like to end by suggesting that for an Indian reader like myself the novel's underlying themes – the freedom struggle, the loss of an old feudal, semi-aristocratic order, life and love behind the purdah, and the other details included in this family saga – add up eventually to an exotic story, charming primarily for its remoteness from its audience. Nevertheless, this cannot take away the historical interest of the story, both for the development of the Indian novel in English and as a representation of a way of life that is unknown to most of its readers. Laila stands as a metaphor for that middle state – an isthmus between larger and almost overwhelming forces – that many Indian women found themselves in during the 1930s and 1940s. For many Indian women readers now, the interest, however, goes beyond the historical; in its imagining of Laila they see their own situation today.

Questions and exercises

1   From the histories of India that you have been reading, trace the key events in the development of the Indian independence movement as one demanding separate Hindu and Muslim states. What role would you expect literature to play in this process?

2   On the basis of your reading of works by contemporary Indian women writers (including at least one writing in India about India), consider the evidence for the notion that in India the 'sociocultural context ... remains by and large conservative and orthodox' (p.124 above).

3   'In considering Indian women's accounts of how they have struggled for freedom we should be particularly conscious of the need to consider cultural difference.' Discuss this comment, drawing on as wide a range of examples of women's writing from India as you can.

4   Compare the representation of Partition in Bhisham Sahni, 'The Train Has Reached Amritsar', Saadat Hasan Manto, 'Toba Tek Singh', and Part Four of *Sunlight on a Broken Column*. Consider overall how far these texts provide evidence for the view that imagining the events of 1947 was very difficult for writers.

5   Compare the presentation of the social structures of India in *Sunlight on a Broken Column* and *Kanthapura*. Can these structures be seen as an important element in the structure of 'the nation' as it was imagined by those seeking independence?

10 A POST-COLONIAL WORLD: LOOK BACK IN ANGER *AND* THE ENIGMA OF ARRIVAL

by Richard Allen

Introduction

In a famous speech delivered in Africa in 1958 the British Prime Minister Harold Macmillan declared that a 'wind of change' was sweeping through the continent. Nationalism in the colonies was no longer something to be contested or absorbed but something to be recognized as simple political fact. For Britain and its colonies the post-colonial world had arrived. Consideration of events before and after 1958 suggests, however, that the adjective 'post-colonial' needs to be thought of as applying to a process happening over time rather than to a simple culture- or history-changing event. Those listening to Macmillan's speech, for example, could hardly forget the Suez crisis of barely two years before. In an almost Victorian imperialist gesture, Britain and France (with Israel) had invaded Egypt with the aim of seizing the Suez Canal. Twenty-six years later, as if to prove the empire were still a living thing, Britain sent not just a gunboat but an entire fleet to the South Atlantic to 'reclaim' the Falkland Islands from Argentina.

The Suez crisis is generally acknowledged to be a pivotal point in the remaking of British national identity. The events are described in all general histories of Britain covering this period: see, for example, Keith Robbins, *The Eclipse of a Great Power: Modern Britain 1870–1992* (London: Longman, 1994). A more detailed study written closer to the time is Hugh Thomas, *The Suez Affair: The Story of Suez* (London: Weidenfeld & Nicolson, 1967). Equally interesting are accounts by those involved, especially Anthony Nutting, *No End of a Lesson* (London: Constable, 1967), and Evelyn Shuckburgh, *Descent to Suez: Diaries 1951–56*, selected by John Charmley (London: Weidenfeld & Nicolson, 1986). Two particular aspects of the affair are worth mentioning here. First, although the events of 1956 had their specific causes in 1956, there was inevitably an element of 'looking back' because of the symbolic resonances the Suez Canal and Egypt had carried for the British Empire. The opening of the canal had cut the travelling time to India dramatically, allowing for a closeness of access and control in government which were vital both to British rule there and to the ease of trade within the Anglophone areas on which the structure of the empire rested. Maintaining what was in effect a controlling interest in Egypt was – according to most historical accounts – a driving force in British policies during the dividing up of Africa amongst the colonial powers after 1880. President Nasser's nationalizing of the Suez Canal Company in 1956 was presented by some in the West at the time as a threat to the Western capitalist free world. The British and French invasion might, more cynically, be seen as an attempt to protect British and French property – by owning the Suez Canal Company, Britain and France owned a piece of Egypt just as much as Cecil Rhodes had owned Rhodesia. The invasion might also be seen as a final act of nostalgia for the empire in Britain and France.

The second aspect of the affair I want to refer to here is connected to the question of how far it was possible for this 'nostalgia' to be successfully turned into reality in the 1950s; this is to do with the power of the USA, and its willingness to exercise that power in the world. In the later part of the nineteenth century the European powers divided Africa and ruled the Indian subcontinent without any intervention from the USA beyond an occasional anti-imperialist protest. By 1956 the situation was quite different. Through the first half of the twentieth century the USA had become increasingly active politically and militarily outside its own borders. In the aftermath of the Second World War, furthermore, US economic power was so great that neither Britain, France nor Israel could ignore US policies. The British and French governments acted secretly in planning the invasion of Egypt, knowing that the American government would be hostile. Once the invasion began, the USA brought all influence to bear to stop it and – to put matters bluntly – two almost-failing imperial powers gave way to a new one.

That the ramifications of the Suez crisis and the ensuing crisis of identity for British ruling culture (and particularly the ruling Conservative Party) were not more extreme may as much as anything be due to the fact that elsewhere the empire did continue to exist. Decolonization was beginning, particu-larly in the Caribbean, but the British presence in East Africa, in Aden and in Cyprus was still strong. There were other counter-balancing events too, particularly associated with economic recovery in Britain. There had been rationing of almost all consumer goods during the war but these measures persisted long after as Britain attempted to recover from its victory. Food rationing was finally ended in 1954, a year after the coronation of Queen Elizabeth II. Through all kinds of cultural events the new queen's reign was evoked as a return to the high success of the era of Elizabeth I, and the full panoply of colonial and Commonwealth allegiance was put on view to support the assertion of British importance in the world.

Many qualifications, needless to say, have to be added to this broad-brush account of the context for literature in Britain in the 1950s. It is axiomatic that such events are differently experienced according to class, gender, race and ethnicity. Equally, the effect of other cultures and economies beyond the empire needs to be taken into account. Some groups were clearly and dramatically influenced by events in the empire, notably those men and their families who had served in the Indian Civil Service or in the Indian Army. The repatriation and resettlement of these people after 1947 had quite a marked effect on the social structure of certain areas of southern and rural Britain. It impinges briefly but importantly in *Look Back in Anger*. In Act 2, Jimmy remembers Alison's father at their wedding, 'upright and unafraid, dreaming of his days among the Indian Princes, and unable to believe he'd left his horsewhip at home' (John Osborne, *Look Back in Anger*,

London: Faber & Faber, 1996, pp.55–6). Almost everyone in some way felt the effects of changes in the empire through, for example, the changing patterns of trade which affected manufacturing and consumption, and through what appeared in newsreels, on radio and on television. P.J. Cain and A.G. Hopkins speak of the effects of the empire (with the exception of India) being 'reglued' economically after the end of the war before becoming 'unstuck' again in the mid-1950s (*British Imperialism: Crisis and Deconstruction 1914–1990*, London: Longman, 1993 p.285). A similar process can be said to have happened in other areas of life.

Equally, there were myriad differences within the newly decolonized states and between them. Of particular interest here, though a minor element in the whole picture, is the situation of those who had identified themselves with the colonizer, particularly through education and government service. Here V.S. Naipaul can stand as an example of the process and its intricacy. His family had arrived in Trinidad from India very much as servants of the empire, to work on the sugar plantations. Naipaul himself was born in 1932. Through his application at school he achieved the accolade of winning a scholarship to go from the 'periphery' to the 'metropolitan centre' of the empire to study English at Oxford University. This is a story of success for the colonial subject and for the colonizing power. An Oxford education opened the door to opportunity and prosperity for anyone from the colonies just as the evidence of the continuing pull of British culture testified to the continuing power of the colonial hegemony. But it is not a tale without ironies. First there is the near coincidence of Naipaul completing his studies at Oxford in 1954 and Trinidad becoming self-governing in political terms in 1956. Then there is a complication in this particular drama of colonial identity and belonging. Conventionally for someone moving to education in England there were competing answers to the question, 'where are you at home?'. Perhaps 'home' involved going back – to your birthplace or your parents' house. But equally it might be to do with the culture into which you have been absorbed – the country whose culture produced the literature that filled your mind and conditioned your imagination.

For Naipaul, there was a third answer, which enabled him to break out of this dilemma and yet which fixed him still more firmly in the inheritance of imperialism. His father had been brought to Trinidad to work as an indentured labourer on the sugar plantations; by race, then, home was somehow neither Trinidad nor Britain but India. However, he can still stand as representative, this time of another process whereby cultural and political relationships have shifted from being a series of colonizer/ colonized relationships to being a set of relationships between a number of different independent countries. It is almost certainly overly Anglocentric to see everything in the British colonial world – trade, politics, culture – as having been exclusively focused on London. But there is enough truth in the notion to make a contrast with what happened after colonies started to become more independent. Of course discrepancies of power persisted, keeping Britain in a favoured place economically and culturally, but there was a greater recognition of English as a language that could have distinct and valuable forms outside Britain and an increased rejection of the notion that certain cultures were inferior or primitive and hence rightly silenced. This process is parallel to the political one whereby under the Thatcher government of the 1980s it became customary for the Commonwealth meetings to speak of Britain as just another member of the group.

Contrasting post-colonial worlds

One possibility for this chapter would have been to explore how British writers (writers born in Britain or born in India in British families) wrote about India after 1947. Comparisons would have been made with the work of Kipling and Forster and continuities and discontinuities identified. We have chosen a different route from this one, but you may be interested to follow the British-India tradition yourself. If so, a straightforward way of doing this would be through analysis and exploration of the work of Paul Scott (1920–78). Though he lived for a relatively short time in India almost all of his fiction is set there, beginning with *Johnnie Sahib* (1952) and *The Alien Sky* (1953). His most famous work is the sequence of novels known as 'the Raj Quartet', which begins with *The Jewel in the Crown* (1966) and was adapted for television under that name in 1982. Scott's work is interestingly discussed in Margaret Scanlon, *Traces of Another Time: History and Politics in Postwar British Fiction* (Princeton: Princeton University Press, 1990), and Michael Gorra, *After Empire: Scott, Naipaul and Rushdie* (London: University of Chicago Press, 1997). It also features in a longer time frame in Sujit Mukherjee, *Forster and Further: The Tradition of Anglo-Indian Fiction* (Hyderabad: Orient Longman, 1993). There are many other writers less well known (or pretty much forgotten) in Britain of whom I will mention just two. First – and in the 'pretty much forgotten' class – there is Christine Weston, who was born in India in 1904 and lived there until 1923 before moving to the USA. Weston published a number of novels, including *Indigo* (1943), and stories such as 'A Game of Halma' (1948) and 'Be Still, She Sleeps' (see Text 10.1). (This last might form an intriguing comparison with certain parts of *The Enigma of Arrival* since in both the search for identity is imagined through memory and a visit to an old house.) A second better-known writer is Ruskin Bond (b.1934), who is still publishing regularly in India; among the works that might seem particularly relevant here are stories such as 'The Man Who Was Kipling' and 'The Last Time I Saw Delhi' (see Texts 10.2 and 10.3).

Our decision, however, was to focus on *Look Back in Anger* and *The Enigma of Arrival*, and since this is the first time we have focused on two texts in a chapter a word of explanation as to our aims is in order. Both *Look Back in Anger* and *The Enigma of Arrival* can be said to have some link with our *Literature and Nation: Britain and India* theme. Osborne's play is generally recognized as part of the canon of English Literature and was written in a context of change after the Second World War and at a time of progressive decolonization; *The Enigma of Arrival* is by a writer of Indian descent whose life and work generally have been marked by colonial cultural processes. But each also offers something of a challenge.

Naipaul – Indian by descent, Trinidadian by birth and education – has become what might be described as 'international' or perhaps 'mixed-national', a hybrid of Caribbean, English and Indian. Moreover, *The Enigma of Arrival* pretty much eschews mention of either the Caribbean or India. It is plainly very different from *Kanthapura* or *Sunlight on a Broken Column*, which are rooted in the cultures they depict and from which they emerge; it has little in common either with *Midnight's Children*, discussed in the next chapter. So part of the reason for including *The Enigma of Arrival* is to provide you with a different kind of opportunity to think again about the validity of the hypothesis put forward in Chapter 1, 'if the particular text under discussion comes from a period of colonialism or decolonization, then it follows that the particular text must be marked in some way by colonialism or decolonization' (p.11).

Look Back in Anger offers a more extreme test of the hypothesis. From its first production it has been read as primarily reacting to – and attempting to fracture – class attitudes in Britain. References to the overseas world do occur, but the whole play is severely fixed in one room in the Midlands in Britain. Maybe here you will feel the hypothesis does fail. If so, that would itself be provocative of thought. Is *Look Back in Anger* perhaps evidence of a kind of ghetto of 'little England' culture which turns inwards from the problems of decolonization? Or was the British Empire by the 1950s just no longer important in British culture?

Approaching Look Back in Anger

The text and other resources

Look Back in Anger was first performed on 8 May 1956 at the Royal Court Theatre, London. It was published by Faber & Faber in the following year; at the time of writing the current edition is John Osborne, *Look Back in Anger* (London: Faber & Faber, 1996). The play is also available in *Plays One* (London: Faber & Faber, 1998), one of a series of compendium volumes of Osborne's works. The most entertaining account of Osborne's life is his own, to be found in his two volumes of autobiography, *A Better Class of Person: An Autobiography 1929–1956* and *Almost a Gentleman: An Autobiography 1955–1966* (London: Faber, 1981 and 1991). Also available is a collection of Osborne's prose writings, *Damn You, England* (London: Faber, 1994). Osborne's plays attracted considerable academic attention when they were first performed and some of these early books still offer a good introduction to his work at this time; see, for example, Martin Banham, *John Osborne* (Edinburgh: Oliver and Boyd, 1969), or Simon Trussler, *The Plays of John Osborne: An Assessment* (London: Gollancz, 1969). Early assessments and reactions specifically to *Look Back in Anger* are collected in John Russell Taylor, *John Osborne's 'Look Back in Anger': A Casebook* (London: Macmillan, 1975). A more recent general reference book is *John Osborne: A Reference Guide*, ed. by Cameron Northouse and Thomas P. Walsh (Boston: G.K. Hall, 1994).

Look Back in Anger, *England and a new kind of drama*

Contemporary writers regularly credited *Look Back in Anger* with creating a new kind of drama on the English stage. The situation seemed a little akin to the way in which earlier in the century Modernism had supposedly made everything new and banished for ever the older ways of writing. In both cases, such evaluations seem in retrospect to tell us as much about the attitudes of those detecting a new world as they do about the works they wrote about. Was this new world identified as in any way post-colonial? Looking back to contemporary reactions to the play, it seems not. The emphasis was on matters of class and on the outraging of social and theatrical conventions. Critics compared *Look Back in Anger* with the contemporary commercial theatre, declaring that Osborne's play rendered more or less everything about the latter obsolete. In the comparison the old world was often taken to be represented by the plays of Terence Rattigan. Rattigan's first major success – *French without Tears* – dated back to 1936; in the 1950s he was one of the senior figures of British theatre, whose work was familiar to theatre audiences from well-dressed and well-spoken plays such as *The Winslow Boy* (1948) and *The Browning Version* (1951) and films such as *The Way to the Stars* (1945). These were clearly serious works but they seemed resolutely middle-class. Particularly in the Second World War films scripted by Rattigan there was an assertion of a nation able to come together to defeat a common enemy and to stand for common decencies. In this world, the notion that seriousness might involve showing a woman ironing in a bedsit, as in *Look Back in Anger*, seemed unthinkable. In such a context Osborne's work could only seem avant-garde.

It is surely possible, however, to make a link with British imperial identity here, even though it seems sometimes as if the empire risks being written out of British imaginings in favour of the Second World War. Surely the kind of high seriousness that was portrayed by Rattigan as being at the heart of the British military victory was the same seriousness that imbued the ideology of imperial service, carrying the white man's burden and decent government across the globe. If so, then Osborne's avant-garde perspective declares that these values too lie in the past, that hope now lies with Jimmy Porter and not Arthur Winslow. However, one should perhaps not accept this assessment of Osborne and Rattigan too easily. Alongside the genuinely realistic elements in *Look Back in Anger* is there not a kind of emotional melodrama which seems much less radical? Rattigan's work has also been reassessed; his portrayals of moral dilemmas perhaps now seem as 'modern' as those presented by Osborne. Comparison of *Look Back in Anger* and

Rattigan's 'Table by the Window', the first part of *Separate Tables* (1954; in *The Collected Plays of Terence Rattigan*, 4 vols, London: Hamish Hamilton, 1953–78; III, 1964), for example, might produce a different result from that which has been conventionally accepted.

Look Back in Anger might also be set beside another icon of innovation in drama from the same period, Samuel Beckett's *Waiting for Godot* (first performed in French in Paris in 1953 and then in English in August 1955). In literary-historical accounts, as Osborne's play is representative of a new realism on the stage, so Beckett's is representative of the 'theatre of the absurd'. Other names associated with this kind of drama are Arthur Adamov, Eugène Ionesco, Jean Genet and Harold Pinter. In a classic account of this movement – Martin Esslin, *The Theatre of the Absurd* (1961; 3rd edn, Harmondsworth: Penguin, 1980) – the 'absurd' is described as follows:

> In one of its aspects it castigates, satirically, the absurdity of lives lived unaware and unconscious of ultimate reality ... In its second, more positive aspect, behind the satirical exposure of the absurdity of inauthentic ways of life, the Theatre of the Absurd is facing up to a deeper layer of absurdity – the absurdity of the human condition itself in a world where the decline of religious belief has deprived man of certainties. When it is no longer possible to accept complete closed systems of values and revelations of divine purpose, life must be faced in its ultimate, stark reality. (pp.400–01)

This seems to suggest again that we are dealing with another kind of literature which has little to do with politics or nation. The absurd can readily be described in the kind of almost metaphysical language used by Esslin, drawing, for example, on the idea that the existential philosophy of Jean-Paul Sartre is a key influence. (The possibility of a similar reading of Osborne's work is explored in E.G. Prater, *An Existential View of John Osborne*, Freeman, SD: Pine Hill, 1993.) But it can be argued that to read the absurd in this way involves largely rejecting the notion of the forming power of 'context'. Taking that 'context' more into account can bring the movement closer to issues of literature and nation. For example, the absurd drama emerged as much as anywhere in France, that is, from a society marked by the liberation of 1945 but also by the continuing memory of the conflicts of the Vichy regime (Beckett himself had played a significant part in the Resistance in Paris). The year 1954 is, meanwhile, the date of the French defeat by the Vietnamese at the Battle of Dien Bien Phu. The battle marked the end of attempts to re-establish French colonial power in South East Asia after the defeat of the Japanese in 1945. It is also the start of the final phase of the struggle for independence in Algeria, France's nearest colonial possession. Maybe the more apt questions, then, are akin to ones raised already, namely, are we are dealing here with literature that exists in a ghetto isolated from the questions of nation and identity that press outside, or is it that these issues are embedded in the texts but indirectly and in encoded ways?

In summary, I am aiming to suggest that it is possible to acknowledge the different styles of these writers – Rattigan's seriousness, Osborne's anger and Beckett's absurdity – while seeing all three as engaged within the same kind of matrix of ideological and historical issues. What then might we see as the particular inflection offered by Osborne's 'anger'? An early discussion of this topic is Michael Anderson, *Anger and Detachment: A Study of Arden, Osborne and Pinter* (London: Pitman, 1976). More recently the issues have been explored by Aleks Sierz in 'John Osborne and the Myth of Anger' (*New Theatre Quarterly*, 12.46 (May 1996), pp.136–46). Towards the end of the article, Sierz writes, 'the audience for the new drama is usually characterised as being young, lower middle class, and left liberal. For this group, the myth of anger offered a radical identity which helped them cope with the insecurity of rapid social change' (p.145). Sierz then takes issue with this, suggesting that the drama remained the property of a more traditional middle-class audience: 'audiences might flatter themselves by thinking that "working class" drama could help change society, but all it did was to change drama. Cultural images of the working class were a place where the *middle class* worked out its idea' (p.145; original italics).

That is to say, perhaps what we witness in *Look Back in Anger* is not so much an outbreak of working-class anger on the stage but, by a sleight of hand, an outburst of anger in the middle-class theatrical establishment that had produced the play and in the middle class that constituted the majority of its audience at the Royal Court. The anger was prompted by a sense of social crisis and change that was particularly relevant to the middle class – arising from the collapse of ideologies of imperial Britain, shifts in national identity, the growing assertiveness and economic power of the young – but which was then projected onto the working-class characters on the stage. It was all very different from the vision of social harmony and optimism that was central to the idea this was a new Elizabethan age.

Finally, you might wish to think about whether these possible readings and linkings are peculiar to the theatre. Critics of the novel in Britain in the 1950s regularly also make references to the development of a new realist style in that genre, so connections with 'anger' and Osborne seem possible there (see, for example, John Braine, *Room at the Top*, 1957, and Alan Sillitoe, *Saturday Night and Sunday Morning*, 1958). But what of poetry? The 1950s saw the publication of, for example, Philip Larkin, *The Less Deceived* (1955), Ted Hughes, *Hawk in the Rain* (1957), and Geoffrey Hill, *For the Unfallen* (1959). Decolonization and the changing nature of Britain's role in the world seem even less prominent here. Maybe it is just that poetry as a genre lacks an engagement with politics from that of prose or drama. But an alternative view is possible which would involve decoding apparently unpolitical language and metaphors to reveal political meanings. Maybe for example one could put the angry emotions that are often present in Hughes's poetry alongside the anger which is a keynote of Osborne's play and see both as responding to contemporary changes and events. In this way poetry could be seen to show signs of the same kind of link between politics and culture that we can see in prose and drama, contributing just as much to the development of new metaphors, new imaginings of community and new inventings of tradition to represent the British nation. In this latter context it might be interesting to follow up the emphasis on history in Geoffrey Hill's work, for example, or the new attention to the lower orders in Larkin, or – in all three poets – the way nature figures in their work.

Sex, the kitchen sink and empire

In 1956 *Look Back in Anger* shocked London audiences not just through its presentation of lower-class life but also because of the sexual promiscuity that seemed to go on there. In all sorts of ways the Second World War had disrupted family life in Britain, and much public policy thereafter was dedicated to reassembling the family as a coherent form, by attempting to re-establish that the woman's place was in the home, for example. With hindsight it seems that Osborne is arguing quite accurately that this ideological endeavour would fail. (The 1999 National Theatre revival of the play brought this aspect of the play to the fore, suggesting that this was the element of the play that had survived best.) Through Alison he offers a highly critical account of the home-making woman. He also presents the 'family' as being anything but domestic through the sexual tension that runs through the play. Osborne has Alison say that Jimmy wants women to be 'a kind of cross between a mother and a Greek courtesan, a henchwoman, a mixture of Cleopatra and Boswell' (p.97). The allusive language present here runs alongside the realistic dialogue throughout the play, and both warrant further study. The sexual radicalism in the play seems, however, distinctly heterosexual – an issue which has also provoked comment. In his biography of Terence Rattigan, Geoffrey Wansell suggests that there was a 'distaste' for Rattigan's work amongst the key members of the English Stage Company at the Royal Court because of his homosexuality and that this worked in favour of *Look Back in Anger* (*Terence Rattigan: A Biography*, London: Fourth Estate, 1996, p.409). This might seem ironic given that some of the scenes between Jimmy and Cliff in Osborne's play have the potential to be played in a quite erotic way (but in a way which is very different from the covert and camp gay world associated with Rattigan). If the sexual radicalism of *Look Back in Anger* interests you, then you may be interested to compare this first-performed play of Osborne's with one produced when his reputation was assured and he was able to be freer, namely *A Patriot for Me* (1965). As written – it was censored for performance – this play presents homosexuality on stage far more radically and directly than heterosexuality is shown in *Look Back in Anger*; one scene opens with a younger man creeping from the bed of the older central character after what has obviously been a one-night stand.

Again, however, we need to come back to the question, why should these matters be of interest for our investigation of literature and nation? The most direct answer would be that Osborne and others writing in the 1950s offer representations of a changing aspect of the British nation, a step on the way from the 'stiff upper lip' of the British Empire to the post-colonial 'swinging sixties' perhaps. There might also be a connection to be made with the notion discussed in relation to *A Passage to India* above that writings about the empire had offered a place for the open expression of desires which it was taboo to connect with 'home'. Other examples of this kind of writing are Rumer Godden, *Black Narcissus* (1938, filmed 1947), and John Masters, *Bhowani Junction* (1954, filmed 1955). Ronald Hyam, *Empire and Sexuality: The British Experience* (Manchester: Manchester University Press, 1991), and Gail Ching-Liang Low, *White Skins / Black Masks: Representation and Colonialism* (London: Routledge, 1996), offer complementary accounts of the colonial experience in this context.

Approaching The Enigma of Arrival

The text and other resources

V.S. Naipaul began to write and to publish in the mid-1950s but his reputation was fully established by his fourth novel, *A House for Mr Biswas* (1961), which has rapidly acquired a canonical status and a place on school and college syllabuses. Naipaul's fiction has been honoured by the award of a conspicuously large number of literary prizes, including the Somerset Maugham Award in 1959 for *Miguel Street*, the W.H. Smith Award in 1968 for *The Mimic Men*, and the Booker Prize in 1971 for *In a Free State*. *The Enigma of Arrival* dates from 1987 (paperback edn, London: Penguin, 1987). Naipaul has also been a regular contributor to newspapers and magazines and has published a number of books of travel writings (see below for details of those about India). Naipaul himself has edited a collection of his letters to his father (V.S. Naipaul, *Letters Between a Father and a Son*, London: Little, Brown, 1999). Academic writing about Naipaul's work began to appear around 1971 with, for example, William Walsh, *V.S. Naipaul* (Edinburgh: Oliver and Boyd, 1973), and Landeg White, *V.S. Naipaul: A Critical Introduction* (London: Macmillan, 1975). More recent general studies include three works all entitled simply *V.S. Naipaul*, by Bruce King (London: Macmillan, 1993), Fawzia Mustafa (Cambridge: Cambridge University Press, 1995) and Suman Gupta (Plymouth: Northcote House, 1999). Discussions of his work from a more specialized perspective include Selwyn Cudjoe, *V.S. Naipaul: A Materialist Reading* (Amherst: University of Massachusetts Press, 1988), and Rob Nixon, *London Calling: V.S. Naipaul, Postcolonial Mandarin* (Oxford: Oxford University Press, 1992).

Naipaul, the 'enigma' and Britain

From the beginning, readers of *The Enigma of Arrival* are likely to feel surrounded by enigma and puzzle. Instinctively, perhaps they will feel that their key task is to solve that puzzle, to understand the novel's form (why it is so explicitly declared to be 'A novel in five sections'), its meaning and its style. At the very beginning, for example, what are we to make of the way the first section begins? It seems unliterary, almost child-like. Yet a moment's reflection suggests the opposite may be the case and that the opening pages of *The Enigma of Arrival* carry echoes of two of the most literary of all novels. The preponderance of short sentences seems almost consciously to evoke the opening pages of James Joyce's *A Portrait of the Artist as a Young Man*. Compare for example the two paragraphs begin-ning 'And then one afternoon it began to snow ...' (*Enigma*, p.12) with those beginning 'The wide playgrounds ...' (*A Portrait of the Artist as a Young Man*, Harmondsworth: Penguin, 1960, p.8). A little later in *The Enigma of Arrival* there is an allusion – which is, if anything, apparently more self-conscious – to the *Swann's Way* part of Marcel Proust's *A la recherche du temps perdu*. Naipaul's narrator refers to there being 'two ways to the cottage' (p.13); paradoxically given that they go to the same place, for one he turns left from the road while for the other he turns right. Proust's narrator refers to 'two "ways"' both leading to a local village, 'so diametrically opposed that we would leave the house by a different door according to the way we had chosen' (Marcel Proust, *Swann's Way*, trans. by C.K. Scott-Moncrieff, London: Chatto & Windus, 1943, p.182; here and later I quote from Moncrieff's classic translation completed by Stephen Hudson, as the one Naipaul himself is likely to have read, rather than from the more recent revised versions).

Then there is the puzzle of how to connect the parts. One of the threads seems to be Naipaul himself, but how are we to be sure the 'I' of the novel is really Naipaul? Such details as we have about Naipaul's life suggest that he has heavily adapted the reality for his fiction. However that may be, a good deal of the emotional seriousness of the novel rests with our involvement with the first-person narrator, as for example, in the following extract from the end of 'Jack's Garden':

> I had thought that because of my insecure past – peasant India, colonial Trinidad, my own family circumstances, the colonial smallness that didn't consort with the grandeur of my ambition, my uprooting of myself for a writing career, my coming to England with so little, and the very little I had to fall back on – I had thought because of this I had been given an especially tender or raw sense of an unaccommodating world. (p.87)

The closeness of this account to the facts of Naipaul's life and the emotional rawness involved in 'arrival' at this point in the narrative are striking. How are we to reconcile them with the coolness of the title of the novel? Perhaps overall the prevailing mood is not this rawness but a mixture of emotion and detachment that is much closer to De Chirico's work (see p.91 for the narrator's description of the particular painting).

Unravelling the relationship between the narrator and the fictional world he inhabits and creates is one of the most interesting projects so far as *The*

Enigma of Arrival is concerned. Equally intriguing for me is the way the realist world of the novel (matters of geography and history, of facts and evidence) runs together with something different – a whole set of ideologies and metaphors that are embodied in the buildings and landscapes. Examples of what I mean occur throughout the novel, but you might look at the page or so following 'The rutted droveway...' in the 'Ivy' section (p.169), or later in the same section the paragraphs beginning 'The Manor...' (p.198). As the realistic details resonate with metaphorical implications, Hobsbawm's 'invented tradition' and Anderson's 'imagined community' (see Chapter 1, p.14 above) persistently come to mind. So complete and compelling are both strands that eventually it is almost as if I am reading two novels at the same time; one in which the language appears transparently to record the everyday life of rural England, the other in which every detail can be read as carefully symbolic of post-colonial identity and culture and in which there is a continual harping on some of the most crucial images of past British culture. In the centre, holding them together, is the narrator 'Naipaul'. The resulting style of writing, in its different way, seems to me every bit as complex as the magic realist style developed by Salman Rushdie which is discussed in the next chapter. In the way it manages to combine – both realistically and through allusions – different time frames *The Enigma of Arrival* might be interestingly compared with two of Tom Stoppard's plays, *Arcadia* (London: Faber & Faber, 1993), which deals with ideas of British identity, and *Indian Ink*, which deals directly with the British experience in India (see Text 10.4).

The way of writing I am describing here is discussed further in John Thieme, *The Web of Tradition: Uses of Allusion in V.S. Naipaul's Fiction* (London: Hansib, 1987). By way of a closer analysis of the style, consider the brief sentence early on when the narrator says of Jack, 'I saw him as a remnant' (p.20). A 'remnant' may be a collective noun – we might speak of the remnant of the army – but it can also be singular – the final piece off a roll of cloth which is too small to be of any proper use. In the world of the 1980s it is, then, rather as if Britain has made up all the proper garments into the imperial culture; the job is finished, all that is left is something which is to be thrown away or perhaps used up for some odd purpose. The idea of Jack as a remnant also sets resonating cultural images that we can most obviously anchor in the poetry of Wordsworth. In *Lyrical Ballads* (1798), for example, Wordsworth gives a new value to the beggar or the old woman in the stark rural landscape, not just as a person but as a central point of value in the English Romantic tradition and in the English national identity (Naipaul refers specifically to Wordsworth on page 26 of the novel). Once established, this kind of detail becomes a source of further meanings later in the book. It lends a resonance, for example, to the details towards the end of the 'Jack's Garden' section, creating something of a parody of the Wordsworthian principle. After Jack's death, rather than his widow remaining enduring and alone in her cottage, with hardly a pause the building is dismantled and she leaves for the town: 'For her, Jack's wife, the move away from the cottage had been good. She saw her life as a small success story. Father a forester, a gamekeeper of sorts; Jack the farm worker, the gardener; and now she half a townswoman' (p.88).

If you wish to explore a further example for yourself, I suggest you take the manor house at the centre of the story, the various descriptions of which seem to me particularly rich in possibilities for metaphorical reading. As I read, 'The house was not old ... but built to look old' (p.184), for example, I feel Naipaul has picked up on just that characteristic of British and imperial culture which is caught in the title of Francis Hutchins, *The Illusion of Permanence: British Imperialism in India* (Princeton: Princeton University Press, 1967). Equally, reading about the manor my mind is carried back to the country-house gentry culture of *Mansfield Park* (see Chapter 3 above); by the twentieth century this world has become fragile indeed: 'a boiler exploded in the manor one day; another time a bit of the roof was blown off' (p.235).

Naipaul and India

Putting *The Enigma of Arrival* alongside Naipaul's non-fiction writing can be as interesting as putting it alongside others of his novels. Chief among these non-fiction writings are the three books he has written about India – *An Area of Darkness* (1964; Harmondsworth: Penguin, 1969), *India: A Wounded Civilisation* (1977; Harmondsworth: Penguin, 1979) and *India: A Million Mutinies Now* (1990; London: Minerva, 1991). At first we seem to be dealing with contrasts; these books are closer to serious journalism and travel writing than fiction and they deal with India and not Britain. Just who is telling the story seems unproblematic since here we can be in no doubt that we are dealing with direct transcriptions of Naipaul's experiences. As soon as we start reading, however, connections emerge. Naipaul does not, for example, seem to me to think that different styles are required for fiction and non-fiction. Consider, for example, the two following paragraphs:

> For the first four days it rained. I could hardly see where I was. Then it stopped raining and beyond the lawn and outbuildings in front of my cottage I saw fields with stripped trees on the boundaries of each field; and far away, depending on the light, glints of a little river, glints which sometimes appeared, oddly, to be above the level of the land.
>
> (*Enigma*, p.11)

> Traffic into the city moved slowly because of the crowd. When at certain intersections the traffic was halted, by lights or by policemen or by the two together, the pavement seethed the more, and such a torrent of people swept across the road, in such a bouncing froth of light-coloured lightweight clothes, it seemed as if some invisible sluice gate had been opened ...
>
> (*India: A Million Mutinies Now*, p.1)

The 'torrent' of people and the 'light-coloured lightweight clothes' give away that the second of these is about India. But in both there is the same combination of the very short simple sentence and the longer extended and quite highly wrought one, the same detached tone in the narration, and the same almost poetic elements in the description ('stripped trees', 'bouncing froth').

There are also thematic connections to be made. Once past the 'Traveller's Prelude' section of *An Area of Darkness* we find Naipaul writing that India is 'the background of my childhood' (p.27), something that he describes in the evocative title of the section as 'A resting place for the imagination'. India is Naipaul's racial home as England (through education and through his scholarship to Oxford) is his cultural and figurative home. In both respects 'home' and 'identity' are bound together. In *An Area of Darkness* Naipaul's journey to India seems to involve the kind of searching for an essential identity that Stuart Hall describes in the extract I analyse in Chapter 1 (see pp.18–20); in the last chapter of *An Area of Darkness* Naipaul gets to his own 'great aporia' when he finally visits his ancestral village. The result is deeply dissatisfying for him. (For a further discussion of 'home' and identity in Naipaul, see Timothy Weiss, *On the Margins: The Art of Exile in V.S. Naipaul*, Amherst: University of Massachusetts Press, 1992.)

The first publication of *An Area of Darkness* provoked an outcry in India; readers there saw only hostility and an almost ultra-European fastidious- ness in Naipaul's portrayal of people and customs. The shared feelings of independence and commonwealth between post-colonial peoples seemed not to have worked. Where there should have been concord and sympathy between colonial voices, all that we hear from Naipaul is mimicry of the old colonial world. It is sometimes suggested that there is a racial as well as a cultural element in Naipaul's work beyond *The Enigma of Arrival* that deserves investigation (for example in *In a Free State* and *A Bend in the River*), but questions should also perhaps be prompted about how, particu- larly in a post-colonial world, different inventions of the same culture can more easily be in play at the same time. A reference to *The Enigma of Arrival* seems possible here. British readers' reactions to Naipaul's imagined England are likely to be less stridently rejecting than the Indian readers of *An Area of Darkness* who found their country imagined as a place of dirt, inefficiency and trickery. But those who begin by seeing a nostalgic 'National Trust' world in *The Enigma of Arrival* are likely to end up thinking Naipaul breaks the fine china even while he fondles it.

I want to end this section by putting *An Area of Darkness* and *The Enigma of Arrival* together to suggest a line of thought relating to the last section of the novel. Schematically, during the period of colonialism literature works in the interest of the colonizing power and – as suggested in the title of Gauri Viswanathan's book on the topic, *Masks of Conquest* (London: Faber, 1990) – conceals that it does so. The remaking of traditions and histories is a silent process. Naipaul's relationship with India begins as an attempt to get past that process, but the result of his first endeavours is in fact a different kind of silence – in *An Area of Darkness* he writes, 'I had learned my separateness from India, and was content to be a colonial, without a past, without ancestors' (p.252). At the risk of tidying Naipaul into a simple and coherent narrative, perhaps by the end of *The Enigma of Arrival* both the silencing of history and the denial of the past have been transmuted into something else. The book is bracketed by memorials; Naipaul's opening dedication is to the memory of his brother, Shiva Naipaul, and he ends the book with a recollection of a journey back to Trinidad for the funeral of his younger sister, Sati. He writes that 'at her death there was ... a wish for old [Hindu] rites, for things that were felt specifically to represent us and our past' (p.316). Here perhaps Naipaul is coming close to an unravelling of the enigma, a statement of what specifically represents him. After the ceremony an old man offers a different representation, a historical account of Trinidad which might be described as a pack of lies but which the narrator dignifies with the lightly ironic phrase 'a composite history', adding:

> Men need history; it helps them to have an idea of who they are ... we remade the world for ourselves; every generation does that, as when we came together for the death of this sister and felt the need to honour and remember. (p.318)

It seems now that to have a past is valuable and necessary but that the past is not a simple and static thing to be discovered but something to be 'remade'. This seems a quite dynamic possibility, and the idea of remaking the world for ourselves, surely, has a clear post-colonial ring – a sense of the narrator taking charge. The novel continues towards its end in this vein with a strong forward movement as the narrator now lays 'aside [his] drafts and hesitations' to write his book (p.318). But with the last words the enigma of arrival returns. Just what is the significance of this new project being the book we have just read? Perhaps we are left with the sense of the solving of the puzzle of meaning that has run through the sections. But equally, maybe we catch an echo of Proust here at the end to match that at the beginning. Towards the end of the final volume of the *In Search of Lost Time* sequence Proust's narrator writes, 'I intended to start afresh from the next day to live in solitude but, this time, with a real object', namely the writing of his book about time and memory (Marcel Proust, *Time Regained*, trans. by Stephen Hudson, London: Chatto & Windus, 1944, p.359). If so, the message is that knowledge is a circling and circular process. Maybe the enigma is that both possibilities are true. We learn that literature can be a quest in which we remake ourselves, our history and our nation; simultaneously we learn that the journey is circular and self-consuming.

Questions and exercises

1   Read, say, three accounts of Britain in the 1950s. Do they offer any consensus as to whether this was a period in which Britain remained bound to its past (the empire, the Second World War etc.) or one in which it was forging a new set of political and cultural identities?

2   Consider the exchanges between Cliff and Jimmy (*Look Back in Anger*, p.89) in the light of the competing ideas (a) that the audience was different from the traditional West End commercial theatre audience and (b) that the audience for Osborne's play was the same as that for the commercial theatre (see p.145 above).

3   Compare *Look Back in Anger* with Harold Pinter's 'absurd' play *The Birthday Party* of 1958. Do the plays seem equally concerned with the same idea of Britain?

4   How does V.S. Naipaul use gardens to create realistic and metaphorical meaning in *The Enigma of Arrival*, pp.198–206?

5   Compare the content and style of the section 'A Doll's House on the Dal Lake' from V.S. Naipaul's *An Area of Darkness*, and the section 'A House on the Lake: A Return to India' from his later *India: A Million Mutinies Now*.

11 POST-COLONIAL HYBRIDITY: MIDNIGHT'S CHILDREN

by Harish Trivedi

Introduction

Salman Rushdie is perhaps the best-known contemporary writer in the world, famous not only for his literary works but also for the controversy caused by his novel *The Satanic Verses*. He has given a new turn both to the Indian novel in English and to the long literary relationship between India and Britain by inaugurating a new 'post-colonial' phase of it, and by exercising a pervasive influence on several younger Indian novelists, such as Amitav Ghosh, Rohinton Mistry, Mukul Kesavan and even a Hindi novelist such as Alka Saraogi (see p.159 below). Ambitious in scope, his novels not only represent individual characters or even a society as a whole, as fiction traditionally had done, but also attempt to 'narrate the nation', in Homi Bhabha's formulation (see *Nation and Narration*, ed. by Homi Bhabha, London: Routledge, 1990). This chapter focuses on his first major work, *Midnight's Children*, to suggest several (con)textual and theoretical ways of engaging with it.

Text and bibliography

Midnight's Children was published in 1981 in London and has subsequently been reprinted in paperback editions in both the UK and the USA, but not in India. (All references here are to the Vintage paperback edition, 1982). It was the second novel by Rushdie; the first was *Grimus* (1975,) a curious fantasy set outside of space and time, which got savage reviews on publication and has not been rescued by Rushdie's later success. *Midnight's Children* won the Booker prize and instantly established Rushdie as a major novelist. His third novel was *Shame* (1983), a satirical account of an unnamed country much like Pakistan; it is considerably shorter than all his other sprawling novels. His fourth novel, *The Satanic Verses* (1988), was largely about Indian characters in England but also contained, as indicated in the title, an account of the early period of Islam and of some supposedly apocryphal verses in the Koran thought to have been interpolated by the Devil. His irreverent treatment gave offence to many Muslims, leading to riots and deaths; the book was banned in several countries including India and Pakistan, and, in February 1989, the Ayatollah Khomeini of Iran issued a *fatwa* calling for the execution of Rushdie, upon which he had to go into prolonged hiding with the help of state security. (The *fatwa* was officially lifted in 1998.)

Undaunted, Rushdie continued to publish throughout the 1990s. *Haroun and the Sea of Stories* (1990) was a book for children which has a story-teller who loses his voice. A substantial collection of his essays followed, *Imaginary Homelands* (1991), as well as a collection of his short stories, *East, West* (1994). *The Moor's Last Sigh* (1995), a big novel again, returned to Bombay for its setting though it also took in south India, where the first contact between India and the West had taken place, and Moorish Spain. His latest work, *The Ground Beneath Her Feet* (1999), is again international in range, encompassing India, England and the USA, and incorporating a notable component of rock 'n' roll through a reworking of the myth of Orpheus.

Much of what has been published so far on Rushdie and on the 'Rushdie affair' has been in newspapers and periodicals, and given his contemporaneity and his still unfolding career, critical discussions of his work are to be found largely in scholarly journals. A useful guide to this material is the extensive *Salman Rushdie Bibliography* by Joel Kuortti (New York: Peter Lang, 1997); it lists works by Rushdie as well as those about him. Of the books published on Rushdie, Timothy Brennan's *Salman Rushdie and the Third World: Myths of the Nation* (London: Macmillan, 1989), which categorizes him as a 'Third World cosmopolitan', provides a stimulating account in a framework especially relevant to this course. Three introductory monographs are each titled *Salman Rushdie*: these are by Catherine Cundy (Manchester: Manchester University Press, 1996), who also offers a comparison of Rushdie and V.S. Naipaul; by D.C.R.A. Goonetilleke (London: Macmillan, 1998), who seeks especially to explicate the Indian context and references; and by Damian Grant in the British Council's Writers and their Work series (Plymouth: Northcote House, 1999). *Reading Rushdie: Perspectives on the Fiction of Salman Rushdie*, ed. by M.D. Fletcher (Amsterdam: Rodopi, 1994), and *Critical Essays on Salman Rushdie*, ed. by M. Keith Booker (New York: G.K. Hall, 1999), both contain a wide range of essays on his works. A more specifically focused selection is *Rushdie's 'Midnight's Children': A Book of Readings*, ed. by Meenakshi Mukherjee (Delhi: Pencraft International, 1999), comprising ten essays on the novel and an early interview; this is of special interest as besides the editor, six of the contributors are Indian.

Rushdie's novels contain perhaps an exceptionally high proportion of real historical events, directly represented or readily recognizable public figures, and constant resemblances to the known facts of his own life. The most extensive and reliable biographical account so far is by Ian Hamilton, 'The First Life of Salman Rushdie' (*The New Yorker*, 25 December 1995 – 1 January 1996), which stops at the publication of *Midnight's Children*.

Approaching Midnight's Children

Rushdie and India

Reportedly, when Martin Amis, one of the prominent British novelists of Rushdie's own generation, was once asked what Rushdie had and he had not, he succinctly answered: 'India.' India has been not only the setting but the grand theme of Rushdie's fiction so far, a theme which he has exploited like no Indian novelist before; but at the same time, the space India occupies in the Western literary world has been considerably enhanced through his representation of it. For many Western readers, in fact, Rushdie speaks for India in a way which seems not only representative but authoritative, and his version of India is often taken to be the 'real' India. The publication of *Midnight's Children* was 'like a continent finding its voice' (*New York Times*) – as if the three thousand years of continuous literary tradition had not existed; the novel was 'a fascinating history lesson as well as an engrossing story' (*Philadelphia Enquirer*); and its story 'was nothing less than that of modern India' (*Publishers Weekly*; all quoted on the covers of the paperback editions). Even an academic specializing in Indian Studies, Robin J. Lewis, has stated that Rushdie has 'altered our vision of the Indian sub-continent', to the extent that all the previous literary representations both by British writers such as Kipling and Forster and by Indians such as Raja Rao and R.K. Narayan have been 'simultaneously subsumed into, and surpassed by, Rushdie's passionate evocation of the recent history of India and Pakistan' (in *Masterworks of Asian Literature in Comparative Perspective*, ed. by Barbara Stoler Miller, Armonk, NY: M.E. Sharpe, 1994, pp.178–9).

Rushdie's relationship with India and the nature of his affiliation with it thus become critically significant issues in themselves. He was born in Bombay on 20 June 1947, close enough to 15 August 1947, the day India became free, when his hero in *Midnight's Children* Saleem Sinai and his 1,000 coevals are born. His parents were Westernized middle-class Muslims who migrated to Pakistan seventeen years later and subsequently to England. Meanwhile, unlike his fictional hero, Rushdie himself was sent at the age of thirteen to England to attend Rugby School, and later went to Cambridge where he did a degree in history which included an optional course on the history of Islam. He has said that he faced racial discrimination at school where he was unhappy, but also that his pale skin and pukka British accent later made him more or less indistinguishable from Englishmen. His upper-crust English education may have come about due to parental inclination and affluence, but he himself seems to have been keen enough and quite ready for the move:

> I grew up with an intimate knowledge of, and even a sense of friendship with, a certain kind of England; a dream England ... I wanted to come to England. I couldn't wait. And to be fair, England has done all right by me.
>
> (*Imaginary Homelands*, p.18)

Even if modulated by a tone of self-deprecating irony, the statement reveals a significant truth. Rushdie went back briefly to Pakistan after Cambridge, found the country distinctly uncongenial, came back, and has stayed in England ever since as a British citizen.

Recently, Rushdie has spoken of himself as having been 'exiled' by India, and in 1998 he expressed his own resolve to turn even imaginatively away from the country: 'I will never write about India again' (quoted in Mukherjee, p.15). Earlier, when he was fully engaged as a writer with the subject of India, he had, speaking on behalf of 'those of us who write from outside India', seemed to contemplate the question of ethical responsibility: 'are we just dilettantes in such affairs, because we are not involved in their day-to-day unfolding, because by speaking out we take no risks, because our personal safety is not threatened? What right do we have to speak at all?' (*Imaginary Homelands*, p.14). But these turned out to be merely rhetorical questions, for the answer Rushdie went on to provide was that from the outside, a writer like himself had a privileged double vision: 'we are not willing to be excluded from any part of our heritage ... Our identity is at once plural and partial ... If literature is in part the business of finding new angles at which to enter reality, then once again our distance, our long geographical perspective, may provide us with such angles' (*Imaginary Homelands*, p.15).

As can be seen, though he continues to be widely regarded in the West as the chief literary spokesman for India, Rushdie in fact stands at an acute angle to the country of his birth, perhaps even at a tangent. His growing vexation with India is quite the opposite of the yearning and nostalgia with which Raja Rao, for example, regards India (see Chapter 8 above). Rao's continuing if wishful project even now to write in an Indian language such as Kannada or even Sanskrit is in fact directly to be contrasted with Rushdie's editorial comment in his introduction to *The Vintage Book of Indian Writing*, ed. by Salman Rushdie and Elizabeth West (London: Vintage, 1997), brought out to mark the fifty years of Indian independence, that Indian writing in English during this period had been 'stronger and more important' than what had been produced in all the other eighteen Indian languages. Besides being an aggrandizement of his own kind of writing, this sweeping statement is also remarkable, as Meenakshi Mukherjee puts it, for 'the aggressiveness' of his 'empty claim based on ignorance' (Mukherjee, p.26).

In fact, such erasure of the indigenous literary culture is reflected widely in the present critical discourse on post-colonial literature which almost by definition is literature written in English, the language of the erstwhile colonizers, by the colonized even after the moment of political (if not cultural) decolonization. Some of these writers come from a social background which was so Westernized that they lost the local language as they acquired more and more English and would not have been able to write in it even if they wanted to, as in the case of Rushdie himself and probably most of the younger Indians writing in English. But some others, who remained effectively bilingual, still wrote in English in order to have the benefits of addressing a larger global audience. Incidentally, the use of English has been an issue of contention also among African writers. The Kenyan writer Ngugi wa Thiong'o actually switched in mid-career to begin writing and publishing in his native Gikuyu but in his case, this could be no more than a symbolic or even paradoxical gesture, for he then proceeded to translate his own Gikuyu works into English. (See the extract from his book, *Decolonising the Mind*, and also a contrasting moderate statement on the question of language from another African writer, Chinua Achebe, both reprinted in *Colonial Discourse and Post-Colonial Theory*, ed. by Patrick Williams and Laura Chrisman (London: Harvester Wheatsheaf, 1993, pp.428–55.) In India the decision to write in English looks quite different inside the country from the way it may look in the West. Where over 70 per cent of the population is now literate but where knowledge of English is still confined to not more than 5 per cent of the people at a generous estimate, few would even begin to doubt that the eighteen major Indian languages still have a viable and vibrant literary culture – though his anglicized upbringing and his recent constrained circumstances may not make Rushdie the best-placed person to know this.

Hybridity

Rushdie's stance, his works, and – if one may bring in the personal in the case of so patently autobiographical a writer – his own formation are an embodiment of the extent and the depth to which a colonizing culture can penetrate that of the colonized. While the colonizer and the colonized are both infected by each other through their historical conjunction and mutual cultural discovery – for example, the British in India up to the eighteenth century were often seen to 'go native' and were (even in English) called 'nabobs' – the coercive weight of assimilation ultimately falls rather more on the colonized. As each interacts with the Other (in the deeper psychic sense of the word expounded by Jacques Lacan; see Chapter 1 above, p.24), each ceases to remain what it previously was and becomes 'hybrid'. There is of course a philosophical sense in which everything is always and already hybrid, for (as the deconstructionist Jacques Derrida has argued) the pure and pristine origin is a myth and the search for it must grow ever more recessive or deferred. The profoundly complex political, racial and cultural transaction that takes place between the colonizer and the colonized and the several distinct phases of nationalism that it goes through, from imitation and assimilation to resistance and finally to post-colonial internationalization, was expounded with passionate engagement by Frantz Fanon in his widely influential works *Les Damnés de la terre* (1961; trans. by Constance Farrington as *The Wretched of the Earth*, London: Penguin, 1967) and *Peau noire, masques blancs* (1952; trans. by C.L. Markmann as *Black Skin, White Masks*, London: Pluto Press, 1986). One contemporary post-colonial critic who has reformulated with exceptional sophistication the concepts of colonial hybridity, 'mimicry', 'sly civility' and 'in-betweenness' is Homi Bhabha, in his collection of essays *The Location of Culture* (London: Routledge, 1994), which also includes a piece containing a discussion of Fanon. (Extracts from both Fanon and Bhabha appear in Williams and Chrisman, pp.36–52, 112–23.)

The persistence of the colonial intermixed with the post-colonial is reflected in *Midnight's Children* in a number of ways. The conditions on which the 'departing Englishman' William Methwold sells his 'Estate' in Bombay by partitioning it among four ethnically varied Indian families are that they must retain all his furniture and fittings and carry on just as he did; to make the self-proclaimed 'allegory' (*Midnight's Children*, pp.95–7) even more explicit, he later turns out to be one of Saleem's several fathers. When Ahmad Sinai's skin begins to turn pale and he is presently 'transformed into a white man', he is secretly rather pleased for, as he explains: 'All the best people are white under the skin; I have merely given up pretending.' A 'theory' which the narrator advances here is that in the first decade of India's independence, 'the gargantuan (even heroic) efforts involved in taking over from the British' had similarly turned the businessmen of India 'white' as well (p.179). Another instance of continued post-colonial anglicization in the novel is the narrator's upbringing and education: 'In India we've always been vulnerable to Europeans ... I was being sucked into a grotesque mimicry of European literature ... Perhaps it would be fair to say that Europe repeats itself, in India, as farce' (p.185).

Perhaps it would be fair to add that these statements are made by exceptionally Westernized characters who seem only too willing to be 'sucked into' a reverent imitation of Europe. There are, of course, other contrasting versions of the way the West has impacted on large segments of the post-colonial Indian society which were not as completely hybridized as Saleem Sinai's world seems to be, or whose hybridization produced a different and more resistant effect on them. For these, we may turn to some instances of writing in the Indian languages. Those dependent on translations might begin to get a sense of this very rich field through my translations of Hindi writings such as Sharad Joshi's story 'Who Isn't Afraid of Virginia Woolf?' (see Text 11.2) or Kamaleshwar's 'The Nose of King George the Fifth' (see Text 11.1). Nirmal Verma's stories are also available in *The Crow of Deliverance: Stories*, trans. by Kuldip Singh and Jai Ratan (London: Readers International, 1991). More recently, and still only partially, translated is Alka Saraogi, *Kali-katha: Via Bypass* (see Text 11.3).

Even lower down in the colonial cultural order and more widespread was the social stratum which remained relatively exempt from the range of colonial permeation, comprising the 'subalterns' who could not speak, or who spoke in very different modes and languages which could not be registered in the discourse of their colonial masters. (See 'Can the Subaltern Speak?', 1988, by Gayatri Chakravorty Spivak, repr. in Williams and Chrisman, pp.66–111). As Spivak clarifies in a revision and elaboration of her argument, the subaltern is distinguished from the 'elite' precisely by his/her 'inhabiting a space of difference' (see her *Critique of Postcolonial Reason*, Cambridge, MA: Harvard University Press, 1999, p.271, n.118).

Rushdie's fictional world in *Midnight's Children*, even if presented with intermittent irony, remains the world of the Indian elite, who are not only more 'vulnerable' to being hybridized but who perhaps are the elite because they have been so hybridized in the first place. The term 'hybridity' here may in fact stand as a euphemism for aspiration to Englishness. As Richard Cronin has argued in an unsettling comparative reading of *Midnight's Children*:

> Salman Rushdie has more in common with Rudyard Kipling than with Premchand or Bankim Chandra Chatterjee. It is an ancestry that he resists as energetically as Saleem resists the notion that his real father is an Englishman ... but, for all his efforts, *Midnight's Children* is better seen as a post-independence version of *Kim*.
>
> ('The Indian English Novel: *Kim* and *Midnight's Children*', *Modern Fiction Studies*, 33.2 (Summer 1987); repr. in Mukherjee, pp.134–48)

History as fiction and magic realism

As has been seen, *Midnight's Children* has been read at least in the West as being not only a novel but also a 'history lesson'. Nor can such a reading be called a wilful misreading, for the hero Saleem claims on the very first page that he was born 'mysteriously handcuffed to history' (p.9) at the precise moment that India attained freedom. This is the governing trope of the novel and is kept up throughout with a device whereby the novelist cuts back to Saleem's life to show what was happening to him whenever a historical event of national significance occurred. On the whole, though, this results in simple juxtaposition; the nation does not intersect, much less determine, the lives of the characters here in any important way. Nor is *Midnight's Children* really comparable with traditional historical novels, from *A Tale of Two Cities* and *War and Peace* to *Gone with the Wind*, where the focus is largely on the personal relationships between individual characters as their lives are played out against the backdrop of momentous historical events but are at crucial junctures interrupted and disrupted by them. In *Midnight's Children*, Saleem's life and the life of the nation run rather as two parallel streams, each on its own fairly watertight course.

Interestingly, Rushdie himself later claimed that he never intended his novel to be read as history:

> [Saleem's] story is not history, but it plays with historical shapes. Ironically, the book's success – its Booker Prize, etc. – initially distorted the way in which it was read. Many readers wanted it to be the history, even the guide-book, which it was never meant to be.
>
> (*Imaginary Homelands*, p.25)

This sounds very much like E.M. Forster's claim that *A Passage to India* is not a political novel: 'the book is not really about politics, though it is the political aspect of it that caught the general public and made it sell' (*The Hill of Devi and Other Indian Writings*, ed. by Elizabeth Heine, London: Edward Arnold, 1983, p.298). But a book is in effect just how it is read; what the author wished it to be has been called 'the intentional fallacy'. In any case, we know that Rushdie wrote some passages of his novel more or

less out of Stanley Wolpert's *A New History of India*, and many other parts apparently came out of newspaper reports and other documentary sources; in fact, at one point, the narrator even challenges the reader: 'If you don't believe me, check' (quoted by Neil ten Kortenaar, *'Midnight's Children* and the Allegory of History', *Ariel*, 26.2 (April 1995), repr. in Mukherjee, pp.28–48).

A radically different way of looking at the correlation between history and fiction is the post-structuralist one, according to which nothing exists naturally or objectively but everything is 'constructed' through and in language. Thus, neither history nor fiction is simply 'given'; rather, both are 'narratives' with their own procedure of selection, omissions and biases, according to the 'subject-position' of the person who narrates them. To hold that anything can exist outside its representation is to be an 'essentialist', i.e. to believe that things have an unmediated essence. It is in this sense, for example, that nations are not real but 'imagined communities' (see Chapter 1, p.14) and are no more or other than what they are narrated to be: 'Nations, like narratives ... fully realize their horizons in the mind's eye ... To study the nation through its narrative address does not merely draw attention to its language and rhetoric; it also attempts to alter the conceptual object itself' (Homi Bhabha, 'Introduction' to *Nation and Narration*, pp.1, 3). As if all this were not 'ambivalent' enough, the language in which the nation is narrated is held to be equally a construction: 'It is the project of *Nation and Narration* to explore the Janus-faced ambivalence of language itself in the construction of the Janus-faced discourse of the nation' (Bhabha, p.3).

There has over the years evolved an uncanny intertextuality between the theoretical articulations of Bhabha and the fictional narratives of Rushdie which may make it particularly apt to read Rushdie in terms of Bhabha. But such a reading will have to leave out of account all those other reading practices according to which General Dyer in this novel has more of a verifiable historical reality to him than Ahmad Sinai, and Jawaharlal Nehru is not a construction in the same sense as is Saleem. For many readers, the fact of India becoming free at the stroke of midnight of 14/15 August exists not on the same plane of credibility as Saleem being born at just that moment (the midnight being more historical than the children), and the Emergency which Indira Gandhi imposed is simply more real than anything Padma can do or say. Curiously, Rushdie himself has attempted to conflate the ambivalences of post-structuralism with the contingencies of post-colonialism; he speaks of himself as someone 'forced by cultural displacement to accept the provisional nature of all truths, all certainties' (*Imaginary Homelands*, p.12). This would seem to imply that for those not culturally displaced like him, truth is still truth and certainty certainty.

When *Midnight's Children* first came out it was often described as a work of magic realism. This term had earlier been used to describe the mode of fictional representation adopted by some Latin American novelists, most

notably Gabriel García Márquez, author of *One Hundred Years of Solitude* (1967; trans. 1971), and also by some European novelists such as Milan Kundera. In this mode, the largely realistic tenor of the novel is punctuated with episodes and descriptions which are clearly fantastic; an obvious example from *Midnight's Children* would be the characteristics and function of Saleem's nose. Related to this is the bending of reality achieved through the use of the grotesque, an eminent example of such a work being Günter Grass's *The Tin Drum* (1959), which is narrated by Oskar, a dwarf who has physical deformities quite comparable to Saleem's. Rushdie's fiction can be seen to bear the clear influence of both these styles: '*Midnight's Children* owes its magic', as Patricia Merivale has stated, 'to García Márquez and its realism to Günter Grass' ('Saleem Fathered by Oskar: Intertextual Strategies in *Midnight's Children* and *The Tin Drum*', *Ariel*, 21.3 (July 1990), repr. in Mukherjee, p.116). Rushdie himself has acknowledged the importance for him of both Márquez and Grass, by suggesting that Márquez's kind of magic realism 'expresses a genuinely "Third World" consciousness', and by recalling that his reading of *The Tin Drum* when he was twenty gave him 'permission' to become the kind of writer he had it in himself to be (*Imaginary Homelands*, pp.301, 276).

Style and form

There are thus many close non-Indian literary antecedents for *Midnight's Children*, and some more have been adduced, such as Sterne's *Tristram Shandy*. The style of the novel is marked by constant word-play, especially punning, and this, together with the thin line dividing his fiction from autobiography, has reminded many readers of James Joyce. In fact, Rushdie himself has described the style of his early fiction as 'sub-Joyce' (quoted in Hamilton, p.100). Yet the novel reads distinctively Indian as much in form and style as in theme, mainly because it is marked on almost every page with a confident unselfconscious deployment of Indian words and phrases and social and cultural allusions. Rushdie's use of a mixed, hybridized English has been seen as a liberating strategy not only for himself but also for numerous subsequent Indian writers, some of whom have also attempted similarly to narrate the nation. This has marked a departure from earlier modes of Indian writing in English, though it must not be forgotten that novelists such as Raja Rao and Mulk Raj Anand had even earlier attempted to appropriate English in their own ways (see Chapter 8 above). G.V. Desani, a writer whose example Rushdie acknowledges, made comparable appropriations in his novel *All About H. Hatterr* (1948), where the initial in the hero's assumed name stands for '*Hindustaniwalla*' (G.V. Desani, *All About H. Hatterr*, repr. Harmondsworth: Penguin, 1972, p.33).

With characteristic exuberance and radical bravado, Rushdie has claimed that his use of English is a form of a final fight against colonialism:

> Those of us who do use English do so in spite of our ambiguity
> towards it, or perhaps because of that, perhaps because we can find
> in that linguistic struggle a reflection of other struggles taking place
> in the real world ... To conquer English may be to complete the
> process of making ourselves free.
>
> (*Imaginary Homelands*, p.17)

There is, of course, another way of looking it, which is that to go on writing
in the language of the colonizer, however inventively and 'subversively', is
still to remain colonized and to enlist oneself 'in a foreign if not enemy
camp, that of the colonizer' (John Updike, review of *The God of Small Things*
by Arundhati Roy, *New Yorker*, 23–30 June 1997).

If Rushdie's extensive use of Indian allusions and Hindi-Urdu words does
not quite 'conquer' English, it does serve at least to 'chutneyfy' it. It also
underlines the fact that his intended reader is clearly a Westerner and not an
Indian, for many of his habitual stylistic devices do not work equally well
for someone who knows any Hindi or Urdu. One of the most frequent of
these is the use of a Hindi word as a kind of authenticating strategy, to show
that Rushdie knows his India from the inside as the reader does not and has
the reliability of a native informant. (This is a familiar literary practice; for
example, in their oriental tales Robert Southey, Thomas Moore and Lord
Byron had all used Eastern words and allusions, supported by scholarly
authorities cited in the footnotes, to heighten their credibility.) Though
Rushdie does not have footnotes or a glossary, he often does stop to provide
the English equivalent immediately afterwards. 'Godown, gudam, ware-
house, call it what you like' (p.71) is a characteristically prolix example, in
which the first word is from Indian English, the second from Hindi, and the
third from British English (rarely used in India), all to describe the same
object. Even more remarkable is his strategy in a sentence such as 'I do not
need to tell you that aag means fire' (p.71) or the following passage:

> Talaaq! Talaaq! Talaaq!
>
> The English lacks the thunderclap sound of Urdu and anyway you
> know what it means.
>
> I divorce thee, I divorce thee, I divorce thee. (p.62)

But this is disingenuous, for if the reader knew what it meant Rushdie
wouldn't need to provide the translation.

In another category altogether are the many palpable and elementary errors
in Rushdie's use of Indian words and allusions which were pointed out
after the novel was published. Resourceful as ever, Rushdie then wrote an
essay to explain that these errors had been planted by him in the novel to
establish that his narrator Saleem was an 'unreliable narrator'! (See 'Errata:
Or, Unreliable Narration in *Midnight's Children'*, in *Imaginary Homelands*,
pp.22–5.) But unreliable narrators usually are unreliable, as with Nelly
Dean in *Wuthering Heights* or Marlow in *Heart of Darkness*, because we

are not supposed to endorse their perceptions and judgements, and not because they get their 'facts' wrong.

Rushdie was born an Indian and has grown to be an Englishman – by education, place of residence and work, and in terms of his national affiliation. His books have been differently (and generally better) received in the West than in India. For example, while *Midnight's Children* has been read by many in the West as an affectionate celebration of India, *India Today* described it as 'one of the most ferocious indictments of India's evolution since independence' (this is quoted – ironically, to market the book – on the cover of the Picador paperback edition). In wider terms, he represents the post-colonial globalization of the world through migrancy and assimilation in a new phase of neo-colonialism. By the same token, perhaps, work like his does not represent that other larger, but proportionately under-represented, segment of the post-colonial peoples of the world who are not migrants and who, though necessarily affected by colonization (or hybridized) in their own way, continue to be rather more local than global where they are.

In the long history of the national and literary interaction between India and Britain, Rushdie, born on the post-colonial cusp like his midnight's children, expresses acutely the almost intractable complexity of both colonization and decolonization. He perhaps also marks the end of an era, the span of two hundred years in which Britain was the most important nation for India in the English-speaking world, as the generation of Indian writers in English after Rushdie have tended to migrate more to the USA and Canada than to Britain. Rushdie's latest novel, *The Ground Beneath Her Feet*, offers some symbolic moments here. It is the first of his novels where the story brings together events in India, Britain and the USA. The novel comes to the reader with an endorsement by Toni Morrison, the Nobel prize winning Black American writer, who describes the book as showing Rushdie 'at his absolute, almost insolently global best'. Just as British literature is not likely in the future to be as concerned, or even as little concerned, with India as it may have been in the past, so Indian literature, especially Indian writing in English, looks like moving beyond Britain and the colonial connection to attempt to address a new readership in the new neo-colonial centre of the world, the USA. This signals a post-colonial realignment of positions for Britain as well as India.

Questions and exercises

1 Trace the manifestations of post-colonial hybridity in Rushdie's work, beginning with *Midnight's Children* and going on through *The Satanic Verses* and *The Moor's Last Sigh*.

2 Examine Rushdie's fictional representation of modern Indian history with reference to historical works or works by other novelists, e.g. Shashi Tharoor, Rohinton Mistry and Mukul Kesavan.

3   Analyse Rushdie's style, especially in terms of innovation and accessibility.

4   Examine the ways in which Rushdie can be considered an 'Indian' writer, especially when compared with other Indian writers in this course, including those who write in the Indian languages.

5   Develop a comparison between Rushdie and V.S. Naipaul as post-colonial writers, beginning, if you like, with the analysis offered by Catherine Cundy in *Salman Rushdie* (Manchester: Manchester University Press, 1996).

RELATED TEXTS

A NOTE ON THE TEXTS

In the texts brought together here, we have normalized certain typographical conventions such as the use of single quotation marks and the position of punctuation marks within them. We have placed any additional comments or pieces of information that are not part of the original text in square brackets; an ellipsis in square brackets indicates where material has been omitted. We have not retained the old spellings where these might act as a barrier between the modern reader and the argument – for example we have substituted *s* for the long *s* used in some of the earlier pieces – and we have standardized the layout. In some instances we have amended or omitted footnotes and on occasion inserted punctuation for clarity, but in general we have not edited the texts except for length. The translation of Indian names into English gives rise to many variations. In these texts, rather than standardize spellings as we have in the preceding chapters, we have retained the spellings used in each source.

1.1 THE BRITISH PENETRATION OF INDIA

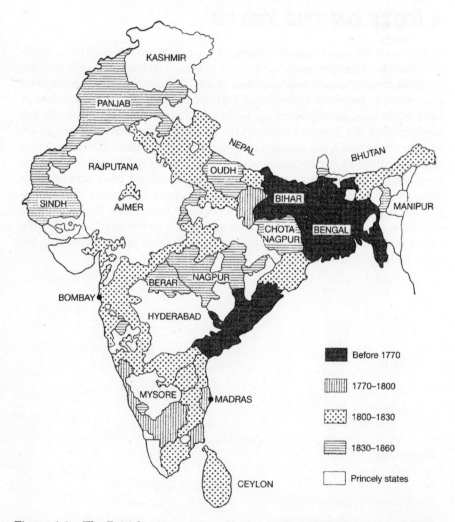

Figure 1.1   The British penetration of India (1750–1860). Reproduced from Herman Kulke and Dietmar Rothermund, *A History of India*, 3rd edn, London: Routledge, 1998, p.371, Map 13.

1.2 THE REPUBLIC OF INDIA

Figure 1.2   The Republic of India (after modification and definition of state boundaries between 1956 and 1972). For clarity the names of certain states in north-east India are omitted; Kashmir is now usually referred to as Jammu and Kashmir. Reproduced from Herman Kulke and Dietmar Rothermund, *A History of India*, 3rd edn, London: Routledge, 1998, p.372, Map 14.

2.1 PREFACE TO CHARLES WILKINS'S TRANSLATION OF THE BHAGAVAD-GITA

Warren Hastings

Source: Warren Hastings, Preface to *The Bhagavad-Gita*, trans. by Charles Wilkins, London, 1785, pp.5–15.

[The preface is in the form of an address to Nathaniel Smith of the East India Company, dated 4 October 1784.]

Sir,

To you, as to the first member of the first commercial body, not only of the present age, but of all the known generations of mankind, I presume to offer, and to recommend through you, for an offering to the public, a very curious specimen of the Literature, the Mythology, and Morality of the ancient Hindoos. It is an episodical extract from the 'Mahabharat', a most voluminous poem, affirmed to have been written upwards of four thousand years ago, by Kreeshna Dwypayen Veiâs, a learned Bramin; to whom is also attributed the compilation of 'The Four Vêdes, or Bêdes', the only existing original scriptures of the religion of Brahmâ; and the composition of all the Poorâns, which are to this day taught in their schools, and venerated as poems of divine inspiration. Among these, and of superior estimation to the rest, is ranked the Mahabharat [...]

The Mahabharat contains the genealogy and general history of the house of Bhaurut, so called from Bhurrut its founder; the epithet Mahâ, or Great, being prefixed in token of distinction: but its more particular object is to relate the dissentions and wars of the two great collateral branches of it, called Kooroos and Pandoos; both lineally descended in the second degree from Veecheetraveerya, their common ancestor, by their respective fathers Dreetrarashtra and Pandoo [...]

The Preface of the Translator will render any further explanation of the Work unnecessary. Yet something it may be allowable for me to add respecting my own judgement of a Work which I have thus informally obtruded on your attention, as it is the only ground on which I can defend the liberty which I have taken.

Might I, an unlettered man, venture to prescribe bounds to the latitude of criticism, I should exclude, in estimating the merit of such a production, all rules drawn from the ancient or modern literature of Europe, all references to such sentiments or manners as are become the standards of propriety for opinion and action in our own modes of life, and equally all appeals to our revealed tenets of religion, and moral duty. I should exclude them, as by no means applicable to the language, sentiments, manners, or morality appertaining to a system of society with which we have been for ages unconnected, and of an antiquity preceding even the first efforts of civilization in our own quarter of the globe, which, in respect to the general diffusion and common participation of arts and sciences, may be now considered as one community.

I would exact from every reader the allowance of obscurity, absurdity, barbarous habits, and a perverted morality. Where the reverse appears, I would have him receive it (to use a familiar phrase) as so much clear gain, and allow it a merit proportioned to the disappointment of a different expectation.

In effect, without bespeaking this kind of indulgence, I could hardly venture to persist in my recommendation of this production for public notice [...]

With the deductions, or rather qualifications, which I have thus premised, I hesitate not to pronounce the Geeta a performance of great originality; of a sublimity of conception, reasoning, and diction, almost unequalled; and [with] a single exception, among all the known religions of mankind, of a theology accurately corresponding with that of the Christian dispensation, and most powerfully illustrating its fundamental doctrines.

It will not be fair to try its relative worth by a comparison with the original text of the first standards of European composition; but let these be taken even in the most esteemed of their prose translations; and in that equal scale let their merits be weighed. I should not fear to place, in opposition to the best French versions of the most admired passages of the Iliad or Odyssey, or of the 1st and 6th Books of our own Milton, highly as I venerate the latter, the English translation of the Mahabharat.

One blemish will be found in it, which will scarcely fail to make its own impression on every correct mind; and which for that reason I anticipate. I mean, the attempt to describe spiritual existences by terms and images which appertain to corporeal forms. Yet even in this respect it will appear less faulty than other works with which I have placed it in competition; and, defective as it may at first appear, I know not whether a doctrine so elevated above common perception did not require to be introduced by such ideas as were familiar to the mind, to lead it by a gradual advance to the pure and abstract comprehension of the subject. This will seem to have been, whether intentionally or accidentally, the order which is followed by the author of the Geeta; and so far at least he soars far beyond all competitors in this species of composition [...]

It now remains to say something of the Translator, Mr. Charles Wilkins. This Gentleman, to whose ingenuity, unaided by models for imitation, and by artists for his direction, your government is indebted for its printing-office, and for many official purposes to which it has been profitably applied, with an extent unknown in Europe, has united to an early and successful attainment of the Persian and Bengal languages, the study of the Sanskreet. To this he devoted himself with a perseverance of which there are few examples, and with a success which encouraged him to undertake the translation of the Mahabharat. This book is said to consist of more than one hundred thousand metrical stanzas, of which he has at this time translated more than a third; and, if I may trust to the imperfect tests by which I myself have tried a very small portion of it, through the medium of another language, he has rendered it with great accuracy and fidelity. Of its elegance, and the skill with which he has familiarized (if I may so express it) his own native language to so foreign an original, I may not speak, as from the specimen herewith presented, whoever reads it, will judge for himself.

Mr. Wilkins's health having suffered a decline from the fatigues of business, from which his gratuitous labors allowed him no relaxation, he was advised to try a change of air for his recovery. I myself recommended that of Banaris, for the sake of the additional advantage which he might derive from a residence in a place which is considered as the first seminary of Hindoo learning; and I promoted his application to the Board, for their permission to repair thither, without forfeiting his official appointments during the term of his absence.

I have always regarded the encouragement of every species of useful diligence, in the servants of the Company, as a duty appertaining to my office; and have severely regretted that I have possessed such scanty means of exercising it, especially to such as required an exemption from official attendance; there being few emoluments in this service but such as are annexed to official employment, and few offices without employment. Yet I believe I may take it upon me to pronounce, that the service has at no period more abounded with men of cultivated talents, of capacity for business, and liberal knowledge; qualities which reflect the greater lustre on their possessors, by having been the fruit of long and laboured application, at a season of life, and with a licence of conduct, more apt to produce dissipation than excite the desire of improvement.

Such studies, independently of their utility, tend, especially when the pursuit of them is general, to diffuse a generosity of sentiment, and a disdain of the meaner occupations of such minds as are left nearer to the state of uncultivated nature; and you, Sir, will believe me, when I assure you, that it is on the virtue, not the ability of their servants, that the Company must rely for the permanency of their dominion.

Nor is the cultivation of language and science, for such are the studies to which I allude, useful only in forming the moral character and habits of the service. Every accumulation of knowledge, and especially such as is obtained by social communication with people over whom we exercise a dominion founded on the right of conquest, is useful to the state: it is the gain of humanity: in the specific instance which I have stated, it attracts and conciliates distant affections; it lessens the weight of the chain by which the natives are held in subjection; and it imprints on the hearts of our own countrymen the sense and obligation of benevolence. Even in England, this effect of it is greatly wanting. It is not very long since the inhabitants of India were considered by many, as creatures scarce elevated above the degree of savage life; nor, I fear, is that prejudice yet wholly eradicated, though surely abated. Every instance which brings their real character home to observation will impress us with a more generous sense of feeling for their natural rights, and teach us to estimate them by the measure of our own. But such instances can only be obtained in their writings: and these will survive when the British dominion in India shall have long ceased to exist, and when the sources which it once yielded of wealth and power are lost to remembrance.

If you, Sir, on the perusal of Mr. Wilkins's performance, shall judge it worthy of so honorable a patronage, may I take the further liberty to request that you will be pleased to present it to the Court of Directors, for publication by their authority, and to use your interest to obtain it? Its public reception will be the test of its real merit, and determine Mr. Wilkins in the prosecution or cessation of his present laborious studies. It may, in the first event, clear the way to a wide and unexplored field of fruitful knowledge; and suggest, to the generosity of his honorable employers, a desire to encourage the first persevering adventurer in a service in which his example will have few followers, and most probably none, if it is to be performed with the gratuitous labor of years lost to the provision of future subsistence: for the study of the Sanskreet cannot, like the Persian language, be applied to official profit, and improved with the official exercise of it. It can only derive its reward, beyond the breath of fame, in a fixed endowment. Such has been the fate of his predecessor, Mr. Halhed, whose labors and incomparable genius, in two useful productions, have been crowned with every success that the public estimation could give them; nor will it detract from the no less original merit of Mr. Wilkins, that I ascribe to another the title of having led the way, when I add, that this example held out to him no incitement to emulate it, but the prospect of barren applause. To say more, would be disrespect; and I believe that I address myself to a gentleman who possesses talents congenial with those which I am so anxious to encourage, and a mind too liberal to confine its beneficence to such arts alone as contribute to the immediate and substantial advantages of the state.

I think it proper to assure you, that the subject of this address, and its design, were equally unknown to the person who is the object of it; from whom I originally obtained the translation for another purpose, which on a second revisal of the work I changed, from a belief that it merited a better destination.

A mind rendered susceptible by the daily experience of unmerited reproach, may be excused if it anticipates even unreasonable or improbable objections. This must be my plea for any apparent futility in the following observation. I have seen an extract from a foreign work of great literary credit, in which my name is mentioned, with very undeserved applause, for an attempt to introduce the knowledge of Hindoo literature into the European world, by forcing or corrupting the religious consciences of the Pundits, or professors of their sacred doctrines. This reflexion was produced by the publication of Mr. Halhed's translation of the Poottee, or code of Hindoo laws; and is totally devoid of foundation. For myself I can declare truly, that if the acquisition could not have been obtained but by such means as have been supposed, I should never have sought it. It was contributed both cheerfully and gratuitously, by men of the most respectable characters for sanctity and learning in Bengal, who refused to accept more than the moderate daily subsistence of one rupee each, during the term that they were employed on the compilation; nor will it much redound to my credit, when I add, that they have yet received no other reward for their meritorious labors. Very natural causes may be ascribed for their reluctance to communicate the mysteries of their learning to strangers, as those to whom they have been for some centuries in subjection, never enquired into them, but to turn their religion into derision, or deduce from them arguments to support the intolerant principles of their own. From our nation they have received a different treatment, and are no less eager to impart their knowledge than we are to receive it. I could say much more in proof of this fact, but that it might look too much like self-commendation.

2.2 PREFACE TO SACONTALÁ

Sir William Jones

Source: *Sacontalá; or, The Fatal Ring, An Indian Drama by Cálidás* **(1789), trans. by Sir William Jones, in** *The Works of Sir William Jones,* **2 vols, New York and London: Garland, 1984, I, 365–73.**

In one of the letters which bear the title of EDIFYING, though most of them swarm with ridiculous errours, and all must be consulted with extreme diffidence, I met, some years ago, with the following passage: 'In the north of India there are many books, called Nátac, which, as the Bráhmens assert, contain a large portion of ancient history without any mixture of fable'; and having an eager desire to know the real state of this empire before the conquest of it by the Savages of the North, I was very solicitous, on my arrival in Bengal, to procure access to those books, either by the help of translations, if they had been translated, or by learning the language in which they were originally composed, and which I had yet a stronger inducement to learn from its connection with the administration of justice to the Hindûs; but when I was able to converse with the Bráhmens, they assured me that the Nátacs were not histories, and abounded with fables; that they were extremely popular works, and consisted of conversations in prose and verse, held before ancient Rájás in their publick assemblies, on an infinite variety of subjects, and in various dialects of India: this definition gave me no very distinct idea; but I concluded that they were dialogues on moral or literary topicks; whilst other Europeans, whom I consulted, had understood from the natives that they were discourses on dancing, musick, or poetry. At length a very sensible Bráhmen, named Rádhácánt, who had long been attentive to English manners, removed all my doubts, and gave me no less delight than surprise, by telling me that our nation had compositions of the same sort, which were publickly represented at Calcutta in the cold season, and bore the name, as he had been informed, of plays. Resolving at my leisure to read the best of them, I asked which of their Nátacs was most universally esteemed; and he answered without hesitation, Sacontalá, supporting his opinion, as usual among the Pandits, by a couplet to this effect: 'The ring of Sacontalá, in which the fourth act, and four stanzas of that act, are eminently brilliant, displays all the rich exuberance of Cálidása's genius.' I soon procured a correct copy of it; and, assisted by my teacher Rámalóchan, began with translating it verbally into Latin, which bears so great a resemblance to Sanscrit, that it is more convenient than any modern language for a scrupulous interlineary version: I then turned it word for word into English, and afterwards, without adding or suppressing any material sentence, disengaged it from the stiffness of a foreign idiom, and prepared the faithful translation of the Indian drama, which I now present to the publick as a most pleasing and authentick picture of old Hindû manners, and one of the greatest curiosities that the literature of Asia has yet brought to light.

Dramatick poetry must have been immemorially ancient in the Indian empire: the invention of it is commonly ascribed to Bheret, a sage believed to have been inspired, who invented also a system of musick which bears his name; but this opinion of its origin is rendered very doubtful by the universal belief, that the first Sanscrit verse ever heard by mortals was pronounced in a burst of resentment by the great Válmic, who flourished in the silver age of the world, and was author of an Epick Poem on the war of his contemporary, Ráma, king of Ayódhyà; so that no drama in verse could have been represented before his time; and the Indians have a wild story, that the first regular play, on the same subject with the Rámáyan, was composed by Hanumat or Pávan, who commanded an army of Satyrs or Mountaineers in Ráma's expedition against Lancà: they add, that he engraved it on a smooth rock, which, being dissatisfied with his composition, he hurled into the sea; and that, many years after, a learned prince ordered expert divers to take impressions of the poem on wax, by which means the drama was in great measure restored; and my Pandit assures me that he is in possession of it. By whomsoever or in whatever age this species of entertainment was invented, it is very certain, that it was carried to great perfection in its kind, when Vicramáditya, who reigned in the first century before Christ, gave encouragement to poets, philologers, and mathematicians, at a time when the Britons were as unlettered and unpolished as the army of Hanumat: nine men of genius, commonly called the nine gems, attended his court, and were splendidly supported by his bounty; and

Cálidás is unanimously allowed to have been the brightest of them. – A modern epigram was lately repeated to me, which does so much honour to the author of Sacontalá, that I cannot forbear exhibiting a literal version of it:

> Poetry was the sportful daughter of Válmic, and, having been educated by Vyása, she chose Cálidás for her bridegroom after the manner of Viderbha: she was the mother of Amara, Sundar, Sanc'ha, Dhanic; but now, old and decrepit, her beauty faded, and her unadorned feet slipping as she walks, in whose cottage does she disdain to take shelter?

All the other works of our illustrious poet, the Shakespeare of India, that have yet come to my knowledge, are a second play, in five acts, entitled Urvasí; an heroic poem, or rather a series of poems in one book, on the Children of the Sun; another, with perfect unity of action, on the Birth of Cumára, god of war; two or three love tales in verse; and an excellent little work on Sanscrit Metre, precisely in the manner of Terentianus; but he is believed by some to have revised the works of Válmic and Vyása, and to have corrected the perfect editions of them which are now current: this at least is admitted by all, that he stands next in reputation to those venerable bards; and we must regret, that he has left only two dramatick poems, especially as the stories in his Raghuvansa would have supplied him with a number of excellent subjects. – Some of his contemporaries, and other Hindû poets even to our own times, have composed so many tragedies, comedies, farces, and musical pieces, that the Indian theatre would fill as many volumes as that of any nation in ancient or modern Europe: all the Pandits assert that their plays are innumerable; and, on my first inquiries concerning them, I had notice of more than thirty, which they consider as the flower of their Nátacs, among which the Malignant Child, the Rape of Ushá, the Taming of Durvásas, the Seizure of the Lock, Málati and Mádhava, with five or six dramas on the adventures of their incarnate gods, are the most admired after those of Cálidás. They are all in verse, where the dialogue is elevated; and in prose, where it is familiar: the men of rank and learning are represented speaking pure Sanscrit, and the women Prácrit, which is little more than the language of the Bráhmens melted down by a delicate articulation to the softness of Italian; while the low persons of the drama speak the vulgar dialects of the several provinces which they are supposed to inhabit.

The play of Sacontalá must have been very popular when it was first represented; for the Indian empire was then in full vigour, and the national vanity must have been highly flattered by the magnificent introduction of those kings and heroes in whom the Hindûs gloried; the scenery must have been splendid and beautiful; and there is good reason to believe, that the court at Avanti was equal in brilliancy during the reign of Vicramáditya, to that of any monarch in any age or country. – Dushmanta, the hero of the piece, appears in the chronological tables of the Bráhmens among the Children of the Moon, and in the twenty-first generation after the flood; so that, if we can at all rely on the chronology of the Hindûs, he was nearly contemporary with Obed, or Jesse; and Puru, his most celebrated ancestor, was the fifth in descent from Budha, or Mercury, who married, they say, a daughter of the pious king, whom Vishnu preserved in an ark from the universal deluge: his eldest son Bheret was the illustrious progenitor of Curu, from whom Pándu was lineally descended, and in whose family the Indian Apollo became incarnate; whence the poem, next in fame to the Rámáyan, is called Mahábhárat.

As to the machinery of the drama, it is taken from the system of mythology, which prevails to this day, and which it would require a large volume to explain; but we cannot help remarking, that the deities introduced in the Fatal Ring are clearly allegorical personages. Maríchi, the first production of Brahmá, or the Creative Power, signifies light, that subtil fluid which was created before its reservoir, the sun, as water was created before the sea; Casyapa, the offspring of Maríchi, seems to be a personification of infinite space, comprehending innumerable worlds; and his children by Aditi, or his active power (unless Aditi mean the primeval day, and Diti, his other wife, the night), are Indra, or the visible firmament, and the twelve Adityas, or suns, presiding over as many months.

On the characters and conduct of the play I shall offer no criticism; because I am convinced that the tastes of men differ as much as their sentiments and passions, and that, in feeling the beauties of art, as in smelling flowers, tasting fruits, viewing prospects, and hearing melody, every individual must be guided by his own sensations and the incommunicable associ- ations of his own ideas. This only I may add, that if Sacontalá should ever be acted in India, where alone it could be acted with perfect knowledge of Indian dresses, manners, and scenery, the piece might easily be reduced to five acts of a moderate length, by throwing the third act into the second, and the sixth into the fifth; for it must be confessed that the whole of Dushmanta's conversation with his buffoon, and great part of his courtship in the hermitage, might be omitted without any injury to the drama.

It is my anxious wish that others may take the pains to learn Sanscrit, and may be persuaded to translate the works of Cálidás: I shall hardly again employ my leisure in a task so foreign to my professional (which are, in truth, my favourite) studies; and have no intention of translating any other book from any language, except the Law Tract of Menu, and the new Digest of Indian and Arabian laws; but, to show, that the Bráhmens, at least, do not think polite literature incompatible with jurisprudence, I cannot avoid mentioning, that the venerable compiler of the Hindû Digest, who is now in his eighty-sixth year, has the whole play of Sacontalá by heart; as he proved when I last conversed with him, to my entire conviction. Lest, however, I should hereafter seem to have changed a resolution which I mean to keep inviolate, I think it proper to say, that I have already translated four or five other books, and among them the Hitópadésa, which I under- took, merely as an exercise in learning Sanscrit, three years before I knew that Mr. Wilkins, without whose aid I should never have learnt it, had any thought of giving the same work to the publick.[1]

2.3 ON THE ORIGIN AND FAMILIES OF NATIONS

Sir William Jones

Source: Sir William Jones, 'Discourse the Ninth: On the Origin and Families of Nations', in *The Works of Sir William Jones*, 2 vols, New York and London: Garland, 1984, II, 185–204.

[This discourse was delivered to the Asiatic Society of Bengal, 23 February 1792.]

You have attended, gentlemen, with so much indulgence to my discourses on the five *Asiatick* nations, and on the various tribes established along their several borders or interspersed over their mountains, that I cannot but flatter myself with an assurance of being heard with equal attention, while I trace to one centre the three great families, from which those nations appear to have proceeded, and then hazard a few conjectures on the different courses, which they may be supposed to have taken toward the countries, in which we find them settled at the dawn of all genuine history.

Let us begin with a short review of the propositions, to which we have gradually been led, and separate such as are morally certain, from such as are only probable: that the first race of *Persians* and *Indians*, to whom we may add the *Romans* and *Greeks*, the *Goths*, and the old *Egyptians* or *Ethiops*, originally spoke the same language and professed the same popular faith, is capable, in my humble opinion, of incontestable proof; that the *Jews* and *Arabs*, the *Assyrians*, or second *Persian* race, the people who spoke *Syriack*, and a numerous tribe of *Abyssinians*, used one primitive dialect wholly distinct from the idiom just mentioned, is, I believe, undisputed, and, I am sure, indisputable; but that the settlers in *China* and *Japan* had a common origin with the *Hindus*, is no more than highly probable; and, that all the *Tartars*, as they are inaccurately called, were primarily of a third separate branch, totally differing from the two others in language, manners, and features, may indeed be plausibly conjectured, but cannot, for the reasons alledged in a former essay, be perspicuously shown, and for the present therefore must be merely assumed. Could these facts be verified by the best attainable evidence, it would not, I presume, be doubted, that the whole earth was peopled by a variety of shoots from the *Indian, Arabian,* and *Tartarian* branches, or by such intermixtures of them, as, in a course of ages, might naturally have happened.

[1] The 'Mr. Wilkins' mentioned here is Charles Wilkins, who translated *The Bhagavad-Gita*, for which Warren Hastings wrote a preface.

Now I admit without hesitation the aphorism of LINNAEUS, that 'in the beginning GOD created one pair only of every living species, which has a diversity of sex'; but, since that incomparable naturalist argues principally from the wonderful diffusion of vegetables, and from an hypothesis, that the water on this globe has been continually subsiding, I venture to produce a shorter and closer argument in support of his doctrine. That *Nature*, of which simplicity appears a distinguishing attribute, *does nothing in vain*, is a maxim in philosophy; and against those, who deny maxims, we cannot dispute; but *it is vain* and superfluous *to do by many means what may be done by fewer*, and this is another axiom received into courts of judicature from the schools of philosophers: *we must not*, therefore, says our great NEWTON, *admit more causes of natural things, than those, which are true, and sufficiently account for natural phenomena*; but it is true, that one pair *at least* of every living species must at first have been created; and that one human pair was sufficient for the population of our globe in a period of no considerable length (on the very moderate supposition of lawyers and political arithmeticians, that every pair of ancestors left on an average two children, and each of them two more), is evident from the rapid increase of numbers in geometrical progression, so well known to those, who have ever taken the trouble to sum a series of as many terms, as they suppose generations of men in two or three thousand years. It follows, that the Author of Nature (for all nature proclaims its divine author) created but one pair of our species; yet, had it not been (among other reasons) for the devastations, which history has recorded, of water and fire, wars, famine, and pestilence, this earth would not now have had room for its multiplied inhabitants. If the human race then be, as we may confidently assume, of one natural species, they must all have proceeded from one pair; and if perfect justice be, as it is most indubitably, an essential attribute of GOD, that pair must have been gifted with sufficient wisdom and strength to be virtuous, and, as far as their nature admitted, happy, but intrusted with freedom of will to be vicious and consequently degraded: whatever might be their option, they must people in time the region where they first were established, and their numerous descendants must necessarily seek new countries, as inclination might prompt, or accident lead, them; they would of course migrate in separate families and clans, which, forgetting by degrees the language of their common progenitor, would form new dialects to convey new ideas, both simple and complex; natural affection would unite them at first, and a sense of reciprocal utility, the great and only cement of social union in the absence of publick honour and justice, for which in evil times it is a general substitute, would combine them at length in communities more or less regular; laws would be proposed by a part of each community, but enacted by the whole; and governments would be variously arranged for the happiness or misery of the governed, according to their own virtue and wisdom, or depravity and folly; so that, in less than three thousand years, the world would exhibit the same appearances, which we may actually observe on it in the age of the great *Arabian* impostor.

On that part of it, to which our united researches are generally confined, we see *five* races of men peculiarly distinguished, in the time of MUHAMMED, for their multitude and extent of dominion; but we have reduced them to *three*, because we can discover no more, that essentially differ in language, religion, manners, and other known characteristicks: now those three races, how variously soever they may at present be dispersed and intermixed, must (if the preceding conclusions be justly drawn) have migrated originally from a central country, to find which is the problem proposed for solution. Suppose it solved; and give any arbitrary name to that centre: let it, if you please, be *Iràn*. The three primitive languages, therefore, must at first have been concentrated in *Iràn*, and there only in fact we see traces of them in the earliest historical age; but, for the sake of greater precision, conceive the whole empire of *Iràn*, with all its mountains and valleys, plains and rivers, to be every way infinitely diminished; the first winding courses, therefore, of all the nations proceeding from it by land, and nearly at the same time, will be [...] without intersections, because those courses could not have thwarted and crossed one another: if then you consider the seats of all the migrating nations as points in a surrounding figure, you will perceive, that the several rays, diverging from *Iràn*, may be drawn to them without any intersection; but this will not happen, if you assume as a centre *Arabia*, or *Egypt*; *India*, *Tartary*, or *China*: it follows, that *Iràn*, or *Persia* (I contend for *the meaning, not the name*), was the central country, which we sought. This mode of reasoning I have adopted not from any affectation (as you will do me the justice to believe) of a scientifick diction, but for the sake of conciseness and variety, and from a wish to avoid repetitions; the substance of my argument having been detailed in a different form at the close of another discourse; nor does the argument in any form rise to demonstration, which the question by no means admits: it amounts, however, to such a proof, grounded on written evidence and credible testimony, as all mankind hold sufficient for decisions affecting property, freedom, and life.

Thus then have we proved, that the inhabitants of *Asia*, and consequently, as it might be proved, of the whole earth, sprang from three branches of one stem: and that those branches have shot into their present state of luxuriance in a period comparatively short, is apparent from a fact universally acknowledged, that we find no certain monument, or even probable tradition, of nations planted, empires and states raised, laws enacted, cities built, navigation improved, commerce encouraged, arts invented, or letters contrived, above twelve or at most fifteen or sixteen centuries before the birth of CHRIST, and from another fact, which cannot be controverted, that seven hundred or a thousand years would have been fully adequate to the supposed propagation, diffusion and establishment of the human race.

The most ancient history of that race, and the oldest composition perhaps in the world, is a work in *Hebrew*, which we may suppose at first, for the sake of our argument, to have no higher authority than any other work of equal antiquity, that the researches of the curious had accidentally brought to light: it is ascribed to MUSAH; for so he writes his own name, which, after the *Greeks* and *Romans*, we have changed into MOSES; and, though it was manifestly his object to give an historical account of a single family, he has introduced it with a short view of the primitive world, and his introduction has been divided, perhaps improperly, into *eleven* chapters. After describing with awful sublimity the creation of this universe, he asserts, that one pair of every animal species was called from nothing into existence; that the human pair were strong enough to be happy, but free to be miserable; that, from delusion and temerity, they disobeyed their supreme benefactor, whose goodness could not pardon them consistently with his justice; and that they received a punishment adequate to their disobedience, but softened by a mysterious promise to be accomplished in their descendants. We cannot but believe, on the supposition just made of a history uninspired, that these facts were delivered by tradition from the first pair, and related by MOSES in a figurative style; not in that sort of allegory, which rhetoricians describe as a mere assemblage of metaphors, but in the symbolical mode of writing adopted by eastern sages, to embellish and dignify historical truth; and, if this were a time for such illustrations, we might produce the same account of the *creation* and the *fall*, expressed by symbols very nearly similar, from the *Puránas* themselves, and even from the *Vèda*, which appears to stand next in antiquity to the five books of MOSES [...]

Three sons of the just and virtuous man, whose lineage was preserved from the general inundation, travelled, we are told, as they began to multiply, in *three* large divisions variously subdivided: the children of YA'FET seem, from the traces of *Sklavonian* names, and the mention of their being *enlarged*, to have spread themselves far and wide, and to have produced the race, which, for want of a correct appellation, we call *Tartarian*; the colonies, formed by the sons of HAM and SHEM, appear to have been nearly simultaneous; and, among those of the latter branch, we find so many names incontestably preserved at this hour in *Arabia*, that we cannot hesitate in pronouncing them the same people, whom hitherto we have denominated *Arabs*; while the former branch, the most powerful and adventurous of whom were the progeny of CUSH, MISR, and RAMA (names remaining unchanged in *Sanscrit*, and highly revered by the *Hindus*), were, in all probability, the race, which I call *Indian*, and to which we may now give any other name, that may seem more proper and comprehensive.

The general introduction to the *Jewish* history closes with a very concise and obscure account of a presumptuous and mad attempt, by a particular colony, to build a splendid city and raise a fabrick of immense height, independently of the divine aid, and, it should seem, in defiance of the divine power; a project, which was baffled by means appearing at first view inadequate to the purpose, but ending in violent dissention among the projectors, and in the ultimate separation of them: this event also seems to be recorded by the ancient *Hindus* in two of their *Puránas*; and it will be proved, I trust, on some future occasion, that *the lion bursting from a pillar to destroy a blaspheming giant*, and *the dwarf, who beguiled and held in derision* the magnificent BELI, are one and the same story related in a symbolical style.

Now these primeval events are described as having happened between the *Oxus* and *Euphrates*, the mountains of *Caucasus* and the borders of *India*, that is, within the limits of *Iràn*; for, though most of the *Mosaick* names have been considerably altered, yet numbers of them remain unchanged: we still find *Harrán* in *Mesopotamia*, and travellers appear unanimous in fixing the site of ancient *Babel*.

Thus, on the preceding supposition, that the first eleven chapters of the book, which it is thought proper to call *Genesis*, are merely a preface to the oldest civil history now extant, we see the truth of them confirmed by antecedent reasoning, and by evidence in part highly probable, and in part certain; but the *connection* of the *Mosaick* history with that of the Gospel by a chain of sublime predictions unquestionably ancient, and apparently fulfilled, must induce us to think the *Hebrew* narrative more than human in its origin, and consequently true in every substantial part of it, though possibly expressed in figurative language; as many learned and pious men have believed, and as the most pious may believe without injury, and perhaps with advantage, to the cause of revealed religion. If MOSES then was endued with supernatural knowledge, it is no longer probable only, but absolutely certain, that the whole race of man proceeded from *Iràn*, as from a centre, whence they migrated at first in three great colonies; and that those three branches grew from a common stock, which had been miraculously preserved in a general convulsion and inundation of this globe [...]

From the testimonies adduced in the six last annual discourses, and from the additional proofs laid before you, or rather opened, on the present occasion, it seems to follow, that the only human family after the flood established themselves in the northern parts of *Iràn*; that, as they multiplied, they were divided into three distinct branches, each retaining little at first, and losing the whole by degrees, of their common primary language, but agreeing severally on new expressions for new ideas; that the branch of YA'FET was *enlarged* in many scattered shoots over the north of *Europe* and *Asia*, diffusing themselves as far as the western and eastern seas, and, at length in the infancy of navigation, beyond them both: that they cultivated no liberal arts, and had no use of letters, but formed a variety of dialects, as their tribes were variously ramified; that, secondly, the children of HAM, who founded in *Iràn* itself the monarchy of the first *Chaldeans*, invented letters, observed and named the luminaries of the firmament, calculated the known *Indian* period of *four hundred and thirty-two thousand years*, or an *hundred and twenty* repetitions of the *saros* [or 3,600-year cycle], and contrived the old system of Mythology, partly allegorical, and partly grounded on idolatrous veneration for their sages and lawgivers; that they were dispersed at various intervals and in various colonies over land and ocean; that the tribes of MISR, CUSH, and RAMA settled in *Africk* and *India*; while some of them, having improved the art of sailing, passed from *Egypt, Phenice,* and *Phrygia,* into *Italy* and *Greece,* which they found thinly peopled by former emigrants, of whom they supplanted some tribes, and united themselves with others; whilst a swarm from the same hive moved by a northerly course into *Scandinavia,* and another, by the head of the *Oxus,* and through the passes of *Imaus,* into *Cashghar* and *Eighúr, Khatá* and *Khoten,* as far as the territories of *Chin* and *Tancút,* where letters have been used and arts immemorially cultivated; nor is it unreasonable to believe, that some of them found their way from the eastern isles into *Mexico* and *Peru,* where traces were discovered of rude literature and Mythology analogous to those of *Egypt* and *India*; that, thirdly, the old *Chaldean* empire being overthrown by the *Assyrians* under CAYUMERS, other migrations took place, especially into *India,* while the rest of SHEM'S progeny, some of whom had before settled on the Red Sea, peopled the whole *Arabian* peninsula, pressing close on the nations of *Syria* and *Phenice*; that, lastly, from all the three families were detached many bold adventurers of an ardent spirit and a roving disposition, who disdained subordination and wandered in separate clans, till they settled in distant isles or in deserts and mountainous regions; that, on the whole, some colonies might have migrated before the death of their venerable progenitor, but that states and empires could scarce have assumed a regular form, till fifteen or sixteen hundred years before the *Christian* epoch, and that, for the first thousand years of that period, we have no history unmixed with fable, except that of the turbulent and variable, but eminently distinguished, nation descended from ABRAHAM.

My design, gentlemen, of tracing the origin and progress of the five principal nations, who have peopled *Asia,* and of whom there were considerable remains in their several countries at the time of MUHAMMED'S birth, is now accomplished; succinctly, from the nature of these essays; imperfectly, from the darkness of the subject and scantiness of my materials, but clearly and comprehensively enough to form a basis for subsequent researches: you have seen, as distinctly as I am able to show, *who* those nations originally were, *whence* and *when* they moved toward their final stations; and, in my future annual discourses, I propose to enlarge on the *particular advantages* to our country and to mankind, which may result from our sedulous and united inquiries into the history, science, and arts, of these *Asiatick* regions, especially of the *British* dominions in *India,* which we may consider as the centre (not of the human race, but) of our common exertions to promote its true interests; and we shall concur, I trust, in opinion, that the race of man, to advance whose manly happiness is our duty and will of course be our endeavour, cannot long be happy without virtue, nor actively virtuous without freedom, nor securely free without rational knowledge.

2.4 INDIAN POETRY IN ENGLISH

Source: *The Golden Treasury of Indo-Anglian Poetry*, ed. by Vinayak Krishna Gokak, Delhi: Sahitya Akademi, 1992, pp.53–6, 61–7.

Henry L.V. Derozio

To the Pupils of the Hindu College

Expanding like the petals [of] young flowers
I watch the gentle opening of your minds,
And the sweet loosening of the spell that binds
Your intellectual energies and powers
That stretch (like young birds in soft summer hours)
Their wings to try their strength. O how the winds
Of circumstances and freshening April showers
Of early knowledge and unnumbered kinds
Of new perceptions shed their influence,
And how you worship truth's omnipotence!
What joyance rains upon me when I see
Fame in the mirror of futurity,
Weaving the chaplets you have yet to gain,
Ah then I feel I have not lived in vain.

The Harp of India

Why hang'st thou lonely on yon withered bough?
Unstrung for ever, must thou there remain;
Thy music once was sweet – who hears it now?
Why doth the breeze sigh over thee in vain?
Silence hath bound thee with her fatal chain;
Neglected, mute, and desolate art thou,
Like ruined monument on desert plain:
O! many a hand more worthy far than mine
Once thy harmonious chords to sweetness gave,
And many a wreath for them did Fame entwine
Of flowers still blooming on the minstrel's grave:
Those hands are cold – but if thy notes divine
May be by mortal wakened once again,
Harp of my country, let me strike the strain!

Chorus of Brahmins, from *The Fakeer of Jungheera*

Scatter, scatter flowerets round,
Let the tinkling cymbal sound;
Strew the scented orient spice,
Prelude to the sacrifice;
Bring the balm, and bring the myrrh,
 Sweet as is the breath of her
Who upon the funeral pyre
Shall, ere Surya sets, expire.

Let pure incense to the skies
Like the heart's warm wishes rise,
Till, unto the lotus throne
Of the great Eternal One
High ascending, it may please
Him who guides our destinies.
Bring the pearl of purest white,
Bring the diamond flashing light;
Bring your gifts of choicest things,
Fans of peacocks, starry wings'
Gold refined, and ivory,
Branches of the sandal tree,
Which their fragrance still impart
Like the good man's injured heart,
This its triumph, this its boast,
Sweetest 'tis when wounded most!
Ere he sets, the golden sun
Must with richest gift be won,
Ere his glorious brow he lave
In yon sacred yellow wave,
Rising through the realms of air
He must hear the widow's prayer. –
Haste ye, haste, the day declines
Onward, onward while he shines,
Let us press, and all shall see
Glory of our Deity.

Song of the Hindustanee Minstrel

I

With surmah[2] [line] the black eye's fringe,
 'Twill sparkle like a star;
With roses dress each raven tress,
 My only loved Dildar!

II

Dildar! There's many a valued pearl
 In richest Oman's sea;
But none, my fair Cashmerian girl!
 O! none can rival thee.

III

In Busrah there is many a rose
 Which many a maid may seek,
But who shall find a flower which blows
 Like that upon thy cheek?

[2] The custom of blackening the eyelashes in oriental nations is now well-known. In Hindoostan, Kajal, or lampblack, is generally used. Surmah is crude antimony, and more in vogue among the Georgians and Circassians, as well as among the natives of Lahore, Cabul and Cashmere.

IV

In verdant realms, 'neath sunny skies,
  With witching minstrelsy,
We'll favour find in all young eyes,
  And all shall welcome thee.

V

Around us now there's but the night,
  The heaven alone above;
But soon we'll dwell in cities bright,
  Then cheer thee, cheer thee, love!

VI

The heart eternally is blest
  Where hope eternal springs;
Then hush thy sorrows all to rest,
  We'll treat the courts of kings.

VII

In palace halls our strains we'll raise,
  There all our songs shall flow;
Come cheer thee, sweet! for better days
  Shall down upon our woe.

VIII

Nay weep not, love! thou shouldst not weep,
  The world is all our home;
Life's watch together we shall keep,
  We'll love where'er we roam.

IX

Like birds from land to land we'll range,
  And with our sweet sitar,[3]
Our hearts the same, though worlds may change,
  We'll live, and love, Dildar!

Michael Madhusudan Dutt

Satan

A form of awe he was – and yet it seemed
A sepulchre of beauty – faded, gone,
Mouldering where memory, fond mourner, keeps
Her lonesome vigils sad – to chronicle
The Past – and tell its tale of coming years.
Or like a giant tree in mighty war
With storm on whirlwind car and fierce array
Blasted and crushed – of all its pride bereft.

[3] A stringed musical instrument.

Or like a barque which oft had walked the deep
In queenlike majesty – and proudly brave –
But by the fiery hand of some dread fiend
Nursed in starless caves of ocean, shorn
Of all its beauty in the boundless surge
A phantom of departed splendour lone.

The Queen of Delhi's Dream, from *The Captive Ladie*

The following tale is founded on a circumstance pretty generally known in India, and, if I mistake not, noticed by some European writers. A little before the famous Indian expedition of Mahmud Ghuzni, the King of Kanauj celebrated the 'Raj-shooio Jugum' or, as I have translated it in the text, the 'Feast of Victory'. Almost all the contemporary Princes, being unable to resist his power, attended it, with the exception of the King of Delhi, who, being a lineal descendant of the great Pandu Princes – the heroes of the far-famed Mahabharat of Vyasa – refused to sanction by his presence the assumption of a dignity – for the celebration of this Festival was an universal assertion of claims to being considered as the lord paramount over the whole country – which by right of descent belonged to his family alone. The King of Kanauj, highly incensed at this refusal, has an image of gold made to represent the absent chief. On the last day of the Feast, the King of Delhi, having, with a few chosen followers, entered the palace in disguise, carried off this image, together, as some say, with one of the Princesses Royal whose hand he had once solicited but in vain, owing to his obstinate maintenance of the rights of his ancient house. The fair Princess, however, was retaken and sent to a solitary castle to be out of the way of the pugnacious lover, who eventually effected her escape in the disguise of a Bhat or Indian Troubadour. The King of Kanauj never forgave this insult, and, when Mahmud invaded the Kingdom of Delhi, sternly refused to aid his son-in-law in expelling a foe, who soon after crushed him also. I have slightly deviated from the above story in representing my heroine as sent to confinement before the celebration of the 'Feast of Victory'. The queen of Delhi burnt herself on the funeral pyre with her dead husband. The dream mentioned in the following presages the disaster.

Methought there came a warrior-maid,
With blood-stain'd brow and sheathless blade;
Dark was her hue, as darkest cloud,
Which comes the Moon's fair face to shroud,
And 'round her waist a hideous zone
Of hands with charnel lightnings shone,
And long the garland which she wore
Of heads all bath'd in streaming gore:
How fierce the eyes by Death unseal'd,
And blasting gleams which they reveal'd.
I shudder'd – tho' I knew 'twas she,
The awful, ruthless Deity,
On whose dread altar like a flood,
There flows for aye her victim's blood!

I shudder'd – for, methought, she came,
With eyes of bright consuming flame,
'Daughter,' – she said, – 'farewell! – I go:
'The time is come, – it must be so:
'Leave thee and thine I will to-night,' –
Then vanish'd like a flash of light!
Again I dreamt: – I saw a pyre
Blaze high with fiercely gleaming fire;
And one there came, – a warrior he, –
Tho' faint, yet bold, – undauntedly,
And plung'd – oh! God! into the flame
Which like a hungry monster rose,
And circl'd round his quivering frame,
A hideous curtain waving close!
I shriek'd – but, tell me why that start,
And paler brow and heaving heart?
Oh! tell me, hath my royal sire
Forgot his deep and ruthless ire,
And come and crush'd our foe-men dire?

King Porus – A Legend of Old

'I shall never look upon his like again'– *Shakespeare*

'When shall such a hero live again?' – *Byron*

I

Loudly the midnight tempest sang,
Ah! it was thy dirge, fair Liberty!
And clouds in thundering accents roar'd
Unheeded warning from on high;
The rain in darksome torrents fell,
Hydaspes' waves did onward sweep,
Like fiery Passion's headlong flow,
To meet th' awaken'd calling deep;
The lightning flashed bright – dazzling, like
Fair woman's glance from 'neath her veil;
And on the heaving, troubled air,
There was a moaning sound of wail!
But, Ind! Thy unsuspecting sons
Did heedless slumber, – while the foe
Came in stealthy step of death, –
Came as the tiger, noiseless, slow,
To close at once its victim's breath!
Alas! they knew not 'midst this gloom,
This war of elements, was nurst, –
Like to an earthquake in the womb
Of a volcano, – deep and low –
A deadlier storm – on them to burst!

II

'Twas morn; the Lord of Day
From gold Sumero's palace bright,
Look'd on his own sweet clime,
But, lo! the glorious flag,
To which the world in awe once bow'd,
There in defiance waved
On India's gales – triumphant – proud! –
Then, rose the dreadful yell, –
Then lion-like, each warrior brave
Rushed on the coming foe,
To strike for freedom – or the grave!
Oh Death! upon thy glory altar
What blood-libations freely flow'd!
Oh Earth! on that bright morn, what thousands
Rendered to thee the dust they ow'd!
But 'fore the Macedonians driven,
Fell India's hardy sons, –
Proud mountain oaks by thunders riven, –
That for their country's freedom bled –
And made on gore their glorious bed!

III

But dauntlessly there stood
King Porus, towering 'midst the foe,
Like a Himala-peak
With its eternal crown of snow:
And on his brow did shine
The jewell'd regal diadem.
His milk-white elephant
Was deck'd with many a brilliant gem.
He reck'd not of the phalanx
That 'round him closed – but nobly fought,
And like the angry winds that blow
And lofty mountain pines lay low,
Amidst them dreadful havoc wrought,
And thinn'd his crown and country's foe!
The hardiest warriors, at his deeds,
Awe-struck quail'd like wind-shaken reeds:
They dared not look upon his face.
They shrank before his burning gaze,
For in his eye the hero shone
That feared not death: – but high – alone –
A being as if of lightning made,
That scorch'd all that is gazed upon –
Trampling the living with the dead.

IV

Th' immortal Thund'rer's son,
Astonish'd eyed the heroic king;
He saw him bravely charge

Like his dread father, – fulmining: –
Tho' thousands 'round him clos'd,
He stood – as stands the ocean rock
Amidst the lashing billows,
Unmoved at their fierce thundering shock
But when th' Emathian conqueror
Saw that with gaping wounds he bled,
'Desist – desist!' – he cried –
'Such noble blood should not be shed!'
Then a herald was sent
Where bleeding and faint,
Stood, 'midst the dying and the dead,
King Porus, – boldly, undismayed:
'Hail, brave and warlike prince!
Thy gen'rous rival bids thee cease –
Behold! there flies the flag,
That lulls dread war, and wakens peace!'

*   *   *   *

V

Like to a lion chain'd,
That tho' faint – bleeding – stands in pride –
With eyes, where unsubdued
Yet flash'd the fire – looks that defied;
King Porus boldly went
Where 'midst the gay and glittering crowd
Sat god-like Alexander;
While 'round, Earth's mightiest monarchs bow'd.
King Porus was no slave;
He stooped not – bent not there his knee, –
But stood, as stands an oak,
In Himalayan majesty.
'How should I treat thee?' ask'd
The mighty king of Macedon:
'Ev'n as a King,' replied
In royal pride, Ind's haughty son,
The conq'ror pleas'd,
Him forth releas'd:
Thus India's crown was lost and won.

VI

But where, oh! where is Porus now?
And where the noble hearts that bled
For freedom – with the heroic glow
In patriot bosoms nourished –
– Hearts, eagle-like that recked not death,
But shrank before foul Thraldom's breath?
And where art thou – Fair Freedom! – thou
Once goddess of Ind's sunny clime!
When glory's halo round her brow
Shone radiant, and she rose sublime,

Like her own towering Himalye
To kiss the blue clouds thron'd on high!
Clime of the sun! – how like a dream –
How like bright sun-beams on a stream
That melt beneath gray twilight's eye –
That glory hath now flitted by!
The crown that once did deck thy brow
It's trampled down – and thou sunk low:
Thy pearl, thy diamond and thy mine
Of glistening gold no more is thine.
Alas! – each conquering tyrant's lust
Has robb'd thee of thy very dust!
Thou standest like a lofty tree
Shorn of fruits – blossoms – leaves and all –
Of every gale the sport to be,
Despised and scorned e'en in thy fall!

2.5 ON EDUCATION IN INDIA

Raja Rammohan Roy

Source: Raja Rammohan Roy, 'Address To His Excellency The Right Honourable William Pitt, Lord Amherst' (1823), in *The Essential Writings of Raja Rammohan Ray* [sic], ed. by Bruce Carlisle Robertson, Delhi: Oxford University Press, 1999, pp.260–63.

My lord,

Humbly reluctant as the natives of India are to obtrude upon the notice of the Government the sentiments they entertain on any public measure, there are circumstances when silence would be carrying this respectful feeling to culpable excess. The present Rulers of India, coming from a distance of many thousand miles to govern a people whose language, literature, manners, customs, and ideas are almost entirely new and strange to them, cannot easily become so intimately acquainted with their real circumstances, as the natives of the country are themselves. We would therefore be guilty of a gross dereliction of duty to ourselves, and afford our Rulers just ground of complaint at our apathy, did we omit on occasions of importance like the present to supply them with such accurate information as might enable them to devise and adopt measures calculated to be beneficial to the country, and thus second by our local knowledge and experience their declared benevolent intentions for its improvement.

The establishment of a new Sangscrit School in Calcutta evinces the laudable desire of Government to improve the Natives of India by Education, a blessing for which they must ever be grateful; and every well wisher of the human race must be desirous that the efforts made to promote it should be guided by the most enlightened principles, so that the stream of intelligence may flow into the most useful channels.

When this Seminary of learning was proposed, we understood that the Government in England had ordered a considerable sum of money to be annually devoted to the instruction of its Indian subjects. We were filled with sanguine hopes that this sum would be laid out in employing European Gentlemen of talents and education to instruct the natives of India in Mathematics, Natural Philosophy, Chemistry, Anatomy and other useful Sciences, which the Nations of Europe have carried to a degree of perfection that has raised them above the inhabitants of other parts of the world.

While we looked forward with pleasing hope to the dawn of knowledge thus promised to the rising generation, our hearts were filled with mingled feeling of delight and gratitude; we already offered up thanks to Providence for inspiring the most generous and enlightened of the Nations of the West with the glorious ambitions of planting in Asia the Arts and Sciences of modern Europe.

We now find that the Government are establishing a Sangscrit school under Hindoo Pundits to impart such knowledge as is already current in India. This seminary (similar in character to those which existed in Europe before the time of Lord Bacon) can be expected to load the minds of youth with grammatical niceties and metaphysical distinctions of little or no practicable use to the possessors or to society. The pupils will there acquire what was known two thousand years ago, with the addition of vain and empty subtleties since produced by speculative men, such as is already commonly taught in all parts of India.

The Sangscrit language, so difficult that almost a life time is necessary for its perfect acquisition, is well known to have been for ages a lamentable check on the diffusion of knowledge; and the learning concealed under this almost impervious veil is far from sufficient to reward the labour of acquiring it. But if it were thought necessary to perpetuate this language for the sake of the portion of the valuable information it contains, this might be much more easily accomplished by other means than the establishment of a new Sangscrit College; for there have been always and are now numerous professors of Sangscrit in the different parts of the country engaged in teaching this language as well as the other branches of literature, which are to be the object of the new Seminary. Therefore their more diligent cultivation, if desirable, would be effectually promoted by holding out premiums and granting certain allowances to those eminent Professors, who have already undertaken on their own account to teach them and would by such rewards be stimulated to still greater exertions.

From these considerations, as the sum set apart for the instruction of the Natives of India was intended by the Government of England, for the improvement of its Indian subjects, I beg leave to state, with due deference to your Lordship's exalted situation, that if the plan now adopted be followed, it will completely defeat the object proposed; since no improvement can be expected from inducing young men to consume a dozen of years of the most valuable period of their lives in acquiring the niceties of the Byakurun of Sangscrit Grammar. For instance, in learning to discuss such points as the following: Khad signifying to eat, Khaduti, he or she or it eats. Query, whether does the word Khaduti taken as a whole, convey the meaning he, she, or it eats or are separate parts of this meaning conveyed by distinct portions of the word? As if in the English language it were asked, how much meaning is there in the eat, how much in the S? and is the whole meaning of the word conveyed by those two portions of it distinctly, or by them taken jointly?

Neither can such improvement arise from such speculations as the following, which are the themes suggested by the Vedant: In what manner is the soul absorbed into the deity? What relation does it bear to the divine essence? Nor will youths fitted to be better members of society by the Vedantic doctrines which teach them to believe that all visible things have no real existence; that as father, brother, etc. have no actual entirety, they consequently deserve no real affection and therefore the sooner we escape from them and leave the world the better – Again no essential benefit can be derived by the student of the *Meemangsa* from knowing what it is that makes the killer of a goat sinless on pronouncing certain passages of the *Veds*, and what is the real nature and operative influence of passages of *Ved* etc.

Again the student of Nyaya Shastra cannot be said to have improved his mind after he has learned into how many ideal classes the objects in the Universe are divided, and what speculative relation the soul bears to the body, the body to the soul, the eye to the ear etc.

In order to enable your Lordship to appreciate the utility of encouraging such imaginary learning as above characterised, I beg your Lordship will be pleased to compare the state of Science and literature in Europe before the time of Lord Bacon with the progress of knowledge made since he wrote.

If it had been intended to keep the British nation in ignorance of real knowledge the Baconian philosophy would not have been allowed to displace the system of the schoolmen, which was the best calculated to perpetuate ignorance. In the same manner the Sangscrit system of education would be best calculated to keep this country in darkness if such had been the policy of the British Legislature. But as the improvement of the native population is the object of the Government, it will consequently promote a more liberal and enlightened system of instruction, embracing mathematics, natural philosophy, chemistry and anatomy with other useful sciences which may be accomplished with the sum proposed by employing a few gentlemen of talents and learning, educated in Europe, and providing a college furnished with the necessary books, instruments and other apparatus.

In representing this subject to your Lordship I conceive myself discharging a solemn duty which I owe to my countrymen and also to that enlightened Sovereign and Legislature which have extended their benevolent cares to this distant land actuated by a desire to improve its inhabitants and I therefore humbly trust you will excuse the liberty I have taken in thus expressing my sentiments to your Lordship.

2.6 ON BRITISH MOVES TO ABOLISH THE PRACTICE OF FEMALE SACRIFICES

Raja Rammohan Roy

Source: Raja Rammohan Roy, 'Some remarks in vindication of the resolution passed by the Government of Bengal in 1829 abolishing the practice of female sacrifices in India' (1832), in *The Essential Writings of Raja Rammohan Ray* [sic], ed. by Bruce Carlisle Robertson, Delhi: Oxford University Press, 1999, pp.166–72.

The practice of burning Hindoo widows, on the funeral piles of their husbands, was abolished by the government of Bengal on the 4th of December, 1829, in consequence of which these unfortunate and deluded persons have been completely saved from destruction, for a period of two years and upwards. Certain Hindoo inhabitants of Calcutta, who find this humane measure detrimental to their interest, have under the advice of an attorney of the Supreme Court, at the Presidency of Fort William, thought proper to bring the subject before the Privy Council, with the view of having the Regulation rescinded and the practice renewed.

As to the propriety, or justice, or humanity or re-establishing such a cruel usage, it may safely be left to the wisdom and discretion of the exalted individuals, before whom in this Christian country and enlightened age, the subject is to be discussed.

With regard to the question of policy, which to many statesmen seems paramount to justice, humanity, conscience, law and religion; It might have been alleged that the abolition would be an interference with the religious rites of the Hindoos, and would cause insurrection, perhaps revolution in the country, and terminate in the loss of the British possessions in India. On this point I beg to offer a few remarks.

First, if there had been any chance of popular commotion being excited by such abolition, it might have been expected immediately after the measure was adopted in the latter end of the year 1829. About two years and upwards have passed, and no accounts have been received that any widow has been burnt, in opposition to the determinations of government, or even that any attempt at commotion has ever been made.

Secondly, from a reference to the printed official returns (laid before Parliament) of the number of Suttees within the territories of the Presidency of Fort William, from 1815 to 1828, inclusive, it appears that within the province of Bengal, including the city of Benares, (to which place an immense number of the Bengalees, male and female, retire from religious prejudices, to end their days) and Patna, which is adjacent, and has been long united to Bengal, by political connection as well as by close and constant intercourse, the number of female sacrifices has mounted to 7941, whereas in the whole extent of the upper provinces, classed under the heading of Bareilly, we find only 203 in a period of 14 years (on an average about 14 in each year): consequently had there been any chance of popular commotion, it might have been dreaded in Bengal particularly, where the practice chiefly prevailed [...]

Thirdly, even in Bengal a great number of the most intelligent and inflential of the natives, landholders, bankers, merchants, and others, felt so much gratified by the removal of the odium, which the practice had attached to their character as a nation, that they united in presenting an address of thanks and congratulation, on the subject, to the Governor General, Lord William Bentinck, on the 18th of January 1830, and in like manner, when his Lordship, in his progress through the upper provinces, arrived at Buxar (situated between Patna, and Benares), persons of the highest rank and respectability, supported by numerous inhabitants, presented another address, expressive of their satisfaction at the abolition of the horrible custom, as will appear by the *Calcutta Government Gazette* of November 15th, 1830.

Fourthly, it was not religious devotion alone which prompted the generality of the natives of Bengal, who carried on the practice of widow burning to such an extent; nor is that their motive for wishing its re-establishment. But it is their worldly interest, which many wish to preserve under the cloak of religion. Since according to their law of inheritance (the *Dayabhaga*) a widow is entitled to inherit the property of her deceased husband, without regard to his condition in life, and therefore is a complete bar to the claims of the father, mother, brothers, sisters and daughters of the deceased, who have all consequently a direct interest in the destruction of the widow. But in the upper provinces, where the *Mitakshara* is respected as the law of inheritance, according to which the rights of the surviving wife are more circumscribed, the relatives of the husband are not much interested in her death; and in these provinces it is found that the Suttees are comparatively very rare.

Fifthly, hence, it is obvious, that as the adherence of the Bengalees to this practice generally springs from selfish considerations of a worldly nature, the abolition of such a fertile source of intrigue and calculating cruelty cannot excite any apprehension of religious enthusiasm in those persons who are conscious of the unworthiness of the cause they advocate; even if the Bengalees had possessed physical energy, and a warlike education. These considerations (and many others might be added) are sufficient to shew, that policy by no means requires the re-establishment of the open perpetration of suicide and murder.

It might be alleged, that the British government has pledged itself not to interfere with the religious rights of its Indian native subjects; but, it must not be forgotten, that according to common sense, as well as from a reference to precedent and the practice of the local government, during the whole period of its dominion in India, it is clear, that this rule was always unequivocally meant to apply to religious observances which are considered incumbent on the people, according to the principles of their own faith, and which are not a nuisance and outrage to public feeling. On this principle, the government, from time to time, prohibited various practices performed in the name of religion; such as the perambulation of the streets by Nagas (or naked devotees), infanticide and suicide under the car of Juggannath, the self-destruction and public burning of lepers, human sacrifices, etc. etc.; it being found that these practices were only partially observed and consequentially merely optional, not incumbent, since their omission involved no loss of civil rights, nor did it bring reproach on those who failed to observe them; while their observance was highly offensive, a nuisance to the public, and a reproach to a civilised government. The case is precisely the same with respect to widow burning. For, first, in regard to the number of widows burning in the province of Bengal, only one widow out of perhaps thirty, and in the upper provinces, one out of nine hundred and ninety-nine could be prevailed on to perform this horrid sacrifice; while all the rest lived in the enjoyment of their civil rights and social respect (as shewn by thousands of judicial decrees): and again, on the score of nuisance, it is a source of greater offence and disgust to the public than the rest, from it being performed with more publicity and tumult, and exhibiting the most helpless of human beings expiring under the great sufferings. Therefore, a regard to consistency and its own character compelled the government to deal with this practice as they had done with the others before mentioned.

In addition to its local observation of the option exercised by widows, of either living an austere life, or of burning themselves with the corpse of their husband, government was furnished with the verdicts of the Pandits of the [native court of the] Sudder Dewanee Adawlut, and of the supreme court of Calcutta; who notwithstanding their enthusiastic zeal in favour of the practice of concremation, felt compelled by the force of truth to acknowledge, that at most it was entirely optional; nay, that an austere life was more meritorious.

Firstly, in reply to the question submitted to the Hindoo Law Officers of the Sudder Dewanee Adawlut, in March 1817, it was stated (p.174), that 'the woman who wishes to accompany her deceased husband, let her ascend the funeral pile'. In some cases, the widow may be laid on the funeral pile, before it is lighted, by the side of her husband. But (p.175) 'if she be destitute of the wish to perform the act of sahagamun (concremation) she must be lifted off'. Again (p.175), 'If having arrived at the place of burning, she determine to burn, the ceremony of depositing the widow must be again gone through.' 'If she afterwards express a wish to rise, she must be lifted off.'

Secondly, the Pandit of the supreme court (Mrityoonjay) states (p.178) that according to the *Jutta Mala Bilas* 'ascending the funeral pile is a voluntary act and not an indispensable one' (p.182). 'The alternative of leading an austere life being mentioned and any objection averse to it, being removed by the comparison cited in the text, this alternative seems evidently to be recommended by the favoured side of the argument' (p.182). 'In a person who is careless about absorption and desirous to obtain a paradise of temporary and inconsiderable bliss, the act of anoogaman (following the husband) is justifiable, but from this reasoning it appears evident that the leading of a virtuous life is preferred as the superior alternative, and that the act of anoogaman 'is held to be of inferior merit' (p.182). No difference prevails with regard to the propriety of leading a life of austerity' (p.183). 'Not the slightest offence attaches either to the women who depart from their resolution (of burning), or to those who persuade them to relinquish their intentions' (p.183).

If we look further into the consequences arising from the successful exertions of European Orientalist, in translating Sanscrit works, in various branches of literature, into the English language, we find that, the Public is now no longer left entirely at the mercy of the Brahmans, in the interpretation of the Hindoo law, and Religious doctrines. For example, the translation of the institutes of Menu, by Sir William Jones, which is before the public, and which to use the language of that immortal translator, of an immortal work, is a 'system of duties, religious and civil, and of law, in all its branches, which the Hindoos firmly believe to have been promulged in the beginning of time by Menu, the son, or grandson of Brahma, or in plain language, the first of created beings, and not the oldest only, but the holiest of the legislators, a system so comprehensive and so minutely exact, that it may be considered as the institutes of Hindoo law' (Sir W. Jones's Works, vol.vii. p.76, Preface).

This great legislator, in describing the duties of widows, thus ordains: 'Let her (the widow) continue till death, forgiving all injuries, performing harsh duties, avoiding every sensual pleasure, and cheerfully practising the incomparable rules of virtue, which have been followed by such women, as were devoted to one only husband' (Chap. v, verse 158, p.271). 'And like those abstemious men, a virtuous wife ascends to heaven, though she have no child, if after the decease of her lord, she devote herself to pious austerity' (Ver.160). 'But a widow who from a wish to bear children, slights her deceased husband, by marrying again, brings disgrace upon herself here below, and shall be excluded from the seat of her lord' (Ver.161).

Here Menu by the expression 'let her continue till death', imperatively commands the widows to live a life of virtue, piety and austerity, discountenances her marrying again, and does not admit the idea of any such alternative as that of burning with the corpse of her husband [...]

Then, whence, it may be asked, arose a practice so repugnant to reason, and so contrary to the most ancient, and highest legislative authority of the

Hindoos? Only (I reply) from the jealousy of their Princes, who were unable to tolerate the idea of their wives proving forgetful of them, and associating with other men after their deaths; and their dependants were induced to follow their footsteps, actuated by the same motives, and also by the influence of example; while their surviving relations did not fail to encourage the practice, for the reasons above explained, to promote their own interests; and literary men of similar feelings have not been wanting, to support their views, by interpolations and inventions, under the name of traditions, and quotations, from the *Pooorans* and *Tantras*, which all acknowledge to have no limit, or certain standard. But fortunately, it is an established rule, that every doctrine founded on these, is to be rejected, when on a fair critical examination, it proves to be inconsistent with Menu, the only safe rule to guard against endless corruptions, absurdities, and human caprices [...]

2.7 ON EDUCATION FOR INDIA

Thomas Babington Macaulay

Source: 'Thomas Babington Macaulay on Education for India', in *Imperialism*, ed. by Philip D. Curtin, New York: Harper and Row, 1971, pp.181–91.

[A shortened version of Macaulay's 'Minute on Education', dated 2 February 1835, and addressed to Lord Bentinck, the Governor-General.]

[...] We now come to the gist of the matter. We have a fund to be employed as Government shall direct for the intellectual improvement of the people of this country. The simple question is, what is the most useful way of employing it?

All parties seem to be agreed on one point, that the dialects commonly spoken among the natives of this part of India contain neither literary nor scientific information, and are moreover so poor and rude that, until they are enriched from some other quarter, it will not be easy to translate any valuable work into them. It seems to be admitted on all sides, that the intellectual improvement of those classes of the people who have the means of pursuing higher studies can at present be effected only by means of some language not vernacular amongst them.

What then shall that language be? One-half of the committee maintain that it should be the English. The other half strongly recommend the Arabic and Sanscrit. The whole question seems to me to be – which language is the best worth knowing?

I have no knowledge of either Sanscrit or Arabic. But I have done what I could to form a correct estimate of their value. I have read translations of the most celebrated Arabic and Sanscrit works. I have conversed, both here and at home, with men distinguished by their proficiency in the Eastern tongues. I am quite ready to take the oriental learning at the valuation of the orientalists themselves. I have never found one among them who could deny that a single shelf of a good European library was worth the whole native literature of India and Arabia. The intrinsic superiority of the Western literature is indeed fully admitted by those members of the committee who support the oriental plan of education.

It will hardly be disputed, I suppose, that the department of literature in which the Eastern writers stand highest is poetry. And I certainly never met with any orientalist who ventured to maintain that the Arabic and Sanscrit poetry could be compared to that of the great European nations. But when we pass from works of imagination to works in which facts are recorded and general principles investigated, the superiority of the Europeans becomes absolutely immeasurable. It is, I believe, no exaggeration to say that all the historical information which has been collected from all the books written in the Sanscrit language is less valuable than what may be found in the most paltry abridgments used at preparatory schools in England. In every branch of physical or moral philosophy, the relative position of the two nations is nearly the same.

How then stands the case? We have to educate a people who cannot at present be educated by means of their mother-tongue. We must teach them some foreign language. The claims of our own language it is hardly necessary to recapitulate. It stands pre-eminent even among the languages of the West. It abounds with works of imagination not inferior to the noblest which Greece has bequeathed to us – with models of every species of eloquence, – with historical compositions which, considered merely as narratives, have seldom been surpassed, and which, considered as vehicles of ethical and political instruction, have never been equalled, – with just and lively representations of human life and human nature, – with the most profound speculations on metaphysics, morals, government, jurisprudence, trade, – with full and correct information respecting every experimental science which tends to preserve the health, to increase the comfort, or to expand the intellect of man. Whoever knows that language has ready access to all the vast intellectual wealth which all the wisest nations of the earth have created and hoarded in the course of ninety generations. It may safely be said that the literature now extant in that language is of greater value than all the literature which three hundred years ago was extant in all the languages of the world together. Nor is this all. In India, English is the language spoken by the ruling class. It is spoken by the higher class of natives at the seats of Government. It is likely to become the language of commerce throughout the seas of the East. It is the language of two great European communities which are rising, the one in the south of Africa, the other in Australasia, – communities which are every year becoming more important and more closely connected with our Indian empire. Whether we look at the intrinsic value of our literature, or at the particular situation of this country, we shall see the strongest reason to think that, of all foreign tongues, the English tongue is that which would be the most useful to our native subjects.

The question now before us is simply whether, when it is in our power to teach this language, we shall teach languages in which, by universal confession, there are no books on any subject which deserve to be compared to our own, whether, when we can teach European science, we shall teach systems which, by universal confession, wherever they differ from those of Europe differ for the worse, and whether, when we can patronize sound philosophy and true history, we shall countenance, at the public expense, medical doctrines which would disgrace an English farrier, astronomy which would move laughter in girls at an English boarding school, history abounding with kings thirty feet high and reigns thirty thousand years long, and geography made of seas of treacle and seas of butter.

We are not without experience to guide us. History furnishes several analogous cases, and they all teach the same lesson. There are, in modern times, to go no further, two memorable instances of a great impulse given to the mind of a whole society, of prejudices overthrown, of knowledge diffused, of taste purified, of arts and sciences planted in countries which had recently been ignorant and barbarous.

The first instance to which I refer is the great revival of letters among the Western nations at the close of the fifteenth and the beginning of the six-teenth century. At that time almost everything that was worth reading was contained in the writings of the ancient Greeks and Romans. Had our ancestors acted as the Committee of Public Instruction has hitherto acted, – had they neglected the language of Thucydides and Plato, and the language of Cicero and Tacitus, had they confined their attention to the old dialects of our own island, had they printed nothing and taught nothing at the universities but chronicles in Anglo-Saxon and romances in Norman French, – would England ever have been what she now is? What the Greek and Latin were to the contemporaries of More and Ascham, our tongue is to the people of India. The literature of England is now more valuable than that of classical antiquity. I doubt whether the Sanscrit literature be as valuable as that of our Saxon and Norman progenitors. In some departments – in history for example – I am certain that it is much less so.

Another instance may be said to be still before our eyes. Within the last hundred and twenty years, a nation which had previously been in a state as barbarous as that in which our ancestors were before the Crusades has gradually emerged from the ignorance in which it was sunk, and has taken its place among civilised communities. I speak of Russia. There is now in that country a large educated class abounding with persons fit to serve the State in the highest functions, and in nowise inferior to the most accomplished men who adorn the best circles of Paris and London. There is reason to hope that this vast empire which, in the time of our grandfathers, was probably behind the Punjab, may in the time of our grandchildren, be pressing close on France and Britain in the career of improvement. And how was this change effected? Not by flattering national prejudices; not by feeding the mind of the young Muscovite with the old women's stories which his rude fathers had believed; not by filling his head with lying legends about St. Nicholas; not by encouraging him to study the great question, whether the world was or not created on the 13th of September; not by calling him 'a learned native' when he had mastered all these points of knowledge; but by teaching him those foreign languages in which the greatest mass of information had been laid up, and thus putting all that information within his reach. The languages of western Europe civilised Russia. I cannot doubt that they will do for the Hindoo what they have done for the Tartar.

And what are the arguments against that course which seems to be alike recommended by theory and by experience? It is said that we ought to secure the co-operation of the native public, and that we can do this only by teaching Sanscrit and Arabic.

I can by no means admit that, when a nation of high intellectual attainments undertakes to superintend the education of a nation comparatively ignorant, the learners are absolutely to prescribe the course which is to be taken by the teachers. It is not necessary however to say anything on this subject. For it is proved by unanswerable evidence, that we are not at present securing the co-operation of the natives. It would be bad enough to consult their intellectual taste at the expense of their intellectual health. But we are consulting neither. We are withholding from them the learning which is palatable to them. We are forcing on them the mock learning which they nauseate.

This is proved by the fact that we are forced to pay our Arabic and Sanscrit students while those who learn English are willing to pay us. All the declamations in the world about the love and reverence of the natives for their sacred dialects will never, in the mind of any impartial person, outweigh this undisputed fact, that we cannot find in all our vast empire a single student who will let us teach him those dialects, unless we will pay him.

I have now before me the accounts of the Mudrassa for one month, the month of December, 1833. The Arabic students appear to have been seventy-seven in number. All receive stipends from the public. The whole amount paid to them is above 500 rupees a month. On the other side of the account stands the following item:

> Deduct amount realized from the out-students of English for the months of May, June, and July last – 103 rupees.

I have been told that it is merely from want of local experience that I am surprised at these phenomena, and that it is not the fashion for students in India to study at their own charges. This only confirms me in my opinions. Nothing is more certain than that it never can in any part of the world be necessary to pay men for doing what they think pleasant or profitable. India is no exception to this rule. The people of India do not require to be paid for eating rice when they are hungry, or for wearing woollen cloth in the cold season. To come nearer to the case before us: – The children who learn their letters and a little elementary arithmetic from the village schoolmaster are not paid by him. He is paid for teaching them. Why then is it necessary to pay people to learn Sanscrit and Arabic? Evidently because it is universally felt that the Sanscrit and Arabic are languages the knowledge of which does not compensate for the trouble of acquiring them. On all such subjects the state of the market is the decisive test.

Other evidence is not wanting, if other evidence were required. A petition was presented last year to the committee by several ex-students of the Sanscrit College. The petitioners stated that they had studied in the college ten or twelve years, that they had made themselves acquainted with Hindoo literature and science, that they had received certificates of proficiency. And what is the fruit of all this? 'Notwithstanding such testimonials,' they say, 'we have but little prospect of bettering our condition without the kind assistance of your honourable committee, the indifference with which we are generally looked upon by our countrymen leaving no hope of encouragement and assistance from them.' They therefore beg that they may be recommended to the Governor-General for places under the Government – not places of high dignity or emolument, but such as may just enable them to exist. 'We want means,' they say, 'for a decent living, and for our progressive improvement, which, however, we cannot obtain without the assistance of Government, by whom we have been educated and maintained from childhood.' They conclude by representing very pathetically that they are sure that it was never the intention of Government, after behaving so liberally to them during their education, to abandon them to destitution and neglect.

I have been used to see petitions to Government for compensation. All those petitions, even the most unreasonable of them, proceeded on the supposition that some loss had been sustained, that some wrong had been inflicted. These are surely the first petitioners who ever demanded com-pensation for having been educated gratis, for having been supported by the public during twelve years, and then sent forth into the world well furnished with literature and science. They represent their education as an injury which gives them a claim on the Government for redress, as an injury for which the stipends paid to them during the infliction were a very inadequate compensation. And I doubt not that they are in the right. They have wasted the best years of life in learning what procures for them neither bread not respect. Surely we might with advantage have saved the cost of making these persons useless and miserable. Surely, men may be brought up to be burdens to the public and objects of contempt to their neighbours at a somewhat smaller charge to the State. But such is our policy. We do not even stand neuter in the contest between truth and falsehood. We are not content to leave the natives to the influence of their own hereditary prejudices. To the natural difficulties which obstruct the progress of sound science in the East, we add great difficulties of our own making. Bounties and premiums, such as ought not to be given even for the propagation of truth, we lavish on false texts and false philosophy.

By acting thus we create the very evil which we fear. We are making that opposition which we do not find. What we spend on the Arabic and Sanscrit Colleges is not merely a dead loss to the cause of truth. It is bounty-money paid to raise up champions of error. It goes to form a nest not merely of helpless place-hunters but of bigots prompted alike by passion and by interest to raise a cry against every useful scheme of education. If there should be any opposition among the natives to the change which I recommend, that opposition will be the effect of our own system. It will be headed by persons supported by our stipends and trained in our colleges. The longer we persevere in our present course, the more formidable will that opposition be. It will be every year reinforced by recruits whom we are paying. From the native society, left to itself, we have no difficulties to apprehend. All the murmuring will come from that oriental interest which we have, by artificial means, called into being and nursed into strength.

There is yet another fact which is alone sufficient to prove that the feeling of the native public, when left to itself, is not such as the supporters of the old system represent it to be. The committee have thought fit to lay out above a lakh of rupees in printing Arabic and Sanscrit books. Those books find no purchasers. It is very rarely that a single copy is disposed of. Twenty-three thousand volumes, most of them folios and quartos, fill the libraries or rather the lumber-rooms of this body. The committee contrive to get rid of some portion of their vast stock of oriental literature by giving books away. But they cannot give so fast as they print. About twenty thousand rupees a year are spent in adding fresh masses of waste paper to a hoard which, one should think, is already sufficiently ample. During the last three years about sixty thousand rupees have been expended in this manner. The sale of Arabic and Sanscrit books during those three years has not yielded quite one thousand rupees. In the meantime, the School Book Society is selling seven or eight thousand English volumes every year, and not only pays the expenses of printing but realizes a profit of twenty per cent. on its outlay.

The fact that the Hindoo law is to be learned chiefly from Sanscrit books, and the Mahometan law from Arabic books, has been much insisted on, but seems not to bear at all on the question. We are commanded by Parliament to ascertain and digest the laws of India. The assistance of a Law Commission has been given to us for that purpose. As soon as the Code is promulgated the Shasters and the Hedaya will be useless to a moonsiff or a Sudder Ameen [i.e. the traditional Indian books of law will be of no use to Indian judges]. I hope and trust that, before the boys who are now entering at the Mudrassa and the Sanscrit College have completed their studies, this great work will be finished. It would be manifestly absurd to educate the rising generation with a view to a state of things which we mean to alter before they reach manhood.

But there is yet another argument which seems even more untenable. It is said that the Sanscrit and the Arabic are the languages in which the sacred books of a hundred millions of people are written, and that they are on that account entitled to peculiar encouragement. Assuredly it is the duty of the British Government in India to be not only tolerant but neutral on all religious questions. But to encourage the study of a literature, admitted to be of small intrinsic value, only because that literature inculcates the most serious errors on the most important subjects, is a course hardly reconcilable with reason, with morality, or even with that very neutrality which ought, as we all agree, to be sacredly preserved. It is confessed that a language is barren of useful knowledge. We are to teach it because it is fruitful of monstrous superstitions. We are to teach false history, false astronomy, false medicine, because we find them in company with a false religion. We abstain, and I trust shall always abstain, from giving any public encouragement to those who are engaged in the work of converting the natives to Christianity. And while we act thus, can we reasonably or decently bribe men, out of the revenues of the State, to waste their youth in learning how they are to purify themselves after touching an ass or what texts of the Vedas they are to repeat to expiate the crime of killing a goat?

It is taken for granted by the advocates of oriental learning that no native of this country can possibly attain more than a mere smattering of English. They do not attempt to prove this. But they perpetually insinuate it. They designate the education which their opponents recommend as a mere spelling-book education. They assume it as undeniable that the question is between a profound knowledge of Hindoo and Arabian literature and science on the one side, and superficial knowledge of the rudiments of English on the other. This is not merely an assumption, but an assumption contrary to all reason and experience. We know that foreigners of all nations do learn our language sufficiently to have access to all the most abstruse knowledge which it contains sufficiently to relish even the more delicate graces of our most idiomatic writers. There are in this very town natives who are quite competent to discuss political or scientific questions with fluency and precision in the English language. I have heard the very question on which I am now writing discussed by native gentlemen with a liberality and an intelligence which would do credit to any member of the Committee of Public Instruction. Indeed it is unusual to find, even in the literary circles of the Continent, any foreigner who can express himself in English with so much facility and correctness as we find in many Hindoos. Nobody, I suppose, will contend that English is so difficult to a Hindoo as Greek to an Englishman. Yet an intelligent English youth, in a much smaller number of years than our unfortunate pupils pass at the Sanscrit College, becomes able to read, to enjoy, and even to imitate not unhappily the compositions of the best Greek authors. Less than half the time which enables an English youth to read Herodotus and Sophocles ought to enable a Hindoo to read Hume and Milton [...]

In one point I fully agree with the gentlemen to whose general views I am opposed. I feel with them that it is impossible for us, with our limited means, to attempt to educate the body of the people. We must at present do our best to form a class who may be interpreters between us and the millions whom we govern – a class of persons Indian in blood and colour, but English in tastes, in opinions, in morals and in intellect. To that class we may leave it to refine the vernacular dialects of the country, to enrich those dialects with terms of science borrowed from the Western nomenclature, and to render them by degrees fit vehicles for conveying knowledge to the great mass of the population.

I would strictly respect all existing interests. I would deal even generously with all individuals who have had fair reason to expect a pecuniary provision. But I would strike at the root of the bad system which has hitherto been fostered by us. I would at once stop the printing of Arabic and Sanscrit books. I would abolish the Mudrassa and the Sanscrit College at Calcutta. Benares is the great seat of Brahminical learning; Delhi of Arabic learning. If we retain the Sanscrit College at Benares and the Mahometan College at Delhi we do enough, and much more than enough in my opinion, for the Eastern languages. If the Benares and Delhi Colleges should be retained, I would at least recommend that no stipends shall be given to any students who may hereafter repair thither, but that the people shall be left to make their own choice between the rival systems of education without being bribed by us to learn what they have no desire to know. The funds which would thus be placed at our disposal would enable us to give larger encouragement to the Hindoo College at Calcutta [where teaching was in English], and establish in the principal cities throughout the Presidencies of Fort William and Agra schools in which the English language might be well and thoroughly taught.

If the decision of His Lordship in Council should be such as I anticipate, I shall enter on the performance of my duties with the greatest zeal and alacrity. If, on the other hand, it be the opinion of the Government that the present system ought to remain unchanged, I beg that I may be permitted to retire from the chair of the committee. I feel that I could not be of the smallest use there. I feel also that I should be lending my countenance to what I firmly believe to be a mere delusion. I believe that the present system tends not to accelerate the progress of truth but to delay the natural death of expiring errors. I conceive that we have at present no right to the respectable name of a Board of Public Instruction. We are a Board for wasting the public money, for printing books which are of less value than the paper on which they are printed was while it was blank – for giving artificial encouragement to absurd history, absurd metaphysics, absurd physics, absurd theology – for raising up a breed of scholars who find their scholarship an incumbrance and blemish, who live on the public while they are receiving their education, and whose education is so utterly useless to them that, when they have received it, they must either starve or live on the public all the rest of their lives. Entertaining these opinions, I am naturally desirous to decline all share in the responsibility of a body which, unless it alters its whole mode of proceedings, I must consider, not merely as useless, but as positively noxious.

3.1 FROM THE CURSE OF KEHAMA

Robert Southey

Source: *The Curse of Kehama* (1810), in *Poems of Robert Southey*, ed. by
Maurice H. Fitzgerald, MA, Henry Frowde and Oxford University Press:
London, 1909, pp.117–24.

Original preface

In the religion of the Hindoos, which of all false religions is the most
monstrous in its fables, and the most fatal in its effects, there is one remarkable peculiarity. Prayers, penances, and sacrifices are supposed to possess
an inherent and actual value, in no degree depending upon the disposition
or motive of the person who performs them. They are drafts upon Heaven,
for which the Gods cannot refuse payment. The worst men, bent upon the
worst designs, have in this manner obtained power which has made them
formidable to the Supreme Deities themselves, and rendered an *Avatar* or
Incarnation of Veeshnoo the Preserver, necessary. This belief is the
foundation of the following Poem. The story is original; but, in all its
parts, consistent with the superstition upon which it is built: and however
startling the fictions may appear, they might almost be called credible when
compared with the genuine tales of Hindoo mythology.

No figures can be imagined more anti-picturesque, and less poetical, than
the mythological personages of the Bramins. This deformity was easily kept
out of sight: – their hundred hands are but a clumsy personification of
power; their numerous heads only a gross image of divinity, 'whose countenance', as the Bhagvat-Geeta expresses it, 'is turned on every side'. To the
other obvious objection, that the religion of Hindostan is not generally
known enough to supply fit machinery for an English poem, I can only
answer, that, if every allusion to it throughout the work is not sufficiently
self-explained to render the passage intelligible, there is a want of skill in
the poet. Even those readers who should be wholly unacquainted with the
writings of our learned Orientalists, will find all the preliminary knowledge
that can be needful, in the brief explanation of mythological names prefixed
to the Poem.

BRAMA, the Creator.

VEESHNOO, the Preserver.

SEEVA, the Destroyer.

These form the Trimourtee, or Trinity, as it has been called, of the Bramins. The allegory is obvious, but has been made for the Trimourtee; not the Trimourtee for the allegory; and these Deities are regarded by the people as three distinct and personal Gods. The two latter have at this day their hostile sets of worshippers; that of Seeva is the most numerous; and in this Poem, Seeva is represented as Supreme among the Gods. This is the same God whose name is variously written as Seeb, Sieven, and Siva, Chiven by the French, Xiven by the Portuguese, and whom European writers sometimes denominate Eswara, Iswaren, Mahadeo, Mahadeva, Rutren, – according to which of his thousand and eight names prevailed in the country where they obtained their information.

INDRA, God of the Elements.

The SWERGA, his Paradise, – one of the Hindoo heavens.

YAMEN, Lord of Hell, and Judge of the Dead.

PADALON, Hell, – under the Earth, and, like the Earth, of an octagonal shape; its eight gates are guarded by as many Gods.

MARRIATALY, the Goddess who is chiefly worshipped by the lower casts.

POLLEAR, or Ganesa, – the Protector of Travellers. His statues are placed in the highways, and sometimes in a small lonely sanctuary, or in the streets and in the fields.

CASYAPA, the Father of the Immortals.

DEVETAS, the Inferior Deities.

SURAS, Good Spirits.

ASURAS, Evil Spirits, or Devils.

GLENDOVEERS, the most beautiful of the Good Spirits, the Grindouvers of Sonnerat.

I The Funeral

1

Midnight, and yet no eye
Through all the Imperial City closed in sleep!
Behold her streets a-blaze
With light that seems to kindle the red sky,
Her myriads swarming through the crowded ways!
Master and slave, old age and infancy,
All, all abroad to gaze;
House-top and balcony
Clustered with women, who throw back their veils
With unimpeded and insatiate sight
To view the funeral pomp which passes by,
As if the mournful rite
Were but to them a scene of joyance and delight.

2

Vainly, ye blessed twinklers of the night,
You feeble beams ye shed,
Quench'd in the unnatural light which might out-stare
Even the broad eye of day;
And thou from thy celestial way
Pourest, O Moon, an ineffectual ray!
For lo! ten thousand torches flame and flare
Upon the midnight air,
Blotting the lights of heaven
With one portentous glare.
Behold the fragrant smoke in many a fold,
Ascending, floats along the fiery sky,
And hangeth visible on high,
A dark and waving canopy.

3

Hark! 'tis the funeral trumpet's breath,
'Tis the dirge of death!
At once ten thousand drums begin,
With one long thunder-peal the ear assailing;
Ten thousand voices then join in,
And with one deep and general din
Pour their wild wailing.
The song of praise is drown'd
Amid the deafening sound;
You hear no more the trumpet's tone,
You hear no more the mourner's moan,
Though the trumpet's breath, and the dirge of death,
Swell with commingled force the funeral yell.
But rising over all in one acclaim
Is heard the echoed and re-echoed name,
From all that countless rout;
Arvalan! Arvalan!
Arvalan! Arvalan!
Ten times ten thousand voices in one shout
Call Arvalan! The overpowering sound,
From house to house repeated rings about,
From tower to tower rolls round.

4

The death-procession moves along;
Their bald heads shining to the torches' ray,
The Bramins lead the way,
Chaunting the funeral song.
And now at once they shout,
Arvalan! Arvalan!
With quick rebound of sound,
All in accordance cry,
Arvalan! Arvalan!
The universal multitude reply.

In vain ye thunder on his ear the name;
Would ye awake the dead?
Borne upright in his palankeen,
There Arvalan is seen!
A glow is on his face, . . a lively red;
It is the crimson canopy
Which o'er his cheek a reddening shade hath shed;
He moves, . . he nods his head, . .
But the motion comes from the bearers' tread,
As the body, borne aloft in state,
Sways with the impulse of its own dead weight.

5

Close following his dead son, Kehama came,
Nor joining in the ritual song,
Nor calling the dear name;
With head deprest and funeral vest,
And arms enfolded on his breast,
Silent and lost in thought he moves along.
King of the World, his slaves, unenvying now,
Behold their wretched Lord; rejoiced they see
The mighty Rajah's misery;
That Nature in his pride hath dealt the blow,
And taught the Master of Mankind to know
Even he himself is man, and not exempt from woe.

6

O sight of grief! the wives of Arvalan,
Young Azla, young Nealliny, are seen!
Their widow-robes of white,
With gold and jewels bright,
Each like an Eastern queen.
Woe! woe! around their palankeen,
As on a bridal day,
With symphony, and dance, and song,
Their kindred and their friends come on.
The dance of sacrifice! the funeral song!
And next the victim slaves in long array,
Richly bedight to grace the fatal day,
Move onward to their death;
The clarions' stirring breath
Lifts their thin robes in every flowing fold,
And swells the woven gold,
That on the agitated air
Flutters and glitters to the torch's glare.

7

A man and maid of aspect wan and wild,
Then, side by side, by bowmen guarded, came;
O wretched father! O unhappy child!
Them were all eyes of all the throng exploring . .

Is this the daring man
Who raised his fatal hand at Arvalan?
Is this the wretch condemn'd to feel
Kehama's dreadful wrath?
Then were all hearts of all the throng deploring;
For not in that innumerable throng
Was one who loved the dead; for who could know
What aggravated wrong
Provoked the desperate blow!

8

Far, far behind, beyond all reach of sight,
In order'd files the torches flow along,
One ever-lengthening line of gilding light:
Far . . far behind,
Rolls on the undistinguishable clamour,
Of horn, and trump, and tambour;
Incessant as the roar
Of streams which down the wintry mountain pour,
And louder than the dread commotion
Of breakers on a rocky shore,
When the winds rage over the waves,
And Ocean to the Tempest raves.

9

And now toward the bank they go,
Where winding on their way below,
Deep and strong the waters flow.
Here doth the funeral pile appear
With myrrh and ambergris bestrew'd,
And built of precious sandal wood.
They cease their music and their outcry here,
Gently they rest the bier;
They wet the face of Arvalan,
No sign of life the sprinkled drops excite;
They feel his breast, . . no motion there;
They feel his lips, . . no breath;
For not with feeble, nor with erring hand,
The brave avenger dealt the blow of death.
Then with a doubling peal and deeper blast,
The tambours and the trumpets sound on high,
And with a last and loudest cry,
They call on Arvalan.

10

Woe! woe! for Azla takes her seat
Upon the funeral pile!
Calmly she took her seat,
Calmly the whole terrific pomp survey'd;
As on her lap the while
The lifeless head of Arvalan was laid.

11

Woe! woe! Nealliny,
The young Nealliny!
They strip her ornaments away,
Bracelet and anklet, ring, and chain, and zone;
Around her neck they leave
The marriage knot alone, . .
That marriage band, which when
Yon waning moon was young,
Around her virgin neck
With bridal joy was hung.
Then with white flowers, the coronal of death,
Her jetty locks they crown.

12

O sight of misery!
You cannot hear her cries, . . their sound
In that wild dissonance is drown'd; . .
But in her face you see
The supplication and the agony, . .
See in her swelling throat the desperate strength
That with vain effort struggles yet for life;
Her arms contracted now in fruitless strife
Now wildly at full length
Towards the crowd in vain for pity spread, . .
They force her on, they bind her to the dead.

13

Then all around retire;
Circling the pile, the ministering
Bramins stand,
Each lifting in his hand a torch on fire.
Alone the Father of the dead advanced
And lit the funeral pyre.

14

At once on every side
The circling torches drop,
At once on every side
The fragrant oil is pour'd,
At once on every side
The rapid flames rush up.
Then hand in hand the victim band
Roll in the dance around the funeral pyre;
Their garments' flying folds
Float inward to the fire;
In drunken whirl they wheel around;
One drops, . . another plunges in;
And still with overwhelming din
The tambours and the trumpets sound;
And clap of hand, and shouts, and cries,

From all the multitude arise;
While round and round, in giddy wheel,
Intoxicate they roll and reel,
Till one by one whirl'd in they fall,
And the devouring flames have swallow'd all.

15

Then all was still; the drums and clarions ceased;
The multitude were hush'd in silent awe:
Only the roaring of the flames was heard.

II   The Curse

1

Alone towards the Table of the Dead
Kehama moved; there on the altar-stone
Honey and rice he spread.
There with collected voice and painful tone
He call'd upon his son.
Lo! Arvalan appears;
Only Kehama's powerful eye beheld
The thin ethereal spirit hovering nigh;
Only the Rajah's ear
Received his feeble breath.
And is this all? the mournful Spirit said,
This all that thou canst give me after death?
This unavailing pomp,
These empty pageantries that mock the dead!

2

In bitterness the Rajah heard,
And groan'd, and smote his breast, and o'er his face
Cowl'd the white mourning vest.

3

ARVALAN

Art thou not powerful, . . even like a God?
And must I, through my years of wandering,
Shivering and naked to the elements,
In wretchedness await
The hour of Yamen's wrath?
I thought thou wouldst embody me anew,
Undying as I am, . .
Yea, re-create me! . . Father, is this all?
This all? and thou Almighty!

4

But in that wrongful and upbraiding tone,
Kehama found relief.
For rising anger half supprest his grief.

Reproach not me! he cried,
Had I not spell-secured thee from disease,
Fire, sword, . . all the common accidents of man, . .
And thou! . . fool, fool . . to perish by a stake!
And by a peasant's arm! . .
Even now, when from reluctant Heaven,
Forcing new gifts and mightier attributes,
So soon I should have quell'd the Death-God's power.

5

Waste not thy wrath on me, quoth Arvalan,
It was my hour of folly! Fate prevail'd,
Nor boots it to reproach me that I fell.
I am in misery, Father! Other souls
Predoom'd to Indra's Heaven, enjoy the dawn
Of bliss, . . to them the temper'd elements
Minister joy: genial delight the sun
Sheds on their happy being, and the stars
Effuse on them benignant influences;
And thus o'er earth and air they roam at will,
And when the number of their days is full,
Go fearlessly before the aweful throne.
But I, . . all naked feeling and raw life, . .
What worse than this hath Yamen's hell in store?
If ever thou didst love me, mercy, Father!
Save me, for thou canst save . . the Elements
Know and obey they voice.

6

KEHAMA

The Elements
Shall sin no more against thee; whilst I speak
Already dost thou feel their power is gone.
Fear not! I cannot call again the past,
Fate hath made that its own; but Fate shall yield
To me the future; and thy doom be fix'd
By mine, not Yamen's will. Meantime all power
Whereof thy feeble spirit can be made
Participant, I give. Is there aught else
To mitigate thy lot?

ARVALAN

Only the site of vengeance. Give me that!
Vengeance, full, worthy, vengeance! . . not the stroke
Of sudden punishment, . . no agony
That spends itself and leaves the wretch at rest,
But lasting long revenge.

KEHAMA

What, boy? is that cup sweet? then take thy fill!

7

So as he spake, a glow of dreadful pride
Inflamed his cheek, with quick and angry stride
He moved toward the pile,
And raised his hand to hush the crowd, and cried,
Bring forth the murderer! At the Rajah's voice,
Calmly, and like a man whom fear had stunn'd,
Ladurlad came, obedient to the call;
But Kailyal started at the sound,
And gave a womanly shriek, and back she drew,
And eagerly she roll'd her eyes around,
As if to seek for aid, albeit she knew
No aid could there be found.

8

It chanced that near her on the river brink,
The sculptured form of Marriataly stood;
It was an Idol roughly hewn of wood,
Artless, and mean, and rude;
The Goddess of the poor was she;
None else regarded her with piety.
But when that holy Image Kailyal view'd,
To that she sprung, to that she clung,
On her own Goddess, with close-clasping arms,
For life the maiden hung.

9

They seized the maid; with unrelenting grasp
They bruised her tender limbs;
She, nothing yielding, to this only hope
Clings with the strength of frenzy and despair.
She screams not now, she breathes not now,
She sends not up one vow,
She forms not in her soul one secret prayer,
All thought, all feeling, and all powers of life
In the one effort centering. Wrathful they
With tug and strain would force the maid away; . .
Didst thou, O Marriataly, see their strife,
In pity didst thou see the suffering maid?
Or was thine anger kindled, that rude hands
Assail'd thy holy Image? . . for behold
The holy image shakes!

10

Irreverently bold, they deem the maid
Relax'd her stubborn hold,
And now with force redoubled drag their prey;
And now the rooted Idol to their sway
Bends, . . yields, . . and now it falls.
But then they scream,

For lo! they feel the crumbling bank give way,
And all are plunged into the stream.

11

She hath escaped my will, Kehama cried,
She hath escaped, . . but thou art here,
I have thee still,
The worser criminal!
And on Ladurlad, while he spake, severe
He fix'd his dreadful frown.
The strong reflection of the pile
Lit his dark lineaments,
Lit the protruded brow, the gathered, front,
The steady eye of wrath.

12

But while the fearful silence yet endured,
Ladurlad roused himself;
Ere yet the voice of destiny
Which trembled on the Rajah's lips was loosed,
Eager he interposed,
As if despair had waken'd him to hope;
Mercy! oh mercy! only in defence . .
Only instinctively, . .
Only to save my child, I smote the Prince;
King of the world, be merciful!
Crush me, . . but torture not!

13

The Man-Almighty deign'd him no reply,
Still he stood silent; in no human mood
Of mercy, in no hesitating thought
Of right and justice. At the length he raised
His brow yet unrelax'd, . . his lips unclosed,
And uttered from the heart,
With the whole feeling of his soul enforced,
The gathered vengeance came.

14

I charm thy life
From the weapons of strife,
From stone and from wood,
From fire and from flood,
From the serpent's tooth,
And the beasts of blood:
From Sickness I charm thee,
And Time shall not harm thee;
But Earth which is mine,
Its fruits shall deny thee;
And Water shall hear me,
And know thee and fly thee;

And the Winds shall not touch thee
When they pass by thee,
And the Dews shall no wet thee,
When they fall nigh thee:
And thou shalt seek Death
To release thee, in vain;
Thou shalt live in thy pain
While Kehama shall reign,
With a fire in thy heart,
And a fire in thy brain;
And Sleep shall obey me,
And visit thee never,
And the Curse shall be on thee
For ever and ever.

15

There where the Curse had stricken him,
There stood the miserable man,
There stood Ladurlad, with loose-hanging arms,
And eyes of idiot wandering.
Was it a dream? alas,
He heard the river flow,
He heard the crumbling of the pile,
He heard the wind which shower'd
The thin white ashes round.
There motionless he stood,
As if he hoped it were a dream,
And feared to move, lest he should prove
The actual misery;
And still at times he met Kehama's eye,
Kehama's eye that fastened on him still.

3.2 *FROM* LALLA ROOKH

Thomas Moore

Source: Thomas Moore, *Lalla Rookh* (1817), London: G.G. Harrap, n.d., pp.193–205.

'Haste, haste!' she cried, 'the clouds grow dark,
But still, ere night, we'll reach the bark;
And by to-morrow's dawn – oh bliss!
  With thee upon the sun-bright deep,
Far off, I'll but remember this,
  As some dark vanish'd dream of sleep;
And thou ——' but ah! – he answers not –
Good Heav'n! – and does she go alone?
She now has reach'd that dismal spot,
  Where, some hours since, his voice's tone
Had come to soothe her fears and ills,

Sweet as the angel ISRAFIL'S,
When every leaf on Eden's tree
Is trembling to his minstrelsy –
Yet now – oh, now, he is not nigh. –
'HAFED! My HAFED! – if it be
Thy will, thy doom this night to die,
 Let me but stay to die with thee,
And I will bless thy loved name,
Till the last life-breath leave this frame,
Oh! let our lips, our cheeks be laid
But near each other while they fade:
Let us but mix our parting breaths,
And I can die ten thousand deaths!
You too, who hurry me away
So cruelly, one moment stay –
 Oh! stay – one moment is not much –
He yet may come – for *him* I pray –
HAFED! dear HAFED!' – all the way
 In wild lamentings, that would touch
A heart of stone, she shriek'd his name
To the dark woods – no HAFED came: –
No – hapless pair – you've look'd your last: –
 Your hearts should both have broken then:
The dream is o'er – your doom is cast –
 You'll never meet on earth again!

Alas for him, who hears her cries!
 Still half-way down the steep he stands,
Watching with fix'd and feverish eyes
The glimmer of those burning brands,
That down the rocks, with mournful ray,
Light all he loves on earth away!
Hopeless as they who, far at sea,
 By the cold moon have just consign'd
The corse of one, lov'd tenderly,
 To the bleak flood they leave behind;
And on the deck still ling'ring stay,
And long look back, with sad delay,
To watch the moonlight on the wave,
That ripples o'er that cheerless grave.
 But see – he starts – what heard he then?
That dreadful shout! – across the glen
From the land-side it comes, and loud
Rings through the chasm; as if the crowd
Of fearful things, that haunt that dell,
Its Gholes and Dives and shapes of hell,
Had all in one dread howl broke out,
So loud, so terrible that shout!
'They come – the Moslems come!' – he cries,
His proud soul mounting to his eyes, –
'Now, Spirits of the Brave, who roam
Enfranchis'd through yon starry dome,

Rejoice – for souls of kindred fire
Are on the wing to join your choir!'
He said – and, light as bridegrooms bound
   To their young loves, reclimb'd the steep
And gain'd the Shrine – his Chiefs stood round –
   Their swords, as with instinctive leap,
Together, at that cry accurst,
Had from their sheaths, like sunbeams, burst.
And hark! – again – again it rings;
Near and more near its echoings
Peal through the chasm – oh! who that then
Had seen those list'ning warrior-men,
With their swords grasp'd, their eyes of flame
Turn'd on their Chief – could doubt the shame,
The' indignant shame with which they thrill
To hear those shouts, and yet stand still?

He read their thoughts – they were his own –
   'What! while our arms can wield these blades,
Shall we die tamely? die alone?
   Without one victim to our shades,
One Moslem heart, where, buried deep,
The sabre from its toil may sleep?
No – God of IRAN's burning skies!
Thou scorn'st the' inglorious sacrifice.
No – though of all earth's hope bereft,
Life, swords, and vengeance still are left.
We'll make yon valley's reeking caves
   Live in the awe-struck minds of men,
Till tyrants shudder, when their slaves
   Tell of the Gheber's [Zoroastrian's] bloody glen.
Follow, brave hearts! – this pile remains
Our refuge still from life and chains;
But his the best, the holiest bed,
Who sinks entomb'd in Moslem dead!'

Down the precipitous rocks they sprung,
While vigour, more than human, strung
Each arm and heart. – The' exulting foe
Still through the dark defiles below,
Track'd by his torches' lurid fire,
   Wound slow, as through GOLCONDA'S vale
The mighty serpent, in his ire,
   Glides on with glitt'ring, deadly trail,
No torch the Ghebers need – so well
They know each myst'ry of the dell,
So oft have, in their wanderings,
Cross'd the wild race that round them dwell,
   The very tigers from their delves
Look out, and let them pass, as things
   Untam'd and fearless like themselves!
There was a deep ravine, that lay

Yet darkling in the Moslem's way;
Fit spot to make invaders rue
The many fall'n before the few.
The torrents from that morning's sky
Had fill'd the narrow chasm breast-high,
And, on each side, aloft and wild,
Huge cliffs and toppling crags were pil'd, –
The guards with which young Freedom lines
The pathways to her mountain-shrines.
Here, at this pass, the scanty band
Of IRAN'S last avengers stand;
Here wait, in silence like the dead,
And listen for the Moslem's tread
So anxiously, the carrion-bird
Above them flaps his wing unheard!

They come – that plunge into the water
Gives signal for the work of slaughter.
Now, Ghebers, now – if e'er your blades
  Had point or prowess, prove them now –
Woe to the file that foremost wades!
  They come – a falchion greets each brow,
And, as they tumble, trunk on trunk,
Beneath the gory waters sunk,
Still o'er their drowning bodies press
New victims quick and numberless;
Till scarce an arm in HAFED'S band,
  So fierce their toil, hath power to stir,
But listless from each crimson hand
  The sword hangs, clogg'd with massacre.
Never was horde of tyrants met
With bloodier welcome – never yet
To patriot vengeance hath the sword
More terrible libations pour'd!

All up the dreary, long ravine,
By the red, murky glimmer seen
Of half-quench'd brands, that o'er the flood
Lie scatter'd round and burn in blood,
What ruin glares! what carnage swims!
Heads, blazing turbans, quiv'ring limbs,
Lost swords that, dropp'd from many a hand
In that thick pool of slaughter stand: –
Wretches who wading, half on fire
  From the toss'd brands that round them fly,
'Twixt flood and flame in shrieks expire: –
  And some who, grasp'd by those that die,
Sink woundless with them, smother'd o'er
In their dead brethren's gushing gore!

But vainly hundreds, thousands bleed,
Still hundreds, thousands more succeed;
Countless tow'ards some flame at night

The North's dark insects wing their flight,
And quench or perish in its light,
To this terrific spot they pour –
Till, bridg'd with Moslem bodies o'er,
It bears aloft their slipp'ry tread,
And o'er the dying and the dead,
Tremendous causeway! on they pass. –
Then, hapless Ghebers, then, alas,
What hope was left for you? for you,
Whose yet warm pile of sacrifice
Is smoking in their vengeful eyes; –
Whose swords how keen, how fierce they knew,
And burn with shame to find how few?

Brush'd down by that vast multitude,
Some found their graves where first they stood;
While some with hardier struggle died,
And still fought on by HAFED'S side,
Who, fronting to the foe, trod back
Tow'rds the high towers his gory track;
And, as a lion swept away
 By sudden swell of JORDAN'S pride
From the wild covert where he lay,
Long battles with the' o'erwhelming tide,
So fought he back with fierce delay,
And kept both foes and fate at bay.

But whither now? their track is lost,
Their prey escap'd – guide, torches gone –
By torrent-beds and labyrinths crost,
 The scatter'd crowd rush blindly on –
'Curse on those tardy lights that wind,'
They panting cry, 'so far behind;
Oh for a bloodhound's precious scent,
To track the way the Gheber went!'
Vain wish – confusedly along
They rush, more desp'rate as more wrong:
Till, wilder'd by the far-off lights,
Yet glitt'ring up those gloomy heights,
Their footing, maz'd and lost, they miss,
And down the darkling precipice
Are dash'd into the deep abyss;
Or midway hang, impal'd on rocks,
A banquet, yet alive, for flocks
Of rav'ning vultures, – while the dell
Re-echoes with each horrible yell.

Those sounds – the last, to vengeance dear,
That e'er shall ring in HAFED'S ear, –
Now reach'd him, as aloft, alone,
Upon the steep way breathless thrown,
He lay beside his reeking blade,
 Resign'd, as if life's task were o'er,

Its last blood-offering amply paid,
  And IRAN'S self could claim no more.
One only thought, one ling'ring beam
Now broke across his dizzy dream
Of pain and weariness – 'twas she,
  His heart's pure planet, shining yet
Above the waste of memory,
  When all life's other lights were set.
And never to his mind before
Her image such enchantment wore.
It seem'd as if each thought that stain'd,
  Each fear that chill'd their loves was past,
And not one cloud of earth remain'd
  Between him and her radiance cast; –
As if to charms, before so bright,
  New grace from other worlds was giv'n,
And his soul saw her by the light
  Now breaking o'er itself from heav'n!
A voice spoke near him – 'twas the tone
Of a lov'd friend, the only one
  Of all his warriors, left with life
From that short night's tremendous strife. –
'And must we then, my Chief, die here?
Foes round us, and the Shrine so near!'
These words have rous'd the last remains
  Of life within him – 'what; not yet
Beyond the reach of Moslem chains!'
  The thought could make ev'n Death forget
His icy bondage – with a bound
He springs, all bleeding, from the ground,
And grasps his comrade's arm, now grown
Ev'n feebler, heavier than his own,
And up the painful pathway leads,
Death gaining on each step he treads.
Speed them, thou God, who heardst their vow!
They mount – they bleed – oh save them now –
The crags are red they've clamber'd o'er,
The rock-weed's dripping with their gore; –
Thy blade too, HAFED, false at length,
Now breaks beneath thy tott'ring strength!
Haste, haste – the voices of the Foe
Come nearer and nearer from below –
One effort more – thank Heav'n! 'tis past,
They've gain'd the topmost steep at last.
And now they touch the temple's walls,
  Now HAFED sees the Fire divine –
When, lo! – his weak, worn comrade falls
  Dead on the threshold of the shrine.
'Alas, brave soul, too quickly fled!
  And must I leave thee with'ring here,
The sport of every ruffian's tread,

The mark for every coward's spear?
No, by yon altar's sacred beams!'
He cries, and, with a strength that seems
Not of this world, uplifts the frame
Of the fall'n Chief, and tow'rds the flame
Bears him along; – with death-damp hand
  The corpse upon the pyre he lays,
Then lights the consecrated brand,
  And fires the pile, whose sudden blaze
Like lightning bursts o'er OMAN'S Sea.–
'Now, Freedom's God! I come to Thee,'
The youth exclaims, and with a smile
Of triumph vaulting on the pile,
In that last effort, ere the fires
Have harm'd one glorious limb, expires!

What shriek was that on OMAN'S tide?
  It came from yonder drifting bark,
That just hath caught upon her side
  The death-light – and again is dark.
It is the boat – ah, why delay'd? –
That bears the wretched Moslem maid;
Confided to the watchful care
  Of a small veteran band, with whom
Their gen'rous Chieftain would not share
  The secret of his final doom,
But hop'd when HINDA, safe and free,
  Was render'd to her father's eyes,
Their pardon, full and prompt, would be
  The ransom of so dear a prize. –
Unconscious, thus, of HAFED'S fate,
And proud to guard their beauteous freight,
Scarce had they clear'd the surfy waves
That foam around those frightful caves,
When the curst war-whoops, known so well,
Came echoing from the distant dell –
Sudden each oar, upheld and still,
  Hung dripping o'er the vessel's side,
And, driving at the current's will,
  They rock'd along the whisp'ring tide;
While every eye, in mute dismay,
  Was tow'rd that fatal mountain turn'd,
When the dim altar's quiv'ring ray
  As yet all lone and tranquil burn'd.

Oh! 'tis not HINDA, in the pow'r
  Of Fancy's most terrific touch
To paint thy pangs in that dread hour –
  Thy silent agony – 'twas such
As those who feel could paint too well,
But none e'er felt and liv'd to tell!
  'Twas not alone the dreary state

Of a lorn spirit, crush'd by fate,
When, though no more remains to dread,
  The panic chill will not depart; –
When, though the inmate Hope be dead,
  Her ghost still haunts the mould'ring heart;
No – pleasures, hopes, affections gone,
The wretch may bear, and yet live on,
Like things, within the cold rock found
Alive, when all's congealed around.
But there's a blank repose in this,
A calm stagnation, that were bliss
To the keen, burning, harrowing pain,
Now felt through all thy breast and brain; –
That spasm of terror, mute, intense,
That breathless, agonis'd suspense,
From whose hot throb, whose deadly aching,
The heart hath no relief but breaking!
Calm is the wave – heav'n's brilliant lights
  Reflected dance beneath the prow; –
Time was when, on such lovely nights,
  She who is there, so desolate now,
Could sit all cheerful, though alone,
  And ask no happier joy than seeing
That star-light o'er the waters thrown –
No joy but that, to make her blest.
  And the fresh, buoyant sense of Being,
Which bounds in youth's yet careless breast, –
Itself a star, not borrowing light,
But in its own glad essence bright.
How different now! – but, hark, again
The yell of havoc rings – brave men!
In vain, with beating hearts, ye stand
On the bark's edge – in vain each hand
Half draws the falchion from its sheath;
  All's o'er – in rust your blades may lie; –
He, at whose word they've scatter'd death,
  Ev'n now, this night, himself must die!
Well may ye look to yon dim tower,
  And ask, and wond'ring guess what means
The battle-cry at this dead hour –
  Ah! she could tell you – she who leans
Unheeded there, pale, sunk, aghast,
With brow against the dew-cold mast; –
  Too well she knows – her more than life,
Her soul's first idol and its last,
  Lies bleeding in that murd'rous strife.
But see – what moves upon the height?
Some signal! – 'tis a torch's light.
  What bodes its solitary glare?
In gasping silence tow'rd the Shrine
All eyes are turn'd – thine, HINDA, thine

Fix their last fading life-beams there.
'Twas but a moment – fierce and high
The death-pile blaz'd into the sky,
And far away, o'er rock and flood
 Its melancholy radiance sent;
While HAFED, like a vision stood
Reveal'd before the burning pyre,
Tall, shadowy, like a Spirit of Fire
 Shrin'd in its own grand element
"Tis he!' – the shudd'ring maid exclaims, –
 But, while she speaks, he's seen no more;
High burst in air the funeral flames,
 And IRAN'S hopes and hers are o'er!
One wild, heart-broken shriek she gave;
 Then sprung, as if to reach that blaze,
 Where still she fix'd her dying gaze,
And, gazing, sunk into the wave, –
 Deep, deep, – where never care or pain
 Shall reach her innocent heart again!

4 LITERATURE, NATION AND REVOLUTION

4.1 ACCOUNTS OF THE EVENTS OF 1857

Source: *A Companion to the 'Indian Mutiny' of 1857* ed. by P.J.O. Taylor, Delhi: Oxford University Press, 1996, pp.53, 22, 174, 9, 303, 300–01, 223–4.

[*We have added headings to the text for guidance.*]

The 'massacre of the ladies' at Kanpur [Cawnpore]

Letter of 17 July 1857

[T]he Nana had all the ladies whom he had saved from the former massacre murdered in cold blood. May God in his mercy, my dear Beadon, preserve me from ever witnessing again such a sight as I have seen this day. The house they were kept in was close to the hotel – opposite the theatre – it was a native house – with a courtyard in the middle, and an open room with pillars – opposite the principal entrance. The whole of the court and this room was literally soaked with blood and strewn with bonnets and those large hats worn by ladies – and there were long tresses of hair glued with clotted blood to the ground – all the bodies were thrown into a dry well and looking down – a map of naked arms legs and gashed trunks was visible. My nerves are now so deadened with horror that I write this quite calmly. It is better you should know the worst – I am going this moment to fill the well up and crown its mouth with a mound. Let us mention the subject no more – silence and prayer alone seem fitting. Ever sincerely yours J.W. Sherer.

The view from 'home'

Illustrated London News, *8 August 1857*

'Atrocities – Burning family alive – Killing by inches – cutting off noses, ears, fingers, toes; they violated mothers in the presence of their children – Bareilly bungalow fired and 40 killed as they ran out – Shahjehanpore church – 'all' murdered at Sunday service and heads and feet of the women and children strewn about the road. Jhansi women publicly violated then murdered and hacked to pieces. Delhi – six European women in one room; one hid under the sofa. Others violated and beheaded, blood trickled under the sofa – she screamed with terror, dragged out and sent to the King of Delhi's harem. Little children 1 year old thrown into the air and caught on bayonets. The Beresfords father, mother and 6 babes murdered: the throats of the children cut with pieces of glass to increase their suffering. At Raee a wretch seized a lady from Delhi, stripped her, violated and then murdered her brutally, first cutting off her breasts. Another hiding under a bridge ditto. Party of fugitives from Delhi found a pair of boots evidently of a girl 6 or 7 years old – with the feet still in them. We select these facts at random from the Indian newspapers and the private correspondence published in London, and could add other details as incredible but unfortunately as true ... And shall there be mercy to such fiends?

Contrasting accounts of the events of 1857

'Judex', an anonymous correspondent, The Times, 29 January 1858

I thoroughly believe that the rebels have aimed at the extermination of our race, but that they have not, as a rule, especially studied our dishonour, that by far the greater part of the stories of dishonour and torture are pure inventions, and that the mutineers have generally, in their blind rage, made no distinction between men and women in any way whatever ... After having visited almost every place from which such stories could have come, I have not learnt one instance in which anyone has survived to tell of injuries suffered. I believe there is not one mutilated, tortured, or, so far as I can gather, dishonoured person now alive ... At Delhi for months the belief was that men, women, and children had been horribly and indiscriminately massacred, but no more. I never heard there a story of dishonour pretending to anything like authenticity ... I *did* hear when I was on the Delhi side that the most horrible and too unmentionable atrocities had been committed at Cawnpore. Well, I went to Cawnpore; what did I hear there from impartial and well-informed persons? Why, simply this, that the matter had been particularly inquired into, and that the result was the assurance that there had not been dishonours or prolonged torture, but that the women and children had been all together massacred and thrown into a well. 'But,' it was added, 'though it has not been here there is no doubt that it was so at Delhi and those places ...' I do not assert that no unnecessary cruelty in the course of murder and no dishonour occurred, it would be opposed to human nature if, in this saturnalia of blood, it had been so, but I *do* express my strong belief that, under the known circumstances of the outbreak, there is rather to be remarked the absence, so far as we can discover, of the amount of female dishonour which might have been anticipated, than an excessive tendency that way. In short, so far as I have been able to learn, the object has throughout been ... extermination rather than dishonour; and the distinction is important ... A Caesar may be murdered; it is only a slave-driver who is tortured and deliberately dishonoured by his victims.

T.E.H., The Times, 1 April 1858

Everyone who was in the camp at Alipore, 35 miles from Delhi, on the 5th of last June [1857] may remember the trial of a zemindar for the rape and subsequent mutilation of an English lady escaping from Delhi ... [he had found the lady] wandering in the fields almost exhausted, she, poor girl, having walked nearly 40 miles under a burning sun – thermometer 110 deg. in the sun [shade]. He then stripped her and made her sit under a tree in front of the village for all the villagers to stare at, and after two hours of this torture, led her away into a clump of trees, where, after enduring every indignity which could be heaped upon a woman, she was murdered. The brute, when brought before the Court, not only did not deny the charge, but boasted of the manner in which he had slain the innocent.

An account of the fate the British met at the hands of the rebels at Jhansi

Bombay Times, *31 March 1858*

Shortly after, the whole of the European community, men women and children, were forcibly brought out of their homes: in the presence of the Ranee they were stripped naked. Then commenced a scene unparalleled in historical times. She who styles herself Ranee ordered as a preliminary step, the blackening of the faces with a composition of soot and oil, then, their being tied to trees at a certain distance from each other, and having directed the innocent little children to be hacked to pieces before the eyes of their agonised parents she gave the women into the hands of the rebel sepoys to be dishonoured first by them, and then handed over to the rabble. The maltreatment was enough to kill them, and several died ere the whole of the brutal scene had transpired; but those still lingering were put to death with the greatest cruelty, being severed limb from limb. The death the men were subject to was by no means so intensely cruel: they fell victim to the insatiate thirst for blood of the hellish Ranee and her fiendish myrmidons.

[Taylor comments that this story attributed to the Earl of Shaftesbury is supported by no evidence and seems an embellishment of a situation where 'the adult males were first slain, then the women and children. After their death the bodies were stripped, not to dishonour them, but to get possession of their clothing which might bring a few rupees to its possessor' (p.303).]

A later account of the fate the rebels met at the hands of the British at the Secunder bagh at Lucknow

St George's Gazette, *31 July 1894*

Close by the spot we halted at, there was a small hole, made by one of Peel's heavy guns, in the walls of the Secunder Bagh, and an officer standing by, said, 'just peep through there', which I did, and an awful sight presented itself to me. There were hundreds of dead and dying sepoys, lying in the small courtyard, where they had been caught by our troops, and from whence there was no exit for them to escape, and I believe not a soul got away. Some little time before we arrived, the building had been stormed by the 53rd, 93rd, and the Siekhs [sic], and after a severe struggle had been captured. Three almost entire sepoy regiments had held this building, to say nothing of other troops, and almost all fell: no quarter was asked, and no quarter was given. The Secunder Bagh is a small palace, standing at the north extremity of a small garden, which is surrounded by high walls: at each corner of the walls there is what may be called a semi-circular bastion or tower, and in the centre of the south wall, the gate leading to the garden and the palace stands; opposite to this is the palace, which stretches across the northern end of the garden ... the 53rd were in readiness to dash at the gates, which the Commander in Chief had given directions were to be blown open with powderbags. The officer of the Engineers on whom this duty devolved told me he had arranged to have the bags ready for this purpose, but that when the moment had arrived, the man with whom he had entrusted the powderbags was not forthcoming. You may imagine the poor fellow's feelings, and important duty to perform and his inability to fulfil it. Fortunately he had not too many seconds to wait, for the moment the troops entered through the breach, those of the enemy who were guarding the gate, made an attempt at escape by throwing it open, when they were met by the gallant 53rd, and a short hand-to-hand conflict ensued, which ended with the slaughter of everyone opposing them.

The fate of Miss Wheeler at Kanpur

A later account adapted from P.J.O. Taylor, A Star Shall Fall (1993)

[The story of the courage and death of Ulrica Wheeler, daughter of Major General Sir Hugh Wheeler, commander of the British troops at Cawnpore as told in 1857] is a typical contemporary tale made up to suit the mood, or inflame the lust for revenge; it was widely believed [...] One tale circulated in Kanpur itself for some weeks before it went out in to the wider world, there to be accepted as the definitive account of 'What happened to Miss Wheeler?' for many a long year. It is said that Ulrica Wheeler [daughter of Major General Sir Hugh Wheeler, commander of British troops at Cawnpore] was dragged from the boat at the Satichaura Ghat by a trooper of the mutinous 2nd Cavalry, by name Ali Khan, and taken to his house where, in the best tradition of savage warfare he had his evil way with her, but paid for it dramatically. Thus speaks the *Friend of India* [newspaper] on 3 September 1857 'she remained with this man till night when he went out and came home drunk; so soon as he was asleep she took a sword and cut off his head, his brother's head, his wife's and two children's. She then went out and seeing other sowars said to them, "Go in and see how nicely I have been rubbing the Resaldar's feet." They went inside and Miss Wheeler then jumped down a well and was killed' [...] Another version of the same tale is slightly more credible in that a revolver is substituted for the sword. She is reported to have secreted the revolver of her father and, in place of cutting everyone's head off with a sword, shot her abductor, his family and friends and then killed herself: there is a lurid illustration of Miss Wheeler 'defending her honour' in this way in Charles Ball's account of the mutiny [...] The supposed fate of Miss Wheeler was enacted in theatres and described in books and periodicals all over the world – the sensational accounts always included the 'fact' that she had killed her captor, Ali Khan, and his entire family [...] In fact she married Ali Khan and lived to the early years of the twentieth century: it is said that her descendants still live in Kanpur.

[In another entry in the Companion (pp.342ff.) P.J.O. Taylor recounts researches which led him to conclude that almost certainly Miss Wheeler's mother was the child of a relationship between an Irish officer in the British army and an Indian woman and thus that the archetypal British heroine Miss Wheeler was in fact part Indian.]

4.2   FROM THE INDIAN MUTINY OF 1857

G.B. Malleson

Source: Colonel G.B. Malleson, CSI, *The Indian Mutiny of 1857*, London: Seeley, 1892; repr. Ditton, Kent: R.J. Leach, 1993, pp.328–31, 403–13.

[We have added headings to the text for guidance.]

The British attack on Sikandarábágh

The following morning the troops, having breakfasted, set out at nine o'clock, and after some skirmishing carried the Dilkushá. Not halting there, they pressed on to the Martinière and carried that also. Sir Colin proceeded to secure the position thus gained by placing in the gardens of the Martinière Hope's brigade and Remmington's troop. Russell he placed on the left, in front of the Dilkushá, whilst he directed Little, with the cavalry, to occupy a line drawn from the canal on his right to a wall of the Dilkushá park on his left. With him he posted likewise Bourchier's battery. Somewhat later in the day, Russell, under his orders, occupied, with some companies, two villages on the canal covering the left of the advance.

But the rebels had no intention to allow the British general to remain in peaceful occupation of his line of attack. No sooner had they realised the exact nature of his dispositions than they massed their troops towards their centre, with the intention of making a grand assault. Little, noticing the gathering, sent an officer, Grant, to reconnoitre. On receiving Grant's report he despatched to the front the gallant Bourchier, supporting him with his cavalry. It was seen that the rebels had lined the opposite bank of the canal, and had only been prevented from making their forward movement by the timely occupation by Russell of the two villages above referred to. Bourchier's guns quickly sent back their skirmishers, and his fire reaching their supporting masses, these in their turn also fell back. A second attempt, made about five o'clock, on the Martinière was baffled by the vigilance of Adrian Hope and the successful practice of Remmington's guns. Here, again, Bourchier's battery and Peel's guns rendered splendid service, literally 'crushing,' by their flank fire, the rebels out of their position.

The troops bivouacked for the night in the places they had gained [...] on the morning of the 16th, a strong body of cavalry, with Blunt's horse-artillery and a company of the 53d, forming the advance guard, marched from the right, crossed the canal, then dry, followed for about a mile the bank of the Gúmtí, then, turning sharply to the left, reached a road running parallel to the Sikandarábágh. Sir Colin has so completely deceived the enemy as to his line of advance that this movement, followed though the advance guard was by the main body of the infantry, was absolutely unopposed, until the advance, making the sharp turn mentioned, entered the parallel road. Then a tremendous fire from enclosures near the road, and from the Sikandarábágh, opened on their flank. Their position was very dangerous, for they were literally broadside to the enemy's fire. The danger was apparent to every man of the advance. It served, however, only to quicken the resolve to baffle the rebels. The first to utilise the impulse was the gallant Blunt. Noticing that there was a plateau whence he could assail the Sikandarábágh on the further side of the road, hemmed in by its banks, apparently impossible for artillery to mount, he turned his horses' faces to the right bank, galloped up it, gained the open space on the plateau, and, unlimbering, opened his guns on the Sikandarábágh. It was one of the smartest services ever rendered in war. It at once changed the position.

For, whilst Blunt was drawing on himself the fire of the rebels by his daring act, the infantry of Hope's brigade had come up with a rush and cleared the enclosures bordering the lane and a large building near them. There remained only the Sikandarábágh itself. Against the massive walls of this building the light guns of Blunt's battery, and the heavier metal of those of Travers, who had joined him, were doing their best to effect a breach. No sooner was this breach believed to be practicable than there ensued one of the most wonderful scenes witnessed in that war. Suddenly and simultaneously there dashed towards it the men of the wing of the 93d and the Sikhs, running for it at full speed. A Sikh of the 4th Rifles reached it first, but he was shot dead as he jumped through. A young officer of the 93d, Richard Cooper by name, was more fortunate. Flying, so to speak, through the hole, he landed unscathed. He was closely followed by Ewart of the same regiment, by John I. Lumsden, attached to it as interpreter, by three privates of the same regiment, and by eight or nine men, Sikhs and Highlanders. Burroughs of the 93d had also effected an entrance, for he was in the enclosure before Ewart, but he was almost immediately wounded. The enclosure in which these officers and men found themselves was 150 yards square, with towers at the angles, a square building in the centre, and was held by 2000 armed men. It seemed impossible that one of the assailants should escape alive.

But what will not the sons of this little island do when the occasion demands it? It must suffice here to say that they rushed forward and maintained a not unequal contest till reinforcements poured in through the gate. Lumsden was killed, Cooper received a slash across his forehead at the moment that he laid his antagonist dead at his feet. Ewart, attacked by numbers, preserved his splendid presence of mind and slew many. He was still holding his own against enormous odds when the front gate was burst open and reinforcements dashed in. Then the struggle increased in intensity. It was a fight for life or death between the rebels and the masters against whom they had risen. For, it must not be forgotten, the defenders were all sipáhís who had rebelled. Nor did the struggle cease so long as one man of the 2000 remained alive.

Conclusion

On the 27th of January 1858 the King of Delhí had been brought to trial in the Privy Council chamber of his palace, charged with making war against the British Government, with abetting rebellion, with proclaiming himself as reigning sovereign of India, with causing, or being accessory to, the deaths of forty-nine people of British blood or British descent; and with having subsequently abetted others in murdering Europeans and others. After a patient trial, extending over forty days, the King was declared to be guilty of the main points of the charges, and sentenced to be transported for life. Ultimately he was sent to Pegu, where he ended his days in peace.

Meanwhile, in England, it had been found necessary, as usual, to find a scapegoat for the disasters which had fallen upon India. With a singular agreement of opinion the scapegoat was declared to be the Company which had won for England that splendid appanage. In consequence it was decreed to transfer the administration of India from the Company to the Crown. An Act carrying out this transfer was signed by the Queen on the 2d of August 1858.

Her Majesty thought it right, as soon as possible after the transfer had been thus effected, to issue to her Indian subjects a proclamation declaratory of the principles under which she intended thenceforth to administer their country. To the native princes of India she announced then, in that proclamation, that all treaties in force with them would be accepted and scrupulously maintained; that she would respect their rights, their dignity, and their honour as her own; that she would sanction no encroachments on the rights of any one of them; that the same obligations of duty which bound her to her other subjects would bind her also to them. To the natives of India generally Her Majesty promised not only complete toleration in matters of religion, but admission to office, without question of religion, to all such persons as might be qualified for the same by their education, ability, and integrity. The Queen declared, further, that she would direct that, in administering the law, due attention should be paid to the ancient rights, usages, and customs of India; that clemency should be extended to all offenders (in the matter of the Mutiny) save to those who had been or should be convicted of having taken part in the murder of British subjects; that full consideration should be given to men who had thrown off their allegiance, or who had been moved to action by a too credulous acceptance of the false reports circulated by designing men; that to all others who would submit before the 1st of January 1859 unconditional pardon should be granted [...]

It now remains for me to sum up in a few words the moral of the Mutiny, the lessons which it taught us, and its warnings.

But before I proceed to this summing up, I am anxious to say a word or two to disabuse the minds of those who may have been influenced by rumours current at the period as to the nature of the retaliation dealt out to the rebels by the British soldiers in the hour of their triumph. I have examined all those rumours – I have searched out the details attending the storming of Delhí, of Lakhnao, and of Jhánsí – and I can emphatically declare that, not only was the retaliation not excessive, it did not exceed the bounds necessary to ensure the safety of the conquerors. Unfortunately war is war. It is the meeting in contact of two bodies of men exasperated against each other, alike convinced that victory can only be gained by the destruction of the opponent. Under such circumstances it is impossible to give quarter. The granting of quarter would mean, as was proved over and over and over again, the placing in the hands of an enemy the power to take life treacherously. It was well understood, then, by both sides at the storming of the cities I have mentioned, that no quarter would be granted. It was a necessity of war. But beyond the deaths he inflicted in fair fight, the British soldier perpetrated no unnecessary slaughter [...]

It has been said that, in certain cases, a new kind of death was invented for convicted rebels, and that the punishment of blowing away from guns was intended to deprive the victim of those rites, the want of which doomed him, according to his view, to eternal perdition. Again, I assert that there is absolutely no foundation for this statement. The punishment itself was no new one in India. It was authorised by courts-martial, the members of which were native officers. Its infliction did not necessarily deprive the victim of all hope of happiness in a future life. The fact, moreover, that the Government of India, jealously careful never to interfere with the religious beliefs of the natives, sanctioned it, is quite sufficient to dispel the notion I have mentioned. The blowing away of criminals from guns was a punishment which was resorted to only when it was necessary to strike a terror which should act as a deterrent. It was in this sense that Colonel Sherer had recourse to it at Jalpaigúrí; and it is indisputable that he thus saved thousands of lives, and, possibly, staved off a great catastrophe [...]

I proceed now to deal with the two questions I have indicated in a preceding page – The lessons which the Mutiny has taught us, and its warnings.

The gradual conquest of India by a company of merchants inhabiting a small island in the Atlantic has ever been regarded as one of the most marvellous achievements of which history makes mention. The dream of Dupleix was realised by the very islanders who prevented its fulfilment by his countrymen. But great, marvellous even, as was that achievement, it sinks into insignificance when compared with the reconquest, with small means, of that magnificent empire in 1857–8. In 1857 the English garrison in India was surprised. There were not a dozen men in the country who, on the 1st of May of that year, believed that a catastrophe was impending which would shake British rule to its foundations. The explosion which took place at Mírath ten days later was followed, within five weeks, by similar explosions all over the North-west Provinces and in Oudh, not only on the part of the sipáhís, but likewise on the part of the people. The rebel sipáhís were strong in the possession of many fortified places, of a numerous artillery, of several arsenals and magazines. In trained soldiers they preponderated over the island garrison in the proportion of at least five to one. They inaugurated their revolt by successes which appealed to the imagination of an impulsive people. At Delhí, at Kánhpur, at Jhánsí, in many parts of Oudh, and in the districts around Agra, they proved to them the possibility of expelling the foreign master. Then, too, the majority of the population in those districts, landowners and cultivators alike, displayed a marked sympathy with the revolted sipáhís. For the English, in those first five weeks, the situation was bristling with danger. A false move might have temporarily lost India. In a strictly military sense they were too few in numbers, and too scattered, to attempt an offensive defence. It is to their glory that, disregarding the strictly scientific view, they did attempt it. The men who administered British India recognised at a glance that a merely passive defence would ruin them. They displayed, then, the truest forecast when they insisted that the resources still available in the North-west and in the Panjáb should be employed in an offensive movement against Delhí. That offensive movement saved them. Though Delhí offered a resistance spreading over four months, yet the penning within her walls of the main army of the rebels gave to the surprised English the time necessary to improvise resources, to receive reinforcements, to straighten matters in other portions of the empire.

The secret of the success of the British in the stupendous conflict which was ushered in by the Mutiny at Mírath and the surprise of Delhí, lay in the fact that they never, even in the darkest hour, despaired. When the news of the massacre of Kánhpur reached Calcutta, early in July, and the chattering Bengálís, who would have fainted at the sight of a sword drawn in anger, were discussing which man amongst them was the fittest to be Chancellor of the Exchequer under the King of Delhí,[4] there was not an Englishman in

---

[4] I can personally testify to this fact.

that city who did not feel the most absolute confidence that the cruel deed would be avenged. There was not one cry of despair – not one voice to declare that the star of Great Britain was about to set. In the deepest distress there was confidence that the sons of Britain would triumph. The same spirit was apparent in every corner of India where dwelt an English man or an English woman. It lived in the camp before Delhí, it was strong in the Residency of Lakhnao, it prevailed in every isolated station where the few Europeans were in hourly dangers of attack from rebels who gave no quarter. Nowhere did one of them shrink from the seemingly unequal struggle. As occasion demanded they held out, they persevered, they pressed forward, and, with enormous odds against them, they wore down their enemies, and they won. The spirit which had sustained Great Britain in her long conquest against Napoleon was a living force in India in 1857–8, and produced similar results.

How did they accomplish the impossible? The answer must spring at once to the lips of those who have witnessed the action of our countrymen in every part of the world. The energy and resolution which gave the Britain which Cæsar had conquered to the Anglian race; which almost immediately brought that Britain to a preponderant position in Europe; which, on the discovery of a new world, sent forth its sons to conquer and to colonise; which, in the course of a brief time, gained North America, the islands of the Pacific, and Australasia; which, entering only as third on the field, expelled its European rivals from India; that energy and that resolution, far from giving evidence of deterioration in 1857, never appeared more conspicuously. It was a question of race. This race of ours has been gifted by Providence with the qualities of manliness, of endurance, of a resolution which never flags. It has been its destiny to conquer and to maintain. It never willingly lets go. Its presence in England is a justification of its action all over the world. Wherever it has conquered, it has planted principles of order, of justice, of good government. And the Providence which inspired the race to plant these great principles, endowed it with the qualities necessary to maintain them wherever they had been planted [...]

More than thirty years have elapsed since the Mutiny was crushed, and again we witness a persistent attempt [by the newly formed Indian nationalist movement] to force Western ideas upon an Eastern people. The demands made by the new-fangled congresses for the introduction into India of representative institutions is a demand coming from the noisy and unwarlike races which hope to profit by the general corruption which such a system would engender. To the manly races of India, to the forty millions of Muhammadans, to the Sikhs of the Panjáb, to the warlike tribes on the frontier, to the Rohílás of Rohilkhand, to the Rájputs and Játs of Rájpútáná and Central India, such a system is utterly abhorrent. It is advocated by the adventurers and crochet-mongers of the two peoples. Started by the noisy Bengális, a race which, under Muhammadan rule, was content to crouch and serve, it is encouraged by a class in this country, ignorant for the most part of the real people of India, whilst professing to be in their absolute confidence. The agitation would be worthy of contempt but for the element of danger which it contains. I would impress upon the rulers of India the necessity, whilst there is yet time, of profiting by the experience of the Mutiny. I would implore them to decline to yield to an agitation which is not countenanced by the real people of India. I entreat them to realise that the Western system of representation is hateful to the Eastern races which inhabit the continent of India; that it is foreign to their traditions, their habits, their modes of thought. The people of India are content with the system which Akbar founded, and on the principles of which the English have hitherto mainly governed. Our Western institutions, not an absolute success in Europe, are based upon principles with which they have no sympathy. The millions of Hindustan desire a master who will carry out the principles of the Queen's proclamation of 1858.

4.3 FROM MARIAM: A STORY OF THE INDIAN MUTINY OF 1857

J.F. Fanthorne

Source: J.F.F[anthorne], *Mariam: A Story of the Indian Mutiny of 1857*, Benares: Chandraprabha Press, 1896, pp.151–9.

[*This extract is taken from a novel published anonymously in India for British readers in 1896 and never subsequently reprinted. All the signs are that the fictionalized account is based on the author's own experiences of events.*]

The station-church

The sun rose with unusual splendour. Six o'clock! Presently the Church-bell began to toll, and Church-goers were seen wending towards the house of prayer, – some in conveyances, others on foot.

The little Station-church of Shahjahánpore, dedicated to St. Mary, is situated on the southern boundary of the cantonment, in an ancient mango-grove known as Dúndá-bágh. It has three entrances, – one to the south, overlooking the large compound known as Buller's, with a small portico to it; another to the west, below the steeple; and the vestry-door opening to the north. There is no other opening to the north except windows. A narrow staircase leads up to the steeple from outside the west face of the building. To the east there used to be at the time of which we are writing, open fields sloping down to the river cultivated with the melon. To the west there was an open plain bounded by the civil part of the station, while the parade-ground stretched away to the north until the barracks of the native troops were reached. The bungalows scattered about on the sides of the parade-ground, were those occupied by the regimental officers, except Captains

Lysaght and Sneyd who resided in the Mess, which was located in the large bungalow known as Buller's.

The above description of the Church in its relation to the adjacent country was necessary in order to comprehend the events which we are about to narrate. We have now reached a part of our history which can best be related by an eye-witness. We shall therefore let Miss Lavater speak herself of what she saw and went through since the time she left home with her father, and tripped along by his side, while they both walked with light hearts and happy faces to Church; for as yet Mr. Lavater hadn't the remotest conception of what his experiences were going to be that day. We have seen how up to the last he had been earnestly pressed to seek escape by flight, but had spurned the proposal with indignation.

Miss Lavater's narrative

(The thirty-first of May)

Myself and my dear father had scarcely left the house, when several sepoys of the Regiment crossed the road, going for their morning bath to the river. They looked so strange and fierce as they cast malicious glances at us that I pressed close to my dear father's side, and drew his attention to them: 'See, papa, how fierce they look!' Their appearance did not strike him particularly, however, as the sepoys usually passed that way of a morning in order to perform their ablutions at the Khannaut; and father used I suppose to cross them frequently on his way to office which was close by, and, moreover, could be seen from our house.

We entered the Church, as was our custom, from the portico, and took our seats in the pew which we had always occupied; namely, the last pew to the right as you enter the Church from the south. There were a number of people already arrived. I did not notice them particularly, as every one seemed to be absorbed in devotion. We knelt down for the 'Confession', and were just in the middle of it, when on a sudden a tumult arose from outside as of many persons yelling and threatening, as the sound advanced in our direction. Every one got up from his knees; some of us stood up, others sat down. Father came out of the pew and went and stood at the door; I followed after him. There now appeared to our view six or seven stalwart men. They were muffled up to their noses, and wore tight *dhotís*[5] as if equipped for the gymnasium. They held naked swords in their right hands, and targets in their left. With heated blood and excited passions at the sight of us two, they at once commenced an onslaught. One of them made a cut at us, but the blow missed us both: the sword catching one of the side-posts of the door, and burying itself in the wood. My father was resting his left hand on the door; so when this first blow was struck, I rushed out of the door passing under his arm which formed a kind of arch for me, and so escaped.

[5] Loin-cloth.

A second and a third cut were made at my father by the others, both of which caught him on the right of his face. My father now siezed the weapon of one of his assailants, and with such a firm grip that in drawing it he cut off two digits of his right hand. These were all the cuts he received; but though he did not fall immediately, his wounds bled profusely. All this while I stood looking on from the portico. I was quite bewildered. I asked my dear father what had happened for him to bleed so. He answered: 'Take the handkerchief from my pocket and bandage my face.' I did so, using my own handkerchief also for the purpose. Another piece of cloth was lying there, he told me to use that also. I did so. He now expressed a desire to go home. I held him by his hand and endeavoured to lead him. We came out a short distance from the portico; but the bleeding became so profuse that he began to feel faint, and said to me: 'I can't walk, my dear; take me back to Church.' We retraced the few steps which we had taken, and re-entered the Church. He sat down on the ground, resting his back against the wall near to our pew.

I must leave my father here awhile, and lead the reader through the other events which occurred simultaneously. The armed men made one, and only one, rush through the Church, and finally went off through the vestry-door. After wounding my father, they rushed into, and up through, the length of the building, cutting right and left as they went. The next person whom they cut at was Lieutenant Scott; but his mother bent over and threw herself over him, and in that posture received a blow on her ribs; but her tight clothes protected her from any serious harm. Mr. Ricketts, the Collector, and Mr. MacCullam, the Minister, ran out through the vestry.

The survivors of the first onslaught now climbed up the belfry. I accompanied them. While there, we saw Captain James riding up to the church, but before he could reach it, a shot fired at him by one of the sepoys who were scattered about the parade-ground, struck him and he fell from his horse. Captains Lysaght and Sneyd now came running from the Mess, calling out: *Bàbá log, bábá log kyá karta?*[6] They tried to pacify and restrain their men, but no heed was paid to their words. They joined us in the turret with their weapons in their hands.

At this stage a phæton was sighted coming full speed towards the Church; it was Dr. Bowling's, and bore him, and his wife and child, and nurse. They had of course to cross the parade-ground. A bullet struck the Doctor as he sat on the coach-box: he at once bent down and doubled up in his seat. A sepoy now ran up and made a thrust at Mrs. Bowling; she, however, escaped, but the point of the sword inflicted a wound on her baby. When the phæton at length reached the Church, some of the officers ran down to help Dr. Bowling down from the coach-box. He seemed to struggle for a while, but was stone-dead before he reached the ground.

[6] My children, what are you about?

I had not been long in the turret when I came down quickly, as the officers present began to talk in an undecided tone, saying they had no ammunition, and could not possibly make a stand. They came to the conclusion that they must flee. They made at first for Hakim Mehndi-Ki-Kothi where Lieutenant Key lived, and afterwards for Chitauná-kí-kothí, Powayan-side, the residence of Mr. Ricketts. Mrs. Shields wanted me to go on to Chitauná with them all, but I told her that I preferred to stay with my father.

By this he had stretched himself down next to where Dr. Bowling lay; that is, near to the south entrance of the Church. A large pool of blood had formed where he sat against the wall. My dear father made no complaint; not a groan escaped him, but his lips were parched; he opened and closed his eyes, and was evidently growing fainter and fainter: the blood was not stanched. He now desired me to go home, and ask mother to send a cot and fetch him. Reluctant to leave his side, I yet did not see what I could do for him. At that time I could have given anything for a dooly, but where was I to get it from? I was dumb-founded. I had witnessed so many dreadful sights, had seen my own dear parent wounded and fall, and the sword of the murderer flash as it fell on the young and innocent, that I felt my head in a perfect daze. There wasn't a tear in my eye. I might have shed tears of blood at the sight of the gaping wounds which disfigured my noble father's face, but the very suddenness of the calamity which had befallen me left me no time to think.

I obeyed my dear father's command, and, leaving him where he lay on the bare ground, never, oh, never to see that dear face again! I proceeded homewards. I first went round to the vestry-side; I had no business to go that side, as my road lay in the opposite direction. I cannot tell why I went that side, when a ghastly spectacle met my gaze, which took me quite aback. There – just 12 or 15 feet from the vestry-door – there lay poor Mr. Ricketts cut into two. His murderer had performed a marvel of expert swordsmanship. From the left shoulder the blow had descended diagonally cutting sheer through the trunk, and separating the head and right hand from the rest of the body! Horror-struck I moved back involuntarily from the spot, and began my dreary walk home through Buller's compound. I met nobody in the way. No one challenged me, no one attempted to intercept or molest me. A dead silence prevailed all round. Just as I had reached the opposite end of Buller's compound, I perceived my dear home was in flames. Mr. Redman's house which was next to ours, was also in a blaze: the destruction was very rapid. On reaching the spot which was once our peaceful home, I looked for my mother but in vain. Mother was not there; she had either perished in the fire, or been cut down by one of the miscreants who had wounded my darling father. I looked for my granny whom I loved as tenderly as my parents, but she too was not there. None of the inmates of the house was to be seen, except old Nablé, my father's bearer, Khushál *dhobí*, and Dhani gardener, and his two sons. I descried Làlà Ràmjimal, also, standing some distance. Seeing me in such great perplexity, he came up to me and said: 'Bábá, don't distress yourself, be calm; mother, granny and the others are all safe; I know where they are refuged, I will take you to them.' He led me to a house situated some 30 yards from our old home. It was a mud house, and its entrance which faced the road, was closed. Lálá gave a push to the door with a foil which he held in his hand, but no one seemed to heed the call. At length Lálá whispered through a chink in the door: '*Missy bábá* has come, open'; when the door was opened slowly by my mother. I rushed into her arms; she held me to her breast, and exclaimed but without a tear in her eye: 'Thank God! at least one is spared to me.'

I then said to her: 'Papa lies wounded in Church; send some one to fetch him.' Poor mother was prepared for this news; she cast a piteous look at Lálá as she said: 'Who will go for us, Lálá, but you?' Lálá at once answered: 'Yes, *sarkár*! I will go. Do you all remain close here until I return.' I volunteered to go back to the Church with him, urging as a plea: 'You don't know where he is; let me go with you and assist you to place him on a cot, and bring him away. Poor father! he is so faint with loss of blood!' But Lálá forbade me, saying: 'No, *Missy bábá*, you must not leave your mother now. If you are seen in my company, you are sure to be killed, and I shall not be able to defend you. I will go alone, and will do what I can to assist my *Sarkár*.' So I had to remain back, while the noble-hearted Lálá ventured alone on his hazardous journey; that is, to bring relief to a Christian – a *káfir*, who to all appearance had been done for already by his murderers. He returned to us in the afternoon, several hours after he had gone, but only to tell us that poor father was no more. '*Sáhab to ho chuké*,'[7] said he. 'I only arrived in time to see him die. He did not speak; he evidently could not; his eyes were getting glazed; pools of blood lay around him; he had lost so much blood that it was impossible for him to survive. He did not speak, but he looked at me in a way to convince me that he recognised me. A tear trickled down his eye; he turned away his head, and expired. That one look of his seemed to say: "I leave them to your care"!'

[7] A Hindu term, and a polite way of saying 'Sahab is dead.'

5 THE WHITE MAN'S BURDEN

5.1 FROM GORA

Rabindranath Tagore

Source: Rabindranath Tagore, *Gora* (1924), Delhi: Macmillan Pocket Tagore Edition, 1980, pp.132–9.

This was the first time Gora had seen what the condition of his country was like, outside the well-to-do and cultured society of Calcutta. How divided, how narrow, how weak was this vast expanse of rural India, – how supinely unconscious of its own power, how ignorant and indifferent as to its own welfare! What gulfs of social separation yawned between villages only a few miles apart. What a host of self-imposed imaginary obstacles prevented them from taking their place in the grand commerce of the world. The most trivial things looked so big to them; the least of their traditions seemed so unbreakable. Without such an opportunity to see it for himself, Gora would never have been able even to imagine how inert were their minds, how petty their lives, how feeble their efforts.

One day a fire occurred in one of the villages in which Gora was staying, and he was astounded to see how utterly they failed to combine their resources even when faced by so grave a calamity. All was confusion, every one running hither and thither, weeping and wailing, without the least sign of method anywhere. There was no source of drinking-water near by, the women of the neighbourhood having to bring water from a great distance for their household work, even those who were comparatively well off never dreaming of digging a tank to mitigate this daily inconvenience in their own households. There had been fires before, but as every one had accepted them merely as visitations of Fate, it never occurred to them to try to make some arrangement for a nearer supply of water.

It began to appear ridiculous to Gora for him to be lecturing these people about the condition of their country, when their power of understanding even the most urgent needs of their own neighbourhood was so overcast by blind habit. What, however, astonished him most was to find that neither Motilal nor Ramapati [the two friends with whom he travels] seemed to be the least disturbed by all that they were seeing – rather they appeared to regard Gora's perturbation as uncalled for. 'This is how the poor are accustomed to live,' they said to themselves; 'what to us would be hardship they do not feel at all.' They even thought it mere sentimentality to be so concerned about a better life for them. But to Gora it was a constant agony to be brought face to face with this terrible load of ignorance, apathy and suffering, which had overwhelmed rich and poor, learned and ignorant alike, and clogged their advance at every step.

Then Motilal received news of the illness of a relative and left for home, so that Ramapati alone remained with Gora.

As these two proceeded they came to a Mohammedan village on the bank of a river. After a long search for some place where they could accept hospitality, they discovered at last a solitary Hindu house, – that of a barber. When this man had duly offered welcome to the Brahmin visitors, they saw on entering his house that one of the inmates was a Mohammedan boy whom, they learnt, the barber and his wife had adopted. The orthodox Ramapati was thoroughly disgusted, and when Gora taxed the barber with his un-Hindu conduct, he said: 'What's the difference, sir? We call on Him as Hari, they as Allah, that's all.'

Meanwhile the sun had risen high and had begun to shine fiercely. The river was far off, across a wide stretch of burning sand. Ramapati, tortured with thirst, wondered where he could get any drinking-water, fit for a Hindu. There was a small well near the barber's house, but the water polluted by this renegade's touch could not serve for his need.

'Has this boy no parents of his own?' asked Gora.

'He has both mother and father living, but he is as good as an orphan all the same,' answered the barber.

'How do you mean?'

The barber then related the boy's history.

The estate on which they were living had been farmed out to Indigo Planters, who were always disputing with the agriculturist tenants the rights to till the fertile alluvial land on the river-banks. All the tenants had given in to the *sahibs* except those living in this village of Ghosepara, who refused to be ousted by the Planters. They were Mohammedans, and their leader Faru Sardar was afraid of no one. During these disputes with the Planters he had twice been put in gaol for fighting the police, and he had at length been reduced to such straits that he was practically starving, yet he would not be tamed.

This year the cultivators had managed to reap an early crop off the fresh alluvial deposits by the river-side, but the Planter himself had come later on, only about a month ago, with a band of club-men and forcibly taken away the harvested grain. It was on this occasion that Faru Sardar, in defending his fellow-villagers, had hit the *sahib* such a blow on his right hand that it had to be amputated. Such daring had never been known in these parts before.

From then onwards the police had been engaged in devastating the whole neighbourhood, like a raging fire. No household was safe from their inquisitorial depredations, nor the honour of the women. Others besides Faru had been put away in gaol, and of those who were left, many had fled from the village. In the house of Faru there was no food, and his wife had only one piece of cloth to wear as a *sari*, the condition of which was such that she could not come out in public. Their only son, this boy Tamiz, used to call the barber's wife 'Auntie', and when she saw that he was practically starving, the kind-hearted woman took him away to her own home.

At a distance of about two or three miles were the offices of the Indigo Factory and there the Inspector of Police and his force were quartered. When they would next descend upon the village, and what they would do in the name of investigation, no one could say. Only the previous day they had suddenly appeared in the house of the barber's old neighbour, Nazim. This Nazim had a young brother-in-law who had come from a different district to see his sister. At sight of him the Police Inspector, without rhyme or reason, had remarked: 'Ha, we have a fighting cock here, I see! Throws out his chest, does he?' With which he struck him over the face with his staff, knocking out his teeth and making his mouth bleed. When the man's sister, at sight of this brutality, came running up to tend her brother, she was sent reeling to the ground with a savage blow. Formerly the police had not the courage to commit such atrocities in this quarter, but now that all the able-bodied men had either been arrested or had fled, they could wreak their wrath on the villagers with impunity, and there was no knowing how long their shadow would continue to darken the locality.

Gora could not tear himself away from the barber's recital, but Ramapati had become desperate with thirst, so before the barber had finished his story he repeated his question: 'How far is the nearest Hindu quarter?'

'The rent collector of the Indigo Factory is a Brahmin, by name Madhav Chatterjee,' said the barber. 'He is the nearest Hindu. He lives in the office buildings, two or three miles away.'

'What kind of a man is he?' asked Gora.

'A regular limb of Satan,' replied the barber. 'You couldn't get another scoundrel so cruel, and yet so soft-spoken. He has been entertaining the Police Inspector all these days, but will collect the expenses from us, with a little profit for himself, too!'

'Come, Gora Babu, let's be going,' interposed Ramapati impatiently. 'I can't stand this any longer.' His patience had been brought to breaking point by the sight of the barber's wife drawing water from the well in the courtyard and pouring pitchers full over that wretch of a Mohammedan boy for his bath! His nerves were so set on edge that he felt he could not remain in that house for another moment.

Gora, as he was going, asked the barber: 'How is it that you are lingering on here in spite of these outrages? Have you no relatives to go to, elsewhere?'

'I've been living here all my life,' explained the barber, 'and have got attached to all the neighbours. I am the only Hindu barber near about, and, as I have nothing to do with land, the Factory people don't molest me. Besides, there's hardly another man left in the whole village, and if I went away the women would die of fright.'

'Well, we're off,' said Gora, 'but I'll come and see you again after we've had some food.'

The effect of this long story of oppression on the famished and thirsty Ramapati was to turn all his indignation against the recalcitrant villagers, who had brought all this trouble on their own head. This upraising of the head in the presence of the strong seemed to him the very height of folly and pig-headedness on the part of these Mohammedan roughs. He felt they were served right thus to be taught a lesson, and to have their insolence broken. It is just this class of people, thought he, who always fall foul of the police, and for that they themselves are mainly responsible. Why could not they give in to their lords and masters? What was the use of this parade of independence – where was their foolhardy boasting now? In fine, Ramapati's sympathies were inwardly ranged on the side of the *sahibs*.

As they walked across the burning sand, in the full heat of the mid-day sun, Gora never spoke a single word. When at length the roof of the Indigo Factory's office showed through the trees, he stopped suddenly and said: 'Ramapati, you go and get something to eat, I'm going back to that barber's.'

'Whatever do you mean?' exclaimed Ramapati. 'Aren't you going to eat anything yourself? Why not go after we've had something at this Brahmin's house?'

'I'll take care of myself, don't you worry!' replied Gora. 'You get some food and then go back to Calcutta. I expect I shall have to stay on at that Ghosepara village for a few days, – you'll not be able to do that.'

Ramapati broke out into a cold sweat. He could not believe his ears. How could Gora, good Hindu as he was, even talk of staying in the home of those unclean people? Was he mad, or determined to starve himself to death? But this was not the time to do much thinking; every moment seemed to him an age; and it did not need much persuasion to make him take this opportunity to escape to Calcutta. Before he went in to the office, however, he turned to cast one glance at Gora's tall figure as he strode across the burning, deserted sands.

How lonely he looked!

Gora was almost overcome with hunger and thirst, but the very idea of having to preserve his caste by eating in the house of that unscrupulous scoundrel, Madhav Chatterjee, became more and more unbearable the longer he thought of it. His face was flushed, his eyes bloodshot, his brain on fire with the revolt in his mind. 'What terrible wrong have we been doing,' he said to himself, 'by making purity an external thing! Shall my caste remain pure by eating from the hands of this oppressor of the poor Mahomedans, and be lost in the home of the man who has not only shared their miseries but given shelter to one of them at the risk of being outcasted himself? Let the final solution be what it may, I cannot accept such con-clusion now.'

The barber was surprised to see Gora return alone. The first thing Gora did was to take the barber's drinking-vessel and after carefully cleaning it, fill it with water from the well. After drinking he said: 'If you have any rice and *dal* in the house please let me have some to cook.' His host busied himself in getting everything ready for the cooking, and when Gora had prepared and eaten his meal he said: 'I will stay on with you for a time.'

The barber was beside himself at the idea, and putting his hands together in entreaty, he said: 'I am indeed fortunate that you should think of conde-scending so far, but this house is being watched by the police, and if they find you here it may lead to trouble.'

'The Police won't dare to harm you while I am here, – if they do, I'll take care of you.'

'No, no,' implored the barber. 'Pray don't think of such a thing. If you try to protect me I shall indeed be a lost man. These fellows will think I am trying to get them into trouble by calling in an outsider as witness of their mis-deeds. So far, I've managed to steer clear of them, but once I am a marked man, I'll have to leave, and after that the village will go to rack and ruin.'

It was hard for Gora, who had spent all his days in the city, to comprehend the reason of the man's apprehensions. He had always imagined that you only had to stand firmly enough on the side of right, for evil to be overcome. His sense of duty would not allow him to think of leaving these afflicted villagers to their fate. But the barber fell on his knees and clasped his feet saying: 'You are a Brahmin, sir, have deigned to come as my guest, – to ask you to depart is nothing less than a crime for me. But because I see you really pity us, I make bold to tell you that if you try to prevent any of this police oppression while staying at my house, you will only get me into trouble.

Gora, annoyed at what he considered the unreasonable cowardice of the barber, left him that very afternoon. He even had a revulsion of feeling for having taken food under the roof of this good-for-nothing renegade! Tired and disgusted he arrived towards evening at the Factory office. Ramapati had lost no time in starting for Calcutta after his meal, and was no longer there.

Madhav Chatterjee showed the greatest respect for Gora, and invited him to be his guest, but Gora, full of his angry reflections, broke out with: 'I won't even touch your water!' [...]

Gora was blessed with an appetite of more than the usual dimensions, – he had moreover eaten very little through all that dismal day, but his whole body was afire with indignation, and he simply could not stay on there for anything, so he excused himself, saying that he had business elsewhere.

5.2 *FROM* THE EXPANSION OF ENGLAND

J.R. Seeley

Source: J.R. Seeley, *The Expansion of England* (1884), ed. and with an introduction by John Gross, London: University of Chicago Press, 1971, pp.192–3, 195, 206–9, 212–13, 231–6, 240–41.

[We have added headings to the text for guidance.]

On the British Empire and the example of the Roman Empire

On the whole then we find in India three stages of civilisation, first that of the hill-tribes, which is barbarism, then that which is perhaps sufficiently described as the Mussulman stage, and thirdly the arrested and half-crushed civilisation of a gifted race, but a race which has from the beginning been in a remarkable manner isolated from the ruling and progressive civilisation of the world. Whatever this race achieved it achieved a long time ago. Its great epic poems, which some would compare to the greatest poems of the West, are ancient, though perhaps much less ancient than has been thought, so too its systems of philosophy, its scientific grammar. The country has achieved nothing in modern times. It may be compared to Europe, as Europe would have been if after the irruption of barbarians and the fall of ancient civilisation it had witnessed no revival, and had not been able to protect itself against the Tartar invasions of the tenth and thirteenth centuries. Let us suppose Europe to have vegetated up to the present time in the condition in which the tenth century saw it, exposed to periodical invasions from Asia, wanting in strongly marked nations and vigorous states, its languages mere vernaculars not used for the purposes of literature, all its wisdom enshrined in a dead language and doled out to the people by an imperious priesthood, all its wisdom too many centuries old, sacred texts of Aristotle, the Vulgate, and the Fathers, to which nothing could be added but in the way of commentary. Such seems to be the condition of the Aryans of India, a condition which has no resemblance whatever to barbarism, but resembles strikingly the medieval phase of the civilisation of the West.

The dominion of Rome over the western races was the empire of civilisation over barbarism. Among the Gauls and Iberians Rome stood as a beacon-light; they acknowledged its brightness, and felt grateful for the illumination they received from it. The domination of England in India is rather the empire of the modern world over the medieval. The light we bring is not less real, but it is probably less attractive and received with less gratitude. It is not a glorious light shining in darkness, but a somewhat cold daylight introduced into the midst of a warm gorgeous twilight.

Many travellers have said that the learned Hindu, even when he acknowledges our power and makes use of our railways, yet is so far from regarding us with reverence that he very sincerely despises us. This is only natural. We are not cleverer than the Hindu; our minds are not richer or larger than his. We cannot astonish him, as we astonish the barbarian, by putting before him ideas that he never dreamed of. He can match from his poetry our sublimest thoughts; even our science perhaps has few concep-tions that are altogether novel to him. Our boast is not that we have more ideas or more brilliant ideas, but that our ideas are better tested and sounder. The greatness of modern, as compared with medieval or ancient, civilisation is that it possesses a larger stock of demonstrated truth, and therefore infinitely more of practical power. But the poetical or mystic philosopher is by no means disposed to regard demonstrated truth with reverence; he is rather apt to call it shallow, and to sneer at its practical triumphs, while he revels for his part in reverie and the luxury of un-bounded speculation.

We in Europe however are pretty well agreed that the treasure of truth which forms the nucleus of the civilisation of the West is incomparably more sterling not only than the Brahminic mysticism with which it has to contend, but even than that Roman enlightenment which the old Empire transmitted to the nations of Europe. And therefore we shall hold that the spectacle now presented by India of a superior civilisation introduced by a conquering race is equal in interest and importance to that which the Roman Empire presented [...]

The Roman Empire is in this respect a somewhat extreme case, because the conquering Power was so remarkably small compared to the empire it attached to itself. The light radiated not from a country but from a city, which was not so much a shining disk as a point of intense light. The Roman Republic had institutions which were essentially civic, and which began to break down as soon as they were extended even to the whole of Italy [...] Of all the unparalleled features which the English Empire in India presents, not one is so unique as the slightness of the machinery by which it is united to England and the slightness of its reaction upon England. How this peculiarity has been caused I have already explained. I have shown that our acquisition of India was made by a process so peculiar that it cost us nothing. Had England as a state undertaken to subvert the Empire of the Great Mogul, she would have destroyed her own constitution in the pro-cess, no less than Rome did by the conquest of Europe. For she would evidently have been compelled to convert herself into a military state of the most absolute type. But as England has merely inherited the throne which was founded in India by certain Englishmen who rose to the head of affairs in time of anarchy, she has been but very slightly disturbed in her domestic affairs by this acquisition. It has modified no doubt, as I have said, her foreign policy in a great degree, but it has produced no change in the internal character of the English state. In this respect India has produced as little effect upon England as those Continental States which have been in modern times connected with England in what is called a personal union, Hannover under the Georges, or Holland under William III. The consequence is that in this instance the operation of the higher civilisation on the lower is likely to be far more energetic and continuous than in those ancient examples of the Roman Empire or the Greek Empire in the East [...]

The motives behind the British Empire

If we combine all the facts I have hitherto adduced in order to form a conception of our Indian Empire, the result is very singular. An Empire similar to that of Rome, in which we hold the position not merely of a ruling but of an educating and civilising race (and thus, as in the marriage of Faust with Helen of Greece, one age is married to another, the modern European to the medieval Asiatic spirit); this Empire held at arm's length, paying no tribute to us, yet costing nothing except through the burden it imposes on our foreign policy, and neither modifying nor perceptibly influencing our busy domestic politics; this Empire nevertheless held firmly and with a grasp which does not slacken but visibly tightens; the union of England and India, ill-assorted and unnatural as it might seem to be, nevertheless growing closer and closer with great rapidity under the influence of the modern conditions of the world, which seem favourable to vast political unions; all this makes up the strangest, most curious, and perhaps most instructive chapter of English history. It has been made the subject of much empty boasting, while those who have looked deeper have often been disposed to regard the whole enterprise with despondency, as a kind of romantic adventure which can lead to nothing permanent. But as time passes it rather appears that we are in the hands of a Providence which is greater than all statesmanship, that this fabric so blindly piled up has a chance of becoming a part of the permanent edifice of civilisation, and that the Indian achievement of England as it is the strangest, may after all turn out to be the greatest, of all her achievements.

At this point again we are led to turn our eyes from the present to the past and to inquire how it could happen to us to undertake such an enterprise. I devoted a lecture to the historical question by what force we were able to subdue the people of India to our government; but this question is different. That was the question, how? this is the question, why? We see that without any supernatural force or genius it was possible to raise such an Empire, but what was the motive which impelled us to do it? How many lives, some of them noble and heroic, many of them most laborious, have been spent in piling up this structure of empire! Why did they do it? Or if they themselves looked no further than their instructions, what was the motive of the authority that gave them their instructions? If this was the [East India] Company, why did the Company desire to conquer India, and what could they gain by doing so? If it was the English Government, what could be its object, and how could it justify such an undertaking to Parliament? We may have been at times too warlike, but the principal wars we have waged have borne the appearance at least of being defensive. Naked conquest for its own sake has never had attractions for us. What then did we propose to ourselves?

The English Government assuredly has gained nothing through this acquisition, for if it has not hampered their budgets by the expense of conquest, on the other hand it has not lightened them by any tribute. If we hope to discover the guilty party by the old plan of asking Cui bono? that is, Who profited by it? the answer must be, English Commerce has profited by it. We have here a great foreign trade, which may grow to be enormous, and this trade is secured to us so long as we are masters of the Government of India. Here no doubt is a substantial acquisition, which stands us in good stead now that we find by experience how tenacious of protection foreign Governments are. May it then be assumed that this trade has been our sole object all along?

The hypothesis is plausible, and it is made more plausible still when we remark that our Empire began evidently in commerce. To defend our factories and for no other purpose we took arms in the first instance. Our first wars in India, as they belong to the same time so belong evidently to the same class, as our colonial wars with France. They were produced by the same great cause on which I have insisted so much, the competition of the Western states for the wealth of the regions discovered in the fifteenth century. We had trade-settlements in India as we had trade-settlements in America. In both countries we encountered the same rivals, the French. In both countries English and French traders shook their fists at each other from rival commercial stations. In America our New England and Virginia stood opposed to their Acadie and Canada; and similarly our Madras, Calcutta and Bombay stood opposed in India to their Pondicherry, Chandernagore and Mahee.

The crisis came in America and India at once between 1740 and 1760, when in two wars divided by a very hollow and imperfect peace these two states struggled for supremacy, and in both quarters England was victorious. From victory over France in India we proceeded without a pause to empire over the Hindus. This fact, combined with the other fact equally striking of the great trade which now exists between England and India, leads very naturally to a theory that our Indian Empire has grown up from first to last out of the spirit of trade. We may imagine that after having established our settlements on the coast and defended these settlements both from the native Powers and from the envy of the French, we then conceived the ambition of extending our commerce further inland; that perhaps we met with new States, such as Mysore or the Mahratta Confederacy, which at first were unwilling to trade with us, but that in our eager avarice we had recourse to force, let loose our armies upon them, broke down their custom-houses and flooded their territories in turn with our commodities, that in this way we gradually advanced our Indian trade, which at first was insignificant, until it became considerable, and at last, when we had not only intimidated but actually overthrown every great native Government, when there was no longer any Great Mogul or any Sultan of Mysore or any Peishwa of the Mahrattas or any Nawab Vizir of Oude or any Maharajah and Khalsa of the Sikhs, then, all restraints having been removed, our trade became enormous.

But it will be found on closer examination that the facts do not answer to this theory. True it is that our Empire began in trade, and that lately there has been an enormous development of trade. But the course of affairs in history is not necessarily a straight line, so that when any two points in it are determined its whole course is known. The truth is that if the spirit of English trade had been thus irrepressible and bent upon overcoming all the obstacles which lay in its path, it would not have raised wars in India, for the main obstacle was not there. The main obstacle to English trade was not the jealousy of native Princes, but the jealousy of the East India Company itself. Accordingly there has been no correspondence in time between the increase of trade and the advance of conquest.

Our trade on the contrary continued to be insignificant in spite of all our conquests until about 1813, and it began to advance with great rapidity soon after 1830. These dates point to the true cause of progress in trade, and they show that it is wholly independent of progress in conquest, for they are the dates of the successive Acts of Parliament by which the Company was deprived of its monopoly. Thus it appears that, while it was by the East India Company that India was conquered, it was not by the East India Company, but rather by the destruction of the East India Company, that the great trade with India was brought into existence. Our conquests in India were made by an exclusive chartered Company, but our Indian trade did not greatly prosper until that Company ceased practically to exist [...]

1813 is the date when the [Company's] monopoly was first seriously curtailed and 1833 the date when it was destroyed. Now Macculloch when he speaks of the utter insignificance of our old trade with India has before him the statistics up to the year 1811, and the statistics which show so vast an increase in the modern trade refer to the years after 1813, and especially to those after 1833. In other words, so long as India was in the hands of those whose object was trade, the trade remained insignificant; the trade became great and at last enormous, when India began to be governed for itself and trade-considerations to be disregarded. This might seem a paradox, did we not remember that in dismissing trade-considerations we also destroyed a monopoly. But there is nothing wonderful in the fact that an exclusive Company, even when its first object is trade, carries on trade languidly, nothing wonderful in a vast trade springing up as soon as the shackles of monopoly were removed.

On the other hand we do not find that the increase of trade corresponds at all to the augmentation of our territorial possessions in India.

There have been four great rulers in India to whom the German title of Mehrer des Reichs or Increaser of the Empire might be given. These are Lord Clive, the founder, Lord Wellesley, Lord Hastings [here Francis

Rawdon-Hastings (1754–1826), Governor-General of Bengal 1813–23 – unrelated to Warren Hastings] and Lord Dalhousie. Roughly it may be said that the first established us along the Eastern Coast from Calcutta to Madras; the second and third overthrew the Mahratta power and established us as lords of the middle of the country and of the Western side of the peninsula, and the fourth, besides consolidating these conquests, gave us the northwest and carried our frontier to the Indus. There were considerable intervals between these conquests, and accordingly they fall into separate groups. Thus there was a period of conquest between 1748 and 1765, which we may label with the name of Clive, a second period beginning in 1798, which may be said to have lasted, though with a long pause, till about 1820; this period may bear the names of Wellesley ánd Lord Hastings; and a third period of war between 1839 and 1850, but of this the first part was unfortunate, and only the second part led to conquests, of which it fell to Lord Dalhousie to reap the harvest.

Now there was no correspondence whatever in time between these territorial advances and the advance of trade. Thus we remarked how insignificant the trade of India still was in 1811, and yet this was shortly after the vast annexations of Lord Wellesley. On the other hand trade took a great leap about 1830, and this is one of the peaceful intervals of the history. About the time of the mutiny annexation almost ceased, and yet the quarter of a century in which no conquests have been made has been a period of the most rapid growth in trade.

And thus the assertion which is often made and which seems to be suggested by a rapid survey of the history, the assertion namely that the Empire is the mere result of a reckless pursuit of trade, proves to be as untrue as the other assertion sometimes made, that it is the result of a reckless spirit of military aggression.

Our first step to empire was very plainly taken with a view simply of defending our factories. The Madras Presidency grew out of an effort, which in the first instance was quite necessary, to protect Fort St. George and Fort St. David from the French. The Bengal Presidency grew in a similar way out of the evident necessity of protecting Fort William and punishing the Mussulman Nawab of Bengal, Surajah Dowlah, for his atrocity of the Black Hole.

So far then the causation is clear. In the period which immediately followed, the revolutionary and corrupt period of British India, it is undeniable that we were hurried on by mere rapacity. The violent proceedings of Warren Hastings at Benares, in Oude, and Rohilcund were of the nature of money-speculations. If the later history of British India had been of the same kind, our Empire might fairly be said to be similar to the Empire of the Spanish in Hispaniola and Peru, and to have sprung entirely out of the reckless pursuit of gain.

But a change took place with the advent of Lord Cornwallis in 1785. Partly by the example of his high character, partly by a judicious reform, which

consisted in making the salaries of the servants of the Company considerable enough to remove the excuse for corruption, he purged the service of
its immorality [...]

Conclusion

There are two schools of opinion among us with respect to our Empire, of
which schools the one may be called the bombastic and the other the
pessimistic. The one is lost in wonder and ecstasy at its immense dimensions, and at the energy and heroism which presumably have gone to the
making of it; this school therefore advocates the maintenance of it as a point
of honour or sentiment. The other is in the opposite extreme, regards it as
founded in aggression and rapacity, as useless and burdensome, a kind of
excrescence upon England, as depriving us of the advantages of our insu-
larity and exposing us to wars and quarrels in every part of the globe; this
school therefore advocates a policy which may lead at the earliest possible
opportunity to the abandonment of it. Let us consider then how our studies
[...] have led us to regard these two opposite opinions.

We have been led to take a much more sober view of the Empire than would
satisfy the bombastic school. At the outset we are not much impressed with
its vast extent, because we know no reason in the nature of things why a
state should be any the better for being large, and because throughout the
greater part of history very large states have usually been states of a low
type. Nor again can we imagine why it should be our duty to maintain our
Empire for an indefinite time simply out of respect for the heroism of those
who won it for us, or because the abandonment of it might seem to betray a
want of spirit. All political unions exist for the good of their members and
should be just as large, and no larger, as they can be without ceasing to be
beneficial. It would seem to us insane that if the connexion with the colonies
or with India hampered both parties, if it did harm rather than good,
England should resolve to maintain it to her own detriment and to that
of her dependencies. We find too a confusion of ideas hidden under much of
the bombastic language of this school, for they seem to conceive of the
dependencies of England as of so much property belonging to her, as if the
Queen were like some Sesostris or Solomon of the ancient world, to whom
'Tarshish and the isles brought presents, Arabia and Sheba offered gifts',
whereas the connexion is really not of this kind at all, and England is not,
directly at least, any the richer for it. And further we have ventured to doubt
that the vastness of this Empire necessarily proves some invincible heroism
or supernatural genius for government in our nation. Undoubtedly some
facts may be adduced to show natural aptitude for colonisation and a
faculty of leadership in our race. A good number of Englishmen may be
cited who have exerted an almost magical ascendancy over the minds of the
native races of India, and in Canada again, where the English settlers have
competed directly with the French, they have shown a marked superiority
in enterprise and energy. But though there is much to admire in the history

of Greater Britain, yet the preeminence of England in the New World has certainly not been won by sheer natural superiority. In the heroic age of maritime discovery we did not greatly shine. We did not show the genius of the Portuguese, and we did not produce a Columbus or a Magelhaen. When I examined the causes which enabled us after two centuries to surpass other nations in colonisation, I found that we had a broader basis and a securer position at home than Portugal and Holland, and that we were less involved in great European enterprises than France and Spain. In like manner when I inquired how we could conquer, and that with little trouble, the vast country of India, I found that after all we did it by means mainly of Indian troops, to whom we imparted a skill which was not so much English as European, that the French showed us the way, and that the condition of the country was such as to render it peculiarly open to conquest.

Thus I admitted very much of what is urged by the pessimists against the bombastic school. I endeavoured to judge the Empire by its own intrinsic merits and to see it as it is, not concealing the inconveniences which may attend such a vast expansion or the dangers to which it may expose us, nor finding any compensation for these in the notion that there is something intrinsically glorious in an Empire 'upon which the sun never sets', or, to use another equally brilliant expression, an Empire 'whose morning drum-beat, following the sun and keeping company with the hours, encircles the globe with an unbroken chain of martial airs'. But though there is little that is glorious in most of the great Empires mentioned in history, since they have usually been created by force and have remained at a low level of political life, we observed that Greater Britain is not in the ordinary sense an Empire at all. Looking at the colonial part of it alone, we see a natural growth, a mere normal extension of the English race into other lands, which for the most part were so thinly peopled that our settlers took possession of them without conquest. If there is nothing highly glorious in such an expansion, there is at the same time nothing forced or unnatural about it. It creates not properly an Empire, but only a very large state. So far as the expansion itself is concerned, no one does or can regard it but with pleasure. For a nation to have an outlet for its superfluous population is one of the greatest blessings. Population unfortunately does not adapt itself to space; on the contrary the larger it is the larger is its yearly increment. Now that Great Britain is already full it becomes fuller with increased speed; it gains a million every three years. Probably emigration ought to proceed at a far greater rate than it does, and assuredly the greatest evils would arise if it were checked. But should there be an expansion of the State as well as of the nation? 'No,' say the pessimists, 'or only till the colony is grown-up and ready for independence.' When a metaphor comes to be regarded as an argument, what an irresistible argument it always seems! I have suggested that in the modern world distance has very much lost its effect, and that there are signs of a time when states will be vaster than they have hitherto been. In ancient times emigrants from Greece to Sicily took up their independence at once, and in those parts there were almost as many states as cities. In the eighteenth century Burke thought a federation quite impossible across the Atlantic Ocean. In such times the metaphor of the grown-up son might well harden into a convincing demonstration. But since Burke's time the Atlantic Ocean has shrunk till it seems scarcely broader than the sea between Greece and Sicily. Why then do we not drop the metaphor? I have urged that we are unconsciously influenced by a historic parallel which when examined turns out to be inapplicable. As indeed it is true generally that one urgent reason why politicians should study history is that they may guard themselves against the false historical analogies which continually mislead those who do not study history! These views are founded on the American Revolution, and yet the American Revolution arose out of circumstances and out of a condition of the world which has long since passed away. England was then an agricultural country by no means thickly peopled; America was full of religious refugees animated by ideas which in England had lately passed out of fashion; there was scarcely any flux and reflux of population between the two countries, and the ocean divided them with a gulf which seemed as unbridgeable as that moral gulf which separates an Englishman from a Frenchman. Even then the separation was not effected without a great wrench. It is true that both countries have prospered since, nevertheless they have had a second war and may have a third, and it is wholly an illusion to suppose that their prosperity has been caused or promoted by their separation. At any rate all the conditions of the world are altered now. The great causes of division, oceans and religious disabilities, have ceased to operate. Vast uniting forces have begun to work, trade and emigration. Meanwhile the natural ties which unite Englishmen resume their influence as soon as the counteracting pressure is removed, I mean the ties of nationality, language and religion. The mother-country having once for all ceased to be a step-mother, and to make unjust claims and impose annoying restrictions, and since she wants her colonies as an outlet both for population and trade, and since on the other hand the colonies must feel that there is risk, not to say also intellectual impoverishment, in independence, since finally intercourse is ever increasing and no alienating force is at work to counteract it, but the discords created by the old system pass more and more into oblivion, it seems possible that our colonial Empire so-called may more and more deserve to be called Greater Britain, and that the tie may become stronger and stronger. Then the seas which divide us might be forgotten, and that ancient preconception, which leads us always to think of ourselves as belonging to a single island, might be rooted out of our minds. If in this way we moved sensibly nearer in our thoughts and feelings to the colonies and accustomed ourselves to think of emigrants as not in any way lost to England by settling in the colonies, the result might be, first that emigration on a vast scale might become our remedy for pauperism, and secondly that some organisation might gradually be arrived at which might make the whole force of the Empire available in time of war.

In taking this view I have borne in mind the example of the United States. It is curious that the pessimists among ourselves should generally have been admirers of the United States, and yet there we have the most striking example of confident and successful expansion. Those colonists which, when they parted from us, did not fringe the Atlantic sea-board and had but lately begun to push their settlements into the valley of the Ohio, how steadily, how boundlessly, and with what steadfast self-reliance have they advanced since! They have covered with their States or Territories, first the mighty Mississippi valley, next the Rocky Mountains, and lastly the Pacific coast. They have made no difficulty of absorbing all this territory; it has not shaken their political system. And yet they have never said, as among us even those who are not pessimists say of the colonies, that if they wish to secede, of course they can do so. On the contrary they have firmly denied this right, and to maintain the unity of their vast state have sacrificed blood and treasure in unexampled profusion. They firmly refused to allow their Union to be broken up, or to listen to the argument that a state is none the better for being very large.

Perhaps we are hardly alive to the vast results which are flowing in politics from modern mechanism. Throughout the greater part of human history the process of state-building has been governed by strict conditions of space. For a long time no high organisation was possible except in very small states. In antiquity the good states were usually cities, and Rome herself when she became an Empire was obliged to adopt a lower organisation. In medieval Europe, states sprang up which were on a larger scale than those of antiquity, but for a long time these too were lower organisms and looked up to Athens and Rome with reverence as to the homes of political greatness. But through the invention of the representative system these states have risen to a higher level. We now see states with vivid political consciousness on territories of two hundred thousand square miles and in populations of thirty millions. A further advance is now being made. The federal system has been added to the representative system, and at the same time steam and electricity have been introduced. From these improvements has resulted the possibility of highly organised states on a yet larger scale. Thus Russia in Europe has already a population of near eighty millions on a territory of more than two millions of square miles, and the United States will have by the end of the century a population as large upon a territory of four millions of square miles. We cannot, it is true, yet speak of Russia as having a high type of organisation; she has her trials and her transformation to come, but the United States has shown herself able to combine free·institutions in the fullest degree with boundless expansion.

Now if it offends us to hear our Empire described in the language of Oriental bombast, we need not conclude that the Empire itself is in fault, for it is open to us to think that it has been wrongly classified. Instead of comparing it to that which it resembles in no degree, some Turkish or Persian congeries of nations forced together by a conquering horde, let us compare it to the United States, and we shall see at once that, so far from being of an obsolete type, it is precisely the sort of union which the conditions of the time most naturally call into existence [...]

[In previous chapters] I have led you to consider what may be the effect of our Indian Empire upon India itself. We perhaps have not gained much from it; but has India gained? On this question I have desired to speak with great diffidence. I have asserted confidently only thus much, that no greater experiment has ever been tried on the globe, and that the effects of it will be comparable to the effect of the Roman Empire upon the nations of Europe, nay probably they will be much greater. This means no doubt that vast benefits will be done to India, but it does not necessarily mean that great mischiefs may not also be done. Nay, if you ask on which side the balance will incline, and whether, if we succeed in bringing India into the full current of European civilisation, we shall not evidently be rendering her the greatest possible service, I should only answer, 'I hope so; I trust so.' In the academic study of these vast questions we should take care to avoid the optimistic commonplaces of the newspaper. Our Western civilisation is perhaps not absolutely the glorious thing we like to imagine it. Those who watch India most impartially see that a vast transformation goes on there, but sometimes it produces a painful impression upon them; they see much destroyed, bad things and good things together; sometimes they doubt whether they see many good things called into existence. But they see one enormous improvement, under which we may fairly hope that all other improvements are potentially included, they see anarchy and plunder brought to an end and something like the *immensa majestas Romanae pacis* established among two hundred and fifty millions of human beings.

Another thing almost all observers see, and that is that the experiment must go forward, and that we cannot leave it unfinished if we would. For here too the great uniting forces of the age are at work, England and India are drawn every year for good or for evil more closely together. Not indeed that disuniting forces might not easily spring up, not that our rule itself may not possibly be calling out forces which may ultimately tend to disruption, nor yet that the Empire is altogether free from the danger of a sudden catastrophe. But for the present we are driven both by necessity and duty to a closer union. Already we should ourselves suffer greatly from disruption, and the longer the union lasts the more important it will become to us. Meanwhile the same is true in an infinitely greater degree of India itself. The transformation we are making there may cause us some misgivings, but though we may be led conceivably to wish that it had never been begun, nothing could ever convince us that it ought to be broken off in the middle.

Altogether I hope that our long course of meditation upon the expansion of England may have led you to feel that there is something fantastic in all those notions of abandoning the colonies or abandoning India, which are so freely broached among us. Have we really so much power over the march of events as we suppose? Can we cancel the growth of centuries for a whim, or because, when we throw a hasty glance at it, it does not suit our fancies? [...] But the fancy is but a chimera produced by inattention, one of those monsters, for such monsters there are, which are created not by imagination but by the want of imagination!

6.1 IRISH WRITERS WHO ARE WINNING FAME

W.B. Yeats

Source: W.B. Yeats, *Letters to the New Island*, new edn ed. by George Bornstein and Hugh Witemeyer, Basingstoke and London: Macmillan, 1989, pp.9–12.

[This letter appeared in the Boston Pilot, 3 August 1889, under the heading 'The Celt in London'.]

London, July 10

England is an old nation, the dramatic fervor has perhaps ebbed out of her. However that may be, most of the best dramas on the English stage from the times of Congreve and Sheridan and Goldsmith to our own day have been the work of Irishmen. The most prominent London dramatist at the present time is certainly the Irishman, Mr. W. Wills; his much more renowned countryman, Mr. Dion Boucicault, can hardly any longer be called a London dramatist. The revival of Mr. Wills' *Claudian* at the Princess, previous to its departure for America, has brought up again the old gossip as to the disputed authorship of the famous earthquake incident which concludes the piece. As a matter of fact the whole merit of the originality belongs to Mr. Wills, and dates as far back as the year following the catastrophe at Ischia, when Mr. Wills, being in Rome, wrote the piece in communication with eye witnesses of the kind of incident he was venturing for the first time to introduce into a drama. But rumor would have it that he was a mere poet and incapable of so scenic a conception. His collaborator was also a man of literature and not equal to so great a stage climax. The manager had a brief period of glory, but then it was decided that he was not enough of a machinist. So the carpenter would have ended by keeping all the laurels, but that he was deprived of them in a most unexpected way. A well known dramatist taking his seat in the stalls the other night remarked to the spruce young female attendant who distributed the programmes, 'That earthquake idea was a very fine one of ——' he was not able to finish his sentence. 'Oh, thank you, sir,' she exclaimed with effusion, and retired blushing and triumphant.

A play on King Arthur and his Round Table by Mr. Wills is announced to follow *Macbeth* at the Lyceum, with Ellen Terry as Guinevere. There was a rumor going the rounds some time ago that he had written a *Robert Emmet* for Irving, and that the censor interfered. It is probably a canard.

One day Mr. Burnand, the editor of *Punch* and general critic and wit, was sitting reading a newspaper in the Savile Club, a place of general resort for men of letters, Messrs. Austin Dobson, Edmund Gosse and Herbert Spencer being among its more constant frequenters. Mr. Wills came in. Now Mr. Burnand had just damned a play of his and so was careful to bury his head in the paper. 'I have something to say that very much concerns Mr. Burnand,' said the dramatist, leaning his back against the fire. The editor of *Punch* looked up. Mr. Wills went on: 'You will remember Dutton Cook, and how he was always damning my plays and Miss S——'s acting? [Mr Burnand remembered.] One day I said to Miss S——, "Let us make a little wax image of Dutton Cook"; we made it. "Now, let us melt it before the fire and stick pins in it"; we did so. Next day I met a friend, and he said to me, "Have you heard the news – Dutton Cook is dead?"' Having finished his story, Mr. Wills went out, and since that day Mr. Burnand, who is no less superstitious than witty, is said to have only abused Mr. Wills' plays in reason.

I wonder are all the cheap reprints of good books read as well as bought. A very distinguished poet who has always issued his own poems at very high prices said in my hearing the other day that he believed the cheap books were only bought for their cheapness. A friend of his once purchased, he said, a London Directory twenty years old because he could get it for threepence: it was such a large book for the money. I hope the threepenny reprint of Aubrey de Vere's beautiful *Legends of St. Patrick*, just issued by Cassell, Petter and Galpin, will have a kinder fate and be read as well as bought. It will probably sell by tens of thousands, if one can at all judge by the immense sale of the same publishers' threepenny editions of such poems as Coventry Patmore's *Angel in the House*, and the sculptor Woolner's *Beautiful Lady*. Its being reprinted at all is a sign of the times. A few years ago no Englishman would look at any Irish book unless to revile it. *Ça ira*.

Apropos of poets, the peasant poet is less common in England than with us in Ireland, but I did meet the other day an Englishman who was a true specimen of the tribe. He is a Mr. Skipsey. He is from the coal country – a strange nursing mother for a poet – and taught himself to write by scribbling with a piece of white chalk on the sides of coal shafts and galleries. In the depth of a mine hundreds of feet under the earth he has written many sweetest and tenderest songs. He has not been left to sing his songs to the dull ear of the mine, however. The most sensitive ears of our time have heard them. Rossetti, a little before his death, read and praised these simple poems. The last few months Walter Scott's collection of Mr. Skipsey's mining poems has made new admirers for their author. He is more like a sailor than a miner, but like a sailor who is almost painfully sensitive and refined. He talked to me about Clarence Mangan a good deal. Mangan is a great favourite of his. He recited, for the benefit of a Saxon who stood by, Mangan's 'Dark Rosaleen.' Himself a peasant, he turned for the moment's inspiration to the country where poetry has been a living voice among the people.

There has been some talk lately in the Parnell Commission about the Clondalkin Branch of the National League. Archbishop Walsh in his evidence mentioned it as the only branch whose action he had been compelled to condemn. They had written up a black list of people they did not approve of. When I was last in Ireland I saw a good deal of the main mover in the matter. Not at all a firebrand, one would think, but a quiet shoemaker, who had read and thought a great deal. I used often to stray into his shop to have a chat about books, among the leather clippings. Since then I have seen at odd times in Irish papers sketches and stories of peasant character by him, all full of keen observation. Carlyle, Emerson and Miss Laffan are his favourite authors. When I saw him last he was struggling with Emerson's Over-Soul, but told me that he always read Carlyle when 'wild with the neighbors.' Perhaps his black list was only a piece of Carlylese. The biographer of Frederick did so love the strong hand! Though, indeed, most men of letters seem to have a tendency towards an amateurish love of mere strength. They grow impatient of the slow progress of thought perhaps, and long to touch the hilt of the sword.

I have some literary news from Ireland. Mr. T.W. Rolleston, who has just translated Walt Whitman into German, is now busy on a life of Lessing for Mr. Walter Scott, who published last autumn the shilling reprint of his translation from Epictetus. Mr. Rolleston has just removed to Dublin from his pretty Wicklow house, where for years now he has been busy with his beehives and Walt Whitman. He is a fine Greek scholar and quite the handsomest man in Ireland, but I wish he would devote his imagination to some national purpose. Cosmopolitan literature is, at best, but a poor bubble, though a big one. Creative work has always a fatherland.

Miss O'Leary is preparing for the press a collection of her poems. Her friends, who have undertaken all business matters concerning the book, have decided to have for frontispieces photographs of Miss O'Leary and Mr. John O'Leary. There will be an introduction describing their life and connection with the old Fenian movement, and, by way of appendix, Sir Charles Gavan Duffy's article on Miss O'Leary's poems. They are, indeed, tender and beautiful verses – Irish alike in manner and matter. One of the most, if not the most, distinguished of critics now writing in the English tongue once said to me, though he did not in the least sympathize with her national aspirations, 'Miss O'Leary's poems, like Wordsworth's, have the rarest of all gifts – a true simplicity.' Nothing quite like them has been printed anywhere since Kickham wrote, 'She lived beside the Anner.' They are the last notes of that movement of song, now giving place to something new, that came into existence when Davis, singing, rocked the cradle of a new Ireland. We of the younger generation owe a great deal to Mr. John O'Leary and his sister. What nationality is in the present literary movement in Ireland is largely owing to their influence – an influence all feel who come across them. The material for many a song and ballad has come from Mr. John O'Leary's fine collection of Irish books – the best I know. The whole house is full of them. One expects to find them bulging out of the windows.

He, more clearly than any one, has seen that there is no fine nationality without literature, and seen the converse also, that there is no fine literature without nationality.

6.2 IRELAND AND THE ARTS

W.B. Yeats

Source: 'Ireland and the Arts' (1901), in W.B. Yeats, *Essays and Introductions*, London and Basingstoke: Macmillan, 1961, repr. 1974, pp.203–10.

[This essay was first published in the United Irishman, 31 August 1901.]

The arts have failed; fewer people are interested in them every generation. The mere business of living, of making money, of amusing oneself, occupies people more and more, and makes them less and less capable of the difficult art of appreciation. When they buy a picture it generally shows a long-current idea, or some conventional form that can be admired in that lax mood one admires a fine carriage in or fine horses in; and when they buy a book it is so much in the manner of the picture that it is forgotten, when its moment is over, as a glass of wine is forgotten. We who care deeply about the arts find ourselves the priesthood of an almost forgotten faith, and we must, I think, if we would win the people again, take upon ourselves the method and the fervour of a priesthood. We must be half humble and half proud. We see the perfect more than others, it may be, but we must find the passions among the people. We must baptize as well as preach.

The makers of religions have established their ceremonies, their form of art, upon fear of death, upon the hope of the father in his child, upon the love of man and woman. They have even gathered into their ceremonies the ceremonies of more ancient faiths, for fear a grain of the dust turned into crystal in some past fire, a passion that had mingled with the religious idea, might perish if the ancient ceremony perished. They have re-named wells and images and given new meanings to ceremonies of spring and midsummer and harvest. In very early days the arts were so possessed by this method that they were almost inseparable from religion, going side by side with it into all life. But, to-day, they have grown, as I think, too proud, too anxious to live alone with the perfect, and so one sees them, as I think, like charioteers standing by deserted chariots and holding broken reins in their hands, or seeking to go upon their way drawn by that sexual passion which alone remains to them out of the passions of the world. We should not blame them, but rather a mysterious tendency in things which will have its end some day. In England, men like William Morris, seeing about them passions so long separated from the perfect that it seemed as if they could not be changed until society had been changed, tried to unite the arts once more to life by uniting them to use. They advised painters to paint fewer pictures upon canvas, and to burn more of them on plates; and they tried to persuade sculptors that a candlestick might be as beautiful as a statue. But here in Ireland, when the arts have grown humble, they will find two passions ready to their hands, love of the Unseen Life and love of country. I would have a devout writer or painter often content himself with subjects taken from his religious beliefs; and if his religious beliefs are those of the majority, he may at last move hearts in every cottage; while even if his religious beliefs are those of some minority, he will have a better welcome than if he wrote of the rape of Persephone, or painted the burning of Shelley's body. He will have founded his work on a passion which will bring him to many besides those who have been trained to care for beautiful things by a special education. If he is a painter or a sculptor he will find churches awaiting his hand everywhere, and if he follows the masters of his craft our other passion will come into his work also, for he will show his Holy Family winding among hills like those of Ireland, and his Bearer of the Cross among faces copied from the faces of his own town. Our art teachers should urge their pupils into this work, for I can remember, when I was myself a Dublin art student, how I used to despond, when youthful ardour burned low, at the general indifference of the town.

But I would rather speak to those who, while moved in other things than the arts by love of country, are beginning to write, as I was some sixteen years ago, without any decided impulse to one thing more than another, and especially to those who are convinced, as I was convinced, that art is tribeless, nationless, a blossom gathered in No Man's Land. The Greeks looked within their borders, and we, like them, have a history fuller than any modern history of imaginative events; and legends which surpass, as I think, all legends but theirs in wild beauty, and in our land, as in theirs, there is no river or mountain that is not associated in the memory with some event or legend; while political reasons have made love of country, as I think, even greater among us than among them. I would have our writers and craftsmen of many kinds master this history and these legends, and fix upon their memory the appearance of mountains and rivers and make it all visible again in their arts, so that Irishmen, even though they had gone thousands of miles away, would still be in their own country. Whether they chose for the subject the carrying off of the Brown Bull or the coming of Patrick, or the political struggle of later times, the other world comes so much into it all that their love of it would move in their hands also, and as much, it may be, as in the hands of the Greek craftsmen. In other words, I would have Ireland re-create the ancient arts, the arts as they were under-stood in Judaea, in India, in Scandinavia, in Greece and Rome, in every ancient land; as they were understood when they moved a whole people and not a few people who have grown up in a leisured class and made this understanding their business.

I think that my reader will have agreed with most that I have said up till now, for we all hope for arts like these. I think indeed I first learned to hope for them myself in Young Ireland Societies, or in reading the essays of

Davis. An Englishman, with his belief in progress, with his instinctive preference for the cosmopolitan literature of the last century, may think arts like these parochial, but they are the arts we have begun the making of.

I will not, however, have all my readers with me when I say that no writer, no artist, even though he choose Brian Borúmha or Saint Patrick for his subject, should try to make his work popular. Once he has chosen a subject he must think of nothing but giving it such an expression as will please himself. As Walt Whitman has written:–

> The oration is to the orator, the acting is to the actor and actress, not to the audience:
> And no man understands any greatness or goodness, but his own or the indication of his own.

He must make his work a part of his own journey towards beauty and truth. He must picture saint or hero, or hillside, as he sees them, not as he is expected to see them, and he must comfort himself, when others cry out against what he has seen, by remembering that no two men are alike, and that there is no 'excellent beauty without strangeness'. In this matter he must be without humility. He may, indeed, doubt the reality of his vision if men do not quarrel with him as they did with the Apostles, for there is only one perfection and only one search for perfection, and it sometimes has the form of the religious life and sometimes of the artistic life; and I do not think these lives differ in their wages, for 'The end of art is peace', and out of the one as out of the other comes the cry: *Sero te amavi, Pulchritudo tam antiqua et tam nova! Sero te amavi!*

The Catholic Church is not the less the Church of the people because the Mass is spoken in Latin, and art is not less the art of the people because it does not always speak in the language they are used to. I once heard my friend Mr. Ellis say, speaking at a celebration in honour of a writer whose fame had not come till long after his death, 'It is not the business of a poet to make himself understood, but it is the business of the people to understand him. That they are at last compelled to do so is the proof of his authority.' And certainly if you take from art its martyrdom, you will take from it its glory. It might still reflect the passing modes of mankind, but it would cease to reflect the face of God.

If our craftsmen were to choose their subjects under what we may call, if we understood faith to mean that belief in a spiritual life which is not confined to one Church, the persuasion of their faith and their country, they would soon discover that although their choice seemed arbitrary at first, it had obeyed what was deepest in them. I could not now write of any other country but Ireland, for my style has been shaped by the subjects I have worked on, but there was a time when my imagination seemed unwilling, when I found myself writing of some Irish event in words that would have better fitted some Italian or Eastern event, for my style had been shaped in that general stream of European literature which has come from so many watersheds, and it was slowly, very slowly, that I made a new style. It was years before I could rid myself of Shelley's Italian light, but now I think my style is myself. I might have found more of Ireland if I had written in Irish, but I have found a little, and I have found all myself. I am persuaded that if the Irishmen who are painting conventional pictures or writing conventional books on alien subjects, which have been worn away like pebbles on the shore, would do the same, they, too, might find themselves. Even the landscape-painter, who paints a place that he loves, and that no other man has painted, soon discovers that no style learned in the studios is wholly fitted to his purpose. And I cannot but believe that if our painters of Highland cattle and moss-covered barns were to care enough for their country to care for what makes it different from other countries, they would discover, when struggling, it may be, to paint the exact grey of the bare Burren Hills, and of a sudden, it may be, a new style, their very selves. And I admit, though in this I am moved by some touch of fanaticism, that even when I see an old subject written of or painted in a new way, I am yet jealous for Cuchulain, and for Baile and Aillinn, and for those grey mountains that still are lacking their celebration. I sometimes reproach myself because I cannot admire Mr. Hughes' beautiful, piteous *Orpheus and Eurydice* with an unquestioning mind. I say with my lips, 'The Spirit made it, for it is beautiful, and the Spirit bloweth where it listeth,' but I say in my heart, 'Aengus and Edain would have served his turn'; but one cannot, perhaps, love or believe at all if one does not love or believe a little too much.

And I do not think with unbroken pleasure of our scholars who write about German writers or about periods of Greek history. I always remember that they could give us a number of little books which would tell, each book for some one county, or some one parish, the verses, or the stories, or the events that would make every lake or mountain a man can see from his own door an excitement in his imagination. I would have some of them leave that work of theirs which will never lack hands, and begin to dig in Ireland the garden of the future, understanding that here in Ireland the spirit of man may be about to wed the soil of the world.

Art and scholarship like these I have described would give Ireland more than they received from her, for they would make love of the unseen more unshakable, more ready to plunge deep into the abyss, and they would make love of country more fruitful in the mind, more a part of daily life. One would know an Irishman into whose life they had come – and in a few generations they would come into the life of all, rich and poor – by something that set him apart among men. He himself would understand that more was expected of him than of others because he had greater possessions. The Irish race would have become a chosen race, one of the pillars that uphold the world.

6.3 INTRODUCTION TO RABINDRANATH TAGORE'S GITANJALI

W.B. Yeats

Source: W.B. Yeats, Introduction to Rabindranath Tagore, *Gitanjali*, Delhi: Macmillan, 1913; repr. Delhi: Macmillan Pocket Tagore Edition, 1981, pp.v–xv.

Introduction

A few days ago I said to a distinguished Bengali doctor of medicine, 'I know no German, yet if a translation of a German poet had moved me, I would go to the British Museum and find books in English that would tell me something of his life, and of the history of his thought. But though these prose translations from Rabindranath Tagore have stirred my blood as nothing has for years, I shall not know anything of his life, and of the movements of thought that have made them possible, if some Indian traveller will not tell me.' It seemed to him natural that I should be moved, for he said, 'I read Rabindranath every day, to read one line of his is to forget all the troubles of the world.' I said, 'An Englishman living in London in the reign of Richard the Second had he been shown translations from Petrarch or from Dante, would have found no books to answer his questions, but would have questioned some Florentine banker or Lombard merchant as I question you. For all I know, so abundant and simple is this poetry, the new Renaissance has been born in your country and I shall never know of it except by hearsay.' He answered, 'We have other poets, but none that are his equal; we call this the epoch of Rabindranath. No poet seems to me as famous in Europe as he is among us. He is as great in music as in poetry, and his songs are sung from the west of India into Burma wherever Bengali is spoken. He was already famous at nineteen when he wrote his first novel; and plays, written when he was but little older, are still played in Calcutta. I so much admire the completeness of his life; when he was very young he wrote much of natural objects, he would sit all day in his garden; from his twenty-fifth year or so to his thirty-fifth perhaps, when he had a great sorrow, he wrote the most beautiful love poetry in our language'; and then he said with deep emotion, 'words can never express what I owed at seventeen to his love poetry. After that his art grew deeper, it became religious and philosophical; all the aspirations of mankind are in his hymns. He is the first among our saints who has not refused to live, but has spoken out of Life itself, and that is why we give him our love.' I may have changed his well-chosen words in my memory but not his thought. 'A little while ago he was to read divine service in one of our churches – we of the Brahma Samaj use your word "church" in English – it was the largest in Calcutta and not only was it crowded, people even standing in the windows, but the streets were all but impassable because of the people.'

Other Indians came to see me and their reverence for this man sounded strange in our world, where we hide great and little things under the same veil of obvious comedy and half-serious depreciation. When we were making the cathedrals had we a like reverence for our great men? 'Every morning at three – I know, for I have seen it' – one said to me, 'he sits immovable in contemplation, and for two hours does not awake from his reverie upon the nature of God. His father, the Maha Rishi, would sometimes sit there all through the next day; once, upon a river, he fell into contemplation because of the beauty of the landscape, and the rowers waited for eight hours before they could continue their journey.' He then told me of Mr. Tagore's family and how for generations great men have come out of its cradles. 'Today,' he said, 'there are Gogonendranath and Abanindranath Tagore, who are artists; and Dwijendranath, Rabindranath's brother, who is a great philosopher. The squirrels come from the boughs and climb on to his knees and the birds alight upon his hands.' I notice in these men's thought a sense of visible beauty and meaning as though they held that doctrine of Nietzsche that we must not believe in the moral or intellectual beauty which does not sooner or later impress itself upon physical things. I said, 'In the East you know how to keep a family illustrious. The other day the curator of a museum pointed out to me a little dark-skinned man who was arranging their Chinese prints and said, "That is the hereditary connoisseur of the Mikado, he is the fourteenth of his family to hold the post."' He answered, 'When Rabindranath was a boy he had all round him in his home literature and music.' I thought of the abundance, of the simplicity of the poems, and said, 'In your country is there much propagandist writing, much criticism? We have to do so much, especially in my own country, that our minds gradually cease to be creative, and yet we cannot help it. If our life was not a continual warfare, we would not have taste, we would not know what is good, we would not find hearers and readers. Four-fifths of our energy is spent in the quarrel with bad taste, whether in our own minds or in the minds of others.' 'I understand,' he replied, 'we too have our propagandist writing. In the villages they recite long mythological poems adapted from the Sanskrit in the Middle Ages, and they often insert passages telling the people that they must do their duties.'

II

I have carried the manuscript of these translations about with me for days, reading it in railway trains, or on the top of omnibuses and in restaurants, and I have often had to close it lest some stranger would see how much it moved me. These lyrics – which are in the original, my Indians tell me, full of subtlety of rhythm, of untranslatable delicacies of colour, of metrical invention – display in their thought a world I have dreamed of all my life long. The work of a supreme culture, they yet appear as much the growth of the common soil as the grass and the rushes. A tradition, where poetry and religion are the same thing, has passed through the centuries, gathering from learned and unlearned metaphor and emotion, and carried back again to the multitude the thought of the scholar and of the noble. If the civilization of Bengal remains unbroken, if that common mind which – as one divines – runs through all, is not, as with us, broken into a dozen minds that know nothing of each other, something even of what is most subtle in these verses will have come, in a few generations, to the beggar on the roads. When there was but one mind in England, Chaucer wrote his *Troilus and Cressida*, and though he had written to be read, or to be read out – for our time was coming on apace – he was sung by minstrels for a while. Rabindranath Tagore, like Chaucer's forerunners, writes music for his words, and one understands at every moment that he is so abundant, so spontaneous, so daring in his passion, so full of surprise, because he is doing something which has never seemed strange, unnatural, or in need of defence. These verses will not lie in little well-printed books upon ladies' tables, who turn the pages with indolent hands that they may sigh over a life without meaning, which is yet all they can know of life, or be carried about by students at the university to be laid aside when the work of life begins, but, as the generations pass, travellers will hum them on the highway and men rowing upon rivers. Lovers, while they await one another, shall find, in murmuring them, this love of God a magic gulf wherein their own more bitter passion may bathe and renew its youth. At every moment the heart of this poet flows outward to these without derogation or condescension, for it has known that they will understand; and it has filled itself with the circumstance of their lives. The traveller in the red-brown clothes that he wears that dust may not show upon him, the girl searching in her bed for the petals fallen from the wreath of her royal lover, the servant or the bride awaiting the master's home-coming in the empty house, are images of the heart turning to God. Flowers and rivers, the blowing of conch shells, the heavy rain of the Indian July, or the parching heat, are images of the moods of that heart in union or in separation; and a man sitting in a boat upon a river playing upon a lute, like one of those figures full of mysterious meaning in a Chinese picture, is God Himself. A whole people, a whole civilization, immeasurably strange to us, seems to have been taken up into this imagination; and yet we are not moved because of its strangeness, but because we have met our own image, as though we had walked in Rossetti's willow wood, or heard, perhaps for the first time in literature, our voice as in a dream.

Since the Renaissance the writing of European saints – however familiar their metaphor and the general structure of their thought – has ceased to hold our attention. We know that we must at last forsake the world, and we are accustomed in moments of weariness or exaltation to consider a voluntary forsaking; but how can we, who have read so much poetry, seen so many paintings, listened to so much music, where the cry of the flesh and the cry of the soul seem one, forsake it harshly and rudely? What have we in common with St. Bernard covering his eyes that they may not dwell upon the beauty of the lakes of Switzerland, or with the violent rhetoric of the Book of Revelation? We would, if we might, find, as in this book, words full of courtesy. 'I have got my leave. Bid me farewell, my brothers! I bow to you all and take my departure. Here I give back the keys of my door – and I give up all claims to my house. I only ask for last kind words from you. We were neighbours for long, but I received more than I could give. Now the day has dawned and the lamp that lit my dark corner is out. A summons has come and I am ready for my journey.' And it is our own mood, when it is furthest from à Kempis or John of the Cross, that cries, 'And because I love this life, I know I shall love death as well.' Yet it is not only in our thoughts of the parting that this book fathoms all. We had not known that we loved God, hardly it may be that we believed in Him; yet looking backward upon our life we discover, in our exploration of the pathways of woods, in our delight in the lonely places of hills, in that mysterious claim that we have made, unavailingly, on the women that we have loved, the emotion that created this insidious sweetness. 'Entering my heart unbidden even as one of the common crowd, unknown to me, my king, thou didst press the signet of eternity upon many a fleeting moment.' This is no longer the sanctity of the cell and of the scourge; being but a lifting up, as it were, into a greater intensity of the mood of the painter, painting the dust and the sunlight, and we go for a like voice to St. Francis and to William Blake who have seemed so alien in our violent history.

III

We write long books where no page perhaps has any quality to make writing a pleasure, being confident in some general design, just as we fight and make money and fill our heads with politics – all dull things in the doing – while Mr. Tagore, like the Indian civilization itself, has been content to discover the soul and surrender himself to its spontaneity. He often seems to contrast his life with that of those who have lived more after our fashion, and have more seeming weight in the world, and always humbly as though he were only sure his way is best for him: 'Men going home glance at me and smile and fill me with shame. I sit like a beggar maid, drawing my skirt over my face, and when they ask me, what it is I want, I drop my eyes and answer them not.' At another time, remembering how his life had once a different shape, he will say, 'Many an hour have I spent in the strife of the good and the evil, but now it is the pleasure of my playmate of the empty days to draw my heart on to him; and I know not why is this sudden call to what useless inconsequence.' An innocence, a simplicity that one does not find elsewhere in literature makes the birds and the leaves seem as near to him as they are near to children, and the changes of the seasons great events as before our thoughts had arisen between them and us. At times I wonder if he has it from the literature of Bengal or from religion, and at other times, remembering the birds alighting on his brother's hands, I find pleasure in thinking it hereditary, a mystery that was growing through the centuries like the courtesy of a Tristan or a Pelanore. Indeed, when he is speaking of children, so much a part of himself this quality seems, one is not certain that he is not also speaking of the saints, 'They build their houses with sand and they play with empty shells. With withered leaves they weave their boats and smilingly float them on the vast deep. Children have their play on the seashore of worlds. They know not how to swim, they know not how to cast nets. Pearl fishers dive for pearls, merchants sail in their ships, while children gather pebbles and scatter them again. They seek not for hidden treasures, they know not how to cast nets.'

6.4 TWO POEMS FROM GITANJALI

Rabindranath Tagore

Source: Rabindranath Tagore, *Gitanjali*, Delhi: Macmillan, 1913; repr. Delhi: Macmillan Pocket Tagore Edition, 1981, pp.20, 25.

XXXV

Where the mind is without fear and the head is held high;

Where knowledge is free;

Where the world has not been broken up into fragments by narrow domestic walls;

Where tireless striving stretches its arms towards perfection;

Where the clear stream of reason has not lost its way into the dreary desert sand of dead habit;

Where the mind is led forward by thee into ever-widening thought and action –

Into that heaven of freedom, my Father, let my country awake.

XLII

Early in the day it was whispered that we should sail in a boat, only thou and I, and never a soul in the world would know of this our pilgrimage to no country and to no end.

In that shoreless ocean, at thy silently listening smile my songs would swell in melodies, free as waves, free from all bondage of words.

Is the time not come yet? Are there works still to do? Lo, evening has come down upon the shore and in the fading light the seabirds come flying to their nests.

Who knows when the chains will be off, and the boat, like the last glimmer of sunset, vanish into the night?

6.5 *FROM* NATIONALISM

Rabindranath Tagore

Source: Rabindranath Tagore, *Nationalism* (1917), Delhi: Macmillan Pocket Tagore Edition, 1995, pp.9–28, 64–79.

Nationalism in the West

[...] I have a deep love and a great respect for the British race as human beings. It has produced great-hearted men, thinkers of great thoughts, doers of great deeds. It has given rise to a great literature. I know that these people love justice and freedom, and hate lies. They are clean in their minds, frank in their manners, true in their friendships; in their behaviour they are honest and reliable. The personal experience which I have had of their literary men has roused my admiration not merely for their power of thought or expression but for their chivalrous humanity. We have felt the greatness of this people as we feel the sun; but as for the [Western idea of the] Nation, it is for us a thick mist of a stifling nature covering the sun itself.

This government by the Nation is neither British nor anything else; it is an applied science and therefore more or less similar in its principles wherever it is used. It is like a hydraulic press, whose pressure is impersonal, and on that account completely effective. The amount of its power may vary in different engines. Some may even be driven by hand, thus leaving a margin of comfortable looseness in their tension, but in spirit and in method their differences are small. Our government might have been Dutch, or French, or Portuguese, and its essential features would have remained much the same as they are now. Only perhaps, in some cases, the organisation might not have been so densely perfect, and, therefore, some shreds of the human might still have been clinging to the wreck, allowing us to deal with something which resembles our own throbbing heart.

Before the Nation came to rule over us we had other governments which were foreign, and these, like all governments, had some element of the machine in them. But the difference between them and the government by the Nation is like the difference between the hand-loom and the power-loom. In the products of the hand-loom the magic of man's living fingers finds its expression, and its hum harmonizes with the music of life. But the power-loom is relentlessly lifeless and accurate and monotonous in its production.

We must admit that during the personal government of the former days there have been instances of tyranny, injustice, and extortion. They caused sufferings and unrest from which we are glad to be rescued. The protection of law is not only a boon, but it is a valuable lesson to us. It is teaching us the discipline which is necessary for the stability of civilisation and for continuity of progress. We are realising through it that there is a universal standard of justice to which all men, irrespective of their caste and colour, have their equal claim.

This reign of law in our present Government in India has established order in this vast land inhabited by peoples different in their races and customs. It has made it possible for these peoples to come in closer touch with one another and cultivate a communion of aspiration.

But this desire for a common bond of comradeship among the different races of India has been the work of the spirit of the West, not that of the Nation of the West [...]

In India we are suffering from this conflict between the spirit of the West and Nation of the West. The benefit of the Western civilisation is doled out to us in a miserly measure by the Nation, which tries to regulate the degree of nutrition as near the zero-point of vitality as possible. The portion of education allotted to us is so raggedly insufficient that it ought to outrage the sense of decency of a Western humanity. We have seen in these countries how the people are encouraged and trained and given every facility to fit themselves for the great movements of commerce and industry spreading over the world, while in India the only assistance we get is merely to be jeered at by the Nation for lagging behind. While depriving us of our opportunities and reducing our education to the minimum required for conducting a foreign government, this Nation pacifies its conscience by calling us names, by sedulously giving currency to the arrogant cynicism that the East is east and the West is west and never the twain shall meet. If we must believe our schoolmaster in his taunt that, after nearly two centuries of his tutelage, India not only remains unfit for self-government but unable to display originality in her intellectual attainments, must we ascribe it to something in the nature of Western culture and our inherent incapacity to receive it or to the judicious niggardliness of the Nation that has taken upon itself the white man's burden of civilising the East? [...]

The truth is that the spirit of conflict and conquest is at the origin and in the centre of Western nationalism; its basis is not social co-operation. It has evolved a perfect organization of power, but not spiritual idealism. It is like the pack of predatory creatures that must have its victims. With all its heart it cannot bear to see its hunting-grounds converted into cultivated fields. In fact, these nations are fighting among themselves for the extension of their victims and their reserve forests. Therefore the Western Nation acts like a dam to check the free flow of Western civilisation into the country of the No-Nation. Because this civilisation is the civilisation of power, therefore it is exclusive, it is naturally unwilling to open its sources of power to those whom it has selected for its purposes of exploitation.

But all the same moral law is the law of humanity, and the exclusive civilisation which thrives upon others who are barred from its benefit carries its own death-sentence in its moral limitations. The slavery that it gives rise to unconsciously drains its own love of freedom dry. The helplessness with which it weighs down its world of victims exerts its force of gravitation every moment upon the power that creates it. And the greater part of the world which is being denuded of its self-sustaining life by the Nation will one day become the most terrible of all its burdens, ready to drag it down into the bottom of destruction. Whenever the Power removes all checks from its path to make its career easy, it triumphantly rides into its ultimate crash of death. Its moral brake becomes slacker every day without its knowing it, and its slippery path of ease becomes its path of doom.

Of all things in Western civilisation, those which this Western Nation has given us in a most generous measure are law and order. While the small feeding-bottle of our education is nearly dry, and sanitation sucks its own thumb in despair, the military organisation, the magisterial offices, the police, the Criminal Investigation Department, the secret spy system, attain to an abnormal girth in their waists, occupying every inch of our country. This is to maintain order. But is not this order merely a negative good? Is it not for giving people's life greater opportunities for the freedom of development? Its perfection is the perfection of an egg-shell, who true value lies in the security it affords to the chick and its nourishment and not in the convenience it offers to the person at the breakfast table [...]

This European war of Nations [the First World War] is the war of retribution. Man, the person, must protest for his very life against the heaping up of things where there should be the heart, and systems and policies where there should flow living human relationship. The time has come when, for the sake of the whole outraged world, Europe should fully know in her own person the terrible absurdity of the thing called the Nation.

The Nation has thriven long upon mutilated humanity. Men, the fairest creations of God, came out of the National manufactory in huge numbers as war-making and money-making puppets, ludicrously vain of their pitiful perfection of mechanism. Human society grew more and more into a marionette show of politicians, soldiers, manufacturers and bureaucrats, pulled by wire arrangements of wonderful efficiency.

But the apotheosis of selfishness can never make its interminable breed of hatred and greed, fear and hypocrisy, suspicion and tyranny, an end in themselves. These monsters grow into huge shapes but never into harmony. And this Nation may grow on to an unimaginable corpulence, not of a living body, but of steel and steam and office buildings, till its deformity can contain no longer its ugly voluminousness – till it begins to crack and gape, breathe gas and fire in gasps, and its death-rattles sound in cannon roars. In this war the death-throes of the Nation have commenced [...]

And we of no nations of the world, whose heads have been bowed to the dust, will know that this dust is more sacred than the bricks which build the pride of power. For this dust is fertile of life, and of beauty and worship. We shall thank God that we were made to wait in silence through the night of despair, had to bear the insult of the proud and the strong man's burden, yet all through it, though our hearts quaked with doubt and fear, never could we blindly believe in the salvation which machinery offered to man, but we held fast to our trust in God and the truth of the human soul. And we can still cherish the hope that, when power becomes ashamed to occupy its throne and is ready to make way for love, when the morning comes for cleansing the blood-stained steps of the Nation along the highroad of humanity, we shall be called upon to bring our own vessel of sacred water – the water of worship – to sweeten the history of man into purity, and with its sprinkling make the trampled dust of the centuries blessed with fruitfulness.

Nationalism in India

[...] India has never had a real sense of nationalism. Even though from childhood I had been taught that idolatry of the Nation is almost better than reverence for God and humanity, I believe I have outgrown that teaching, and it is my conviction that my countrymen will truly gain their India by fighting against the education which teaches them that a country is greater than the ideals of humanity.

The educated Indian at present is trying to absorb some lessons from history contrary to the lessons of our ancestors. The East, in fact, is attempting to take unto itself a history, which is not the outcome of its own living. Japan, for example, thinks she is getting powerful through adopting Western methods, but, after she has exhausted her inheritance, only the borrowed weapons of civilisation will remain to her. She will not have developed herself from within.

Europe has her past. Europe's strength therefore lies in her history. We, in India, must make up our minds that we cannot borrow other people's history, and that if we stifle our own we are committing suicide. When you borrow things that do not belong to your life, they only serve to crush your life.

And therefore I believe that it does India no good to compete with Western civilisation in its own field. But we shall be more than compensated if, in spite of the insults heaped upon us, we follow our own destiny [...]

We must recognise that it is providential that the West has come to India. And yet someone must show the East to the West, and convince the West that the East has her contribution to make to the history of civilisation. India is no beggar of the West. And yet even though the West may think she is, I am not for thrusting off Western civilisation and becoming segregated in our independence. Let us have a deep association. If Providence wants England to be the channel of that communication, of that deeper association, I am willing to accept it with all humility. I have great faith in human nature, and I think the West will find its true mission. I speak bitterly of Western civilisation when I am conscious that it is betraying its trust and thwarting its own purpose. The West must not make herself a curse to the world by using her power for her own selfish needs, but, by teaching the ignorant and helping the weak, she should save herself from the worst danger that the strong is liable to incur by making the feeble acquire power enough to resist her intrusion. And also she must not make her materialism to be the final thing, but must realise that she is doing a service in freeing the spiritual being from the tyranny of matter.

I am not against one nation in particular, but against the general idea of all nations. What is the Nation?

It is the aspect of a whole people as an organised power. This organisation incessantly keeps up the insistence of the population on becoming strong and efficient. But this strenuous effort after strength and efficiency drains man's energy from his higher nature where he is self-sacrificing and creative. For thereby man's power of sacrifice is diverted from his ultimate object, which is moral, to the maintenance of this organisation, which is mechanical.

Yet in this he feels all the satisfaction of moral exaltation and therefore becomes supremely dangerous to humanity. He feels relieved of the urging of his conscience when he can transfer his responsibility to this machine which is the creation of his intellect and not of his complete moral personality. By this device the people which loves freedom perpetuates slavery in a large portion of the world with the comfortable feeling of pride having done his duty; men who are naturally just can be cruelly unjust both in their act and their thought, accompanied by a feeling that they are helping the world to receive its deserts; men who are honest can blindly go on robbing others of their human rights for self-aggrandisement, all the while abusing the deprived for not deserving better treatment. We have seen in our everyday life even small organisations of business and profession produce callousness of feeling in men who are not naturally bad, and we can well imagine what a moral havoc it is causing in a world where whole peoples are furiously organising themselves for gaining wealth and power.

Nationalism is a great menace. It is the particular thing which for years has been at the bottom of India's troubles. And inasmuch as we have been ruled and dominated by a nation that is strictly political in its attitude, we have tried to develop within ourselves, despite our inheritance from the past, a belief in our eventual political destiny.

There are different parties in India, with different ideals. Some are struggling for political independence. Others think that the time has not arrived for that, and yet believe that India should have the rights that the English colonies have. They wish to gain autonomy as far as possible.

In the beginning of the history of political agitation in India there was not the conflict between the parties which there is today. At that time there was a party known as the Indian Congress; it had no real programme. They had a few grievances for redress by the authorities. They wanted larger representation in the Council House, and more freedom in Municipal government. They wanted scraps of things, but they had no constructive ideal.

Therefore I was lacking in enthusiasm for their methods. It was my conviction that what India most needed was constructive work coming from within herself. In this work we must take all risks and go on doing the duties which by rights are ours, though in the teeth of persecution; winning moral victory at every step, by our failure and suffering. We must show those who are over us that we have in ourselves the strength of moral power, the power to suffer the truth. Where we have nothing to show, we have only to beg. It would be mischievous if the gifts we wish for were granted to us at once, and I have told my countrymen, time and again, to combine for the work of creating opportunities to give vent to our spirit of self-sacrifice, and not for the purpose of begging.

The party, however, lost power because the people soon came to realise how futile was the half policy adopted by them. The party split, and there arrived the Extremists, who advocated independence of action, and discarded the begging method – the easiest method of relieving one's mind from his responsibility towards his country. Their ideals were based on Western history. They had no sympathy with the special problems of India. They did not recognise the patent fact that there were causes in our social organisation which made the Indian incapable of coping with the alien. What should we do if, for any reason, England was driven away? We should simply be victims for other nations. The same social weaknesses would prevail. The thing we in India have to think of is this – to remove those social customs and ideals which have generated a want of self-respect and a complete dependence on those above us – a state of affairs which has been brought about entirely by the domination in India of the caste system, and the blind and lazy habit of relying upon the authority of traditions that are incongruous anachronisms in the present age.

Once again I draw your attention to the difficulties India has had to encounter and her struggle to overcome them. Her problem was the problem of the world in miniature. India is too vast in its area and too diverse in its races. It is many countries packed in one geographical receptacle. It is just the opposite of what Europe truly is, namely, one country made into many. Thus Europe in its culture and growth has had the advantage of the strength of the many as well as the strength of the one. India, on the contrary, being naturally many, yet adventitiously one, has all along suffered from the looseness of its diversity and the feebleness of its unity. A true unity is like a round globe, it rolls on, carrying its burden easily; but diversity is a many-cornered thing which has to be dragged and pushed with all force. Be it said to the credit of India that this diversity was not her own creation; she has had to accept it as a fact from the beginning of her history. In America and Australia, Europe has simplified her problem by almost exterminating the original population. Even in the present age this spirit of extermination is making itself manifest, in the inhospitable shutting out of aliens, by those who themselves were aliens in the lands they now occupy. But India tolerated difference of races from the first, and that spirit of toleration has acted all through her history.

Her caste system is the outcome of this spirit of toleration. For India has all along been trying experiments in evolving a social unity within which all the different peoples could be held together, while fully enjoying the freedom of maintaining their own differences. The tie has been as loose as possible, yet as close as the circumstances permitted. This has produced something like a United States of a social federation, whose common name is Hinduism.

India had felt that diversity of races there must be and should be, whatever may be its drawback, and you can never coerce nature into your narrow limits of convenience without paying one day very dearly for it. In this India was right; but what she failed to realise was that in human beings differences are not like the physical barriers of mountains, fixed for ever – they are fluid with life's flow, they are changing their courses and their shapes and volume.

Therefore in her caste regulations India recognised differences, but not the mutability which is the law of life. In trying to avoid collisions she set up boundaries of immovable walls, thus giving to her numerous races the negative benefit of peace and order but not the positive opportunity of expansion and movement. She accepted nature where it produces diversity, but ignored it where it uses that diversity for its world-game of infinite permutations and combinations. She treated life in all truth where it is manifold, but insulted it where it is ever moving. Therefore Life departed from her social system and in its place she is worshipping with all ceremony the magnificent cage of countless compartments that she has manufactured.

The same thing happened where she tried to ward off the collisions of trade interests. She associated different trades and professions with different castes. This had the effect of allaying for good the interminable jealousy and hatred of competition – the competition which breeds cruelty and makes the atmosphere thick with lies and deception. In this also India laid all her emphasis upon the law of heredity, ignoring the law of mutation, and thus gradually reduced arts into crafts and genius into skill.

However, what Western observers fail to discern is that in her caste system India in all seriousness accepted her responsibility to solve the race problem in such a manner as to avoid all friction, and yet to afford each race freedom within its boundaries. Let us admit India has not in this achieved a full measure of success. But this you must also concede, that the West being more favourably situated as to homogeneity of races, has never given her attention to this problem, and whenever confronted with it she has tried to make it easy by ignoring it altogether. And this is the source of her anti-Asiatic agitations for depriving aliens of their right to earn their honest living on these shores. In most of your colonies you only admit them on condition of their accepting the menial position of hewers of wood and drawers of water. Either you shut your doors against the aliens or reduce them into slavery. And this is your solution of the problem of race-conflict
[...]

Not only in your relation with aliens but with the different sections of your own society you have not achieved harmony of reconciliation. The spirit of conflict and competition is allowed the full freedom of its reckless career. And because its genesis is the greed of wealth and power it can never come to any other end but to a violent death. In India the production of commodities was brought under the law of social adjustments. Its basis was co-operation, having for its object the perfect satisfaction of social needs. But in the West it is guided by the impulse of competition, whose end is the gain of wealth for individuals. But the individual is like the geometrical line; it is length without breadth. It has not got the depth to be able to hold anything permanently. Therefore its greed or gain can never come to finality. In its lengthening process of growth it can cross other lines and cause entanglements, but will ever go on missing the ideal of completeness in its thinness of isolation.

In all our physical appetites we recognise a limit. We know that to exceed that limit is to exceed the limit of health. But has this lust for wealth and power no bounds beyond which is death's dominion? In these national carnivals of materialism are not the Western peoples spending most of their vital energy I merely producing things and neglecting the creation of ideals? And can a civilisation ignore the law of moral health and go on in it its endless process of inflation by gorging upon material things? Man in his social ideals naturally tries to regulate his appetites, subordinating them to the higher purpose of his nature. But in the economic world our appetites follow no other restrictions but those of supply and demand which can be artificially fostered, affording individuals opportunities for indulgence in an endless feast of grossness. In India our social instincts imposed restrictions upon our appetites – maybe it went to the extreme of repression – but in the West the spirit of economic organisation with no moral purpose goads the people into the perpetual pursuit of wealth [...]

The general opinion of the majority of the present-day nationalists in India is that we have come to a final completeness in our social and spiritual ideals, the task of the constructive work of society having been done several thousand years before we were born, and that now we are free to employ all our activities in the political direction. We never dream of blaming our social inadequacy as the origin of our present helplessness, for we have accepted as the creed of our nationalism that this social system has been perfected for all time to come by our ancestors, who had the superhuman vision of all eternity and supernatural power for making infinite provision for future ages. Therefore, for all our miseries and shortcomings, we hold responsible the historical surprises that burst upon us from outside. This is the reason why we think that our one task is to build a political miracle of freedom upon the quicksand of social slavery. In fact we want to dam up the true course of our own historical stream, and only borrow power from the sources of other peoples' history.

Those of us in India who have come under the delusion that mere political freedom will make us free have accepted their lessons from the West as the gospel truth and lost their faith in humanity. We must remember whatever weakness we cherish in our society will become the source of danger in politics. The same inertia which leads us to our idolatry of dead forms in social institutions will create in our politics prison-houses with immovable walls. The narrowness of sympathy which makes it possible for us to impose upon a considerable portion of humanity the galling yoke of inferiority will assert itself in our politics in creating the tyranny of injustice.

When our nationalists talk about ideals they forget that the basis of nationalism is wanting. The very people who are upholding these ideals are themselves the most conservative in their social practice. Nationalists say, for example, look at Switzerland where, in spite of race differences, the people have solidified into a nation. Yet, remember that in Switzerland the races can mingle, they can intermarry, because they are of the same blood. In India there is no common birthright. And when we talk of Western Nationality we forget that the nations there do not have that physical repulsion, one for the other, that we have between different castes. Have we an instance in the whole world where a people who are not allowed to mingle their blood shed their blood for one another except by coercion or for mercenary purposes? And can we ever hope that these moral barriers against our race amalgamation will not stand in the way of our political unity?

Then again we must give full recognition to this fact that our social restrictions are still tyrannical, so much so as to make men cowards. If a man tells me that he has heterodox ideas, but that he cannot follow them because he would be socially ostracised, I excuse him for having to live a life of untruth, in order to live at all. The social habit of mind which impels us to make the life of our fellow-beings a burden to them where they differ from us even in such a thing as their choice of food, is sure to persist in our political organisation and result in creating engines of coercion to crush every rational difference which is the sign of life. And tyranny will only add to the inevitable lies and hypocrisy in our political life. Is the mere name of freedom so valuable that we should be willing to sacrifice for its sake our moral freedom?

The intemperance of our habits does not immediately show its effects when we are in the vigour of our youth. But it gradually consumes that vigour, and when the period of decline sets in then we have to settle accounts and pay off our debts, which leads us to insolvency. In the West you are still able to carry your head high, though your humanity is suffering every moment from its dipsomania of organising power. India also in the hey-day of her youth could carry in her vital organs the dead weight of her social organisations stiffened to rigid perfection, but it has been fatal to her, and has produced a gradual paralysis of her living nature. And this is the reason why the educated community of India has become insensible of her social needs. They are taking the very immobility of our social structures as the sign of their perfection – and because the healthy feeling of pain is dead in the limbs of our social organism they delude themselves into thinking that it needs no ministration. Therefore they think that all their energies need their only scope in the political field. It is like a man whose legs have become shrivelled and useless, trying to delude himself that these limbs have grown still because they have attained their ultimate salvation, and all that is wrong about him is the shortness of his sticks.

So much for the social and the political regeneration of India. Now we come to her industries, and I am very often asked whether there is in India any industrial regeneration since the advent of the British Government. It must be remembered that at the beginning of the British rule in India our industries were suppressed, and since then we have not met with any real help or encouragement to enable us to make a stand against the monster commercial organisations of the world. The nations have decreed that we must remain purely an agricultural people, even forgetting the use of arms for all time to come. Thus India is being turned into so many predigested morsels of food ready to be swallowed at any moment by any nation which has even the most rudimentary set of teeth in its head.

India therefore has very little outlet for her industrial originality. I personally do not believe in the unwieldy organisations of the present day. They very fact that they are ugly shows that they are in discordance with the whole creation. The vast powers of nature do not reveal their truth in hideousness, but in beauty. Beauty is the signature which the Creator stamps upon His works when he is satisfied with them. All our products that insolently ignore the laws of perfection and are unashamed in their display of ungainliness bear the perpetual weight of God's displeasure. So far as your commerce lacks the dignity of grace it is untrue. Beauty and her twin brother Truth require leisure and self-control for their growth. But the greed of gain has no time or limit to its capaciousness. Its one object is to produce and consume. It has pity neither for beautiful nature nor for living human beings. It is ruthlessly ready without a moment's hesitation to crush beauty and life out of them, moulding them into money. It is this ugly vulgarity of commerce which brought upon it the censure of contempt in our earlier days, when men had leisure to have an unclouded vision of perfection in humanity. Men in those times were rightly ashamed of the instinct of mere money-making. But in this scientific age money, by its very abnormal bulk, has won its throne. And when from its eminence of piled-up things it insults the higher instincts of man, banishing beauty and noble sentiments from its surroundings, we submit. For we in our meanness have accepted bribes from its hands and our imagination has grovelled in the dust before its immensity of flesh [...]

This commercialism with its barbarity of ugly decorations is a terrible menace to all humanity, because it is setting up the ideal of power over that of perfection. It is making the cult of self-seeking exult in its naked shamelessness. Our nerves are more delicate than our muscles. Things that are the most precious in us are helpless as babes when we take away from them the careful protection which they claim from us for their very preciousness. Therefore, when the callous rudeness of power runs amuck in the broad-way of humanity it scares away by its grossness the ideals which we have cherished with the martyrdom of centuries.

The temptation which is fatal for the strong is still more so for the weak. And I do not welcome it in our Indian life, even though it be sent by the Lord of the Immortals. Let our life be simple in its outer aspect and rich in its inner gain. Let our civilisation take its firm stand upon its basis of social co-operation and not upon that of economic exploitation and conflict. How to do it in the teeth of the drainage of our life-blood by the economic dragons is the task set before the thinkers of all oriental nations who have faith in the human soul [...]

6.6 SELECTED POEMS

Vallathol Narayana Menon

Source: Vallathol Narayana Menon, *Selected Poems*, Trichur: Kerala Sahitya Akademi, 1978, pp.32–3, 46–50, 79–80, 91–101.

To the Mother Land

In this poem the poet exhorts his countrymen to shed their stupor and to help their allies in their fight against their enemies in the first world war [...]

Oh! revered Mother
Why do you sit with your head bent?
Could it be you are weeping silently?
Though to disasters grievous you are used for long
Do your eyes, even now, smart with tears?
Or though granite-hard in your own grief
Your heart is soft as butter in another's pain?
How can our rough hands
Calloused, holding the spade
Wipe the tears from your gentle face?
Here we dedicate at your feet
The wages of today's labour too.
Send this too.
To your sisters[8] in the peril of war,
Let us do what little we can
Worry not we have to fast, oh! mother
Fasting is an auspicious rite for us,
Your children can live on water
Held in their cupped hand;[9]
They have shown too they could hold

[8] The sisters are the allies.

[9] The Indians who adopt Vanaprastha practise to live on just a handful of water. Austerity is a virtue highly cherished by the Indians.

The oceans of the world
In the hollow of their hand and swallow them.[10]
Held in their hand is self restraint.
Their hands lanky with starvation
Can at one blow suppress mountains.
An urban mansion, or a gloomy wilderness,
A silken bed, or the surface of a rock
Is all the same, Oh! mother
To us, your sons!
Yourself, great soul, have taught your children
The noblest of virtues is sacrifice.
Where else in the world is a man
Who would give up his body to save a bird?
The lullaby that rocks your sons to sleep
Is the joyous song of 'Dharma'.
They grow up ready to renounce all
For the sake of 'Dharma' and truth.
To your sons in the battlefield
Fighting for righteousness's sake
It matters not what they gain
A shower of shots, or a shower of flowers –
Unhappily, for sometime now
Rust encrusts your sword;[11]
Still, to the hosts of your foes
Your sword is the thunderbolt.
Let your enemies
Who their arrogant pride cannot contain
Turn their strength into smoke.
When the mind clears off the smoke
And cleanses bright the firmament
There will flutter against the sun
The flags of victory of your beloved friends.
Their victory, oh! mother is ours too.

Salutation to the Mother

[...] In this poem Vallathol pays tribute to the story of Kerala and inspires its people to stand by one another and work for its freedom. The poem is remarkable for its nature descriptions, rich allusiveness and the patriotic fervour it exudes.

Bow to the mother, bow to the mother,
Bow to her who is great,
Bow to her who grants boons.
Like the gem that long ago

[10] According to the Puranas, Agastya, the sage drank all the waters of the seas.

[11] The reference is to the law that forbids Indians carry weapons.

The sun-god gave to Satrajit[12]
Is not our land a matchless gem,
The Ocean, the home of precious stones
In fond affection bestowed on
Jamadagni's son, supreme in ascetic might?
Bow to the goddess of prosperity[13]
Dear daughter of the ocean.

The mother reclines
Her head on the green-clad Sahya Hills
Her feet encushioned on the sandy beach.
Guarding her on either side
Stand the Lord of Gokarna[14] and the Goddess Kumari.
Bow to the mother, bow to the mother
Bow to her who is worshipped
Even by the gods we worship.

The waves of the ocean
Like attendant maids
Put silver anklets of white foam
On your dainty divine feet.
Dissatisfied they take them off
And try them on again and yet again.
Bow to the mother, bow to the mother
Bow to her who is supreme
In the glory of her fortune.

Dark rain clouds bright with lightning
Are elephants adorned with gold,
Loud thunder is the flourish of trumpets,
Indra's shining rainbow is festive decoration.
Where but in Bhargava's temple
Is such a festival of rains?[15]

Bow to the mother, bow to the mother
Bow to the presiding deity
Of plenty and of prosperity.
The cardmom plants on your hills
Flags that fly aloft your fame,
Gracefully wave in the playful wind
That blows from your sandalwood groves
Far and wide over the world,
They waft your fragrance everywhere.

[12] Syamantakom that the sun God presented to Satrajit. Kerala [in legend] is a jewel that the sea presented to Parasu Rama. Hence the comparison.

[13] Lakshmi, the Goddess of prosperity rose from the sea of milk as it was churned.

[14] Gokarna marks the northern limit of Kerala. The Cape was the southern limit of ancient Kerala. Cape is often represented as a virgin endlessly waiting for her Lord Siva.

[15] The rainy season is represented as a grant festival in a Kerala Temple.

Bow to the mother, bow to the mother
Bow to her whose virtues
Charm the peoples of the world.

The arecanut trees in your garden
United in wedlock to clinging betel vines,
And their heads humbled with weight of fruit
Dance in the wind
In their joy of serving the world.
Bow to the mother, bow to the mother
Bow to her whose hospitality
Is sung aloud by her guests.

Supreme in bewitching beauty
Is this orchard of yours.
Here coconut palms stand bearing
Pitchers of shining gold,
Clusters of coral adorn
Pepper vines in the fruitful days.
Bow to her who is adored
By all who wish for a life auspicious,
Do not turn from us
Your face pale with pain
We swear we shall become
Again, Oh! mother, your children true.
The ship of time ever rushing forward
Yet brings the voyagers back to the starting place.[16]
Bow to the mother, bow to the mother,
Bow to her whose heart is wrung
With love for her offspring.

Her royal sword lies forgotten
Encrusted with mud
Let us take it up and burnish it,
Let it stainless shine,
Let the.sun's effulgent rays
Kiss its spotless blade.
Bow to the mother, bow to the mother,
Bow to her whose breasts
Have nourished heroes great.
Our ancestors in days of old
With sword as well as tongue
Routed mighty foes.
Some drops of their blood still flow in us,
The warmth of that blood stirs us in our sleep.
Our eyes open a little at least now.
Bow to the mother, bow to the mother,
Bow to her who is blessed
With children great, from days of yore.

---

[16] The poet suggests that the wheel has come to a full circle; the time is ripe for the liberation of the motherland.

Can these curtains of mere cobwebs
Make division of our mother's house?
Our breath is enough to blow them off
If we stretch and blow a deep-drawn breath.[17]
Bow to the mother, bow to the mother,
Bow to her who is renowned
As the author of welfare.

Let this our new garland
Woven of many flowers
On the silken thread of brotherhood
Shine for ever, unspoilt, on mother's breast,
Giving her joy ecstatic.
Bow to the mother, bow to the mother,
Bow to her who teaches
The doctrine of 'Advaita'.
Let us take as our Veda mother's words;
Service to her be our noblest yajna,[18]
Brothers dear, let us dedicate unto her
Our cherished lives entire;
What God but the mother is here for us?
Bow to the mother, bow to the mother,
Bow to her whose benevolence grants
All the desires of the heart.

This Way, This Way

In this poem, the poet exhorts his countrymen to stand united under the
leadership of Mahatma Gandhi and to fight for India's freedom [...]

This is the path, this the right course
We have to take, oh my brothers!
Let not confusion sap our strength again!
Let the lofty mansion of wickedness
Hit the sky and dazzle the world, –
Enough the lowly huts of virtue
For us who are poor.

Let the waves in the river grow violent,
Let the wind howl and blow with all its might,
Let the rain come down in torrents, –
Why should we care?
Heart to heart, shoulder to shoulder,
With arms through which the same blood runs,
If we but ply our oars a dozen times in perfect unison,
This great boat of ours will reach the appointed shore!

[17] The suggestion is that Indians shall rise above their petty differences and fight
for freedom, as the children of the self same mother.

[18] The ceremonial sacrifice. It is a ritual prosecuted to propitiate the Gods; at the
time it ennobles the devotee.

He who, inculcating self-discipline, makes the lion a lamb, – [19]
Is not that very Mahatma our helmsman?
Let us seek the blessings of our one and only Mother:
Obeisance to thee Mother, obeisance to thee Ever-blessed
We pray thee, lift up your dauntless and serene head,
Which for long has been bent under the load of sorrow and shame!

Behold our saintly Master – he who has
Conquered all fear and doubt.
Stands before thee, holding aloft in his hand –
Alas! lean and shrivelled with austere penance!
The crown that should appropriately adorn it!
The same holy blood[20] that poured out of your heart
To slake the thirst of the wild demons
Has now turned into the ceremonial saffron water
For your royal consecration.[21]
The eastern horizon turns red at first,
The bright radiance that illumines rises after!
Ineffable jubilation marks this moment of victory!
The ears are regaled by the hymns of heavenly beings;
The goddess of peace takes up here divine veena
In hands soft as the tender leaves of the mango,
And starts playing on it!
The curtain is raised, and Truth takes the stage,
A sweet symphony spreads in the heavens.
Great Queen of World,[22] may the sceptre in your lotus hand
Shed in all quarters the rich radiance
Of the rising sun!

Unity Before Everything Else

This is a reflective poem imbued with patriotism. The poet is deeply moved at the tragic plight of his motherland which has become a bog of abject misery and stark poverty. The majority of the people are victims of exploitation by the few privileged people [...] [T]he poet criticizes the haves and the high-caste people of his country, who ill-treat the have-nots and the casteless.

My feeble head could ill stand
The tidal onslaught of sad thoughts;
In my court-yard, white washed by moon-light,
I lay stretched on my back.
In the far distance above my eyes,
The sea of the sky lay frothing with stars

[19] Reference to Gandhi's non-violence.

[20] It is significant that these lines came to be prophetic [of Ghandi's own death].

[21] After his martyrdom Gandhi was hailed as the father of the nation; Vallathol looked upon him as a living sage [...]

[22] India.

An unseen cool hand – the gentle breeze –
Stroked my limbs again and again.
The bright full moon, too good-natured
To nurse any grouse,
Who decks in silver this earth of man
Which smudges him with its shadow,
Mercifully rubbed my body with camphor.

The goddess of Nature laboured to comfort
Her son with her motherly ministrations;
But even the free flow of her ambrosial affection
Did not bring any relief that night to my burning brow,
Though the rest-giving night had ordained
Undisturbed silence everywhere,
The fierce rumblings in hundreds of thousands
Of starving stomachs burst in upon my ear!

India's skeletons, whose flesh and blood
Had been licked off by others
Suddenly ranged themselves one by one before me! –
My God! who am I to presume to quench with my tears
The thirst of these miserable beings?

The wealth that Father gave in common to all his children
Has become the property of a few who are strong;
These poor brothers may not even go and beg for it,
For they are closed in by the high bastions of caste!
Ah, the strange justice of this ordinance of caste!
Pure are the masters who persecute their own brothers,
And these hapless creatures are unclean, who melt
Their life's energy to mint gold currency for their overlords!

What crime have these poor people done
That they should lie curled up in the dungeons of bondage?
Or, perhaps, they know not the distress of dependence:
We are like grubs that breed in a poisonous brew!
Has not the school come to be the market-place for us
Where slavery is sold for an enormous price?
'Higher Education'[23] – the higher education that is
Sewn into one's clothes! –
Alas! how much hasn't it degraded us!

Oh! where is that inner refinement, where that sense of equality,
Where that grand renunciation, where that constant
Thought of liberation?
'Approach not!', 'Touch not!' – so long as
The din of these shouts
With which we drive away ourselves prevails,
So long shall we fail to hear the hymn
Of our ancient Dharma,

---

[23] Vallathol was one of the first to sense the dangers of higher education which created a new caste of privileged people in India.

So long shall we, exiles, fail to return
To our homeland!

The stars – the souls of the departed guardians
Of Dharma – gazed intently on my face;
There in the heavens some white clouds from
The North together moved southwards;
They did not ask the dark clouds that had
Gathered before them to move away;
In fact they mingled with them!
That union was as beautiful as the confluence
Of the Ganges and Kalindi[24]
Unity is to be sought above everything else!

[24] Ganga stands for the high caste people, Kalindi, for the casteless. Just as the two rivers mix at Prayaga, in the modern India, people should mix and become one nation.

7 LIBERAL DILEMMAS IN ENGLAND AND INDIA

7.1 HOME RULE FOR INDIA: RADICAL IDEAS

Bal Gangadhar Tilak

Source: C.H. Philips, H.L. Singh and B.N. Pandey, *The Evolution of India and Pakistan 1858–1947: Selected Documents*, London: Oxford University Press, 1962, pp.161–3.

On the Swadeshi movement resolution, 1906

It is a mistake to suppose that the Swadeshi movement is not favoured by Mahomedans. It is a mistake to suppose that it requires sacrifice from poor people. We, the middle classes are the greatest offenders in this respect (Hear, hear). The poor Kumbi villagers require not many foreign articles at all, – probably none at all. It is we, the middle classes, who are the consumers of foreign goods; and since this Government is not going to stop the drain by imposing a protective duty it becomes imperatively necessary to adopt a measure by which we can do ourselves what the Government is bound to do and what the Government ought to have done long ago. That one point was self-help: and another point was determination; and the third, sacrifice. You will find that all this included in this resolution, joined with the declaration made in the Presidential address that Swadeshism [the boycott of British goods in favour of Indian] is a forced necessity in India owing to unnatural economic conditions of India, makes up a complete case for you. I trust that that resolution of self-help adopted this year will form the basis of other resolutions of self-help in years to come ...

On the tenets of the new party, 2 January 1907

Two new words have recently come into existence with regard to our politics, and they are *Moderates* and *Extremists*. These words have a specific relation to time, and they, therefore, will change with time. The Extremists of to-day will be Moderates tomorrow, just as the Moderates of to-day were Extremists yesterday. When the National Congress was first started and Mr. Dadabhai's views, which now go for Moderates, were given to the public, he was styled an Extremist, so that you will see that the term Extremist is an expression of progress. We are Extremists to-day and our sons will call themselves Extremists and us Moderates ...

... One thing is granted, *viz.*, that this Government does not suit us. As has been said by an eminent statesman – the Government of one country by another can never be a successful, and therefore, a permanent Government. There is no difference of opinion about this fundamental proposition between the Old and New schools. One fact is that this alien Government has ruined the country ... We believed in the benevolent intentions of the Government, but in politics there is no benevolence. Benevolence is used to sugar-coat the declarations of self-interest, and we were in those days deceived by the apparent benevolent intentions under which rampant self-interest was concealed ...

... It is said there is a revival of Liberalism, but how long will it last? Next year it might be, they are out of power, and are we to wait till there is another revival of Liberalism, and then again if that goes down and a third revival of Liberalism takes place; and after all what can a liberal Government do? I will quote the observation of the father of the Congress, Mr. A.O. Hume. This was made in 1893. Let the Government be Liberal or Conservative, rest sure that they will not yield to you willingly anything [...] So then it comes to this that the whole British electorate must be converted. So you are going to convert all persons who have a right to vote in England, so as to get the majority on your side, and when this is done and when by that majority the Liberal party is returned to Parliament bent upon doing good to India and it appoints a Secretary of State as good as Mr. Morley, then you hope to get something of the old methods. The new Party has realized this position. The whole electorate of Great Britain must be converted by lectures. You cannot touch their pocket or interest, and that man must be a fool indeed who would sacrifice his own interest on hearing a philosophical lecture ... To convert the whole electorate of England to your opinion and then to get indirect pressure to bear upon the Members of Parliament, they in their turn to return a Cabinet favourable to India and the whole Parliament, the Liberal party and the Cabinet to bring pressure on the bureaucracy to yield – we say this is hopeless. You can now understand the difference between the Old and the New parties. Appeals to the bureaucracy are hopeless. On this point both the New and Old parties are agreed. The Old party believes in appealing to the British nation and we do not. That being our position, it logically follows we must have some other method. There is another alternative. We are not going to sit down quiet. We shall have some other method by which to achieve what we want. We are not disappointed, we are not pessimists. It is the hope of achieving the goal by our own efforts that has brought into existence this new New Party.

... We have come forward with a scheme which if you accept, shall better enable you to remedy this state of things than the scheme of the Old school. Your industries are ruined utterly, ruined by foreign rule; your wealth is going out of the country and you are reduced to the lowest level which no human being can occupy. In this state of things, is there any other remedy by which you can help yourself? The remedy is not petitioning but boycott. We say prepare your forces, organise your power, and then go to work so that they cannot refuse you what you demand ... We are not armed, and there is no necessity for arms either. We have a stronger weapon, a political weapon, in boycott. We have perceived one fact, that the whole of this administration, which is carried on by a handful of Englishmen, is carried on with our assistance. We are all in subordinate service. The whole Government is carried on with our assistance and they try to keep us in ignorance of our power of co-operation between ourselves by which that which is in our own hands at present can be claimed by us and administered by us. The point is to have the entire control in our hands. I want to have the key of my house, and not merely one stranger turned out of it. Self-Government is our goal; we want a control over our administrative machinery ... What the New Party wants you to do is to realise the fact that your future rests entirely in your own hands. If you mean to be free, you can be free; if you do not mean to be free, you will fall and be for ever fallen.

7.2 HOME RULE FOR INDIA: MODERATE IDEAS

Gopal Krishna Gokhale

Source: *Speeches and Writings of Gopal Krishna Gokhale*, ed. by R.P. Patwardhan, D.V. Ambekar and D.G. Karve, 3 vols, 1962–7, London: Asia Publishing House, II, 354–7, 386–7.

[From a paper read before the East India Association, London, 11 July 1906.]

Self-government within the Empire

It may be that bureaucracies, like the Bourbons never learn, but it should really not be difficult for Englishmen to realize that you cannot have institutions like the universities working for more than half a century in India, and then expect to be able to govern the people, as though they were still strangers to ideas of constitutional freedom or to the dignity of national aspirations. Those who blindly uphold the existing system, and resist all attempts, however cautious and moderate, to broaden its bases, prefer practically to sacrifice the future to the present. No one denies the undoubted difficulties of the position, but they are by no means so formidable as those who do not want to move at all like to believe. The goal which the educated classes of India have in view is a position for their country in the Empire worthy of the self-respect of civilised people. They want their country to be a prosperous, self-governing integral part of the Empire, like the Colonies, and not a mere poverty-stricken, bureaucratically-held possession of that Empire. The system under which India is governed at present is an unnatural system, and however one may put up with it as a temporary evil, as a permanent arrangement it is impossible, for under such a system 'the noble, free, virile, fearlesslike', to use the words of a well-known American preacher, 'which is the red blood of any nation gradually becomes torpid', and nothing can compensate a people for so terrible a wrong.

Advance from experiment to experiment

Of course, we recognize that the new self-government has to be on Western lines, and therefore the steps by which the goal is reached must necessarily be slow, as, for the advance to be real, it must be from experiment to experiment only. But there is all the difference in the world between such cautious progress and no progress at all; and the bureaucracy which, by standing in the way of all reasonable instalments of reform, hopes to prevent reform altogether, is only undermining its own position by such a short-sighted and suicidal policy. The officials in theory admit the necessity of associating the people with the Government of the country, but they object to admitting only a small proportion of the population to a share in the administration, and they ask us to wait till the mass of the people have been qualified by education to take an intelligent part in public affairs! At the same time, how much or how little is being done to push on mass education may be seen from the fact that, after more or less a century of British rule, and forty years after England herself woke up to the responsibilities of Governments in regard to mass education, seven children out of eight in India are growing up today in ignorance and darkness, and four villages out of five are as yet without a school-house! Moreover, it is ignored that what is asked at the present stage is a voice in the administration, not for the whole population, but only for those who have been qualified by education to exercise their responsibilities in a satisfactory manner. As regards the bulk of the people, it is recognized that education has got to come first, and what is urged is that this educational work should be pushed on in the most vigorous manner possible.

India likely to be another Ireland

It is true, as I have already admitted, that an Oriental country cannot hope to advance on Western lines, except by cautious and tentative steps. But what Japan has been able to achieve in forty years, India should certainly have accomplished in a century. The attitude of the two Governments in the matter has, however, been one of the main elements of difference in the two cases. My concern, however, is more with the present and the future than with the past. And here I repeat that, unless the old faith of the educated classes in the character and ideals of British rule is brought back, England will find on her hands before long another Ireland, only many times bigger, in India. The younger generations are growing up full of what may be called Irish bitterness, and the situation must fill all who believe in the peaceful progress of the country under British rule with anxious apprehensions. If India is to attain self-government within the Empire – an idea which to an increasing proportion of my countrymen appears to be a vain dream – the advance will have to be along several lines more or less simultaneously. Of these in some respects the most important is the admission of Indians to the higher branches of the public service. As long as India continues to be bureaucratically governed, admission to high office will be a test of the position assigned to the Indians in the system of administration. It is not a mere question of careers for young men, – though even that view is entitled to weight, and the bureaucracy certainly behaves at times as though the most important question before it was how to retain and, if possible, increase the existing number of openings for the employment of Englishmen in India – but it is a measure of our advance towards that equality which has been promised us by the Sovereign and by Parliament. Moreover, as the ranks of the bureaucracy come to be recruited more and more from among the Indians, its resistance to the control of taxpayers' representatives will grow less and less. At present only the field of law – there, too, only a portion of it – is freely open to us, and we find Indians there climbing right to the top of the tree. And if my countrymen are thought to be qualified to discharge the duties of Chief Justice and Advocate-General, it is preposterous that they should be kept out of the superior ranks of Excise and Opium and Salt and Customs and Post and Telegraph and Survey, and similar other services.

Reforms urgently needed

Under present arrangements India's true centre of gravity is in London. We protest against this most unnatural arrangement and we urge most strongly that all competitive examinations for recruitment to Indian services should be held, not in London only, but simultaneously in India and in England. And we claim to be admitted now to the executive councils of the Viceroy and the Governors of Madras and Bombay, as also to the Secretary of State's Council in this country. Next, we want district administration – which is the unit of administration in India – to be decentralized. On the one hand, it must be freed from the present excessive control of the secretariat of the central Government and its numerous special departments; and on the other, the people of the district must be provided with opportunities to influence its course more and more largely, till at last the officials become in fact, as they are in theory, the servants of the people. The first step towards this is to associate with the heads of districts, for purposes of general administration, boards of leading men elected by the people, at first, perhaps, merely advisory, but gradually entrusted with increasing powers of control. In this way an administration conducted with the real consent of the governed may, in course of time, be substituted for the present system of administration carried on in the dark and behind the backs of the people concerned, with its attendant evils of confidential reports and police surveillance. Then local self-government must be carried further. It still remains all over the country where it was placed by Lord Ripon a quarter of a century ago, and in some places it has even been pushed back. Local bodies should now be made in the more advanced localities wholly popular assemblies and while the control of the Government over them must not be weakened, they should be freed from all petty and harassing interference on the part of the officials. As regards Legislative Councils, the position is more difficult. Of course, the next instalment, whenever it comes, can, I think, be clearly foreseen. The enlargement of the Councils, the widening of their functions so that Budgets should be really discussed and passed, an increase in the proportion of elected members up to the point at which the officials will still have a small standing majority – these changes may sooner or later appear safe enough even to the official mind. But the advance beyond that is really the thing that will matter, and it is not easy to see how it will come about. As long as the higher branches of the public service continue to be a practical monopoly of Englishmen, there is small chance of the Legislative Councils being entrusted with any substantial share of control over the actions of the Executive, and this consideration emphasizes still further the necessity of steadily Indianizing the service of the country. In the army, too, our position must be generally improved, and the commissioned ranks now thrown open to carefully selected Indians. Side by side with these reforms, mass education must be taken vigorously in hand, so that in twenty years from now, if not earlier, there should be free and compulsory education in the country for both boys and girls.

I think that an earnest and sustained advance along these lines will go far to prevent any further alienation of the educated classes, and even their old goodwill may thus be regained. I cannot say that I have much hope that any such policy will be at once adopted. The struggle before us is, I fear, a long one and, in all probability, it will be a most bitter one. The flowing tide, however, is with us, and such a struggle can have but one issue.

[From an address to the Universal Races Congress, London, July 1911.]

English failure to understand India

It is to be regretted that on the English side there is no corresponding attempt to study and understand India. It is true that individual Englishmen have done monumental work in interpreting India to the West, but neither in England nor among Englishmen in this country [India] is there any sympathetic study of Indian culture and civilisation, with the result that very few Englishmen, in spite of a prolonged stay in this country, acquire any real insight into them. It is a curious fact, and one of no small significance, that in this matter Germany is far ahead of England, and even America bids fair to go beyond her. It is obvious that there is great room for improvement here, and if one result of the present Congress will be to stimulate among Englishmen a study of India's culture and civilisation in a sympathetic spirit, the Congress will have rendered a great service to India. But while it is undoubtedly true that such study, especially if it leads to increased respect for India by Englishmen, will contribute materially to improve the relations between the two sides, there is no getting away from the fact that as the contact between England and India at present is predominantly political, it is on the attitude of Englishmen towards the political advancement of India that the future of these relations will turn. The question, therefore, how to promote 'the most friendly feelings' between the East and the West in India, resolves itself largely into how England may assist India's political advancement.

Representative government in India

The political evolution to which Indian reformers look forward is representative government on a democratic basis. The course of this evolution must necessarily be slow in India, though it need not be as slow as some people imagine. It is true, as Lord Morley pointed out three years ago, that a long time must elapse before India takes those countless, weary steps that are necessary to develop a strong political personality. But a beginning has been made and the movement can now only be forward and not backward. The difficulties that tend to retard the movement are undoubtedly great and at times they threaten to prove quite overwhelming. But everyday the forces urg[ing] us grow stronger and in the end the difficulties will be overcome. It is unnecessary to say that it is largely in England's power to hasten or delay this evolution. If England wants to play her part nobly in this mysterious and wonderful drama, her resolve to help forward this advance must be firm and irrevocable and not dependent on the view, predilections or sympathies of individual administrators, whom she may, from time to time, charge with the direction of Indian affairs. I think the time has come when a definite pronouncement on this subject should be made by the highest authority entitled to speak in the name of England, and the British Government in India should keep such pronouncements in view in all its actions. There is a class of thinkers and writers amongst Englishmen with whom it is an axiom that Oriental people have no desire, at any rate, no capacity for representative institutions. This cool and convenient assumption is not standing the test of experience and in any case no self-respecting Indian will accept it; and it is astonishing that those men who thus seek to shut the door in the face of Indian aspirations, do not realise how thereby they turn the Indian mind against those very interests for whose support they probably evolve the theories.

7.3 THE INDIAN PRINCES AND THE FUTURE OF INDIA

Source: *Speeches of Indian Princes on Politics*, Allahabad: Prince and Press, 1919, pp.21–2, 143–4.

[Report of a speech delivered at the first session of the Bhavangar Popular Assembly, October 1918.]

Maharaja of Bhavangar, 'On popular rule'

His Highness the Maharaja in opening the proceedings, offered a cordial welcome to the people's representatives. He said that with the exercise of moderation and restraint, and with the realisation of a correct sense of duty on their part, he entertained high hopes and expectations of the future development of this new experiment to the benefit alike of the ruler and the ruled. He added that one essential condition for the eventual success of such assemblies was that the leaders of the people should endeavour to enter into the difficulties and responsibilities of the executive officers, and to help and co-operate with them in the discharge of their onerous duties. The political education of any people was necessarily slow in growth and not as easy of attaining as it was generally supposed to be. Those who aspired to be leaders of men had got gradually to cultivate the habit of estimating one another's merits and the interests of the masses above those of individuals. To his officers his Highness enjoined the practice of toleration in cases of differences of opinion, and a dispassionate and impartial consideration of other people's point of view. He concluded by blessing the assembly with his good wishes for success and further development. The speech was much appreciated.

[Speech delivered at the Maratha Educational Conference, January 1918.]

Maharaja of Kolapur, 'On home rule'

At present the great city is [alive with discussion] about Home Rule. The question of questions is whether we are fit for it. We really do want to have Home Rule. It will give us what we may say is life-blood. It is the British Government who have instilled the idea of Home Rule in us, and they are not at all averse to the advancement of subject races and have not prevented progress like many, for which we are grateful to them. Nay, they have been always anxious to see us progress. The present is not the occasion to treat so important and wide question as Home Rule in all its details. I am inclined however to agree generally with Lord Syndenham's [*sic*; perhaps Lord Sydenham, Governor of Bombay 1907–13] views in this respect. Lord Syndenham's idea is that so long as India remains caste-ridden her people won't be able to derive the fullest benefit due to the introduction of Home

Rule. For the present all that we have to do to attain our goal is to educate our people and thus prepare their minds. This is the only way to approach this important and momentous question. If castes remain as they are, Home Rule in the sense in which it is meant will result in nothing short of oligarchy. I may repeat once again I am not against Home Rule. Surely we want it. Under present circumstances, however, we must have the protection and guidance of the British Government until the evils of the caste system become ineffective. To prevent Home Rule from culminating into an oligarchy we must have communal representation [i.e. representation in which different religious and caste groups vote separately for their own representatives] at least for ten years. It will teach us what are our rights. Once we know them communal representation can be dispensed with. In the absence of communal franchise we have sad experience of our Municipalities before us. In these institutions representation of lower castes is only nominal. The mistake therefore should not be repeated.

7.4 FROM THE RECONSTRUCTION OF INDIA

Edward Thompson

Source: Edward Thompson, *The Reconstruction of India*, rev. edn, London: Faber & Faber, 1931, pp.162–6, 272–6, 277–8.

The alignment of parties

The [Nehru] Report was flung out decisively, December 31st, 1928, by the All-India Moslem Conference. This Conference carried a series of resolutions, belligerently framed with a brevity that makes them sound like a series of rifle-shots. The questions over which the Nehru Report havers and bargains – such as the proposed separation of Sind from Bombay, the giving of at least a beginning of self-government to the North-West Frontier Province – all these are settled with ultimatum-like directness. Among the more interesting items in this uncompromising document are the demand for a federal constitution, the statement that the separate election of Moslems is 'essential in order to bring into existence a really representative democratic government', and the insistence that 'Moslems should have their due share in the Central and Provincial Cabinets' and that 'Moslems should be ensured their majority in the provinces in which the Moslem population is in the majority and that in the other provinces their representation should continue as now existing'. H.H. the Aga Khan, in his presidential address, brought out the clear, rigid backbone of Moslem agreement; that (1) it is impossible for Moslems to live happily and peacefully in India if friction and suspicion are to prevail between them and the Hindus; (2) there can be no prosperity and self-government for India so long as Moslems are in doubt as to the safety of their cultural entity; (3) so long as India is dependent on England for protection the latter must continue to claim a dominant share and voice in the Government of India.

Let it be noted, first, that so far no progress whatever has been made in persuading Moslems to set patriotism before religion; second, that resolutions phrased in this unambiguous fashion have behind them, besides conviction, a certain mood of exasperation and despair. The ultimatum comes when argument has failed to bring about a settlement, and the parties align themselves. This is what the last two years have brought about in India. The situation has been untangling itself; from an apparent and temporary unification separate and disparate elements have been emerging. This Moslem Delhi Conference must be considered in relation to the National Congress, to which it made a direct reply and challenge. The Congress, meeting at Calcutta with elaborate pageantry of royalty – Pandit Motilal Nehru, the President, rode in a carriage drawn by thirty-four white horses bestridden by youths – had given Government exactly one calendar year in which to accept the Nehru Constitution, which was so scarred with disagreement and was totally unacceptable to any but the extreme political wing of the Hindu community. The Bengali Extremist, Mr. Subashchandra Bose, moved an amendment establishing Independence, which was lost by 1350 votes to 973. Lala Lajpat Rai, the veteran Hindu Punjab politician, had died some months previously of heart failure. His death was alleged to have been 'accelerated by the injuries received at the hands of the police of Lahore, when leading the boycott procession on the arrival of the Simon Commission'. Since he had gone on with a strenuous round of speaking and working, it may be claimed that he was at least part-author of his own death. Mr. Saunders, a boy of twenty-one, had been in charge of the police in the vicinity of where Mr. Rai was; for his supposed responsibility he was murdered just before the Congress met, a murder of exceptional cruelty and cynicism.

Just as the Lahore Congress (December, 1929) has received more attention than its real importance justified, so this Calcutta Congress, a year earlier, has received less. Most of all, it revealed Mr. Gandhi's failing physical strength. The Sons of Zeruiah proved too hard for him. He fought for a space of two years' delay, instead of one, arguing that one year was insufficient for the purpose of educating and uniting their own people. 'Our Congress roll to-day,' he said (December 28th, 1928), 'is nothing but a bogus affair. Let us face facts. It is worth nothing. We want a living register of the Congress'.[25] He urged his hearers to dismiss from their minds 'the bogey of Independence versus Dominion Status'; there was no essential difference between them. But the young men, the out-and-out zealots for a complete and unqualified break, such men as Subashchandra Bose, Srinivasa Iyengar, and J.M. Sen Gupta, beat him. In the end, he had to command Government to come to heel in twelve months instead of in twenty-four. But he uttered

[25] William I. Hull, *India's Political Crisis*, 163.

the complaint and warning that 'Our National life ... is a struggle not only against environments that seek to crush us, but it is also a struggle within our own ranks, and often a struggle within our ranks more bitter than the struggle with the environment which is outside of ourselves'.[26]

Having ordered Government to accept what they could not persuade their own communities to accept, the Congress stood aside from all attempts to contribute to a settlement, and continues to stand aside. The alignment of political India proceeded apace. The Sikhs were resentful both of the measures of the Nehru Constitution and the tone the Report took to their demands. The Justice Party, representing the Non-Brahman majority of the Madras Presidency; the Indian Christians; the Liberal Party, whose most prominent members in February accepted Sir John Simon's invitation to form an Indian Commission to work with the British Parliamentary one – all these now stood aside, under their own flags. Since the Moslem community had done the same, it remained only for the Princes to complete the alignment of India. This they did, a year later, when it was unanimously carried in the Chamber of Princes (February 13th, 1929), that 'While adhering to their policy of non-intervention in the affairs of British India, and repeating their assurance of sympathy with its continued political progress, the Princes and Chiefs composing this Chamber, in view of the recent pronouncement of a section of British Indian politicians indicative of a drift towards complete independence, desire to place on record that in the light of the mutual obligations arising from their treaties and engagements with the British Crown they cannot assent to any proposals having for their object the adjustment of equitable relations between the States and British India, unless such proposals proceed upon the initial basis of the British Connexion'. Mr. Gandhi, overwhelmingly elected for the Congress Presidency in 1929, had stood down in favour of Jawaharlal Nehru (son of Motilal Nehru), a Harrovian. Pandit Jawaharlal Nehru arrived from Russia in the autumn of 1928, with excessively advanced views. In his presidential address at the Congress in Lahore, December 29th, 1929, he replied to the Princes, whom he called 'puppets', relics of a bygone age, many of them without a single redeeming feature, 'the product of a vicious system which would ultimately have to go'.[27]

Political India being thus sectioned off, it remained to wait, each grouping puzzled as to what the others might do. The leading events of 1929 were two, the first inflammatory, the second conciliatory. In the early autumn Jatindranath Das, one of the young men arrested in connection with the murder of Mr. Saunders, died of hunger-striking. His body was passed from station to station, from Lahore to Calcutta, the subject of enthusiastic demonstration. At the burning there was an attendance second only to that which had come to the obsequies of Mr. C.R. Das. On October 31st, while everyone was wondering what would happen, with the 'year of grace'

[26] William I. Hull, *India's Political Crisis*, 163.

[27] Summary in the *Times*, December 30th, 1929.

given by the Congress for unconditional acceptance or rejection of their Constitution drawing to a close, the Viceroy, in agreement with Mr. Wedgwood Benn, Secretary of State for India, did a thing both brave and magnanimous and, as I believe, entirely statesmanlike. He announced that the definite aim of the Government was 'Dominion Status' and that a Round Table Conference would be held, at which the Government, the Princes, and the people of British India would meet [...]

Ethics of the situation

There is no justification for the kind of charge often made, that England 'stole' India, and so on. These ethical considerations apply to events of recent years – to the way we entered Egypt, if you like, or to anything that has happened in Central America. The eighteenth and nineteenth centuries were a different world, and what the British did, and what Indians did, were the normal conduct of the time. The facts now are, the British are in India, they are the only guarantee of its ordered progress, and events in Palestine (to take only things of yesterday) have proved to everyone that the Indian question is more complex than a choice between 'keeping India in bondage' and 'setting her free'. More fortunate than the United States where the Philippines are concerned, the British have a third choice to those of giving independence and keeping in subjection.

I quote again from Mr. C.R. Das's speech as President of the Bengal Provincial Conference, May 2nd, 1925. To him, he said, the idea of Dominion Status within the Empire was 'specially attractive because of its deep spiritual significance. I believe in world-peace, in the ultimate federation of the world; and I think that the great Commonwealth of Nations called the British Empire – a federation of divers races, each with its distinct mental outlook – if properly led with statesman at the helm, is bound to make a lasting contribution to the great problem that awaits the statesman, the problem of knitting the world into the greatest federation the mind can conceive, the federation of the human race. But only if properly led with statesmen at the helm – for the development of the idea involves apparent sacrifice on the part of the constituent nations, and it certainly involves the giving up for good of the Empire idea with its ugly attribute of domination. I think it is for the good of India, for the good of the world, that India should strive for freedom within the Commonwealth, and so serve the cause of humanity'.

I have no more love for the Empire, as that word and thing are by many understood, than I have for any other manifestation of the spirit of aggression. But to many of us the Empire is a preparation for the peace of all Nations, a commonwealth which will not absorb other peoples but will show the way for all to find the fullest freedom. I do not want the goodwill that has survived so miraculously past all exasperation, and exists between thousands of Indians and Englishmen to-day, to be wasted. I want to convince Indians that their civilisation, however strictly we may measure it, is valued by us. One element in the present estrangement, not mentioned in this book but well known to many of us, is the profound distrust that many of the best Indians feel towards Western civilisation. Will they believe us when we say that we understand this distrust, and that we share it? Mr. Gandhi's experience of the West, though extensive, has been woefully unfortunate. The passions of a gold-mining region [in South Africa], where races have recently engaged in bitter fighting and are still full of memories and suspicion, do not show Europe at its best. When Mr. Gandhi raised his corps of Indian stretcher-bearers and orderlies, in the so-called Zulu Rebellion, he was given the care of the natives whose bodies had been lacerated by the whippings the court-martials had ordered. He has seen even War at its meanest and foulest, not as many of us have seen it – as I have seen it, for example, watching his magnificent fellow-countrymen advancing through the storm of that first day of battle at Istabulat, over an exposed plain. And we can understand why Mr. Gandhi, and many others with him, feel the deepest misgiving as they see India being fast industrialised, and dread the apparent certainty that she must go the way of the rest of the world. We have laughed at his spinning-wheel movement. But we know that there is sense behind it, in more ways than one. Indeed, the whole Indian question is complicated by there being involved with it a deeper struggle, where our sympathies divide them and us, cutting across all racial lines. It is hard to see how India can support her vast population without industrialisation. But she will be cursed by it when it has spread, even as we have been cursed by it. Mr. Gandhi has persuaded himself that the fight of the spinning-wheel and the village industries is against the mills of Lancashire. A glance at the trade figures of any year will show that it is not at all against Lancashire, but against the mills of Bombay and Japan. This does not change the fact that India has seen something she dreads, and is right to dread. Her poverty, if it could be raised above the subsistence-level, to a place where distress and famine disappear, is a thing she may well prefer to keep, rather than lose her peace.

All the same, there is a greater wisdom in the attitude of Tagore, who has seen Western civilisation at its best, and knows that it is a finely spiritual thing as well as a grossly materialistic one. India might help to save more than herself, if she could keep her simplicity, fling away her indigenous follies, and accept Western dentistry and surgery and freedom of spirit and thought and person. Part of this freedom is common sense, which would (for example) understand perfectly *why* the worship of the cow came into being but would recognize it under present circumstances as a silly and degrading superstition. Tagore has recently spoken frankly of Mr. Gandhi's forcing the *charka* (native spinning-wheel) on the women, when it is an outmoded tool. Gandhi's defence, when this was pointed out to him for-merly, was that the women would have wastes of idle time on their hands, if they used a more efficient model. But why need free time and leisure always be a curse to Indian women?

I believe that to many Indians the thought of leaving the Empire, even for the possible but untested glories of Independence, comes with some sadness. We have built up something not altogether unlike that Roman majesty of strength and law which so held the imagination of St. Paul the Hebrew. Not a few Englishmen are reluctant to let India go, not because of the tribute foreigners believe us to draw from it, but for the entirely unpractical reason that it has fired our dreams and that our best of manhood has gone in her service. I myself, a pacifist to the core, regret most of all to think that the Indian Army, which men of my blood trained and made and which has fought side by side with our own Army on so many fields, must soon cease to be a place where the English can serve. I find it infinitely easier to let every Governorship and every Commissionership go. Mr. Gandhi, for his part, when he wrote, during the Amritsar bitterness, 'to every Englishman', claimed nothing but bare fact, stating that 'no Indian has co-operated with the British Government more than I have for an unbroken period of twenty-nine years of public life in the face of circumstances that might well have turned any other man into a rebel ... It was free and voluntary co-operation, based on the belief that the sum-total of the British Government was for the benefit of India.' Let us see where this co-operation led him. It is a story our people do not know as well as they should.

The future historian will distinguish four stages in Britain's work in India. The first, up to 1857, was the period of conquest and settlement. The second, which between 1895 and 1914 began to overlap the third, was the period of administration, when men did the job as it came to hand, without philosophy or overmuch co-operation and investigation. The third, which we see ending, was a double effort – to get at the sources of plague, poverty, famine, not merely to handle their acute phases; and to train Indians to take over their own government. Both efforts were sincere and valuable, but handicapped by coming so late. The fourth, that is beginning before our eyes (for proof, read such books as Mr. Brayne's Remaking of an Indian Village and Mr. M.L. Darling's Rusticus Loquitur), will see the British accepting the task of service and guidance, whose reward will be the knowledge that they are doing the work of centuries in a few years.

I believe that by remaining in the Empire India can most effectively use her own qualities. East and West are by no means as apart as many represent. The historical and cultural contact of Great Britain and India has laid down a causeway, which should be used. Our own language was once fed by French and Italian. India has vernaculars as unspoiled as was Elizabethan English. Many a time, driving my own thought along the grooves of a language already worn by a thousand better minds than mine, I have wished I had such a new-minted vocabulary and syntax, fresh from the roads and as yet not rubbed into obscurity by four centuries of literary use. It is almost impossible to write a paragraph of English that is not spiky with clichés. There is a great future before the Indian vernaculars. And Indians have English as their highway to the whole modern world of the West.

8 GANDHIAN NATIONALISM

8.1 SPEECHES AND WRITINGS OF MOHANDAS KARAMCHAND GANDHI

Source: 'Satyagraha – Not Passive Resistance', 'Some Rules of Satyagraha', 'Independence', 'Speech at Women's Conference, Sojitra', 'What is Woman's Role', 'Speech at a Prayer Meeting', 'Excerpt from Gandhi's Prayer Speeches', in *The Penguin Gandhi Reader*, ed. by Rudrangshu Mukherjee, Delhi: Penguin, 1993, pp.125–30, 157–60, 83–5, 181–3, 195–6, 277–8, 279.

On 'Satyagraha', 2 September 1917

The force denoted by the term 'passive resistance' and translated into Hindi as *nishkriya pratirodha* is not very accurately described either by the original English phrase or by its Hindi rendering. Its correct description is 'satyagraha'. Satyagraha was born in South Africa in 1908. There was no word in any Indian language denoting the power which our countrymen in South Africa invoked for the redress of their grievances. There was an English equivalent, namely, 'passive resistance', and we carried on with it. However, the need for a word to describe this unique power came to be increasingly felt, and it was decided to award a prize to anyone who could think of an appropriate term. A Gujarati-speaking gentleman submitted the word 'satyagraha', and it was adjudged the best.

'Passive resistance' conveyed the idea of the Suffragette Movement in England. Burning of houses by these women was called 'passive resistance' and so also their fasting in prison. All such acts might very well be 'passive resistance' but they were no 'satyagraha'. It is said of 'passive resistance' that it is the weapon of the weak, but the power which is the subject of the article can be used only by the strong. This power is not 'passive' resistance; indeed it calls for intense activity. The movement in South Africa was not passive but active. The Indians of South Africa believed that Truth was their object, that Truth ever triumphs, and with this definiteness of purpose they persistently held on to Truth. They put up with all the suffering that this persistence implied. With the conviction that Truth is not to be renounced even unto death, they shed the fear of death. In the cause of Truth, the prison was a palace to them and its doors the gateway to freedom.

Satyagraha is not physical force. A satyagrahi does not inflict pain on the adversary; he does not seek his destruction. A satyagrahi never resorts to firearms. In the use of satyagraha, there is no ill-will whatever.

Satyagraha is pure soul-force. Truth is the very substance of the soul. That is why this force is called satyagraha. The soul is informed with knowledge. In it burns the flame of love. If someone gives us pain through ignorance, we shall win him through love. 'Non-violence is the supreme *dharma* [duty]' is the proof of this power of love. Non-violence is a dormant state. In the waking state, it is love. Ruled by love, the world goes on. In English there is a saying, 'Might is Right'. Then there is the doctrine of the survival of the fittest. Both these ideas are contradictory to the above principle. Neither is wholly true. If ill-will were the chief motive-force, the world would have been destroyed long ago; and neither would I have had the opportunity to write this article nor would the hopes of the readers be fulfilled. We are alive solely because of love. We are all ourselves the proof of this. Deluded by modern Western civilization, we have forgotten our ancient civilization and worship the might of arms [...]

[In Hindu mythology] Rama stands for the soul and Ravana for the non-soul. The immense physical might of Ravana is as nothing compared to the soul-force of Rama. Ravana's ten heads are as straw to Rama. Rama is a *yogi*, he has conquered self and pride. He is 'placid equally in affluence and adversity', he has 'neither attachment, nor the intoxication of status'. This represents the ultimate in satyagraha. The banner of *satyagraha* can again fly in the Indian sky and it is our duty to raise it. If we take recourse to satyagraha, we can conquer our conquerors the English, make them bow before our tremendous soul-force, and the issue will be of benefit to the whole world.

[...] [A] satyagrahi does not fear for his body, he does not give up what he thinks is Truth; the word 'defeat' is not to be found in his dictionary, he does not wish for the destruction of his antagonist, he does not vent anger on him; but has only compassion for him.

A satyagrahi does not wait for others, but throws himself into the fray, relying entirely on his own resources. He trusts that when the time comes, others will do likewise. His practice is his precept. Like air, satyagraha is all-pervading. It is infectious, which means that all people – big and small, men and women – can become satyagrahis. No one is kept out from the army of satyagrahis. A satyagrahi cannot perpetrate tyranny on anyone; he is not subdued through the application of physical force; he does not strike at anyone. Just as anyone can resort to satyagraha, it can be resorted to in almost any situation.

People demand historical evidence in support of satyagraha. History is for the most part a record of armed activities. Natural activities find very little mention in it. Only uncommon activities strike us with wonder. Satyagraha has been used always and in all situations. The father and the son, the man and the wife are perpetually resorting to satyagraha, one towards the other. When a father gets angry and punishes the son, the son does not hit back with a weapon, he conquers his father's anger by submitting to him. The son refuses to be subdued by the unjust rule of his father but he puts up with the punishment that he may incur through disobeying the unjust father. We can similarly free ourselves of the unjust rule of the Government by defying the unjust rule and accepting the punishments that go with it. We do not bear malice towards the Government. When we set its fears at rest, when we do not desire to make armed assaults on the administrators, nor to unseat them from power, but only to get rid of their injustice, they will at once be subdued to our will.

The question is asked why we should call any rule unjust. In saying so, we ourselves assume the function of a judge. It is true. But in this world, we always have to act as judges for ourselves. That is why the satyagrahi does not strike his adversary with arms. If he has Truth on his side, he will win, and if his thought is faulty, he will suffer the consequences of his fault.

What is the good, they ask, of only one person opposing injustice; for he will be punished and destroyed, he will languish in prison or meet an untimely end through hanging. The objection is not valid. History shows that all reforms have begun with one person. Fruit is hard to come by without tapasya [ascetic endeavour for a noble cause]. The suffering that has to be undergone in satyagraha is tapasya in its purest form [...]

It is said that it is a very difficult, if not an altogether impossible, task to educate ignorant peasants in satyagraha and that it is full of perils, for it is a very arduous business to transform unlettered ignorant people from one condition into another. Both the arguments are just silly. The people of India are perfectly fit to receive the training of satyagraha. India has knowledge of *dharma*, and where there is knowledge of *dharma*, satyagraha is a very simple matter. The people of India have drunk of the nectar of devotion. This great people overflows with faith. It is no difficult matter to lead such a people on to the right path of satyagraha. Some have a fear that once people get involved in satyagraha, they may at a later stage take to arms. This fear is illusory. From the path of satyagraha [clinging to truth], a transition to the path of a-satyagraha [clinging to untruth] is impossible. It is possible of course that some people who believe in armed activity may mislead the satyagrahis by infiltrating into their ranks and later making them take to arms. This is possible in all enterprises. But as compared to other activities, it is less likely to happen in satyagraha, for their motives soon get exposed and when the people are not ready to take up arms, it becomes almost impossible to lead them on to that terrible path. The might of arms is directly opposed to the might of satyagraha. Just as darkness does not abide in light, soulless armed activity cannot enter the sunlike radiance of soul-force [...]

Then it is said that much suffering is involved in being a satyagrahi and that the entire people will not be willing to put up with this suffering. The objection is not valid. People in general always follow in the footsteps of the noble. There is no doubt that it is difficult to produce a satyagrahi leader. Our experience is that a satyagrahi needs many more virtues like self-control, fearlessness, etc., than are requisite for one who believes in armed action. The greatness of the man bearing arms does not lie in the superiority of the arms, nor does it lie in his physical prowess. It lies in his determination and fearlessness in face of death. General Gordon was a mighty warrior of the British Empire. In the statue that has been erected in his memory he has only a small baton in his hand. It goes to show that the strength of a warrior is not measured by reference to his weapons but by his firmness of mind. A satyagrahi needs millions of times more of such firmness than does a bearer of arms. The birth of such a man can bring about the salvation of India in no time. Not only India but the whole world awaits the advent of such a man. We may in the meanwhile prepare the ground as much as we can through satyagraha.

How can we make use of satyagraha in the present conditions? Why should we take to satyagraha in the fight for freedom? We are all guilty of killing manliness. So long as our learned Annie Besant is in detention, it is an insult to our manhood. How can we secure her release through satyagraha? It may be that the Government has acted in good faith, that it has sufficient grounds for keeping her under detention. But, at any rate, the people are unhappy at her being deprived of her freedom. Annie Besant cannot be freed through armed action. No Indian will approve of such an action. We cannot secure her freedom by submitting petitions and the like. Much time has passed. We can all humbly inform the Government that if Mrs Annie Besant is not released within the time limit prescribed by us, we will all be compelled to follow her path. It is possible that all of us do not like all her actions; but we find nothing in her actions that threatens the 'established Government' or the vested interests. Therefore we too by participating in her activities will ask for her lot, that is, we shall all court imprisonment. The members of our Legislative Assembly also can petition the Government and when the petition is not accepted, they can resign their membership [...]

Nothing more need be said. Truth alone triumphs. There is no *dharma* higher than Truth. Truth always wins. We pray to God that in this sacred land we may bring about the reign of *dharma* by following satyagraha and that this our country may become an example for all to follow.

Some rules of Satyagraha, 27 February 1930

This necessarily brief explanation of satyagraha will perhaps enable the reader to understand and appreciate the following rules:

As an individual

A satyagrahi, i.e., a civil resister, will harbour no anger.

He will suffer the anger of the opponent.

In so doing he will put up with assaults from the opponent, never retaliate; but he will not submit [...] to any order given in anger.

When any person in authority seeks to arrest a civil resister, he will voluntarily submit to the arrest [...]

If a civil resister has any property in his possession as a trustee, he will refuse to surrender it, even though in defending it he might lose his life. He will, however, never retaliate.

Non-retaliation excludes swearing and cursing.

Therefore a civil resister will never insult his opponent [...]

A civil resister will not salute the Union Jack, nor will he insult it [...]

In the course of the struggle if anyone insults an official or commits an assault upon him, a civil resister will protect such official or officials from the insult or attack even at the risk of his life.

As a prisoner

As a prisoner, a civil resister will behave courteously towards prison officials, and will observe all such discipline of the prison as is not contrary to self-respect [...]

A civil resister will make no distinction between an ordinary prisoner and himself, will in no way regard himself as superior to the rest [...]

A civil resister may not fast for want of conveniences whose deprivation does not involve any injury to one's self-respect.

As a unit

A civil resister will joyfully obey all the orders issued by the leader of the corps [...]

[...] If the sum total of the energy of the corps appears to a member to be improper or immoral, he has a right to sever his connection but being within it, he has no right to commit a breach of its discipline.

No civil resister is to expect maintenance for his dependants [...] A civil resister entrusts his dependants to the care of God [...]

In communal fights

No civil resister will intentionally become a cause of communal quarrels.

In the event of any such outbreak, he will not take sides, but he will assist only that party which is demonstrably in the right. Being a Hindu he will be generous towards Musalmans and others, and will sacrifice himself in the attempt to save non-Hindus from a Hindu attack. And if the attack is from the other side, he will not participate in any retaliation but will give his life in protecting Hindus [...]

On independence, 21 July 1946

Independence of India should mean independence of the whole of India including what is called India of the States and the other foreign powers,

French and Portuguese, who are there, I presume, by British sufferance. Independence must mean that of the people of India, not of those who are today ruling over them. The rulers should depend on the will of those who are under their heels. Thus, they have to be servants of the people, ready to do their will.

Independence must begin at the bottom. Thus, every village will be a republic or Panchayat having full powers. It follows, therefore, that every village has to be self-sustained and capable of managing its affairs even to the extent of defending itself against the whole world. It will be trained and prepared to perish in the attempt to defend itself against any onslaught from without. Thus, ultimately, it is the individual who is the unit. This does not exclude dependence on and willing help from neighbours or from the world. It will be free and voluntary play of mutual forces. Such a society is necessarily highly cultured in which every man and woman knows what he or she wants and, what is more, knows that no one should want anything that others cannot have with equal labour.

This society must naturally be based on truth and non-violence which, in my opinion, are not possible without a living belief in God, meaning a self-existent, all-knowing living Force which inheres every other force known to the world and which depends on none and which will live when all other forces may conceivably perish or cease to act. I am unable to account for my life without belief in this all-embracing living Light.

In this structure composed of innumerable villages, there will be ever-widening, never-ascending circles. Life will not be a pyramid with the apex sustained by the bottom. But it will be an oceanic circle whose centre will be the individual always ready to perish for the village, the latter ready to perish for the circle of villages, till at last the whole becomes one life composed of individuals, never aggressive in their arrogance but ever humble, sharing the majesty of the oceanic circle of which they are integral units [...] Congressmen themselves are not of one mind even on the contents of Independence. I do not know how many swear by non-violence or the charkha [spinning wheel] or, believing in decentralization, regard the village as the nucleus. I know on the contrary that many would have India become a first-class military power and wish for India to have a strong centre and build the whole structure round it. In the medley of these conflicts I know that if India is to be the leader in clean action based on clean thought, God will confound the wisdom of these big men and will provide the villages with the power to express themselves as they should.

On the situation and role of women, 16 January 1925

To women I talk about Ramarajya. Ramarajya is more than swarajya. Let me therefore talk about what Ramarajya will be like – not about swaraj. Ramarajya can come about only when there is likelihood of a Sita arising.

Among the many *shlokas* recited by Hindus, one is on women. It enumerates women who are worthy of being remembered prayerfully early in the morning. Who are these women by taking whose names men and women become sanctified? Among such virtuous women Sita's name is bound to figure. We never say Rama-Sita but Sita-Rama, not Krishna-Radha, but Radha-Krishna. It is thus that we tutor even the parrot. The reason why we think of Sita's name first is that, without virtuous women, there can be no virtuous men. A child will take after the mother, not the father. It is the mother who holds its reins. The father's concerns lie outside the home and that is why I keep saying that, as long as the women of India do not take part in public life, there can be no salvation for the country. Only those can take part in public life who are pure in body and mind [...] What does it mean to participate in public life? Public work does not mean attendance at meetings, but wearing khadi [home-spun] – the symbol of purity – and serving the men and women of India [...] The object of our public life is to serve the visible God, that is, the poor. If you want to serve them, take the name of God, go amidst them and ply the spinning-wheel.

To take part in public life is to serve your poor sisters. Their lot is wretched. I met them on the banks of the Ganga where Janaka lived, where Sitaji lived. They were in a pitiful state. They had scanty clothes, but I could not give them saris because I had not found the charkha then. Indian women remain naked even if they have clothes, because as long as one Indian woman has to go naked it must be said that all are naked. Or even if a woman is adorned in a variety of ways but is of unworthy soul, she would still be naked. We have to think of ways of making them spin, weave and thus covering themselves truly [...]

Were our mothers mad that they used to spin? Now when I ask you to spin, I must appear mad to you. But it is not Gandhi who is mad; it is yourself who are so. You do not have any compassion for the poor. Even so you try to convince yourself that India has become prosperous and sing of that prosperity. If you want to enter public life, render public service, then spin on the charkha, wear khadi. If your body and mind are pure you will become truly swadeshi. Spin in the name of God [...]

The second sign of virtue is service to *Antyajas* [the lowest castes]. Brahmins and gurus of today regard touching an *Antyaja* as sinful. I say that it is a meritorious act, not a sin. I do not ask you to eat and drink with them, but to mix with them in order to render service. It is meritorious to serve sick *Antyaja* boys who are worthy of service. *Antyajas* eat, drink, stand and sit, and so do we all. It is not that doing this is either sinful or meritorious. My mother used to become *Antyaja* for some time and then she would not allow anyone to touch her. My wife similarly used to become a *Antyaja*. At this time she became an untouchable. Our *Bhangis* also become untouchable when they do their work. As long as they do not bathe, one can understand not touching them. But if you would not touch them even when they have bathed and tidied up, for whose sake do they bathe then? [...] [D]id Ramachandraji [the hero of the Ramayana] despise the *Antyajas*? He ate berries already savoured by Shabari and he hugged the king of Nishadas, and they were both untouchables. You can see for yourselves that there is no untouchability in the Hindu religion.

The third sign of virtue is furtherance of friendship with the Muslims. If someone tells you that 'they are Mias' or 'Mia and Mahadev cannot get on', then tell him that you cannot harbour enmity towards the Muslims.

If you do these three things, you will be said to have taken full part in public life. By doing so you will become worthy of being prayerfully remembered early in the morning; and it would be said that you have worked for India's salvation. I beseech you to become thus worthy.

On the situation and role of women, 12 February 1940

[It has been said that women require] treatment different from men. If it is so, I do not think any man will find the correct solution. No matter how much he tries, he must fail because nature has made him different from woman. Only the toad under the harrow knows where it pinches him. Therefore ultimately woman will have to determine with authority what she needs. My own opinion is that, just as fundamentally man and woman are one, their problem must be one in essence. The soul in both is the same. The two live the same life, have the same feelings. Each is a complement of the other. The one cannot live without the other's active help.

But somehow or other man has dominated woman from ages past, and so woman has developed an inferiority complex. She has believed in the truth of man's interested teaching that she is inferior to him. But the seers among men have recognized her equal status.

Nevertheless, there is no doubt that at some point there is bifurcation. Whilst both are fundamentally one, it is also equally true that in the form there is a vital difference between the two. Hence the vocations of the two must also be different. The duty of motherhood, which the vast majority of women will always undertake, requires qualities which man need not possess. She is passive, he is active. She is essentially the mistress of the house. He is the bread-winner, she is the keeper and distributor of the bread. She is the caretaker in every sense of the term. The art of bringing up the infants of the race is her special and sole prerogative. Without her care the race must become extinct.

In my opinion it is degrading both for man and woman that women should be called upon or induced to forsake the hearth and shoulder the rifle for the protection of that hearth. It is a reversion to barbarity and the beginning of the end. In trying to ride the horse that man rides, she brings herself and him down. The sin will be on man's head for tempting or compelling his companion to desert her special calling. There is as much bravery in keeping one's home in good order and condition as there is in defending it against attack from without.

As I have watched millions of peasants in their natural surroundings and as I watch them daily in little Segaon, the natural division of spheres of work has forced itself on my attention. There are no women blacksmiths and carpenters. But men and women work on the fields, the heaviest work being done by the males. The women keep and manage the homes. They supplement the meagre resources of the family, but man remains the main bread-winner.

The division of the spheres of work being recognized, the general qualities and culture required are practically the same for both the sexes.

My contribution to the great problem lies in my presenting for acceptance truth and ahimsa [non-violence] in every walk of life, whether for individuals or nations. I have hugged the hope that in this woman will be the unquestioned leader and, having thus found her place in human evolution, will shed her inferiority complex. If she is able to do this successfully, she must resolutely refuse to believe in the modern teaching that everything is determined and regulated by the sex impulse. I fear I have put the proposition rather clumsily. But I hope my meaning is clear. I do not know that the millions of men who are taking an active part in the war are obsessed by the sex spectre. Nor are the peasants working together in their fields worried or dominated by it. This is not to say or suggest that they are free from the instinct implanted in man and woman. But it most certainly does not dominate their lives as it seems to dominate the lives of those who are saturated with the modern sex literature. Neither man nor woman has time for such things when he or she is faced with the hard fact of living life in its grim reality.

On Hindu–Muslim relations, 7 September 1946

I am a villager. I belong with the villagers. The Congress has accepted power for the sake of these downtrodden villagers. I had taken up the cause of Hindu–Muslim unity long before I joined the Congress. I had a number of Muslim friends when I was at school. I went to South Africa to plead the case of some Muslim friends of my brother. I had gone there to gain my livelihood, but soon after my arrival there I gave the first place to service. As a coolie-barrister I served my friends of the labouring class. I had gone as an employee of a Muslim firm and I served the Hindus through them. My memory of those days is a happy one. It is a matter of deep regret that even in South Africa communal differences have arisen. Nevertheless they are unitedly fighting for the rights of Indians. I still remember those hefty Muslims, and especially Seth Cachalia, who participated in the satyagraha and who said they would rather die than live as slaves. When the Qaid-e-Azam and his followers describe Hindus as their enemies I am surprised and pained. I am not a Muslim but I venture to say that Islam does not preach enmity towards anyone. I think I am as much a Christian, a Sikh and a Jain as I am a Hindu. Religion does not teach one to kill one's brother however different his belief. No one can treat another as his enemy until the latter has become his own enemy. Muslim League leaders were not right when they said that they would compel the Congress, the Hindus and the British to accede to their demand.

I am reminded of an incident during the Khilafat days. I was speaking at a meeting of Hindus. I said to them: 'If you want to protect the cow then protect Khilafat. If required even lay down your lives for it.' When I said this it brought tears of joy to the eyes of the Ali Brothers. But what a tragic change we see today. I wish the day may again come when Hindus and Muslims will do nothing without mutual consultation. I am day and night tormented by the question: what I can do to hasten the coming of that day. I appeal to the League not to regard any Indian as its enemy. I appeal to the English not to nurse the thought that they can divide Hindus and Muslims. If they do they will be betraying India and betraying themselves. Hindus and Muslims are both born of the same soil. They have the same blood, eat the same food, drink the same water and speak the same language. The Qaid-e-Azam says that all the Muslims will be safe in Pakistan. In Punjab, Sind and Bengal we have Muslim League Governments. Can one say that what is happening in those provinces augurs well for the peace of the country? Does the Muslim League believe that it can sustain Islam by the sword? If it does it is committing a great error. The very meaning of the word 'Islam' is peace and I am certain that no religion worth the name can be kept alive except through peace.

After Independence, 26 September 1947

There was a time when India listened to me. Today I am a back number. I have been told I have no place in the new order, where we want machines, navy, air force and what not. I can never be a party to that. If you can have the courage to say that you will retain freedom with the help of the same force with which you have won it [i.e. satyagraha], I am your man. My physical incapacity and my depression will vanish in a moment. The Muslims are reported to have said *'Hanske liya Pakistan, ladke lenge Hindustan'* (Laughing we took Pakistan, fighting we will take Hindustan). If I had my way, I would never let them have it by force of arms. Some dream of converting the whole of India to Islam. That will never happen through war. Pakistan can never destroy Hinduism. The Hindus alone can destroy themselves and their faith. Similarly, if Islam is destroyed, it will be destroyed by the Muslims in Pakistan, not by the Hindus in Hindustan.

[Gandhi was assassinated by a Hindu fanatically opposed to his religious tolerance on 30 January 1948.]

8.2 A SPECIAL HOLI

Premchand

Source: Premchand, 'Vichitra Holi' (1921), in *Mansarovar* ['Collected Short Stories'], 8 vols, Allahabad: Hans Prakashan, 1988, III, 238–41.

[Short story translated from the Hindi by Harish Trivedi for this collection.]

It was the day of Holi, the carnivalesque spring festival. Mr A.B. Cross had gone out hunting, and his groom, orderly, sweeper, waterman, milkman and *dhobi* were all celebrating Holi. No sooner had the Saheb left than they had drunk a deep draught of *bhang* and they were now sitting in the garden singing the lusty songs of *phaag*[28]. They glanced at the gate every now and then to see if the Saheb had returned. But it was Sheikh Noor Ali who presently came and stood before them.

The groom asked him – So Khansamah-ji,[29] when is the Saheb coming back?

Noor Ali said – He can come when he likes, but I am quitting today. I shan't serve him any more.

The orderly said – You will never find a job like this again. The pay is good and you can also make a bit on the side. No reason why you should leave it.

Noor Ali – Hang it all, I say. I shan't be a slave any more. They kick us around all the time and yet we go on slaving for them! I am quitting this place now. But come, let me give all of you a treat first. Follow me into the dining-room, and I shall serve you such fine drinks as will truly cool your hearts.

Groom – What if the Saheb were to return all of a sudden?

Noor Ali – The fellow won't return for a while yet. Come right in.

Servants of British masters are often drunkards themselves. As soon as they enlist to serve the Sahebs, they too become subject to the same affliction. When the master swigs bottle after bottle, why shouldn't the servants do the same? At this invitation then, all of them brightened up. They were already high on *bhang*. They abandoned their drums and cymbals right there and, following Noor Ali, went and sat at the dining-table. Noor Ali opened a bottle of Scotch whisky, filled the glasses and they all began to quaff. When those used to coarser stuff found such fine liquor flowing they began to empty glass after glass. The khansamah did what he could to abet them. In a short while they had lost their heads, and lost all fear too. One started to sing a traditional Holi song, and another joined in. The singing picked up. Noor Ali brought in the drums and cymbals, and a concert was under way. As they sang on, one of them got up and began to dance. Another joined

[28] A type of song.

[29] Head cook or steward

him. Soon all were cavorting around the room. A big hullabalou arose. They proceeded from singing *kabir* to *phaag* to *chautal*[30] to trading abuse and even roughing each other up. Fearless, they felt truly at home. Chairs were knocked down, pictures came off walls, and someone even upturned the table. Another began juggling with plates.

Such were the uproarious goings-on when Lala Ujagarmal, a rich man of the city, arrived. When he saw this strange sight he was dumbfounded. He asked the khansamah – What's all this commotion, Sheikh-ji? What would the Saheb say if he were to see all this?

Noor Ali – But what can we do if these are the Saheb's own orders? He has decreed a feast for all his servants today and asked us to celebrate Holi. We hear the *Lat Saheb*, His Lordship the Viceroy himself, has issued orders to other sahebs to mix with the people and to participate in all their festivals. That's why our Saheb has given this order, though normally he wouldn't even look at us. Come in, please, and be seated. What can I get for you? A new consignment of wines from England has just arrived.

Lala Ujagarmal, who had been awarded the title of Rai Saheb by the British, was a gentleman of liberal ideas. He attended British dinners without any qualms, had adopted a Western life-style, was the moving spirit behind the Union Club, was thick with the British generally and regarded Mr Cross as an especially dear friend. In fact, he had always been close to the District Magistrate, whoever he might have been. On Noor Ali's invitation he took a seat and said – Is that so? Right, then, bring on something special. And let someone sing a *ghazal*.

Noor Ali – Yes sir, anything for you, sir.

The Rai Saheb had already had a couple before leaving home; when he'd had a few more, he asked falteringly – So, Noor Ali, will the Saheb too play Holi today?

Noor Ali – Yes, sir.

The Rai Saheb – But I haven't brought any colours or anything with me. Send someone at once to my bungalow to fetch some, and some water-pistols.

He joked happily with the groom, Ghasite, about what fun it all was.

Ghasite – What fun, what fun. Happy Holi!

The Rai Saheb – (*singing*) I'm going to play Holi with the Saheb today, I'm going to play Holi with the Saheb today, oh I am going to aim my water-pistol at him.

Ghasite – I'll smear him with colours.

Milkman – I'll cover him in a cloud of colour.

---

[30] Different types of songs.

Dhobi – I'll guzzle bottle after bottle.

Orderly – I'll sing *kabir* after *kabir.*

Rai Saheb – I'll play Holi with the Saheb today.

Noor Ali – Hey, watch out everyone! I can hear the Saheb's motor car entering the compound. Rai Saheb, here, I've got your colours and water-pistols, so just start to sing a song now and, as the Saheb enters, shoot your water-pistol at him. All of you now, go ahead and cover his face with colour. The Saheb will be beside himself with joy. The car is in the driveway. Get ready!

II

Mr Cross got out of the car with his gun in hand and began calling out for his servants, but with the *chautal* song in full flow, no one could hear him. Puzzled, he wondered at first what was wrong; then he noticed the sound of singing, which seemed to be coming from his bungalow. This was too much! His face contorted with rage, Mr Cross took hold of his riding whip and approached the dining-room; but before he could step into it, the Rai Saheb discharged his water-pistol straight at him. All Mr Cross's clothes were drenched and the coloured water got into his eyes. As he was wiping his eyes, the groom and the milkman and all the others ran up and got hold of the Saheb, and rubbed coloured powder all over his face. The *dhobi* picked up some oil and soot and plastered the Saheb with it! The Saheb's rage knew no bounds, and he began thrashing around blindly with his whip. The poor souls had thought that the Saheb would be pleased and give them a big tip, but on being whipped instead they quickly came to their senses and ran off in all directions. When Rai Saheb Ujagarmal saw things take such a turn he realized at once that Noor Ali had taken him for a ride. He shrank into a corner. When the room had emptied of all servants the Saheb advanced towards him. The Rai Saheb was scared out of his wits. He bolted out of the room and ran as fast as his feet could carry him, with the Saheb close on his heels. The Rai Saheb's carriage was parked outside the gate. Sensing the commotion, the horse gave a start, pricked its ears and ran off with the carriage behind it. What a scene it was, with the horse and carriage in front, the Rai Saheb chasing it, and Mr Cross chasing him, whip in hand. All three ran as if they had shaken off a yoke. The Rai Saheb tripped over but promptly picked himself up and was off again before the Saheb could catch up. The chase lasted till they were out of the grounds and onto the open road. Finally, the Saheb stopped. To proceed further with soot on his face would be ridiculous. In any case, he thought the Rai Saheb had probably been punished enough. He decided to go and sort out the servants, and so turned back. The Rai Saheb breathed again; in fact, he sat down right where he was to catch his breath. The horse too stuttered to a halt. The coachman got down, attended to the Rai Saheb, picked him up and deposited him in the carriage.

III

Rai Ujagarmal was the leader of the all the cooperators and collaborators in the city. He had complete faith in the continuing goodwill of the British and always sang to the tune of the British Raj, promising it obedience and wishing it well in every way. In all his speeches, he took the non-cooperators to task. Recently he had gone up in the esteem of the British, and had been given several government contracts which had previously been the preserve of British contractors. As cooperation with the British had brought him both honour and wealth, he wished the non-cooperators to carry on with their ways even as he denounced them. He thought of non-cooperation as a passing fad, and was keen to make hay while the sun shone. Even as he carried exaggerated reports of the doings of the non-cooperators, he secretly laughed at the British for giving credence to such reports. As he went up in the esteem of the British, so he went up in his own esteem. He was no longer as timid as before. As he sat in his carriage and his breath returned to normal, he began to reflect on what had just happened. Surely Noor Ali betrayed me, he thought; he must be in league with the non-cooperators. But even if the British do not play Holi, their flying into a rage shows that they do not look on us as any better than dogs. How proud they are of their authority over us! He chased me with a whip! Now I know that whatever little regard he showed for me earlier was merely a pretence. In their hearts they must think of us as low and degraded. That little spurt of red colour from the water-pistol was no bullet; it wouldn't have killed him. Don't we go to church at Christmas and send them baskets of gifts, though that's no festival of ours? But this fellow got so mad just because I squirted some coloured water on him! Oh, what an insult! I should have stood up to him and confronted him. To have run away was cowardice. That's what encourages them to roar like lions. There can be no doubt that through winning some of us over they want to crush the non-cooperators. All their courtesy and civility is only a ruse to serve their self-interest. They are still as proud and they are still as tyrannical; there is no difference.

The Rai Saheb grew more and more agitated. Such utter humiliation! The thought of his insult would not go away and quite overwhelmed him. This is the fruit of all my cooperation, he lamented. This is just what I deserve. How pleased I was at their expressions of goodwill. How stupid of me not to realize that between the master and the slave there can be no friendship. How I laughed at the non-cooperators for wanting to have nothing to do with the British. It turns out that it's not they who were laughable, it's I who am ridiculous.

He did not go home but went straight to the office of the Congress Committee. There he found a huge assembly. The Committee had invited everyone, the high and the low, the touchables and the untouchables, to come together to celebrate Holi. It had arranged for a feast of fruits, so that all castes could partake of it. When he arrived, someone was in the middle of a speech. The Rai Saheb got out of his carriage but felt embarrassed to go and join the meeting straightaway. Dragging his feet, he went and stood in a corner. Everyone was startled to see him there and gazed at him, wondering what on earth this arch-priest of the sycophants thought he was doing here. He should have been at some meeting of collaborators passing a resolution pledging loyalty. Maybe he has come to spy on us, they thought, and to bait him shouted – Victory to Congress!

Ujagarmal shouted loudly – Victory to non-cooperation!

The response came – Down with sycophants!

Ujagarmal shouted even more loudly – Down with lickspittles!

So saying, and filling everyone with amazement, he went up to the platform and said in a grave tone – Gentlemen, friends, forgive me for having non-cooperated with you so far. I beg your forgiveness from the bottom of my heart. Do not think of me as a spy, a betrayer, a defector. Today the veil has been lifted from my eyes. Today, on this sacred day of Holi, I have come to embrace you in love and affection. Kindly treat me with indulgence and generosity. Today I have been punished for having betrayed you. The district officer today humiliated me dreadfully. I was whipped by him and I have come to seek refuge. I have been a traitor to the nation, an enemy of the people. For the sake of my selfishness and because of my distrust of you, I have done a great disservice to the nation and put hurdles in your path. When I think of all my misdeeds I wish I could smash my heart into bits. (A voice piped up – Go ahead! And just let me know if you need any help! The Chairman – This is no time for sarcasm.) No, I need no help from anyone, I can do the job very well myself; but first I must do great penance and atone for all my sins. I hope to spend the rest of my days doing just such penance, in washing the mud off my face. All I beg of you is to give me a chance to reform myself; please trust me and consider me a humble servant of yours. From now on, I dedicate myself to you with body, soul and all that I have.

8.3 FROM RANGABHUMI

Premchand

Source: Premchand, *Rangabhumi* ['The Field of Action'] (1925), 2 vols, Delhi: Hind Pocket Books, 1988, I, 7, II, 250–51, 278.

[Extracts from a novel, translated from the Hindi by Harish Trivedi for this collection.]

Cities are places where the rich live and buy and sell. The land that lies beyond is for them a place of entertainment and amusement. In the heart of the cities are schools for their children and courts of law as arenas for themselves, where in the name of justice they strangle the poor. At the edges of cities are habitations of the poor. In Benares, Pandepur is just such a habitation. The city lights do not reach it nor the swept and washed wide roads of the city nor the piped water of the city. On both sides of the road here are little shops of grocers and sweet-vendors, and behind them the huts of *ekka*-drivers, carters, cowherds and labourers. A couple of house-holds belong to gentlemen fallen on hard times, whose poverty has banished them from the city. Amongst all these people lives a poor and blind beggar whom everyone calls Surdas. In India the blind lack neither a name nor an occupation. Tradition ordains that Surdas be their name [after the blind devotional Hindi poet of the seventeenth century], and begging alms their occupation. Their characteristics and temperamental traits too are already known to all: a flair for singing and playing music, an especially loving and devout heart, a particular bent for spirituality. Eyes wide shut; vision wide open.

Surdas was a very feeble, frail and simple man who looked as though God had created him just to live on alms. Each morning, with the help of a stick, he would grope his way to the high road and there pray for the passers-by. God bless you, for giving! was his refrain, which he kept up all day.

[Some land Surdas owns, which he has allowed to be used as common pasture, is requisitioned for a cigarette factory. He resists, until the police arrive with three cannons trained on his hut. Sophia Sevak, an Indian Christian whose father wants to set up the factory, supports Surdas, and she now challenges the British district officer, Clark, who has in the past been an admirer of hers.]

Clark – We come here to rule, and not just to follow our own inclinations. As soon as we step off the ship, we erase our own individuality. Our justice, our sympathy, our good will, all have just one purpose. Our first and last object is to rule [...]

Sophia – But unjust rule is not rule, it's war.

Clark – Well, you've called a spade a spade! ... I'll see you later. He spurred on his horse.

Sophia shouted – No, never! I don't want to see you ever again!

[The Gurkhas are brought in.] The crowd too was roused; the mice prepared to take on the cats. Surdas had stood quietly by until now. When he heard the commotion he feared for what might happen and said to Bhairon, his constant companion – Brother, raise me on your shoulders so that I may plead with the people once again. Why don't they go away from here? How many times have I asked them to, but no one listens. If the police open fire, there will be greater blood-shed today than before.

Bhairon hoisted Surdas up on his shoulders. He now towered a head above the rest of the crowd. People rushed to him from all sides to hear what he had to say. Hero-worship is a natural attribute of a crowd. He looked as if he were some sightless Greek god surrounded by his devotees.

Surdas looked at the assembled people with his blind eyes and said – Brothers, please go back home. With folded hands I beg of you to go home. No good will come of standing here and taunting our rulers. If I am destined to die I shall die, and not one of you could do a thing about it. If I am not destined to die, I shall escape unscathed from the cannon's mouth. Indeed, your coming here hinders me rather than helps me. Whatever sympathy and righteousness the rulers, the police, the army may have felt for us has turned into anger because all of you have collected here. I would have shown our rulers how a single blind man can force an army to retreat, can spike the muzzle of a gun, can blunt the edge of a sword. I wanted to fight on the strength of righteousness [...]

He could say no more. When Clark had seen the blind fellow get up and speak, he thought he was inciting the crowd to unruly conduct. He believed that as long as this man who was their spirit was alive, the limbs would continue to move. Therefore, it was necessary to destroy this very spirit. Cut off the source and the water will stop flowing. He had looked for an opportunity to implement this plan but Surdas had always been surrounded by a number of people. Now, seeing Surdas's head raised above the crowd, Clark had his chance, that golden opportunity which would ensure the end of the battle. He knew of course what would follow. The infuriated crowd would throw stones, burn houses, ransack government buildings. But he had enough force at his command to put down the trouble. The key was to remove the blind fellow from the field of action – for he was at the heart of it all, the thread that controlled all movement. He pulled out his pistol and shot Surdas. He didn't miss his aim; the arrow found its mark. The bullet hit Surdas in the shoulder, his head dropped, and blood began to flow. Bhairon couldn't support him, and Surdas fell to the ground. Moral force failed to counteract brute force.

[Surdas lingers on for a few days and then dies.] Needless to say, the funeral procession was a grand occasion. There was no band or music, no horses and elephants, but there was no lack of eyes to shed tears, and mouths to sing his praises. Surdas's biggest victory was that even his enemies felt no enmity for him any more. [They all joined in his funeral procession.] His bier was made up of sandalwood; a flag of victory flew on top of it.

[...] On the way back Clark said to Raja Mahendra Kumar – It is my misfortune that such a good man died at my hands.

The Raja Saheb wondered at this and said – Why misfortune and not a job well done?

Clark said – No, truly, Raja Saheb, it is my misfortune. We do not fear people like you, with your wealth and estates, we only fear those who can reign over the hearts of the people. It is our punishment for ruling here that in this country we must kill the kind of person whom in England we would have venerated as god-like [...]

8.4   SPEECHES AND WRITINGS OF JAWAHARLAL NEHRU

Source: *Nehru: The First Sixty Years*, ed. and introduced by Dorothy Norman, foreword by Jawaharlal Nehru, 2 vols, London: Bodley Head, 1965, II, 142, 149–50, 148–9, 336, 337–8, 368–70.

On imperialism [1943]

Since Hitler emerged from obscurity and became the *Führer* of Germany, we have heard a great deal about racialism and the nazi theory of the *Herrenvolk*. That doctrine has been condemned and is today condemned by the leaders of the United Nations. Biologists tell us that racialism is a myth and there is no such thing as a master race. But we in India have known racialism in all its forms ever since the commencement of British rule. The whole ideology of this rule was that of the *Herrenvolk* and the Master Race, and the structure of government was based upon it; indeed the idea of a master race is inherent in imperialism. There was no subterfuge about it; it was proclaimed in unambiguous language by those in authority. More powerful than words was the practice that accompanied them, and generation after generation and year after year India as a nation and Indians as individuals were subjected to insult, humiliation, and contemptuous treatment. The English were an Imperial Race, we were told, with the God-given right to govern us and keep us in subjection; if we protested we were reminded of the 'tiger qualities of an imperial race'. As an Indian, I am ashamed to write all this, for the memory of it hurts, and what hurts still more is the fact that we submitted for so long to this degradation. I would have preferred any kind of resistance to this, whatever the consequences, rather than that our people should endure this treatment. And yet it is better that both Indians and Englishmen should know it, for that is the psychological background of England's connection with India, and psychology counts and racial memories are long.

On religion, philosophy and science [1943]

India must break with much of her past and not allow it to dominate the present. Our lives are encumbered with the dead wood of this past; all that is dead and has served its purpose has to go. But that does not mean a break with, or a forgetting of, the vital and life-giving in that past. We can never forget the ideals that have moved our race, the dreams of the Indian people through the ages, the wisdom of the ancients, the buoyant energy and love of life and nature of our forefathers, their spirit of curiosity and mental adventure, the daring of their thought, their splendid achievements in literature, art, and culture, their love of truth and beauty and freedom, the basic values that they set up, their understanding of life's mysterious ways, their toleration of other ways than theirs, their capacity to absorb other peoples and their cultural accomplishments, synthesize them and develop a varied and mixed culture; nor can we forget the myriad experiences which have built up our ancient race and lie embedded in our subconscious minds. We will never forget them or cease to take pride in that noble heritage of ours. If India forgets them, she will no longer remain India and much that has made her our joy and pride will cease to be.

It is not this that we have to break with, but all the dust and dirt of ages that have covered her up and hidden her inner beauty and significance, the excrescences and abortions that have twisted and petrified her spirit, set it in rigid frames, and stunted her growth. We have to cut away these excrescences and remember afresh the core of that ancient wisdom and adapt it to our present circumstances. We have to get out of traditional ways of thought and living which, for all the good they may have done in a past age, and there was much good in them, have ceased to have significance today. We have to make our own all the achievements of the human race and join up with others in the exciting adventure of Man [...]

On industrialization in India [1943]

I have a partiality for the literary aspects of education and I admire the classics. But I am quite sure that some elementary scientific training in physics and chemistry and especially biology, as also in the applications of science, is essential for all boys and girls. Only thus can they understand and fit into the modern world and develop, to some extent at least, the scientific temper. There is something very wonderful about the high achievements of science and modern technology (which no doubt will be bettered in the near future), in the superb ingenuity of scientific instruments, in the amazingly delicate and yet powerful machines, in all that has flowed from the adventurous inquiries of science and its applications, in the glimpses into the fascinating workshop and processes of nature, in the fine sweep of science, through its myriad workers, in the realms of thought and practice, and above all in the fact that all this has come out of the mind of man ...

The three fundamental requirements of India, if she is to develop industrially and otherwise, are: a heavy engineering and machine-making industry, scientific research institutes, and electric power. These must be the foundations of all planning, and the National Planning Committee laid the greatest emphasis on them. We lacked all three, and bottlenecks in industrial expansion were always occurring. A forward policy could have rapidly removed these bottlenecks, but the government's policy was the reverse of forward and was obviously one of preventing the development of heavy industry in India. Even when World War II started, the necessary machinery was not allowed to be imported; later shipping difficulties were pleaded. There was neither lack of capital nor skilled personnel in India, only machinery was lacking, and industrialists were clamoring for it. If opportunities had been given for the importation of machinery, not only would the economic position of India have been infinitely better, but the whole aspect of the war in the Far Eastern theaters might have changed. Many of the essential articles which had to be brought over, usually by air and at great cost and under considerable difficulties, could have been manufactured in India. India would really have become an arsenal for China and the East, and her industrial progress might have matched that of Canada or Australia. But imperative as the needs of the war situation were, the future needs of British industry were always kept in view, and it was considered undesirable to develop any industries in India which might compete with British industries in the postwar years. This was no secret policy; public expression was given to it in British journals, and there were continuous reference to it and protests against it in India.

On independence achieved

[From a speech to the Constituent Assembly, New Delhi, 14 August 1947.]

Long years ago we made a tryst with destiny, and now the time comes when we shall redeem our pledge, not wholly or in full measure, but very sub-stantially. At the stroke of the midnight hour, when the world sleeps, India will awake to life and freedom. A moment comes, which comes but rarely in history, when we step out from the old to the new, when an age ends, and when the soul of a nation, long suppressed, finds utterance. It is fitting that at this solemn moment we take the pledge of dedication to the service of India and her people and to the still larger cause of humanity.

At the dawn of history India started on her unending quest, and trackless centuries are filled with her striving and the grandeur of her success and her failures. Through good and ill fortune alike she has never lost sight of that quest or forgotten the ideals which gave her strength. We end today a period of ill fortune and India discovers herself again [...]

[From a broadcast speech, 15 August 1947.]

Fellow countrymen, it has been my privilege to serve India and the cause of India's freedom for many years. Today I address you for the first time officially as the First Servant of the Indian people, pledged to their service and their betterment. I am here because you willed it so and I remain here so long as you choose to honour me with your confidence.

We are a free and sovereign people today and we have rid ourselves of the burden of the past. We look at the world with clear and friendly eyes and at the future with faith and confidence.

The burden of foreign domination is done away with, but freedom brings its own responsibilities and burdens, and they can only be shouldered in the spirit of a free people, self-disciplined, and determined to preserve and enlarge that freedom.

We have achieved much; we have to achieve much more. Let us then address ourselves to our new tasks with the determination and adherence to high principles which our great leader has taught us. Gandhiji is fortunately with us to guide and inspire and ever to point out to us the path of high endeavour. He taught us long ago that ideals and objectives can never be divorced from the methods adopted to realize them; that worthy ends can only be achieved through worthy means. If we aim at the big things of life, if we dream of India as a great nation giving her age-old message of peace and freedom to others, then we have to be big ourselves and worthy children of Mother India. The eyes of the world are upon us watching this birth of freedom in the East and wondering what it means.

Our first and immediate objective must be to put an end to all internal strife and violence, which disfigure and degrade us and injure the cause of freedom [...]

Our long subjection and the World War and its aftermath have made us inherit an accumulation of vital problems, and today our people lack food and clothing and other necessaries, and we are caught in a spiral of inflation and rising prices. We cannot solve these problems suddenly, but we cannot also delay their solution [...] We wish ill to none, but it must be clearly understood that the interests of our long-suffering masses must come first and every entrenched interest that comes in their way must yield to them. We have to change rapidly our antiquated land tenure system, and we have also to promote industrialization on a large and balanced scale, so as to add to the wealth of the country, and thus to the national dividend which can be equitably distributed.

Production today is the first priority, and every attempt to hamper or lessen production is injuring the nation, and more especially harmful to our labouring masses. But production by itself is not enough, for this may lead to an even greater concentration of wealth in a few hands, which comes in the way of progress and which, in the context of today, produces instability and conflict. Therefore, fair and equitable distribution is essential for any solution of the problem.

On the death of Gandhi

[From the translation of a speech delivered in Hindustani, 12 February 1948, as Gandhi's ashes were committed to the Ganges ('Ganga' in Hindi) at the sacred point where the Ganges meets the Jumna ('Jamuna' in Hindi) at Allahabad.]

This great tragedy has happened because many persons, including some in high places, have poisoned the atmosphere of this country of ours. It is the duty of the Government as well as the people to root out this poison. We have had our lesson at a terrible cost. Is there anyone amongst us now who will not pledge himself after Gandhiji's death to fulfil his mission – a mission for which the greatest man of our country, the greatest man in the world, has laid down his life?

You and I and all of us will go back from these sands of our noble river, the Ganga. We shall feel sad and lonely. We shall never see Gandhiji again. We used to run to him for advice and guidance whenever we were confronted with any great problem or when we felt ill at ease or in doubt. There is none to advise us now or to share our burdens. It is not I alone or a few of us who looked up to him for help. Thousands and hundreds of thousands of our countrymen considered him their intimate friend and counsellor. All of us felt that we were his children. Rightly he was called the Father of our Nation and in millions of homes today there is mourning as on the passing away of a beloved father.

We shall go away from this river bank sad and lonely. But we shall also think with pride of the high and unique privilege that has been ours to have had for our chief and leader and friend this mighty person, who carried us to great heights on the way to freedom and truth. And the way of struggle that he taught us was also the way of truth. Remember also that the path he showed us was one of fighting for the good and against evil and not the way of sitting quietly on the peaks of the Himalayas. And so we have to fight on and not seek escape or rest. We have to do our duty and fulfil the pledges we have given him. Let us tread the path of truth and Dharma. Let us make India a great country in which goodwill and harmony prevail and every man and woman, irrespective of faith and belief, can live in dignity and freedom.

How often we have shouted, 'Mahatma Gandhi ki Jai'. By shouting this slogan we thought we had done our duty. Gandhiji always felt pained to hear this shouting, for he knew what little it meant and how often it just took the place of action or even of thought. 'Mahatma Gandhi ki Jai' – 'Victory to Mahatma Gandhi', what victory could we wish him or give him? He was the Victorious One in life and in death. It is you and I and this unfortunate country who have to struggle for victory.

Throughout his life he thought of India in terms of the poor and the oppressed and the downtrodden. To raise them and free them was the mission of his life. He adopted their ways of life and dress so that no one in the country might feel lowly. Victory to him was the growth of freedom of these people.

What kind of triumph did Gandhiji wish for us? Not the triumph for which most people and countries strive through violence, fraud, treachery and evil means. That kind of victory is not stable. For the foundations of a lasting victory can only be laid on the rock of truth. Gandhiji gave us a new method of struggle and political warfare and a new kind of diplomacy. He demonstrated the efficacy of truth and goodwill and non-violence in politics. He taught us to respect and co-operate with every Indian as a man and as a fellow-citizen, irrespective of his political belief or religious creed. We all belong to Mother India and have to live and die here. We are all equal partners in the freedom that we have won. Every one of our three or four hundred million people must have an equal right to the opportunities and blessings that free India has to offer. It was not a few privileged persons that Gandhiji strove and died for. We have to strive for the same ideal and in the same way. Then only shall we be worthy to say, 'Mahatma Gandhi ki Jai'.

9.1 CHILDHOOD MEMORIES

Lalithambika Antharjanam

Source: Lalithambika Antherjanam [*sic*], 'Childhood Memories' (1969), in *Cast Me Out If You Will: Stories and Memoir*, translated from the Malayalam and introduced by Gita Krishnankutty, Calcutta: Stree, 1998, pp.133–42.

A valley surrounded by a fortress of hills, all the level ground divided into rice fields, the canal waters foam and whirl against the rocks, and sometimes they snake swiftly down. The hillsides where the cattle graze are filled with country flowers. There are rabbits and mountain squirrels everywhere. The Komaran Rock, which can be seen from every point around, towers over the landscape. Under it is a tiger's lair. Often we saw hunters with a tiger they had shot and hung on a pole, exhibiting it at the Devi temple in the village to the accompaniment of cries and ululations.

Anyone who wanted to get to the village had to walk through nearly four miles of field and hillside. An aristocratic wealthy *tarawad*, full of innumerable members of a vast extended family, stood in the centre of the village. Around it were the houses of the laborers, some of whom were of the upper castes, though most were untouchables or harijans. Many of the villagers were agricultural workers. There were separate communities of washerfolk, carpenters, and blacksmiths.

A little girl was born one morning sixty years ago in this big house that stood isolated from the outside world in the midst of hills. It was the Malayalam year 1084 (AD 1909), the month of Meenam, Friday the thirteenth. The star was Karthika.

Although her society considered it a curse to be born a girl, she was not wholly unwelcome. For one thing, her parents had lost two children and were longing for a baby. For another, she was born at the time when her grandfather, whose star was the same as hers, was praying to the Devi chanting the 'Lalitha Sahasranamam,' the thousand names of the Goddess. And that is how she received her name, Lalithambika, which according to tradition should have been a different one.

Another anecdote that was always told to her along with this one, and was also to do with her birth, affected her very deeply over the years. When her father, a learned man of progressive views, heard that a daughter had been born to him, he exclaimed angrily, 'No, I will not live here any longer. I'll go away, maybe to Madras, become a Christian, and marry an Englishwoman.'

'And what if she has a daughter too?' asked my mother.

'At least I will be allowed to bring her up like a human being. I will have the liberty to educate her, give her the freedom to grow, get her married to a good man.'

She had heard this story many times. Her eighty-year-old mother had repeated it to her just a few days ago. She had not understood its significance at first. Her father took great care not to let her realize that she had been born into a society that did not believe in bringing up girls as human beings. Her mother, who was her first teacher, began to instruct her at a very early age. Her *vidyarambham* ceremony was conducted when she was three years old. She would tug at her mother's *mundu* and take her away to her books until she learned to read herself. After that she began to read on her own: anything she could lay her hands on, newspapers, magazines, books. She read indiscriminately, unceasingly.

Childhood

My very first memory of early childhood is of the sounds I used to hear when I woke up in the morning: the chime of holy bells blending with the chants. I usually lay in bed for some time and listened. When I rose and came out, the *nalukettu* [courtyard] was always enveloped in the smoke of the Ganapathi *homan*. The fragrance of tulasi and sandalwood and of foods prepared for the *naivedyam* would waft out of the thevarappura.

Amma rose very early in the mornings. She would have had a bath and begun the rituals of worship and the preparations for breakfast by the time I awoke. Many of the children would have had their baths. Because it was such a huge extended family, there was a certain lack of order in the routine of the household. But none of us were allowed to have breakfast till we had had a bath and said our prayers. I usually ran to the tank on the eastern side of the house, had a dip in it, dried myself rapidly, and rushed back. As a child of five or six, all I wore was a *konam* made of the spathe of a palm leaf or of red cloth. I first went to the temple, then worshipped all the household deities and prostrated before them. After this, I ate my share of the offerings: the milky sweet made for the worship that day, malar, *trimadhuram*, and slivers of coconut. Then came breakfast, for which I had hot *kanji* with ghee and roasted pappadams.

In the mornings we had lessons with a teacher. All we took to class were a quill pen and a few sheets of paper. Pens with nibs were not very common in those days. We wrote with sharpened ostrich feathers, and made our own ink. We pounded kadukka nuts, mixed copper sulphate into it, added water, and left it in the sun in a frying pan. Sometimes we put in hibiscus flowers to improve the consistency. When the mixture had been sunned for four or five days and grown thick, we strained it and stored it in bottles.

We sat on the floor and wrote on little low desks, which had drawers in them to hold pens and ink. Writing in copybooks was a strict requirement. We began with a lesson in Sanskrit. After that we studied the government textbooks of the period. They were chosen for us according to the class we were suited for. We did arithmetic, geography, and history. In the afternoon, we were free for an hour and started lessons again after lunch only at three. We continued until the sun set. The music teacher came occasionally, in the morning or the evening.

At dusk, we said our prayers again. Achan sat with us after dinner, while we read the Puranams. All this left me very little free time. However, we managed to escape the watchful eyes of the grown-ups to run away and paddle and swim in the tanks, roam through the banana groves, and pick flowers. Wild rabbits played amongst the bushes. You could stand on the hill and watch the lovely sunsets and the green fields lying around. I have breathed the beauty of this landscape so often as a child.

There is a high school building on the hill now, and children instead of rabbits play on the hillside. Roads run all over and cars and buses go down them ceaselessly. Cement structures have been erected everywhere. I watch the children of the new generation and think that the human race has certainly made great progress, but is losing touch with nature. Is this a part of progress? Who are the fortunate ones, they or we? But then concepts like good fortune and happiness are relative after all.

The beginning

There were three portraits in the front room of their guesthouse. The first was of Swami Vivekananda delivering the Chicago address [in 1894]. The next one was of Gandhiji in a big turban, with a shawl around his shoulders. The third was a beautiful painting of Tagore, with eyes as wide as lotus petals, a long beard, and a loose robe. Her father's brother had brought the last two from Madras where he was a student. Discussions on the ideals and activities of the three persons in these portraits – on religion, nationalism, and literature – took place very often in the room where they hung. All three attracted her, but Gandhiji exerted the strongest influence over her. She began to think and write about him, and about the freedom of India. She tore up most of what she had written, but one or two articles were published.

Disturbing news filled the newspapers: the Mapilla Rebellion, the satyagraha at Vaikkam, the protest against land taxes. I recall the little girl engrossed in K.P. Kesava Menon's biography of Mahatma Gandhi, bent almost double on the ground. She cried because she wanted to wear khadar. She bought a spinning wheel. She planted cotton and spun yarn. She put up pictures of the nationalist leaders on the walls of her room.

When she insisted she would wear nothing but khadar, her father asked, 'What is so special about khadar?'

'It is a *swadeshi* product. Gandhiji has asked all of us to wear it.'

Her father replied, 'What about the mundus woven here, in Veliyath and Talachara? Aren't they swadeshi as well? Don't the weavers who make them have to make a living too?'

He was right. Her family always used mundus woven in the rural areas. She thought of the old weaver from Veliyath who usually brought them. His family lived on the paddy he received in exchange for the mundus.

She now perceives that most people who advocated khadar at the time were not truly interested in the ideals that inspired its manufacture, they wore it merely because it was in fashion. Around this time her father bought her a copy of Tagore's *At Home and Outside* [*The House and the World*].

The treasures of memory

She hardly ever left the protective circle of her fortress home, except for an occasional visit to her uncle's house, or, more rarely, to the house of a relative. Such expeditions had to be made in stages. First, there was a tiring walk of three or four miles, and then a journey of nearly four days, partly in a closely covered bullock cart and partly in a country boat.

Her father could be described as a child of the mountains, while her mother must have been the offspring of a water goddess, for she loved water. As a little girl she often saw crocodiles as their boat glided slowly over the Pamba River. Red and white water lilies grew in the fields and lotuses bloomed in profusion in the channels between them. The sand lay knee-deep in summer, and during the monsoon water flowed everywhere, as far as the eye could reach.

Boat rides with her uncle, festivals in the temple, a grandmother who adored her: all these filled her life with novelty and happiness.

As a child she did not think of herself as different from others, and it was only much later that she noticed that the quality that set her apart had certain disadvantages. As if in response to her father's wish, her mother bore no more daughters. She grew up with her brothers for company, learned whatever they did, and behaved no differently from them. Wooden kuradus were not inserted in her earlobes to lengthen them in the customary manner and she never went bare-breasted. As she grew older, she was aware that people disapproved of the way she was being brought up. They thought that a growing girl had no right to so much freedom.

When she looks back now, she understands the meaning of the expression in her father's eyes every time she lingered in the room where literary discussions took place. He obviously could not bear to tell her to go to the inner rooms, to explain to her that she could no longer be with them now that she was growing up.

A caged bird

The event that her parents had dreaded took place at last. The day she reached puberty, the house looked and felt as if someone had died. Her mother wept, so did the rest of the family, and the servant women, and seeing them, she too could not help crying. Even her father, usually confident and assured, lamented: 'I feel as if I have to cage a free bird'.

She was like one dead now, as far as the outside world was concerned. She might not go to the temple, or play under the champakam tree. She might not talk to her favorite swami. She felt the impact of these changes very sharply over the next four days, and began to understand why her father had been so distressed when a daughter had been born to him.

Like everyone else around her, she had to submit to customs that had been observed strictly over many centuries. She knew that no concessions would be made for her, and that she had to bow to the dictates of destiny, no matter how deeply it hurt.

I feel that her real education took place during those two years, when she was confined to the *antahpuram* [purdah-room]. She read a great deal during this period and wrote a little too. She reflected deeply and compassionately on the contradictions, the joys, and the sorrows, the ideals, desires, and experiences of all the people around her: her immediate and extended family, her society and the laborers in the village. The longer she thought about them, the more intensely she shared their joys and sorrows. She often asked herself, 'What if I were in their place?'

Three of her grandfather's sisters, who were child widows, lived with them and she observed them closely. She had heard the story of yet another sister who had been unjustly cast out when she was fifty years old for the crime of having gone out of the house without her umbrella [used to conceal a woman's face] in the midst of a family quarrel. She had taken ill and died untended by the roadside.

Two or three young girls distantly related to her had been sold to people who came from north Kerala, on the pretext of being given in marriage. Nothing had been heard of them since.

She often thought that the souls of these unfortunate women inhabited her. What if I had been one of them, she asked herself.

She wrote a novel in the narrative style of *At Home and Outside*. Poems, plays and stories followed swiftly. She read them over and over again, cried over them, then tore them up.

She had no companions of her age at all.

Marriage

Her parents became increasingly busy with their domestic responsibilities. Her brothers had left home to go to the English school about seven miles away from their village, and now lived in the vicinity of the school. Once she finished her household duties, she read, wrote, and watched the happenings in and around the house through the doors of the *nalukettu*. She never regretted those two years of solitude, which gave her the opportunity to nurture her inner vision and to define her ideals.

Discussions that would eventually decide their daughter's future must have taken place during this period, in the outer rooms and the kitchen of the big house. And that was how a good-looking gentle, affectionate young man came into her life one day, like a messenger from the gods. He held her hand over the glowing flames of the sacrificial fire and said to her, 'I take your hand in the certainty that it will bring good fortune to both of us. Will you follow me?'

She said yes silently in her heart. The priest said to them, 'Your lives are now joined.'

They have been mutually supportive companions now for forty-two years. There have been occasions when they felt too tired to go on, when they were lost and confused. But their griefs and burdens brought them closer together. When the dreamlike responses of the imaginative vision and the practical good sense of everyday reality go hand in hand, a new lineage is born.

Now that she had a comrade to help her to achieve her aims and desires, she grew stronger. Her mind, free of its fetters, longed for complete freedom. It was a period when a group of young revolutionaries were actively engaged in trying to change society. They convened meetings, performed plays, and spoke on public platforms. Her village took part in these activities and organized public speeches and propaganda marches.

People began to see that art could be used as a powerful weapon. The waves of this impassioned social and national struggle swept through the darkest corners of the inner rooms and roused them into a new awareness of freedom.

We cast away our umbrellas

She remembers it perfectly, the day they decided to hold that important meeting in a nearby town. A group of courageous women who had decided to cast away their umbrellas were going to be there. She pretended she was going to a temple, started out with her umbrella and shawl, and threw the umbrella away as soon as she left the house. She then rearranged the mundu that covered her as a saree, and took the bus to the venue of the meeting.

It gives her great pleasure now to think of that inspiring event. But she came back that day to find her mother in tears, sorrowing as if her daughter had died. Her relatives wanted nothing to do with her, and even the servants avoided her. Senior members of the family declared that they could not perform a *shraddha* [memorial prayer] in a house where a woman had been cast out. Others counseled that she be forbidden to enter the kitchen. It began to look as if the matter might lead to a legal dispute, or even partition of the family property. However, her father remained unruffled. 'All right,' he said, 'she and her husband went to a public meeting together. Is that sufficient reason to cast her out? People have done worse things and not been so severely punished.' He refused to be intimidated. And society gradually changed its norms.

I believe that each era evolves its own ideas and goals, and that they also depend on how old one is, the stage of life one has reached. It is the combination of these factors that compels human beings to action. The young woman therefore surrendered to her destiny, which was to express the thoughts and feelings within her. But when she began to put them down in writing, she did not ever think that she might someday become well known in the literary world. A friend came across some of the pieces she had written in her notebook and insisted that she send them to one of the leading Malayalam weeklies, which published them. The editor then asked her for a poem. She gave them a poem and a story. And so it all began ...

She was determined to fulfill her literary and domestic duties, as well as her commitments to society, with an equal degree of dedication. They were all integral parts of her life and she could not bear to neglect any of them. She did not realize at the time that this obstinacy would result in her being unable to accomplish any of her tasks completely.

Meanwhile, there were babies every year. She brought them up. She wrote, read and made speeches. When I look back, I see the young mother crouched on the ground, writing as she rocks the cradle. I see the wilful, ignorant young woman standing on a public platform, holding her baby close to her while she makes a speech – the impudent woman who opposed anyone who did not agree with her, who used her art as a weapon against her adversaries, who stoically accepted the blows and wounds that her enemies in the literary world aimed at her.

She dealt with the world around her solely on the basis on information gleaned from the newspapers, and her vision of life was directed purely by her imagination. She saw the world in the light of her own beliefs – beliefs that changed constantly with the changing pace of the times. Only much later did she see that even the great men of the twentieth century could do little to alter the corrupt nature of the prevalent goals and methods of action, and that truth and justice had no place in political conflict.

Those who use the pen as a weapon often lacerate their own hearts with its needle-sharp point. She became sensitive to criticism and found herself wondering whether readers would be annoyed with her, whether they would misunderstand her. She tormented herself endlessly with self-censure.

But she persisted in her chosen way of action with extraordinary self-confidence, even at the risk of being considered insolent. Human beings are an assortment of defects, misdeeds, and contradictions that they wish upon themselves. Their definitions of defects and misdeeds vary according to the period they live in, the beliefs that guide them, and the circumstances in which they are placed. Who knows what is right and what is wrong? There are religions that believe that all men and women are born sinners. How innocently, how trustingly, they call themselves sinners! I am not prepared to go that far. But I do know that we often bruise and slash each other in order to achieve what we consider good. But who can tell whether what we thus achieve is truly good and right? Sometimes when we try to eliminate what we believe is bad in us, we lose an essential part of our individuality. What we thought of as a defect might well have been our strongest point.

As time went by, her impudence and her outspokenness were repeatedly crushed and she had perforce to learn humility. With that, however, the artistic skills she had acquired began to weaken.

9.2 A LEAF IN THE STORM

Lalithambika Antharjanam

Source: Lalithambika Antharjanam, 'A Leaf in the Storm', translated from the Malayalam by Narayan Chandran, in *Stories about the Partition of India*, ed. by Alok Bhalla, Delhi: HarperCollins, 1994, pp.137–45.

1

She was certainly the most emaciated of the women reclaimed from that obscure village in western Punjab; and the most outraged of them all, too.

She didn't bother to tell them her name or caste. Perhaps she even hesitated to accompany them to the refugee camp. She realized that she would be one of the many to be given in exchange. Fifty bonded girls were to be given away for the fifty 'reclaimed'. The exchange took place on the border, black bundles of rags crawled up and down, like ghosts let loose from the sepulchres. She was the last to come. She halted. She wasn't too sure ...

'From one prison to another? ...'

The transport was ready. The police and the army personnel would accompany them too. The social service volunteers were generous in their consolation. Still, someone had to gently force her into the vehicle bound for the camp.

The women were looked after well in the camp. They rejoiced as though they had been reunited with their lost children. The relatives of some of those women joined them in the camp. Some asked after their kinsfolk. Only one of them sat quietly, all by herself, in a corner. She did not lift her veil. As the lady volunteer approached her with some food, she exploded, 'Damn your crumbs of bread; I want a gun. Or a dagger. Wouldn't mind a little poison either. It's that I want ... first and last ...'

The lady volunteer stood aghast. This woman must have gone mad. Well, who wouldn't under these circumstances? What is indeed amazing is that she is alive. A good many of these women keep crying. Some of them recount their baneful lives. That old woman there – is the mother of nine children, who in turn have given her fifty children of their own. She has indeed been a mother to the whole village, to both Hindus and Muslims. The family decided to stay on because of their mother's insistence that she should breathe her last in her own village. Today, she alone remains. Her children were killed. The girls were abducted. Her house was gutted. And there she stood, in the courtyard, supporting herself on a stick, watching her house burn down to ashes. Yet, she lives on ... She eats, sleeps, and talks ... Hope, passion for life..

There you see another woman, now at her breakfast, chewing hard at dirty bits of chapati. Her cheeks and breasts are swollen. Her clothes are torn. She had been married to a big officer in Sindh. She set out with her three children as soon as the people had been warned of the revolt. Tragedy overtook her car and waylaid her. She was violated in front of her husband's body which lay ripped open and scattered. She could only see the blood-stained hands of her children. Someone reclaimed her body, more dead than alive, from the railway tracks. Alas, she hasn't yet died.

On the other side of the hall, a Sikh girl is consoling a Hindu child. Another child has now dozed off, crying. Loud wails, everywhere, after one's parents. No one answers – Where are those parents?

Among them are people who ran for life, for several miles. Many have arrived with bruised feet, broken limbs and withered bodies. Not to speak of their fear of fever and epidemics. Despite all this, they seem to have got used to this way of life.

She observes everything about her. She doesn't cry now. But her eyes are dim with pity and despair. At times her eyes reflect the hate and cynicism of one who despises the whole world. Her belly remains big even though she hasn't had food for four days. She clenches her fist, aims it at her belly. But, now the occupants of the camp have begun to notice this small woman, good looking and noble, and perhaps born into a well-to-do family. Her frail body evidently cannot stand such torture – the four-day fasting and much else besides. Maybe she was the darling of her parents, the beloved of her husband ... By now, inevitably, the report of her condition must have reached the camp doctor.

The doctor coaxed her to drink milk. He begged her, 'Won't you drink this milk, for me sister? Why don't you realize that this life is also valuable for our beloved country?'

'One life ... one life!' She broke into tears and said, 'Why one life? How many lives have we lost now? Look at me! I am damned too ... You want me to live on still, and sow the seed of damnation?'

She continued sobbing, 'My life ... doctor ... may I ask you something? Tell me, are you able to destroy something which must be destroyed, just as much as you can preserve something you think must be preserved? Now this life bred of damnation – conceived in consequence of inhuman rape and ignorance – tell me doctor, can you destroy this, save another life ... ? Can you do that?'

She raised her eyebrows in question. The doctor turned pale. He wasn't quite prepared to answer something like this when he came to the camp. He was a disciple of the supreme master of ahimsa. It was at his master's instance that he had given up a well-paying job to serve the refugees here.

Her demand was loud and clear. Further, he was trained and adequately equipped for the task. But, still ... But, would it be proper? He was stricken with a kind of moral cowardice. Breaking an egg, and wringing another's neck are taking away lives, in different ways ...

He spoke like a vedantin, 'Sister, who are we to fight the decree of destiny? Look, I'm a doctor. I have no moral right to take away someone's life; I can only redeem it. Look at the lakhs of people in this camp; there are many more like them in other camps too. We will overcome this storm that rages over the east and west of our land. Bharat will endure; are you not a woman of India? Cheer up; here, drink this milk ... '

She said nothing in return. She drank the milk, however. It does not matter whether it was the doctor's sermon or her zest for life that eventually prevailed upon her desperate obstinacy. Since then she has been eating regularly.

The camp register entered her name as 'Jyoti'. It was a Sikh woman who told us that her name is 'Jyotirmoyi Devpal'. We began to hear more and more about her presently – that Jyoti's mother and the Sikh lady came from the same village; that even after coming of age, Jyoti had gone about refusing to veil her face; that she had spurned the proposal for marriage from a zamindar, true to her self-assertive nature, and so on. The women in her village were rather amazed at this girl's independent ways. Maybe now she is paying too high a price for such indulgence!

The crowd in the refugee camp grew day by day. Different costumes ... different languages ... Men, women, children. The young and the old. And the number swelled. And new stories; loud clamour as never before. And in the midst of all these no one bothered about Jyoti. In that ocean of mass movement she was but a wave. She witnessed many births in the camp. More deaths than births. In the camp one could witness all the scenes of human life.

At sunset people gathered under the big leafy tree at the backyard of the camp. They were villagers, who knew little of national politics. They all belonged to that beautiful land of five rivers and sugar-cane fields, the land where the wheat fields swayed in laughter as the breeze blew over them, where the buffaloes grazed in the fields ... Far away, in the desert, a caravan of camels crawled towards the adjacent village. On many evenings like this one, these men had returned home, humming tunes, their work-tools balanced on their shoulders. And those houses ... They have been hounded out of those houses – those ancestral homes they had inherited, and which, they would have passed on to their progeny. They have been driven away from them like stray dogs ... hunted out of them like wild hen. How did this happen? Who was at fault?

They cursed all the well-known leaders. They gnashed their teeth in vengeful rage. Some of them blamed even the 'toothless grandsire' of Indian politics – that kindly soul! Poor people. They were not amongst those who made others suffer, but those who suffered themselves.

In the camps across the border, do the people have the same feelings of outrage?

Jyoti listened to everything. She moved about slowly, trying hard to contain her swollen belly within the folds of her sari. Only a few people knew her secret; that she was pregnant and unmarried, and had been 'reclaimed' by the camp. Her burden grew heavier as the days passed. Those first imperceptible pulsations grew into swollen coils within her, threatening a revolt that might stifle her. What moved within her was a challenge to every cell of her being. It symbolized everything womanhood and humanity found despicable in nature. And that it should grow within her, drawing on her life-blood! It moved and drew breath from her life-breath. One day, it will emerge – this 'cosmic shape' – biding no one's time, seeking no one's permission. Come out it must, willy-nilly.

Pressing her big belly hard against the floor, she bore her pain. What else could she do?

The next day something unusual happened. There lay in the toilet the lifeless body of a child, new born and deserted. A beautiful child it was, round and gleaming, like a thick clot of blood. Its fair skin was like that of an inhabitant of the territorial border. It had brown hair. On its neck was a thick bluish mark resembling a crescent. The scavenger dragged its still warm body away, and put it into his garbage bin. No girl shed a tear. There was no case against anyone.

Jyoti stood and watched all this. She wondered how courageous these people were in practical life – people one could easily mistake for cowards and slaves! They had no qualms. No indecisiveness. Nor did they turn to anyone for advice. Whatever the obstacles, they swept past them and went on ahead.

Faster than those tremors within her belly rose her heart-throbs. So, that's very easy ... and equally trivial ... It shouldn't take more time than it would in nipping off a blade of grass. A second? Maybe, a minute at the most – at midnight she could wipe herself clean of her filth and come out – into a new world of hopes ...!

During the day she wandered about in the open and desolate space outside the camp. At night she preferred to be left alone in a corner. One day, at supper she felt a terrible pain in her back and felt dizzy. The people around had to lift her up and lay her on the cot. Jyoti was worried and anxious. She did not know anything. Was this a prelude to that momentous happening? Ayyo ... and then?

But nothing happened. No one was suspicious either. It was quite normal for some people in the camp to feel sick.

Weeks passed by.

That day, a distinguished guest arrived. Everyone had heard about him. In fact, the message he brought them was well known and appreciated by them all. The guest addressed the people under the shade of the big tree in the backyard of the camp. 'Young men should be prepared to accept abducted women as their mothers, sisters, and even as their wives – Those children ...' Jyoti pricked up her ears, 'those children are indeed the citizens of Indian, the first citizens of a free India ...'

Her face glowed. 'How ironical that would be! Are they citizens of India alone? That is, of India as we conceive of her today? They will grow up ... these children ... as they begin to comprehend the reality, as they come of age ... that blood ... No! The source of that blood is hate, not love ... would it not run amok, driven by the intense desire for vengeance? Even break past the borders? ...'

When Jyoti came to herself, she noticed that there was nobody around her. Perhaps the guest had left. And so had every other listener. It was late night.

She got to her feet hoping to go into the camp from the open yard which was steeped in darkness. It was cold. She couldn't walk, her body was shivering. She felt helpless and weak ... A pain, with the speed of a thousand bolts of lightning, invaded her brain. The overwhelming travail of creation ... She stood clinging to the branch of the big tree, trying to endure the pain. For how long? She couldn't remember. In the meanwhile, hazy memories thronged her mind ...

Far away, in one of those prosperous villages in the Punjab – in a well-to-do household – a mother was in labour ... There, the doctor and the nurses waited at hand ... Her relatives were anxious. The master of the house sat on the bed, his eyes fixed on the clock. They were waiting for the fruit of prolonged medical treatment and their virtuous deeds.

The girl who was born that day was the darling of her kinsfolk and neighbours. She grew up in perfect happiness. No one had faulted her for anything. She joined college, despite the initial objections of her parents whom she won over by her charm. She shocked her people when she decided to give up her purdah. They chose to ignore such aberrations in her. She loved her freedom. That explained her refusal to settle for a marriage, which others considered desirable. The freedom she had earned was not only for herself. It was also the freedom from slavery for her community, indeed for the whole human race. She wanted to free the bonded, those who were enslaved by convention. She wanted to make them happy and contented. She hoped in vain that she could knit together a net of silver threads.

Her dreams had landed her in prison. In her fight to behold her ideals she had to suffer police brutality. For days she had gone without food or rest. Ignoring all warnings, she had dedicated herself to the uplift of women. 'I trust my brothers,' she used to say, when others tried to dissuade her venturesome spirit. And now ... this reward!

Oh my mother!

During those periodic bouts of excruciating pain, she shuddered. Her legs grew weaker and weaker. Her whole body was perspiring. Was she about to throw up? Resting her head against the trunk of the tree, she took a deep sigh. She was utterly exhausted.

Memory ... frightening scenes from memory again ...

2

Fifteen women wearing ghoshah veils were confined in a room, far inside the lady's wing of the palace, in her neighbourhood. The master of that house, Qasim, was a good friend of her father. And Ayesha was her bosom friend. Ayesha had given them refuge. Only Ali, Ayesha's brother, thought otherwise, 'Damn them! Our land will yield gold only when it is soaked by the blood of these kafirs!'

Ayesha tried hard not to rouse suspicion even in her brother. She had concealed those ghoshah ladies with great care. Her plan was to send them across the border when her father's bullock cart went on its usual trip. The refugee camp across the harbour would take care of them. Qasim Sahib's cart had been on its regular trips across the border for fifty years. No one would suspect that it carried women. And no one would stop it on the way.

That night, the miserable journey inside the iron-cage: one felt choked amidst violent bumps and jerks. Loud slogans rent the air ... The air was full of the smell of flesh burning ... the heat of flames ... Qasim Sahib periodically hollered, ignoring other voices, 'Pakistan Zindabad ... Allah-ho-Akbar!'

The travellers thought for a while that they were out of danger. Then suddenly a big row erupted. The cart stopped. Someone pulled out the bundles of hay from the cart, ignoring Qasim Sahib's swearing and protests. Loud, thunderous laughter. Wild shouts. From among the bundles of hay fifteen women were dragged out. One by one, those flowers fell ...

Oh ... how cruel life's traffic is! Overwhelming pain! What could it be – the agony of life, or death?

It seemed her mother, now returned from the dead, was speaking to her – 'Jyoti, I too went through this. My mother and mother's mother ... In fact, all mothers ... '

No woman can evade the tax levied on her life. Suddenly she thought of the prison in which she had lain unconscious. An awful lot of men must have come into that cell. Those devilish faces ... reddened by fanatic hate and frenzy! To which one of those faces does this bear a resemblance?

Jyoti felt a deep convulsion from within. She felt hot ... and thirsty. She breathed hard and her body shook in agony ...

Ho! And so it ends. Was it really the end?

The lamps had gone out in the camp sheds. Here and there the sick groaned. The children cried. No one, however, would really know about this.

She lay on her back on the lawn, a triumphant soldier, fallen in exhaustion on the battlefield. The stars had dimmed in the sky. The young one of a bird cried 'kee ... kee', and fluttered its wings on the tree.

Her first instinct was to close her eyes, grope her way about, and choke it to death with her hands. With that, she might bury the bundle of her misery and shame which she had borne all these months ... there; bury it under that tree, forever ... She wouldn't let the scavenger drag it away. One must carry one's cross oneself.

Jyoti got up and stretched her hand. She felt that mass of flesh ... 'O, how warm it is! Did my body give it so much warmth? I hope its looks are like mine ... Perhaps I should look at it, its small eyes, once ... once only!'

'Oh! it is seeking refuge, stirring its little feet.' That voice didn't resemble hers; in fact it wasn't like anything she had heard so far. Its voice resounded like the assertion of a right, an appeal to nature.

'Perhaps the voice has woken up the camp. The whole universe and its creatures might wake up, hearing this voice. It is so compelling. And so tender!'

She tried to cover its parted lips, to hush its voice. How ticklishly smooth they felt, like the tender leaves. More than compassion, fear overcame her. As though someone had forbidden her, and said, 'No don't stifle that voice! It is not the voice of an individual, but that of the whole world!'

Jyoti drew back with a shudder. She was confused. 'Why not run away from this place of conflicting emotions, of fear and suspicion, and go into hiding?

But where? The place doesn't matter ... to the utmost boundary of this earth, or hell ... wherever ... Will this voice haunt me there too?

Let the child be, amidst the green grass, in the light of the stars. I have heard it said that babes deserted by their mothers are tended to by goddesses. Someone will surely spot the child in the morning. Perhaps, one of those mothers without children ...' And then a doubt crossed her mind – did she have children?

Jyoti was confused. It was rather difficult to sever life's bonds so easily. The scar would remain. The world would suppurate and continue to afflict one's life till the very end. Jyoti returned slowly. The child was still crying. Its voice grew hoarse. Its limbs began to grow limp. There was no time to wait.

The mother swooped the child up into her arms. She warmed its forehead by caressing it gently. Her life-blood flowed like fresh milk.

As the mother walked slowly towards the camp, the stars beamed from heaven. Maybe they had resolved a complicated puzzle.

9.3   THE TRAIN HAS REACHED AMRITSAR

Bhisham Sahni

Source: Bhisham Sahni, 'The Train Has Reached Amritsar', translated from the Hindi by Alok Bhalla, in *Stories about the Partition of India*, ed. by Alok Bhalla, Delhi: HarperCollins, 1994, pp.147–58.

There were very few passengers in the compartment. The Sardarji, sitting opposite me, had been telling me stories about the war. He had fought on the Burmese front, and every time he talked about the white soldiers, he laughed at them derisively. There were also three Pathan traders in the compartment. One of them, who was dressed in green, lay stretched on the upper berth. He was a jovial man who had joked throughout the journey with a frail-looking Babu. That Babu seemed to be from Peshawar, because at times they talked to each other in Pushto. On the berth opposite me and to my right, sat an old woman whose head and shoulders were covered. She had been telling the beads of her rosary for quite sometime. There may have been other passengers in the compartment, but I can't remember them anymore.

The train moved slowly, the passengers gossiped with each other, the wheat fields outside swayed gently in the breeze, and I was happy because I was going to Delhi to watch the Independence Day celebrations.

When I think back on those days they seem to be shrouded in mist. Perhaps, the past always seems hazy. And as the future opens up before us, the past becomes even more indistinct.

The decision to create Pakistan had just been announced, and people speculated about the shape of things to come. But no one could foresee the future clearly. The Sardarji, sitting opposite me, asked me repeatedly whether I thought Jinnah Sahib would continue to live in Bombay or move to Pakistan. My answer was always the same, 'Why should he leave Bombay? What would be the point? He can always go to Pakistan and come back.' There was speculation about which side of the border Lahore and Gurdaspur would find themselves. Nothing had changed in the way people talked to each other or joked together. A few people had abandoned their homes and run away, while those who had chosen to stay back had merely laughed at them. No one knew what to do, what steps to take. Some people rejoiced at the creation of Pakistan, others rejoiced at India's Independence. There had been riots in a few places, but there were also preparations being made for the celebration of freedom in other places. Given the history, everyone felt that after Independence the riots would automatically stop. The golden glow of freedom was surrounded by uncertainty and darkness. Only occasionally did one catch a glimpse of the future through the surrounding haze.

Soon after we crossed the Jhelum, the Pathan sitting on the upper berth, untied a bundle, took out chunks of boiled meat and nan, and offered them to the passengers. In his usual jovial way, he invited the Babu sitting next to me to share them with him, 'Here Babu, eat. You will become strong like us. Your wife will be pleased. Eat it, dalkhor, you are weak because you only eat dal.'

Everyone in the compartment laughed. The Babu smiled, shook his head and said something in Pushto.

The other Pathan joined in the teasing and said, 'O zalim, if you don't want if from our hands, pick it up yourself. I swear it's only goat's meat and nothing else.'

The Pathan sitting on the upper berth chuckled, and added, 'O son of a swine, no one will know. We won't tell your wife. If you share meat with us, we'll "drink" dal with you.'

Everyone laughed. The Babu smiled, shook his head and said something in Pushto again.

'How can we let you sit there and stare at us, while we eat? It's not courteous.' The Pathans were in a good mood.

'He doesn't want to take food from you because you haven't washed your hands,' the fat Sardarji said and tittered at his own joke. He was reclining on the berth and half his belly had spilled over the seat. 'The Babu doesn't want to accept meat from your hands, because you have just woken up and have begun eating. There is no other reason.' As he said that he looked at me, winked and tittered.

'If you don't eat meat, you should travel in the ladies compartment. Why sit here?' Again, the whole compartment laughed.

There were other passengers in the compartment, but a sort of informality had grown between those of us who had been together since the beginning.

'O zalim, come and sit, sit with me. Let's tell each other stories,' one of the Pathans said.

The train stopped at a station and lots of new passengers pushed their way in.

'What station is it?' someone asked.

'Wazirabad, I hope,' I replied, looking out of the window.

The train didn't stop there for long. But before it left, there was a minor incident. A man had got down from the next compartment to get some water. He had just begun to fill his pot, when he suddenly turned around with a start and ran back. Some water spilled out of his pot. But the manner in which he had been startled was revealing in itself. Others who were standing around the tap also ran back towards their compartments. I had seen people run in fear like that before. Within a few seconds, the platform was deserted. Inside our compartment, however, people were still laughing and joking.

'Something is wrong,' the Babu sitting next to me muttered.

Something was certainly wrong. But none of us was able to find out what had happened. Since I had seen many riots, I could sense the slight change in the atmosphere. The sound of doors shutting, people standing on roof-tops and an eerie silence – they were all signs of a riot.

Suddenly, there was an altercation at the door opposite the one that opened onto the platform. Some passengers were trying to get in.

'There is no place in here. Don't try to force your way in,' someone shouted.

'Shut the door. Can't you see there is no place. People think they can push their way in ...' Many passengers shouted at the same time.

As long as a passenger outside tries to force his way in, people inside oppose him. But the moment he gets in, all opposition subsides and he becomes a part of the inner world of the compartment, and at the next station begins to shout and scream at other passengers trying to get in – 'There is no place here, go to the next compartment ... People think they can walk in ...'

The commotion at the door increased. A man, with a drooping moustache, wearing tattered clothes, was trying to squeeze his way into the compart-ment. From his filthy clothes, it appeared that he worked in a halwai's shop. Without paying attention to the protests of the other passengers, he turned around and began pulling in an enormous black trunk.

'Come on, climb in,' he shouted to someone behind him. A thin, frayed woman climbed up, followed by a young, dark girl of sixteen or seventeen. People continued to scream at them. The Sardarji had to get up and sit upon his berth.

'Shut the door ... People barge in as if they are walking into their father's house ... Don't let anyone else in ... What are you doing ... Push him out ...' Everyone shouted at the same time.

The man continued to pull his trunk in, while his wife and daughter stood against the toilet door.

'Couldn't you have found another compartment? ... Did you have to bring women in here too ...'

The man was breathless and his clothes were soaked through his sweat. Having pulled in the trunk, he began hauling in a bundle of wooden legs for his cot.

'I have a ticket. We are not travelling without tickets. I was lucky to reach the station.' Suddenly all the passengers fell silent.

But the Pathan sitting on the lower berth yelled, 'Get out of here! Can't you see there is no room?' Blind with rage, he suddenly got up and tried to kick the man. But, unfortunately, he missed him, and the kick landed on his wife's stomach. She screamed with pain and collapsed on the floor.

That man had not time to argue with the passengers. He was much too busy collecting his luggage. But an ominous silence descended on the compartment. The man began pulling in large bundles packed with his things. Seeing that, the Pathan sitting on the upper berth lost his patience, and yelled, 'Throw him out. Who does he think he is?' The Pathan sitting on the lower berth, got up and threw the man's trunk out of the door of the compartment. It fell at the feet of a coolie in a red uniform.

No one interfered, only the old woman sitting in a corner muttered, 'Have some pity. Be kind to them and let them come in. Come, child, come and sit next to me. We'll somehow manage! Leave them alone, you scoundrels, let them in .'

Before that man could pull all his baggage in, the train began to move.

'My luggage! My luggage has been left behind!' he screamed in despair.

'Father, our luggage is still outside,' the girl standing against the toilet door said, as she trembled with fear.

'Get down, down,' shouted the man in despair. He threw the rest of his luggage out and, holding the iron-bars of the door, jumped down himself. His terrified daughter and his wife, who was still groaning with pain, followed him.

'You are cruel people, that was an awful thing to have done,' the old woman protested loudly. 'There is no pity left in your hearts. He had a young daughter. You are cruel, pitiless people, you pushed them out.'

The train sped past the deserted platform. There was an uneasy silence in the compartment. No one had the courage to defy the Pathans.

Just then, the frail Babu sitting next to me, touched my arm and whispered, 'Fire. Look something is burning.'

The train had left the city behind. We saw flames leaping out of the clouds of smoke which rose above the city.

'A riot. That is why people were scared at the platform. There has been a clash somewhere.'

The city was in flames. The passengers in the compartment rushed to the windows to catch a glimpse of the fire.

After the train left the city far behind there was silence in the compartment. When I turned around to look at the passengers, I noticed that the Babu's face was pale, and that his forehead was covered with sweat. He looked deathly pale. I realized then that each passenger was nervous and suspicious about his neighbour. The Sardarji got up from his seat and sat down next to me. The Pathan on the lower berth climbed up to join his two companions on the upper berth. Perhaps, the condition in the other compartments was also the same. Everyone was tense. The lights had been turned off. The old woman was telling her rosary. The three Pathans on the upper berth quietly watched everyone down below. The passengers were alert to everything around them.

'What station was that?' someone asked.

'Wazirabad,' another person replied.

The name produced a strange reaction amongst the passengers. The Pathans became less tense, the silence amongst Hindus and Sikhs became more ominous. One of the Pathans took some snuff out of a small box and sniffed it. The other Pathans did the same. The old woman continued to tell her beads over and over again and mutter something in a hoarse voice.

There was an ominous silence at the next station where the train stopped. Not even a bird was in sight. A mushqee, however, walked across the deserted platform with a bag full of water on his back, offering some to the passengers. 'Water, come and drink water,' he cried. The women and children sitting in the ladies compartment, stretched out their hands for water.

'There's been a communal riot here. Many people have been killed.' It appeared as if he was the only man who had stepped out to do a good deed.

As soon as the train began to move, people pulled their windows down. One could hear, over the clatter of the wheels, the loud rattle of windows being pulled shut in compartments far away.

The Babu, sitting next to me, was so terrified that he jumped up from his seat and lay down flat on the floor. His face was tense with fear. Seeing him thus, one of the Pathans on the upper berth, mockingly said, 'O coward, are you a man or a woman? Don't lie there on the floor. You are a disgrace to all men.' Then he added something in Pushto and laughed. The Babu lay on the floor without saying anything in reply. The other passengers sat in tense silence. The atmosphere in the compartment was charged with fear.

'We won't let a coward stay in our compartment. O Babu, get down at the next station and go sit in the ladies compartment.'

The Babu's lips were dry. He stammered something and then fell silent. After some time he got up, dusted his clothes and sat on his seat again. I didn't know why he had decided to lie on the floor. Maybe, when he heard the sound of the shutters being pulled down, he thought that people outside were either throwing stones or firing at the train.

I was confused. It was possible that one person had, in panic, pulled the shutters of his window down, and others had instinctively followed his example.

Tense and nervous, we continued on our journey. The night outside grew darker. The passengers watched each other suspiciously. If the train slowed down they stared at each other apprehensively. If it stopped the silence inside became unbearable. Only the Pathans seemed to be unconcerned. After some time, however, they too stopped gossiping because no one was in the mood to talk to them.

A little later the Pathans began to doze, while the other passengers continued to stare anxiously into nothingness. The old woman covered her head, folded her legs up on the seat and went to sleep. One of the Pathans, climbing onto the upper berth once again, pulled out his rosary and began counting the black beads mechanically.

The moon had appeared in the sky by then, and the world outside seemed even more mysterious and even more threatening. Sometimes, in the far distance, we saw flames leaping up into the sky. Cities were burning all around us. There were times when the train screamed through the night; at other times, however, it crawled slowly for miles.

Suddenly the Babu, who had been looking out of the window, shouted excitedly. 'We have crossed Harbanspura!' All the other passengers were startled by his shrill voice. They turned to look at him.

'O Babu, why are you screeching?' the Pathan with the rosary asked in surprise. 'Do you want to get down here? Shall I pull the chain?' He continued to make fun of the Babu. It was obvious that he had neither heard of Harbanspura nor was he aware of its importance for the passengers.

The Babu didn't say anything in reply. He merely shook his head, looked at the Pathan and turned around to look out of the window again.

Everyone in the compartment was silent. The engine blew its whistle and slowed down. There was a loud clatter of the wheels. Perhaps, the train had changed tracks. The Babu continued to lean out of the window and stare ahead.

'We have reached!' he shouted again in excitement. 'We have arrived at Amritsar!' He leapt up, whipped around to face the Pathan and began shouting, 'Come down you bastard. You son of a bitch ... May your mother ...'

The Babu began to hurl filthy curses at the Pathan. The Pathan with the rosary in his hand, turned to look at the Babu and said, 'O Babu, what's the matter? What have I said?'

Seeing the Babu so agitated, the other passengers sat up.

'Come down, you son of a bitch ... You dared to kick a Hindu woman, you bastard ...'

'O Babu, stop cursing and screaming. I'll cut your tongue out, you son of a pig.'

'You dare to abuse me! May your mother...' the Babu shouted as he stood on his seat. He was trembling with rage.

'Enough, enough,' the Sardarji said, 'Don't fight. We don't have far to go now.'

'I'll break your legs. You think the train belongs to you?' the Babu continued to shout.

'O Babu, what have I said? Everyone wanted to throw them out, I pushed them. Why curse me alone? If you don't stop, I'll cut out your tongue.'

The old woman pleaded, 'Please sit down and be calm. Please, in the name of God, be calm.'

The Babu seemed as if he was possessed and was muttering something incoherently. He continued to shout, 'You pretend to be brave like a lion in your own backyard. Now talk, you son of a bitch.'

The train slowly pulled into the Amritsar station. The platform was crowded. The people, who peered into the compartment, wanted to ask only about one thing, 'What's happening back there? Where have the riots broken out?'

The entire platform was buzzing with talk about the riots. The passengers in the train had pounced upon the few hawkers on the platform. They were hungry and thirsty.

A few Pathans appeared at the window of our compartment. The moment they spotted the other Pathans inside they began talking to them in Pushto. I looked around for the Babu. He was nowhere in sight. I was disturbed. He had been trembling with rage. I didn't know what he would do. The Pathans in our compartment collected their bundles and left with the other Pathans to sit in a compartment up ahead. The segregation, which had taken place earlier in our compartment, was now taking place in the entire train.

The crowd around the hawkers began to thin out. People started walking back towards their compartments. I suddenly saw the Babu. His face was still pale and a lock of hair had fallen across his forehead. As he came closer, I noticed that he was carrying an iron rod in his hand. I didn't know where he had found it. Before entering the compartment, he hid the rod behind his back, and as he sat down on the seat next to mine, he slipped it under the berth. When he raised his eyes, he was startled to find that the Pathans were no longer sitting on the upper berth.

'The bastards have run away. The sons of bitches ... they have all escaped.' He stood up and started shouting angrily, 'Why did you let them escape? You are all impotent and cowardly.'

The train was very crowded. Many new passengers had boarded it. No one paid him any attention.

The train began to move and, once again, he sat down on his seat next to me. But he was very upset and was continuously muttering something to himself.

Slowly the train lurched forward. The passengers who had travelled with us, had eaten as many puris as they could have and had quenched their thirst. The train was now passing through a region in which there was no danger to the lives and property of the passengers.

The new passengers were gossiping. The train had begun to move at a steady pace. Soon the passengers began to doze. But the Babu continued to stare into empty space. Repeatedly, he asked me to tell him where the Pathans had gone after getting down from the compartment. He seemed to be possessed.

Soon even I was lulled to sleep by the rhythmic movement of the train. There was no space to lie down in the compartment. I slept where I sat, and my body swayed with the train. Sometimes when I woke up, I heard the Sardarji lying on the opposite berth snoring comfortably. He looked like a corpse. Indeed, I felt, looking at the awkward postures people were reclining in, that I was travelling in a train full of dead bodies. The Babu, however, was restless. He sometimes leaned out of the window and sometimes sat still, with his back erect against the wall.

If the train stopped at a station and the clatter of its wheels ceased, a deep silence fell over everything. In such a silence even the sound of something falling, or the footsteps of someone getting down, startled me out of my sleep.

Once when I woke up, I noticed that the train was moving slowly. It was dark inside the compartment. All the lights had been switched off. I looked out of the window and saw the red light of a signal glowing somewhere far behind. We had recently passed a station, but the train had still not picked up speed.

I heard a vague sound outside the compartment. Then, still half asleep, I saw the shadow of something moving. I stared at it for a while and then forgot about it. It was nearly dawn.

Suddenly, I heard someone outside bang at the door of the compartment. I turned around to look. The door was shut. I again heard someone bang at the door. It seemed as if someone was hitting the door with a stick. When I leaned outside the window, I saw a man on the foot-board of the compartment. He had a lathi in his hand and a bundle over his shoulder. His clothes were dirty and he had a beard. When I looked down, I saw a woman running barefoot alongside the train. She was carrying two bundles in her hand. Because of their weight, she couldn't run fast. The man standing on the foot-board urged her again and again, 'Come on, climb up!'

The man banged at the door with his lathi and called out, 'Open the door. In the name of Allah, open the door.'

He was breathless, 'In the name of Allah, open the door. There is a woman with me. She'll be left behind ...'

Suddenly I saw the Babu jump up from his seat, rush to the window and ask, 'Who is it? There is no place here.'

The man outside pleaded, 'For the sake of Allah, she'll be left behind ...'

The man pushed his hand in through the window and groped for the latch.

'There is no place in here, get down from the train,' the Babu screamed, and the next instant pulled the door open with a jerk.

'Ya Allah,' I heard the man exclaim with relief.

At that very instant, I saw the iron rod flash in the Babu's hand. He gave the man a sharp blow on his head. I was so shocked that I couldn't move. At first I thought that the blow had no effect on the man. He still held onto the bars of the door. The bundle had slipped down his shoulder and hung on his arm.

Suddenly, two or three thin streams of blood began to flow down the man's face. In the faint light of the morning, I saw the man grimace with pain. He uttered 'Ya Allah' a few times, groaned and staggered. He looked at the Babu with eyes which were barely open as if they were trying to ask his assailant what crime he had committed. The shadows of the night scattered. I saw terror on the man's face.

The woman, who was running along the track, was shouting and cursing. She didn't know what had happened. She thought that her husband had staggered under the weight of the bundle he was carrying. Running beside him, she kept trying to place his feet back on the foot-board of the compartment again.

Suddenly, the man's grip on the door-handles loosened and he fell to the ground like a tree which had been chopped down. As soon as he fell, the woman stopped running, as if both of them had reached their journey's end at the same time.

The Babu stood at the door like a statue. The iron bar was still in his hand. His arm didn't seem to have the strength to throw it away. I was still afraid and sat hidden in my corner staring at him.

After sometime the Babu stirred. A strange impulse made him lean out of the door and look back. Somewhere far behind, next to the railway tracks, he saw a dark heap. The train continued on its journey.

The Babu roused himself out of his trance. He threw the iron rod out of the door. Turned around and cast his eyes over the passengers. They were all asleep. He didn't notice me.

Then he closed the door shut. Examined his clothes carefully, checked both his hands and sniffed them to see if they smelled of blood. After that he walked quietly across and sat down on his seat.

Slowly, the morning sun dispelled the darkness. Bright and clear light spread over everything. No one had pulled the chain to stop the train. The body of the man who had fallen had been left miles behind. The wheat fields swayed gently in the breeze.

The Sardarji woke up and scratched his body. The Babu sat quietly with his hands behind his head and stared into space. There was a shadow of a beard on his face.

Seeing the Babu sitting opposite him, the Sardar laughed and said, 'You look frail, Babu, but you are brave. You showed real courage back there. The Pathans got scared of you and ran away. If they had stayed here, you would have smashed the heads of each of them.'

The Babu smiled in reply – it was a terrifying smile. He continued to stare at the Sardar's face for a long time.

9.4 GETTING EVEN

Ajneya [S.H. Vatsayan]

Source: Ajneya [S.H. Vatsayan], 'Getting Even', translated from the Hindi by Alok Rai, in *Stories about the Partition of India*, ed. by Alok Bhalla, Delhi: HarperCollins, 1994, pp.119–25.

Hurriedly shoving her things into the unlit compartment, depositing little Abid on a seat through one of the windows and helping her elder daughter, Zubeida, into the carriage, Suraiya herself barely managed to clamber aboard the train as it was starting to pull out. She heaved a sigh of relief, and had only just bethought herself of the Pure and Merciful One, when she noticed the two forms, all wrapped up in blankets, in the far corner of the compartment. And they weren't her Muslim brethren – they were Sikhs! In the intermittent light that shone in the dark of the compartment as the train moved past successive lights on the station platform, she noticed something inhuman in their pitiless, unblinking eyes. As if their sight were not a whit impeded by the fact of her body, but went clear through it; and in them she noticed a cold hostility, as if beyond all human appeal, so sharp it seemed that it would draw blood from anyone who sought to touch it in any way. Although the light was hardly sufficient to actually see all this, Suraiya imagined she saw clearly that their eyes were bloodshot and ... and ... a fearful tremor passed through her. But the train had picked up speed by then, it was no longer possible to move to another compartment. She would have considered jumping out of the running train, children and all, but then, she thought, being thrown out by one's fellow-passengers couldn't be that much worse, could it? Immersed in these thoughts, and keeping a sharp eye on the handle of the alarm chain dangling above, she sat, uncertain ... but she'd do something about it at the next station ... there shouldn't be anything to fear in just one stop ... at least there had been no incidents on this stretch so far ...

'How far will you be going?'

Suraiya was startled. The older Sikh was asking her something. And what a deep voice he had! Though he might very well kill her and throw her out of the train after a couple of stops, yet he was speaking to her with such elaborate courtesy now – Suraiya reflected upon the irony of this, and so forgot to reply to his question.

The Sikh asked again, 'How far will you be going?'

Suraiya had unveiled her face, but she drew her veil back on, and replied, 'I am going to Etawah.'

The Sikh thought for a moment, 'Is there no one else with you?'

Suraiya speculated about the moment's hesitation that had preceded that last question, 'He is calculating how much time he'll need for killing me ... O Lord, please send some more passengers at the next stop ... and I must surely tell him I have someone with me – that might frighten him a little! Though what good is a travelling companion these days if he isn't in the same compartment ... if you should happen to get stabbed. Just hang on till the next stop – someone will come to the window and ask if there is anything you need ...'

She said, 'There's my brother ... in the next compartment.'

Little Abid piped up smartly, 'What are you saying, Ma! Mamu has gone to Lahore ...'

Suraiya rebuked him sharply, 'Keep quiet!'

After a little while, the Sikh asked again, 'Do you have a family in Etawah?'

'Yes.'

The Sikh remained silent for a while. Then he said, 'Your brother should have been in the same compartment with you. Nobody sits apart from one's near and dear ones these days.'

Suraiya wondered if the old rascal had guessed that there was really no one with her!

The Sikh said, almost as if to himself, 'But no one can be depended upon when things begin to fall apart ... it's everyone for himself ...'

The train had slowed down. It was a small station. Suraiya was unable to decide whether she should move to another compartment, or stay where she was? Two more passengers entered the compartment. Suraiya quickly sized them up – 'Hindus' – and then she really got afraid, and started to gather her things.

The Sikh asked her, 'Are you planning to get down here?'

'I thought, I might go and sit with my brother ...' What strange creatures we are that we try and shelter behind lies even in such situations ... and then, such flimsy lies ... for wouldn't her brother have come himself to help her move? But how could he come, since he wasn't there at all?

The Sikh then said to her, 'Stay where you are. You have nothing to fear here. You are like a sister to me, and these children are as my own. I will see you safely up to Aligarh. There is little danger beyond that point, and anyway some of your own people will also be entraining there.'

One of the Hindus spoke up, 'Sardarji, let her go if that's what she wants. What is it to you?'

Suraiya was unable to decide what to make of this exchange between the Sikh and the Hindu, but the train decided the issue by moving off again. She sat down.

The Hindu asked 'Sardarji, do you come from Punjab?'

'Yes.'

'Where is your home?'

'Used to be in Shekhupura. Now it might as well be here.'

'Here? What do you mean?'

'Wherever I happen to be, there's my home! One corner of a railway compartment.'

The Hindu checked his tone somewhat, and then, as if his voice were a glass and he were stirring a generous dose of sympathy in it before offering it to the Sikh, he said unctuously, 'Then you are a refugee ...'

The Sikh replied dryly, as if declining the proffered glass, though the Hindu gentleman quite missed the subtle resonance of his tone, 'Yes.'

The Hindu gentleman turned to him with somewhat greater interest, 'Terrible things must have happened to your family members –'

There was a flash of anger in the Sikh's eyes, but he did not fall for the bait. He kept quiet.

The Hindu looked in Suraiya's direction and went on, 'They say that in Delhi terrible things have been done to Hindus and Sikhs. Such things people recount, I tell you, one is ashamed even to talk about such things. They stripped the women naked and ...'

The Sikh turned to the wrapped up figure sitting beside him, and said, 'Kaka, go and sleep on the upper berth.' He was obviously the older Sikh's son and, when he got up and stretched his slim young body, the light in the old man's eyes, as he looked up towards the upper berth was unmistakably paternal. The young boy climbed onto the upper berth and lay down, and the old Sikh stretched his legs on the lower one and began staring out of the window.

The Hindu gentleman's recital had been interrupted, and he started again, 'Right in front of their fathers and their brothers, young girls were stripped naked and ...'

The Sikh said, 'Babu Sahib, why tell me things that I have seen myself anyway ...'

This time the sharp dryness in the tone was even clearer, but the Hindu gentleman missed it again. As if encouraged, he started again, 'You are quite right ... How can we ever begin to understand your sorrow. We can but sympathize, and yet what is that sympathy worth which cannot even gauge the depth of another's pain! Just think, how can I even comprehend what those Sikhs went through, before whose very eyes their wives and daughters were ...'

The Sikh could barely control his voice, 'All people have wives and daughters, Babu Sahib.'

The Hindu gentlemen was arrested briefly by something incomprehensible in the Sikh's tone, but not for long. 'Well, now Hindus and Sikhs have also woken up. Of course it's wrong to take revenge, but how long can one be tolerant? In Delhi they have rallied strongly, and in places they have even retaliated in kind, an eye for an eye ... Really speaking, there is no other option. I heard that in Karol Bagh, a Muslim doctor's daughter was ...'

This time it wasn't any longer a dry and subtle resonance in the Sikh's voice, it was a manifest and grating harshness, 'Babu Sahib, a woman's dishonour is a matter of shame for all men. And sister –' he said, turning towards Suraiya, 'I apologize to you for your having to hear all this.'

The Hindu gentlemen was taken aback, 'What, what, what was that about? I haven't said anything to this lady.' And then, getting a grip on himself, he said with a hint of deliberate rudeness, 'Is she – she with you, then?'

The Sikh replied even more harshly, 'Yes! I am escorting her till Aligarh.'

'This poor man,' a voice spoke up inside Suraiya's head 'this poor, good man is going to Aligarh, Aligarh ...' She made so bold as to ask him, 'You will get down at Aligarh?'

'Yes.'

'Do you have anyone in Aligarh?'

'I have no one anywhere. My son's with me.'

'What is taking you there? Will you be staying for some days?'

'No, I return tomorrow.'

'So ... you are going for the fun of it.'

'Fun!' The Sikh repeated in a lost sort of voice, 'Fun!' Then he controlled himself and said, 'No, we're not going anywhere really – we're still thinking about where we might go. And when nothing is stable any longer, the only place one can think at all is in a moving train ...'

Again a voice prompted inside Suraiya's head, 'Aligarh ... Aligarh ... He is a decent sort ...'

She spoke out, 'Aligarh ... it is not such a good place. Why are you going there?'

The Hindu gentleman also spoke up, as if taking pity on someone obviously deranged, 'Just imagine!'

'Good place or bad, what difference can it make to me?'

'Even so – don't you feel afraid? Suppose you get stabbed at night ...'

The Sikh smiled and said, 'Have you ever considered that someone might even welcome that as a deliverance?'

'But that's absurd!'

'And why not? So, who will kill me? It could be a Muslim or a Hindu: If a Muslim kills me, I will only go and join up with the other members of my family, wherever it is that they have gone before me. And if a Hindu should get me, I will console myself with the thought that even this last has been accomplished. The disease which has gripped the whole country has reached its climax – and we can at last start on the road back to health and sanity.'

'But why will a Hindu kill you? A Hindu may well have a million defects, but he will never do such a thing ...'

Suddenly, the Sikh lost his temper. He said contemptuously, 'Go on, Babu Sahib! Only just now you were relating the Delhi incidents with such obvious relish. Now, if you had a knife, and there was no danger to yourself

– would you have spared your fellow-passengers ... these people ... and if I should have dared to intervene, me as well?'

The Hindu gentleman made as if to say something, but the Sikh restrained him with a commanding gesture, 'Since you apparently wish to know about it, prepare to listen well. You presume to give me sympathy because I am a refugee. Sympathy is a big thing, and I would have considered myself fortunate indeed if you had been capable of true sympathy. But how can you even begin to understand my anguish, when in the very same breath you speak of the Delhi happenings with such heartlessness. If you had been capable of giving me sympathy – if you had so much heart, your tongue would have stuck to the roof of your mouth, it would have frozen with shame before you could begin to utter one syllable regarding the things that you were so keen to gossip about – your head would have bowed with shame. A woman's dishonour is a woman's dishonour – it is not a Hindu's shame or a Muslim's shame, in her the mother of all mankind has been dishonoured. Whatever happened to me in Shekhupura ... happened. But I know that I can never take revenge for that, because there can be no adequate vengeance for all that took place there! I can only get even after a fashion – so that whatever happened to me should never happen to another. And that is why I escort people back and forth between Delhi and Aligarh. It helps to pass the days, and I am able to get even just a little. And in this way if someone should happen to kill me some day, the account will at last be closed – it matters little whether the killer is a Muslim, or a Hindu! My only aim is that no one – Hindu, Sikh or Muslim – no one should ever have to see what I have seen. And whatever befell my family members before they died, may it not be the fate of anyone's wives and daughters ever to have to behold!'

For sometime after this, there was complete silence in the compartment. When the train slowed down as it approached Aligarh, Suraiya desperately wanted to say some words of gratitude to the Sikh, but she was unable to make a sound.

The Sardar roused himself and turning towards the upper berth, said, 'Up, Kaka, we're at Aligarh.' Then he turned to the Hindu gentleman and said, 'You must forgive me, Babu Sahib, if I have inadvertently said some harsh things to you. After all we're your refugees now!'

It was clear from the Hindu gentleman's expression that if the Sikh had not been disembarking there, he himself would have moved to another compartment.

9.5   TOBA TEK SINGH

Saadat Hasan Manto

Source: Saadat Hasan Manto, 'Toba Tek Singh', in *Kingdom's End and Other Stories*, translated from the Urdu by Khalid Hasan, London: Verso, 1987, pp.11–18.

A couple of years after the Partition of the country, it occurred to the respective governments of India and Pakistan that inmates of lunatic asylums, like prisoners, should also be exchanged. Muslim lunatics in India should be transferred to Pakistan and Hindu and Sikh lunatics in Pakistani asylums should be sent to India.

Whether this was a reasonable or an unreasonable idea is difficult to say. One thing, however, is clear. It took many conferences of important officials from the two sides to come to this decision. Final details, like the date of actual exchange, were carefully worked out. Muslim lunatics whose families were still residing in India were to be left undisturbed, the rest moved to the border for the exchange. The situation in Pakistan was slightly different, since almost the entire population of Hindus and Sikhs had already migrated to India. The question of keeping non-Muslim lunatics in Pakistan did not, therefore, arise.

While it is not known what the reaction in India was, when the news reached the Lahore lunatic asylum, it immediately became the subject of heated discussion. One Muslim lunatic, a regular reader of the fire-eating daily newspaper *Zamindar*, when asked what Pakistan was, replied after deep reflection: 'The name of a place in India where cut-throat razors are manufactured.'

This profound observation was received with visible satisfaction.

A Sikh lunatic asked another Sikh: 'Sardarji, why are we being sent to India? We don't even know the language they speak in that country.'

The man smiled: 'I know the language of the *Hindostoras*. These devils always strut about as if they were the lords of the earth.'

One day a Muslim lunatic, while taking his bath, raised the slogan '*Pakistan Zindabad*' with such enthusiasm that he lost his footing and was later found lying on the floor unconscious.

Not all inmates were mad. Some were perfectly normal, except that they were murderers. To spare them the hangman's noose, their families had managed to get them committed after bribing officials down the line. They probably had a vague idea why India was being divided and what Pakistan was, but, as for the present situation, they were equally clueless.

Newspapers were no help either, and the asylum guards were ignorant, if not illiterate. Nor was there anything to be learnt by eavesdropping on their conversations. Some said there was this man by the name Mohamed Ali

Jinnah, or the Quaid-e-Azam, who had set up a separate country for Muslims, called Pakistan.

As to where Pakistan was located, the inmates knew nothing. That was why both the mad and the partially mad were unable to decide whether they were now in India or in Pakistan. If they were in India, where on earth was Pakistan? And if they were in Pakistan, then how come that until only the other day it was India?

One inmate had got so badly caught up in this India–Pakistan–Pakistan– India rigmarole that one day, while sweeping the floor, he dropped every- thing, climbed the nearest tree and installed himself on a branch, from which vantage point he spoke for two hours on the delicate problem of India and Pakistan. The guards asked him to get down; instead he went a branch higher, and when threatened with punishment, declared: 'I wish to live neither in India nor in Pakistan. I wish to live in this tree.'

When he was finally persuaded to come down, he began embracing his Sikh and Hindu friends, tears running down his cheeks, fully convinced that they were about to leave him and go to India.

A Muslim radio engineer, who had an M.Sc. degree, and never mixed with anyone, given as he was to taking long walks by himself all day, was so affected by the current debate that one day he took all his clothes off, gave the bundle to one of the attendants and ran into the garden stark naked.

A Muslim lunatic from Chaniot, who used to be one of the most devoted workers of the All India Muslim League, and obsessed with bathing himself fifteen or sixteen times a day, had suddenly stopped doing that and announced – his name was Mohamed Ali – that he was Quaid-e-Azam Mohamed Ali Jinnah. This had led a Sikh inmate to declare himself Master Tara Singh, the leader of the Sikhs. Apprehending serious communal trouble, the authorities declared them dangerous, and shut them up in separate cells.

There was a young Hindu lawyer from Lahore who had gone off his head after an unhappy love affair. When told that Amritsar was to become a part of India, he went into a depression because his beloved lived in Amritsar, something he had not forgotten even in his madness. That day he abused every major and minor Hindu and Muslim leader who had cut India into two, turning his beloved into an Indian and him into a Pakistani.

When news of the exchange reached the asylum, his friends offered him congratulations, because he was now to be sent to India, the country of his beloved. However, he declared that he had no intention of leaving Lahore, because his practice would not flourish in Amritsar.

There were two Anglo-Indian lunatics in the European ward. When told that the British had decided to go home after granting independence to India, they went into a state of deep shock and were seen conferring with each other in whispers the entire afternoon. They were worried about their changed status after independence. Would there be a European ward or would it be abolished? Would breakfast continue to be served or would they have to subsist on bloody Indian chapati?

There was another inmate, a Sikh, who had been confined for the last fifteen years. Whenever he spoke, it was the same mysterious gibberish: 'Uper the gur gur the annexe the bay dhayana the mung the dal of the laltain.' Guards said he had not slept a wink in fifteen years. Occasionally, he could be observed leaning against a wall, but the rest of the time, he was always to be found standing. Because of this, his legs were permanently swollen, something that did not appear to bother him. Recently, he had started to listen carefully to discussions about the forthcoming exchange of Indian and Pakistani lunatics. When asked his opinion, he observed solemnly: 'Uper the gur gur the annexe the bay dhayana the mung the dal of the Government of Pakistan.'

Of late, however, the Government of Pakistan had been replaced by the Government of Toba Tek Singh, a small town in the Punjab which was his home. He had also begun enquiring where Toba Tek Singh was to go. However, nobody was quite sure whether it was in India or Pakistan.

Those who had tried to solve this mystery had become utterly confused when told that Sialkot, which used to be in India, was now in Pakistan. It was anybody's guess what was going to happen to Lahore, which was currently in Pakistan, but could slide into India any moment. It was also possible that the entire subcontinent of India might become Pakistan. And who could say if both India and Pakistan might not entirely vanish from the map of the world one day?

The old man's hair was almost gone and what little was left had become a part of the beard, giving him a strange, even frightening, appearance. However, he was a harmless fellow and had never been known to get into fights. Older attendants at the asylum said that he was a fairly prosperous landlord from Toba Tek Singh, who had quite suddenly gone mad. His family had brought him in, bound and fettered. That was fifteen years ago.

Once a month, he used to have visitors, but since the start of communal troubles in the Punjab, they had stopped coming. His real name was Bishan Singh, but everybody called him Toba Tek Singh. He lived in a kind of limbo, having no idea what day of the week it was, or month, or how many years had passed since his confinement. However, he had developed a sixth sense about the day of the visit, when he used to bathe himself, soap his body, oil and comb his hair and put on clean clothes. He never said a word during these meetings, except occasional outbursts of 'Uper the gur gur the annexe the bay dhayana the mung the dal of the laltain.'

When he was first confined, he had left an infant daughter behind, now a pretty young girl of fifteen. She would come occasionally, and sit in front of him with tears rolling down her cheeks. In the strange world that he inhabited, hers was just another face.

Since the start of this India–Pakistan caboodle, he had got into the habit of asking fellow inmates where exactly Toba Tek Singh was, without receiving a satisfactory answer, because nobody knew. The visits had also suddenly stopped. He was increasingly restless, but, more than that, curious. The sixth sense, which used to alert him to the day of the visit, had also atrophied.

He missed his family, the gifts they used to bring and the concern with which they used to speak to him. He was sure they would have told him whether Toba Tek Singh was in India or Pakistan. He also had a feeling that they came from Toba Tek Singh, where he used to have his home.

One of the inmates had declared himself God. Bishan Singh asked him one day if Toba Tek Singh was in India or Pakistan. The man chuckled: 'Neither in India nor in Pakistan, because, so far, we have issued no orders in this respect.'

Bishan Singh begged 'God' to issue the necessary orders, so that his problem could be solved, but he was disappointed, as 'God' appeared to be preoccupied with more pressing matters. Finally, he told him angrily: '*Uper the gur gur the annexe the mung the dal of Guruji da Khalsa and Guruji ki fateh ... jo boley so nihal sat sri akal.*'

What he wanted to say was: 'You don't answer my prayers because you are a Muslim God. Had you been a Sikh God, you would have been more of a sport.'

A few days before the exchange was to take place, one of Bishan Singh's Muslim friends from Toba Tek Singh came to see him – the first time in fifteen years. Bishan Singh looked at him once and turned away, until a guard said to him: 'This is your old friend Fazal Din. He has come all the way to meet you.'

Bishan Singh looked at Fazal Din and began to mumble something. Fazal Din placed his hand on his friend's shoulder and said: 'I have been meaning to come for some time to bring you news. All your family is well and has gone to India safely. I did what I could to help. Your daughter Roop Kaur...' – he hesitated – 'She is safe too ... in India.'

Bishan Singh kept quiet. Fazal Din continued: 'Your family wanted me to make sure you were well. Soon you will be moving to India. What can I say, except that you should remember me to bhai Balbir Singh, bhai Vadhawa Singh and bahain Amrit Kaur. Tell bhai Bibir Singh that Fazal Din is well by the grace of God. The two brown buffaloes he left behind are well too. Both of them gave birth to calves, but, unfortunately, one of them died after six days. Say I think of them often and to write to me if there is anything I can do.'

Then he added: 'Here, I brought you some rice crispies from home.'

Bishan Singh took the gift and handed it to one of the guards. 'Where is Toba Tek Singh?' he asked.

'Where? Why, it is where it has always been.'

'In India or in Pakistan?'

'In India ... no, in Pakistan.'

Without saying another word, Bishan Singh walked away, murmuring: *'Uper the gur gur the annexe the be dhyana the mung the dal of the Pakistan and Hindustan dur fittey moun.'*

Meanwhile, exchange arrangements were rapidly getting finalized. Lists of lunatics from the two sides had been exchanged between the governments, and the date of transfer fixed.

On a cold winter evening, buses full of Hindu and Sikh lunatics, accompanied by armed police and officials, began moving out of the Lahore asylum towards Wagha, the dividing line between India and Pakistan. Senior officials from the two sides in charge of exchange arrangements met, signed documents and the transfer got under way.

It was quite a job getting the men out of the buses and handing them over to officials. Some just refused to leave. Those who were persuaded to do so began to run pell-mell in every direction. Some were stark naked. All efforts to get them to cover themselves had failed because they couldn't be kept from tearing off their garments. Some were shouting abuse or singing. Others were weeping bitterly. Many fights broke out.

In short, complete confusion prevailed. Female lunatics were also being exchanged and they were even noisier. It was bitterly cold.

Most of the inmates appeared to be dead set against the entire operation. They simply could not understand why they were being forcibly removed, thrown into buses and driven to this strange place. There were slogans of *'Pakistan Zindabad'* and *'Pakistan Murdabad'*, followed by fights.

When Bishan Singh was brought out and asked to give his name so that it could be recorded in a register, he asked the official behind the desk: 'Where is Toba Tek Singh? In India or Pakistan?'

'Pakistan,' he answered with a vulgar laugh.

Bishan Singh tried to run, but was overpowered by the Pakistani guards who tried to push him across the dividing line towards India. However, he wouldn't move. 'This is Toba Tek Singh,' he announced. *'Uper the gur gur the annexe the be dhyana mung the dal of Toba Tek Singh and Pakistan.'*

Many efforts were made to explain to him that Toba Tek Singh had already been moved to India, or would be moved immediately, but it had no effect on Bishan Singh. The guards even tried force, but soon gave up.

There he stood in no man's land on his swollen legs like a colossus.

Since he was a harmless old man, no further attempt was made to push him into India. He was allowed to stand where he wanted, while the exchange continued. The night wore on.

Just before sunrise, Bishan Singh, the man who had stood on his legs for fifteen years, screamed and as officials from the two sides rushed towards him, he collapsed to the ground.

There, behind barbed wire, on one side, lay India and behind more barbed wire, on the other side, lay Pakistan. In between, on a bit of earth which had no name, lay Toba Tek Singh.

10.1 BE STILL, SHE SLEEPS

Christine Weston

Source: Christine Weston, 'Be Still, She Sleeps', in *There and Then*, London: Collins, 1948, pp.124–30.

Monghyr used to be a garrison town on the Ganges, in the Province of Bihar, in India. On the outskirts of the town, there still stand the great houses of Englishmen who have long since gone away; a few preferred to live out their lives and die in these big mansions, which, even two generations ago, were no more than ancestral shells, and their grandchildren and great-grandchildren survive in the region as planters or *rentiers*, living in less pretentious houses on a dwindling scale of wealth and vitality. When I was about fifteen, a friend of my parents offered us her house in Monghyr for the winter, and we children saw the place for the first time. We had often heard about it because my grandfather had been stationed in Monghyr as a subaltern in the Indian Army, in 1860.

My brother and I came to Monghyr filled with anticipation, for, young as we were, antiquity held for us an especial attraction; we moved on tiptoe, with what Flaubert has called 'the historic shudder'. Although no more than three or four hundred miles from our own home in the north, this was like a new country. The vegetation was more tropical and the natives talked an unfamiliar tongue. Our friend's house was made of brick, with deep, cool verandas, and although of fairly recent origin, it seemed already part of the pervading atmosphere of decay. It was surrounded by a magnificent garden, and from the front veranda we could see the river and the opposite shore, greenish yellow, topped by dark toddy palms. Looking eastward from the garden, we saw palm trees, until their outlines were lost in a line of little plum-coloured hills.

At night we listened to the jackals as they shrieked and fought among the cold funeral pyres down on the shore, and one morning we discovered a human skull which the creatures had carried into our shrubbery. With the exception of a few incongruous Americans employed by the local tobacco factory, the white population of Monghyr was composed almost entirely of descendants of that original ancient garrison. They moved in an element peculiar to people who are consciously *descendant*, with a pathos, a dignity, a quietness that made us think of ghosts.

My brother and I shared a passion for exploration, and a few weeks after our arrival we got on our bicycles and started off. I remember that it was an afternoon late in February and that the heat of midday still clung to every-thing. Already the air smelled of summer and we heard the green barbet crying, 'Kutur, kutur, kutur!' followed by the loud 'Tonk!' of its cousin, the coppersmith. We pedalled along a dusty road, past the old cantonments, past the bazaar and the railway station, then turned to follow the river southward. As we rode, we talked about our grandfather's stories of the old days in Monghyr, of the indigo plants and the Mutiny of 1857, of our grandparents and their friends. We joked rather heartlessly about the ante-diluvian cousins whom we'd met – tall, pale old men, with faded eyes and long, white moustaches, who spoke a strange, courtly English, and who smelled, said my brother, like the insides of old books. 'We'll be like that some day,' I murmured, feeling a bit guilty. 'Oh no, we won't,' replied my brother. 'I don't intend to let white ants nest in *my* insides!' His face was freckled and his eyes a vivid blue under the brim of his khaki helmet, which was decorated with the wings of bright-coloured birds and looked like the war bonnet of a Red Indian.

Presently we came on a little side road, which branched off at right angles under a tunnel of trees, and, obeying an infallible instinct, we wheeled into it and pedalled along in a pleasant shade. Wheat was ripening in the fields on either side, but we saw no one and heard nothing except the chirrup of birds and squirrels. Our road began to climb suddenly and we were obliged to dismount and push our bicycles. Now a sort of plan became visible in the lay of the land: rough terraces, worn by neglect and weather, trees which once wore formal shapes. At last we saw a house rise up before us – a great, red brick castle, or so it seemed in our eyes, with a central dome flanked by two smaller ones, a circular veranda supported on sandstone pillars, and tall, pointed windows, from which shutters hung askew. We climbed to the top terrace and found ourselves amongst a confusion of trees and vines, broken-down pomegranate and custard-apple trees, expiring in the shade of the sturdier banyans and palms. In the strong afternoon light the house stood impressive, silent, deserted, and for several moments we did not move, staring around us in wonder. To our right, the tangle of trees opened a little and we could see the river; to our left, trees and plain stretched for miles and we could see nothing else, not even a rooftop.

We left our bicycles propped against the veranda steps, and found our-selves facing an enormous door, fastened with bits of rotting string. For a moment we hesitated, listening, then cried together, '*Quai hai?*' which means 'Anyone home?' An echo answered us and we heard a bat flying about behind the great door.

'There's no one here. Let's go in,' said my brother. The string powdered away under our hands and the door opened ponderously. We stepped into a huge, bare room whose ceiling soared upward like the arch of a cathedral. Light from the tall windows fell across the floor, which was littered with dead bats, dead insects, leaves, and heaven knows what – all the weird accumulation which sifts through the crevices of an empty house. The walls were strained and peeling, except for one corner, where, for some reason, the vegetable paint survived in an oblong of startling, ardent blue. We walked about cautiously, examining a variety of objects stacked against the walls; massive pieces of furniture, crumbling with age and mildew and the forays of white ants. There were trunks, boxes, bundles which, when we touched them, parted softly at their seams and exuded a sort of liquid dust. We found two huge saddles, from which the leather had peeled like wet paper, a bundle of hog spears, and a set of pistols in embossed holsters. Excited and frightened, we ventured into another room, then another, discovering pictures from which the paint had mouldered away, more trunks, more books, strange, personal, forgotten accoutrements.

No one had told us about this house and, as children will, we wondered whether we had made a unique discovery. Might we perhaps stumble on a skeleton or unearth a treasure? Dared we explore further? Dared we make off with any of these fascinating, unguarded, and apparently unwanted objects? My brother eyed the ancient pistols. For my part, I'd noticed an Indian violin, made of polished wood inlaid with mother-of-pearl and enamel. It was stringless, the seams had burst, and as an instrument for making music it was clearly worthless. But I wanted it.

'Let's make sure there isn't a watchman or someone about,' whispered my brother, and his whisper ran round the room like a flutter of dead leaves. 'Yes,' I whispered back, and 'Yes!' whispered the silence round us. We walked from room to room in the shadowy light from the tall windows. We poked into cupboards which gave forth pathetic odours; we peered round corners and down passages and into black, airless godowns. Everything seemed in the act of dying – visibly, inexorably dying. Suddenly glancing at my brother, I saw that his face had a rigid expression; his eyes were staring and colourless. As a very small boy he'd had a terror of darkness and of closed places, and now I saw that terror in his face and saw it grip his body so that he stood transfixed, hardly able to breathe. I was afraid then – not of this great, empty, sad house, but of him and for him, and I knew that we must go at once, away from there, into the sunlight. I took hold of his sleeve and dragged him to the door and down the veranda steps on to the terrace. Outside, the natural world rose bright and reassuring, the sun felt warm on our faces, and we heard the barbet crying, 'Kutur, kutur, kutur!'

The colour came back into my brother's face and he said, rather defiantly, 'Pretty smelly in there, wasn't it? But we might as well see what's on the other side.'

We wheeled our bicycles round to the rear of the house, and from there the ground fell away in a long slope, at the foot of which we saw a small white building, like a well-house or a summer-house, with a door set in one wall. The slope was smooth and inviting, and my brother, swinging on to his bicycle, cried, 'Race you!'

We sped down the hill and dismounted beside the building. Set into the door was a plaster plaque, protected by a piece of glass now stained and broken. On the plaque was a single sentence which admonished us simply, 'Be still, she sleeps.' Inside the door, we found a grave made of white-washed masonry, no longer white, crumbling a little at the edges, and with no headstone, no inscription, no clue to the sleeper buried there.

Later we heard the story. About the middle of the last century, the house had belonged to an English officer who had married the daughter of an Indian noble. She was sixteen, high-spirited, and a fine horsewoman. They had not been married long when one day her husband laughingly challenged her to race with him, as a test of her horsemanship, down the slope and to jump a gate at the bottom. She accepted the challenge and they raced together down the hill. At the gate her horse fell and she was thrown and killed. He husband buried her where she had fallen. He had loved her very much and could not forget her, so he resigned from the Army, left his house exactly as it was, and disappeared. No one ever heard what became of him. No one came to claim the house or its contents. One by one, old friends and servants died or went away, and people said that no thief ever touched stick or stone. The place just stood there as we had found it, empty, silent, waiting for him to come back and for her to awaken.

10.2 THE MAN WHO WAS KIPLING

Ruskin Bond

Source: Ruskin Bond, 'The Man Who Was Kipling', in *The Best of Ruskin Bond*, Delhi: Penguin, 1994, pp.53–6.

I was sitting on a bench in the Indian Section of the Victoria and Albert Museum in London, when a tall, stooping, elderly gentleman sat down beside me. I gave him a quick glance, noting his swarthy features, heavy moustache, and horn-rimmed spectacles. There was something familiar and disturbing about his face, and I couldn't resist looking at him again.

I noticed that he was smiling at me.

'Do you recognize me?' he asked, in a soft pleasant voice.

'Well, you do seem familiar,' I said. 'Haven't we met somewhere?'

'Perhaps. But if I seem familiar to you, that is at least something. The trouble these days is that people don't *know* me anymore – I'm a familiar, that's all. Just a name standing for a lot of outmoded ideas.'

A little perplexed, I asked 'What is it you do?'

'I wrote books once. Poems and tales ... Tell me, whose books do you read?'

'Oh, Maugham, Priestley, Thurber. And among the older lot, Bennett and Wells ...' I hesitated, groping for an important name, and I noticed a shadow, a sad shadow, pass across my companion's face.

'Oh yes, and Kipling,' I said, 'I read a lot of Kipling.'

His face brightened up at once, and the eyes behind the thick-lensed spectacles suddenly came to life.

'I'm Kipling,' he said.

I stared at him in astonishment, and then, realizing that he might perhaps be dangerous, I smiled feebly and said, 'Oh, yes?'

'You probably don't believe me. I'm dead, of course.'

'So I thought.'

'And you don't believe in ghosts?'

'Not as a rule.'

'But you'd have no objection to talking to one, if he came along?'

'I'd have no objection. But how do I know you're Kipling? How do I know you're not an imposter?'

'Listen, then:

> When my heavens were turned to blood,
> When the dark had filled my day,
> Furthest, but most faithful, stood
> That lone star I cast away.
> I had loved myself, and I
> Have not lived and dare not die.

'Once,' he said, gripping me by the arm and looking me straight in the eye. 'Once in life I watched a star; but I whistled her to go.'

'Your star hasn't fallen yet,' I said, suddenly moved, suddenly quite certain that I sat beside Kipling. 'One day, when there is a new spirit of adventure abroad, we will discover you again.'

'Why have they heaped scorn on me for so long?'

'You were too militant, I suppose – too much of an Empire man. You were too patriotic for your own good.'

He looked a little hurt. 'I was never very political,' he said. 'I wrote over six hundred poems, and you could only call a dozen of them political. I have been abused for harping on the theme of the White Man's burden but my only aim was to show off the Empire to my audience – and I believed the Empire was a fine and noble thing. Is it wrong to believe in something? I never went deeply into political issues, that's true. You must remember, my seven years in India were very youthful years. I was in my twenties, a little immature if you like, and my interest in India was a boy's interest. Action appealed to me more than anything else. You must understand that.'

'No one has described action more vividly, or India so well. I feel at one with Kim wherever he goes along the Grand Trunk Road, in the temples at

Banaras, amongst the Saharanpur fruit gardens, on the snow-covered Himalayas. *Kim* has colour and movement and poetry.'

He sighed, and a wistful look came into his eyes.

'I'm prejudiced, of course,' I continued. 'I've spent most of my life in India – not *your* India, but an India that does still have much of the colour and atmosphere that you captured. You know, Mr Kipling, you can still sit in a third-class railway carriage and meet the most wonderful assortment of people. In any village you will still find the same courtesy, dignity and courage that the Lama and Kim found on their travels.'

'And the Grand Trunk Road? Is it still a long winding procession of humanity?'

'Well, not exactly,' I said, a little ruefully. 'It's just a procession of motor vehicles now. The poor Lama would be run down by a truck if he became too dreamy on the Grand Trunk Road. Times *have* changed. There are no more Mrs Hawksbees in Simla, for instance.'

There was a far-away look in Kipling's eyes. Perhaps he was imagining himself a boy again; perhaps he could see the hills or the red dust of Rajputana; perhaps he was having a private conversation with Privates Mulvaney and Ortheris, or perhaps he was out hunting with the Seonce wolfpack. The sound of London's traffic came to us through the glass doors, but we heard only the creaking of bullock-cart wheels and the distant music of a flute.

He was talking to himself, repeating a passage from one of his stories. 'And the last puff of the daywind brought from the unseen villages the scent of damp wood-smoke, hot cakes, dripping undergrowth, and rotting pine-cones. That is the true smell of the Himalayas, and if once it creeps into the blood of a man, that man will at the last, forgetting all else, return to the hills to die.'

A mist seemed to have risen between us – or had it come in from the streets? – and when it cleared, Kipling had gone away.

I asked the gatekeeper if he had seen a tall man with a slight stoop, wearing spectacles.

'Nope,' said the gatekeeper. 'Nobody been by for the last ten minutes.'

'Did someone like that come into the gallery a little while ago?'

'No one that I recall. What did you say the bloke's name was?'

'Kipling,' I said.

'Don't know him.'

'Didn't you ever read *The Jungle Books*?'

'Sounds familiar. Tarzan stuff, wasn't it?'

I left the museum, and wandered about the streets for a long time, but I couldn't find Kipling anywhere. Was it the boom of London's traffic that I heard, or the boom of the Sutlej river racing through the valleys?

10.3 THE LAST TIME I SAW DELHI

Ruskin Bond

Source: Ruskin Bond, 'The Last Time I Saw Delhi', in *The Best of Ruskin Bond*, **Delhi: Penguin, 1994, pp.57–61.**

I'd had this old and faded negative with me for a number of years and had never bothered to make a print from it. It was a picture of my maternal grandparents. I remembered my grandmother quite well, because a large part of my childhood had been spent in her house in Dehra after she had been widowed; but although everyone said she was fond of me, I remembered her as a stern, somewhat aloof person, of whom I was a little afraid.

I hadn't kept many family pictures and this negative was yellow and spotted with damp.

Then last week, when I was visiting my mother in hospital in Delhi, while she awaited her operation, we got talking about my grandparents, and I remembered the negative and decided I'd make a print for my mother.

When I got the photograph and saw my grandmother's face for the first time in twenty-five years, I was immediately struck by my resemblance to her. I have, like her, lived a rather spartan life, happy with my one room, just as she was content to live in a room of her own while the rest of the family took over the house! And like her, I have lived tidily. But I did not know the physical resemblance was so close – the fair hair, the heavy build, the wide forehead. She looks more like me than my mother!

In the photograph she is seated on her favourite chair, at the top of the veranda steps, and Grandfather stands behind her in the shadows thrown by a large mango tree which is not in the picture. I can tell it was a mango tree because of the pattern the leaves make on the wall. Grandfather was a slim, trim man, with a drooping moustache that was fashionable in the twenties. By all accounts he had a mischievous sense of humour, although he looks unwell in the picture. He appears to have been quite swarthy. No wonder he was so successful in dressing up 'native style' and passing himself off as a street-vendor. My mother tells me he even took my grandmother in on one occasion, and sold her a basketful of bad oranges. His character was in strong contrast to my grandmother's rather forbidding personality and Victorian sense of propriety; but they made a good match.

But here's the picture, and I am taking it to show my mother who lies in the Lady Hardinge Hospital, awaiting the removal of her left breast.

It is early August and the day is hot and sultry. It rained during the night, but now the sun is out and the sweat oozes through my shirt as I sit in the back of a stuffy little taxi taking me through the suburbs of Greater New Delhi.

On either side of the road are the houses of well-to-do Punjabis, who came to Delhi as refugees in 1947 and now make up more than half the capital's population. Industrious, flashy, go-ahead people. Thirty years ago, fields extended on either side of this road, as far as the eye could see. The Ridge, an outcrop of the Aravallis, was scrub jungle, in which the black buck roamed. Feroz Shah's fourteenth century hunting lodge stood here in splendid isolation. It is still here, hidden by petrol pumps and lost within the sounds of buses, cars, trucks and scooter-rickshaws. The peacock has fled the forest, the black buck is extinct. Only the jackal remains. When, a thousand years from now, the last human has left this contaminated planet for some other star, the jackal and the crow will remain, to survive for years on all the refuse we leave behind.

It is difficult to find the right entrance to the hospital, because for about a mile along the Panchkuin Road the pavement has been obliterated by tea-shops, furniture shops, and piles of accumulated junk. A public hydrant stands near the gate, and dirty water runs across the road.

I find my mother in a small ward. It is a cool, dark room, and a ceiling fan whirrs pleasantly overhead. A nurse, a dark pretty girl from the South, is attending to my mother. She says 'In a minute,' and proceeds to make an entry on a chart.

My mother gives me a wan smile and beckons me to come nearer. Her cheeks are slightly flushed, due possibly to fever; otherwise she looks her normal self. I find it hard to believe that the operation she will have tomorrow will only give her, at the most, another year's lease on life.

I sit at the foot of her bed. This is my third visit, since I flew back from Jersey, using up all my savings in the process; and I will leave after the operation, not to fly away again, but to return to the hills which have always called me back.

'How do you feel?' I ask.

'All right. They say they will operate in the morning. They've stopped my smoking.'

'Can you drink? Your rum, I mean.'

'No. Not until a few days after the operation.'

She has a fair amount of grey in her hair, natural enough at fifty-four. Otherwise she hasn't changed much; the same small chin and mouth, lively brown eyes. Her father's face, not her mother's.

The nurse has left us. I produce the photograph and hand it to my mother.

The negative was lying with me all these years. I had it printed yesterday.

'I can't see without my glasses.'

The glasses are lying on the locker near her bed. I hand them to her. She puts them on and studies the photograph.

'Your grandmother was always very fond of you.'

'It was hard to tell. She wasn't a soft woman.'

'It was her money that got you to Jersey, when you finished school. It wasn't much, just enough for a ticket'.

'I didn't know that.'

'The only person who ever left you anything. I'm afraid I've nothing to leave you, either.'

'You know very well that I've never cared a damn about money. My father taught me to write. That was inheritance enough.'

'And what did I teach you?'

'I'm not sure ... Perhaps you taught me how to enjoy myself now and then.'

She looked pleased at this. 'Yes, I've enjoyed myself between troubles. But your father didn't know how to enjoy himself. That's why we quarrelled so much. And finally separated.'

'He was much older than you.'

'You've always blamed me for leaving him, haven't you?'

'I was very small at the time. You left us suddenly. My father had to look after me, and it wasn't easy for him. He was very sick. Naturally I blamed you.'

'He wouldn't let me take you away.'

'Because you were going to marry someone else.'

I break off; we have been over this before. I am not there as my father's advocate, and the time for recrimination has passed.

And now it is raining outside, and the scent of wet earth comes through the open doors, overpowering the odour of medicines and disinfectants. The dark eyed nurse comes in again and informs me that the doctor will soon be on his round. I can come again in the evening, or early morning before the operation.

'Come in the evening,' says my mother. 'The others will be here then.'

'I haven't come to see the others.'

'They are looking forward to seeing you.' 'They' being my stepfather and half-brothers.

'I'll be seeing them in the morning.'

'As you like ...'

And then I am on the road again, standing on the pavement, on the fringe of a chaotic rush of traffic, in which it appears that every vehicle is doing its best to overtake its neighbour. The blare of horns can be heard in the corridors of the hospital, but everyone is conditioned to the noise and pays no attention to it. Rather, the sick and the dying are heartened by the thought that people are still well enough to feel reckless, indifferent to each other's safety! In Delhi there is a feverish desire to be first in line, the first to get anything ... This is probably because no one ever gets around to dealing with second-comers.

When I hail a scooter-ricksaw and it stops a short distance away, someone elbows his way past me and gets in first. This epitomizes the philosophy and outlook of the Delhi-wallah.

So I stand on the pavement waiting for another scooter, which doesn't come. In Delhi, to be second in the race is to be last.

I walk all the way back to my small hotel, with a foreboding of having seen my mother for the last time.

10.4 FROM INDIAN INK

Tom Stoppard

Source: Tom Stoppard, *Indian Ink*, London: Faber & Faber, 1995, pp.1–6.

Act one

Dusk. FLORA *sits alone on a moving train. Her suitcase is on the rack above her head. The train is approaching a station.* FLORA, *already speaking, stands to lift down her suitcase. By the end of her first speech, she is on the station platform at Jummapur.*

FLORA
'Jummapur, Wednesday, April the second. Darling Nell, I arrived here on Saturday from Bombay after a day and a night and a day in a Ladies Only, stopping now and again to be revictualled through the window with pots of tea and proper meals on matinee trays, which, remarkably, you hand back through the window at the next station down the line where they do the washing up; and from the last stop I had the compartment to myself, with the lights coming on for me to make my entrance on the platform at Jummapur. The President of the Theosophical Society was waiting with several members of the committee drawn up at a respectful distance, not quite a red carpet and brass band but garlands of marigolds at the ready, and I thought there must be somebody important on the train – '

COOMARASWAMI
(*Interrupting*) Miss Crewe!

FLORA
' – and it turned out to be me.'

COOMARASWAMI
Welcome to Jummapur!

FLORA
'which was very agreeable.' Thank you!
(*And as she is garlanded by* COOMARASWAMI)
How nice! Are you Mr Coomar ...

COOMARASWAMI
Coomaraswami! That is me! Is this your only luggage?!
Leave it there!
(*He claps his hands imperiously for assistance, and then shakes hands
enthusiastically with* FLORA.)
How do you *do*, Miss *Crewe*!
(*The handshake which begins on the station platform ends on the verandah
of the 'Dak Bungalow', or guesthouse. The guesthouse requires a verandah
and an interior which includes, or comprises, a bedroom. On the verandah
is a small table with at least two chairs. There is an electric light, unlit,
and an oil lamp, lit. The bedroom contains a bed under a mosquito net, a
washstand, a bedside table, an electric fan and a 'punkah'. There is a door
to a bathroom off-stage.
A servant,* NAZRUL, *carries Flora's suitcase into the bedroom, and then
retreats to his quarters, out of sight.*)

FLORA
(*Completing the handshake*) Thank you!

COOMARASWAMI
Welcome, my dear Miss Crewe! And farewell! A day of rest!

FLORA
Thank you – you were so kind to ...

COOMARASWAMI
I will leave you! Tomorrow, a picnic! Do you like temples?

FLORA
Well, I don't know ... I'm sure I ...

COOMARASWAMI
Leave everything to me!
(COOMARASWAMI *leaves her, shouting in Hindi for his buggy-driver.
The Shepperton garden is now visible. Here,* MRS SWAN *and* PIKE *are
having tea while occupied with a shoebox of Flora's letters.*)

FLORA

'And in no time at all I was installed in a little house, two good-sized rooms under a tin roof ... with electric light ... (*She tries the electric light switch without result.*) ... and an oil lamp just in case ...'
(*She looks out from the verandah.*) '... a verandah looking out at a rather hopeless garden ... but with a good table and chair which does very well for working ...'
(*She tries out the chair and the table.*) '... and a wicker sofa of sorts for not working ... and round the back ...'
(*She has a brief look around the corner of the verandah where it goes out of sight, while* MRS SWAN *turns a page of the letter.*)
(*Reappearing*) '... a kitchen bit with a *refrigerator*! But Nazrul, my cook and bottle-washer, disdains the electric stove and makes his own arrangements on a little verandah of his own.'
(*She goes into the interior, into the bedroom, where she tries the switch for the ceiling fan, again without result.*)
'My bedroom, apart from the ceiling fan, also has a punkah which is like a pelmet worked by a punkah-wallah who sits outside and flaps the thing by a system of ropes and pulleys, or would if he were here, which he isn't. And then off the bedroom ...'
(*She disappears briefly through a door.*
MRS SWAN *passes the page to* PIKE *and they continue to read in silence.*)
(*Reappearing*) '... is a dressing room and bathroom combined, with a tin tub, and a shower with a head as big as a sunflower – a rainflower, of course ...'
(PIKE *grunts approvingly*)
'... and all this is under a big green tree with monkeys and parrots in the branches, and it's called a duck bungalow ...'

MRS SWAN
Dak bungalow.

FLORA
'... although there is not a duck to be seen.'
(*She disappears into the bathroom with her suitcase.*)

MRS SWAN
Dak was the post; they were post-houses, when letters went by runner.

PIKE
Ah ...

MRS SWAN
I wish I'd kept the envelopes, they'd be worth something now, surely, the Indian ones at least.

PIKE
Oh, but it's the wine, not the bottles! These letters are a treasure. They may be the only *family* letters anywhere.

MRS SWAN
I dare say, since I'm the only family. I like to have two kinds of cake on the go. The Madeira is my own.

PIKE
I'm really not hungry.

MRS SWAN
I wouldn't let that stop you, Mr Pike, if you hope to get on my good side.

PIKE
I would love some. The Madeira. (*She cuts him a slice.*) And won't you please call me Eldon? (*He takes the slice of cake.*) Thank you. (*He takes the bite and gives a considered verdict.*) Wonderful.

MRS SWAN
I should think so.

PIKE
It's the excitement. There's nothing like these in the British Library, you know!

MRS SWAN
(*Amused*) The British Library!

PIKE
The University of Texas has Flora Crewe indexed across twenty-two separate collections! And I still have the Bibliothèque Nationale next week. The *Collected Letters* are going to be a year of my life!

MRS SWAN
A whole year just to collect them?

PIKE
(*Gaily*) The notes, the notes! The notes is where the fun is! You can't just *collect* Flora Crewe's letters into a book and call it 'The Collected Letters of Flora Crewe', I'm not even sure if it's legal where I come from.

MRS SWAN
America?

PIKE
The Department of English Studies, University of Maryland. Luckily, the correspondence of well-known writers is mostly written without a thought for the general reader. I mean, they don't do their own footnotes. So there's an opportunity here. Which you might call a moral enterprise. No, okay, an opportunity. Edited by E. Cooper Pike. There isn't a page which doesn't need – look – you see here? – 'I had a funny dream last night about the Queen's Elm.' Which Queen? What elm? Why was she dreaming about a *tree*? So this is where I come in, wearing my editor's hat. To lighten the darkness.

MRS SWAN
It's a pub in the Fulham Road.

PIKE
Thank you. This is why God made writers, so the rest of us can publish. Would that be a *chocolate* cake?

MRS SWAN
Why, would you ...?

PIKE
No, I just thought: did your sister like chocolate cake particularly?

MRS SWAN
What an odd thing to think. Flora didn't like chocolate in any form.

PIKE
Ah. That's interesting. May I?
(PIKE *takes the next page of the letter from the tea-table.*
FLORA *approaches, accompanied by* COOMARASWAMI, *who has a yellow parasol, furled.*)

FLORA
'The sightseeing with picnic was something of a Progress with the president of the Theosophical Society holding a yellow parasol over me while the committee bicycled alongside, sometimes two to a bike, and children ran before and behind – I felt like a carnival float representing Empire – or, depending how you look at it, the Subjugation of the Indian People, and of course you're right, darling, but I never saw anyone less subjugated than Mr Coomaraswami.'

COOMARASWAMI
We have better temples in the south. I am from the south. You are right to be discriminating!

FLORA
(*Apologetically*) Did I seem discriminating? I'm sure it wasn't their fault. The insides of churches ...

COOMARASWAMI
I understand you completely, Miss Crewe!

FLORA
But I don't know what I'm trying to say!

COOMARASWAMI
That is not a requirement.

FLORA
I'm afraid I'm without religion, you see.

COOMARASWAMI
I *do* see! Which religion are you afraid you are most without?

FLORA
Now, Mr Coomaraswami, turning a phrase may do for Bloomsbury
but I expect better from *you*.
'And I told him about Herbert's lady decorator being asked on her
deathbed what was her religion and telling the priest, "I'm afraid I
worship mauve".'

COOMARASWAMI
(*Thoughtfully*) For me, it is grey.

FLORA
'I'm going to like India.'

PIKE
(*With letter*) Who was Herbert?

MRS SWAN
Wells.

PIKE
Ah. (*Catching on*) H.G. Wells? Really? (*Cautiously*) You don't mean
he and Flora ...?

MRS SWAN
You should see your face. Flora met him not long before she went
out.

PIKE
Out?

MRS SWAN
To India. It must have been round Christmas or New Year. I think
I got a postcard from Paris (*She delves into the shoebox.*) Flora loved
Paris. Here, look ... is that it?

PIKE
Paris, yes ... no, 1924 ... it's a souvenir of the Olympic Games.

MRS SWAN
Oh yes, the hurdler. Flora apologized publicly in the Chelsea Arts
Club. No medals for us in the *hurdles*.

PIKE
Is that *true*, Eleanor?

MRS SWAN
Now, Eldon, you are *not* allowed to write a book, not if you were to
eat the entire cake. The *Collected Poems* was a lovely surprise and
I'm sure the *Collected Letters* will be splendid, but *biography* is the
worst possible excuse for getting people wrong.

FLORA
'So far, India likes me. My lecture drew a packed house, Mr C's
house, in fact, and a much more sensible house than mine, built

round a courtyard with a flat roof all round so I had an audience in
the gods like gods in the audience ...'
(*There is the sound of applause.* coomaraswami *faces the audience with*
FLORA. *It is night.*)
'... and it all went terribly well, until ...'

COOMARASWAMI
Miss Crewe in her wisdom and beauty has agreed to answer
questions!

FLORA
'– and the very first one went –'

QUESTIONER
Miss Crewe, it is said you are an intimate friend of Mr H.G. Wells –

FLORA
'– and I thought, "God, how unfair! – to have come all this way to
be gossiped about as if one were still in the Queen's Elm" –'

PIKE
A public house in the Fulham area of Chelsea.

FLORA
'– but it turned out nothing was meant by it except –'

QUESTIONER
Does Mr Wells write his famous books with a typewriter or with
pen and ink?

FLORA
(*Firmly*) With pen and ink, a Waterman fountain pen, a present from
his wife.
(*There is an appreciative hubbub.*)
'Not that I had the least idea – Herbert showed small inclination to
write his famous books while I was around.'

PIKE
FC had met Wells no earlier than December and the affair was
therefore brief, possibly the weekend of January 7th and 8th; which
she spent in Paris.

FLORA
'After which there was a reception with lemonade and Indian
Scotch ...'
(FLORA *and* COOMARASWAMI *are offered drinks from a tray of drinks.*
They are joined in due course by the questioner.)
'... and delicious snacks and conversation – darling, it's so moving,
they read the *New Statesman* and the *TLS* as if they were the Bible in
parts, well, I don't mean the *Bible* but you know what I mean, and
they know who wrote what about whom; it's like children with
their faces jammed to the railings of an unattainable park. They ask
me –'

11.1 THE NOSE OF KING GEORGE THE FIFTH [31]

Kamaleshwar

Source: Kamaleshwar, 'George Pancham ki Nak' (1960), repr. in Kamaleshwar, *George Pancham ki Nak* (collection of short stories), Delhi: Rajpal & Sons, 1998, pp.9–13.

[Translated from the Hindi by Harish Trivedi for this collection.]

This relates to the time when Queen Elizabeth the Second of England, accompanied by her consort, was about to visit India. The newspapers were full of her. Reports came from the London papers of all the various arrangements which were afoot for the royal visit. The royal tailor was in a quandary about what the Queen would wear on which occasion on her tour of India, Pakistan and Nepal. Her secretary and possibly also a secret agent were to precede her on a whirlwind tour of the subcontinent, for after all, her visit was no joke. As times had changed and the era of sovereigns setting off accompanied by their armies had passed, an army of photographers stood in readiness instead.

Cuttings from the British papers could be seen pasted into the Indian papers the following morning. Reportedly, the Queen had ordered a light blue suit to be made of brocade brought from India. Reportedly, it had cost four hundred pounds.

Queen Elizabeth's horoscope was published. So were the colourful deeds of ` Prince Philip as well as detailed curricula vitae of her servants, chefs, stewards and bodyguards. Even the dogs living it up in the royal palace had their photographs printed in all the newspapers.

There was much ado, much hustle and bustle. A trumpet was blown in England, and it resounded all over India.

The news reports caused a sensation in India. The capital was all in a tizzy. The Queen who descends at the airport wearing a 5,000-rupee suit should

---

[31] In idiomatic Hindi usage 'nose' stands for self-respect, dignity, honour, and is broadly like 'face' in the English phrase 'to lose face' (with the difference that while in English one loses face oneself, in Hindi one's nose is said to be cut off by someone else). Queen Elizabeth II first visited India in 1961, fourteen years after India won independence in 1947, and was only the second British monarch ever to do so after King George V in 1911. Beginning in 1957, a socialist party in the opposition in India had campaigned with notable success for the removal of statues of British figures from public places.

be met with appropriate pomp and circumstance – and perhaps with more than appropriate pomp and circumstance. This was the Queen whose cooks even had distinguished themselves in valour in the First World War, the Queen whose glory and splendour could hardly be described – and this Queen was now coming to visit Delhi.

New Delhi looked at itself and, in the famous words of the Urdu poet Ghalib, exclaimed:

> What grace of God that she should come to my house.
> I now look at her, and now at my house!

And promptly New Delhi began thoroughly to refurbish itself.

No one seemed to order anyone about, no one seemed to notice anyone doing anything, and yet, as if by magic, the roads washed off the dust of ages and grew young again. Public buildings decked themselves up like delicate beauties.

There seemed to be just one little problem, and that was the nose of King George the Fifth. New Delhi had it all, was going to have it all, fully expected to have it all, except for this little difficulty of the nose of King George the Fifth. New Delhi had everything – except the nose.

By this nose hangs a long tale. There had been a time when this nose had stirred up quite a commotion. A political agitation had been launched against it, and resolutions passed by several parties. Funds had been collected, and leaders had got up and given speeches. Hot debates had raged around it, and newspapers had carried whole pages on it. The issue at stake was whether King George the Fifth should be allowed to retain his nose or have it taken off. As happens with all political agitations, some were in favour, some against, and the majority were silent. The silent of course lent strength to both sides.

While the agitation was on, armed guards had been posted to protect the nose of King George the Fifth. How dare anyone get anywhere near it! Similar noses stood high at numerous places all over India, and wherever people could lay their hands on them they had with jubilant ceremony removed them and duly escorted them to museums. A guerrilla war had been waged over royal noses.

Just then a disaster occurred. From the statue on the high pedestal near India Gate in the heart of New Delhi, the nose of King George the Fifth suddenly went missing. The armed guards still stood at their posts and still patrolled all around – while the nose was taken off. King George the Fifth had been denosed.

That the Queen should arrive and the nose still be missing! Here was a cause for worry and anxiety. Action was urgently initiated. A meeting was called of those responsible for running the country to debate what to do.

There was unanimous agreement that if this nose were still to be missing when the Queen arrived, we couldn't be said to have our noses left either.

Consultations were held at the highest level. Heads were scratched and the decision taken that the nose must be had at any cost. A particular sculptor was summoned to present himself in New Delhi at once.

Though this sculptor was truly an artist at heart, he had now fallen on hard times. He came and looked at the faces of all the high officials. A strange kind of worry suffused them, which made some of them look long, some sad and some in a funk. Looking at all of them, the poor sculptor was moved to tears. Just then he heard someone say: 'Sculptor! You've been called here to fix the nose of King George the Fifth.'

The sculptor replied: 'It will be done. But I must first know exactly when this statue was sculpted and where. Where did the stone for this statue come from?'

The officials all looked at each other, as if it was someone else's responsibility to answer. Then, they found a way out. They phoned a clerk and instructed him to conduct a full investigation into the matter. Files of the Department of Archaeology were dissected and disembowelled but yielded nothing. The clerk returned and, trembling, told the committee: 'Sirs, pardon me sirs, but the files have eaten up all the evidence.'

The brows of the dispirited officials were overcast. A special committee was now constituted with responsibility for the nose and with instructions that it simply must resolve the problem somehow or the other. It summoned the sculptor again, who now proceeded to offer a solution. He said: 'It doesn't matter if the stone cannot be identified. I shall go and visit each hill and mountain of India and bring back an identical slab of stone.' The committee breathed again. The chairman proclaimed proudly as they dispersed: 'Is there anything at all which is not to be found in our India? The womb of this country contains everything. We must toil hard to find it but our toil will surely be rewarded, and future generations will live in peace and will prosper.'

His little speech was promptly published in all the newspapers.

The sculptor set off on a tour of all the mountainous areas and stone quarries of India. Some days later he returned disappointed. Looking utterly disgraced and with his head hanging in shame, he reported: 'I have combed each little acre of India but couldn't find a slab of matching stone. The stone must be foreign.'

The chairman flew into a rage and said: 'Shame on you and your way of thinking. We have already embraced all things foreign – customs and manners, way of living, heart and soul. If even ballroom dancing can be found in India, why can't a mere slab of stone?'

The sculptor stood speechless. But suddenly there was a gleam in his eye. He said: 'May I suggest something, sir, on the condition that it must be kept a secret from the press?'

The chairman too now had a gleam in his eye. The peon was ordered to go out closing all the doors behind him. The sculptor then said: 'Throughout our country we also have many statues of our own leaders. If you please, sir, ... what I mean is, ... if any of their noses fits this statue, we could just go and take it off and ...'

The members of the committee each looked at the other. After a moment's initial panic, each eye reflected joy. The chairman said softly, 'But with the greatest possible discretion, of course ...'

The sculptor set off on a tour of the country once again. He had the exact measurements of the missing nose of King George the Fifth. From Delhi he went to Bombay, and there took the measure of the noses of all the leaders – Dadabhai Naoroji, Gokhale, Tilak, Shivaji, Cowasjee Jehangir. He next ran to Gujarat, and assessed the noses of Gandhiji, Sardar Patel, Vithalbhai Patel, Mahadev Desai. In Bengal next, he had a good hard look at Gurudeb Rabindranath Tagore, Subhas Chandra Bose, Raja Rammohun Roy etc., and moved on to Bihar. Passing through Bihar he came to Uttar Pradesh and went round looking at the statues of Chandrashekhar Azad, Ramprasad Bismil, Motilal Nehru and Madan Malviya. Beginning to panic now, he set off for distant Madras, looked at Satyamurthi and others, took in nearby provinces such as Mysore and Kerala and came back up to Panjab, to confront Lala Lajpat Rai and Bhagat Singh. At last he returned to Delhi and confessed his predicament: 'I have now gone and circum-ambulated all the statues of India. I have measured each nose – and each one is bigger than that of King George the Fifth.'

On hearing this finding the committee was greatly disappointed and extremely annoyed. The sculptor tried to console them as best he could: 'I had heard that there stand in front of the Bihar Secretariat statues of the three children who fell as martyrs in the Quit India movement of 1942, so I went there as well to see if a child's nose might fit. But even those three noses proved bigger than the missing one. Now tell me, sirs, what more can I do?'

The capital was now in full readiness. The statue of King George the Fifth had been given a good scrubbing and a fresh shine. Everything was in place, except the nose.

The matter went up to the highest officials again. There was much consternation. If George the Fifth remained denosed, of what use on earth would it be to offer the warmest welcome to the Queen? That would be like having our own noses cut off.

But our sculptor, having fallen on hard times, was hardly one to give up. He now had a most amazing brainwave which he said he could reveal only under the strictest secrecy. So the committee met again behind closed doors and the sculptor put forward his new plan. 'Since it's absolutely essential that the nose be restored, my humble suggestion – er, my modest proposal, sirs – is that out of the four hundred million that we have, a live nose should be cut off and planted.'

This instantly caused a deep hush. After a few moments of silence the chairman looked round at everyone. They all looked perplexed, so after some hesitation the sculptor said gingerly to them: 'But you have no reason to worry. Just leave the whole thing to me. It's my job to choose the right nose. All I need is your permission.'

After some whispered consultation the sculptor was granted permission.

The newspapers reported merely that the matter of the nose had been resolved and the statue of King George the Fifth on Rajpath (till yesterday called King's Way) at the India Gate was soon to get its nose.

Before the nose could be restored, armed guards were put on duty again. The ornamental pond surrounding the statue was drained and cleaned. All the weeds and sediment were taken out and fresh water put in so that the live nose which was to be planted should not dry up. No one of course had the slightest inkling, and all the arrangements were completely hush-hush. The day of the Queen's arrival drew nearer. Meanwhile, the sculptor seemed to be at his wits' end trying to implement the solution he had himself proposed. To procure a live nose he now asked the committee for some more assistance, which was promptly granted. On the condition, of course, that the nose would be in place on an appointed day, well before the Queen arrived.

The appointed day dawned.

King George the Fifth had his nose again.

All the newspapers reported that the nose which King George the Fifth had got was so life-like it didn't look made of stone at all.

But there was something else worthy of note in the newspapers that day. That day, there were no reports of any inaugurations in the whole country. No one had cut any ribbons. No public meetings had been held. No one had been felicitated and there had been no occasion to present anyone with a scroll of honour. No welcome ceremony had taken place at any railway station or airport. In fact, there were no reports or photographs of anyone doing anything at all.

But for the report on the nose, the newspapers were all blank.

One wondered why this should have been so.

After all, only one nose had been wanted, and that too by a stone statue.

11.2   WHO ISN'T AFRAID OF VIRGINIA WOOLF?

Sharad Joshi

Source: Sharad Joshi, 'Who Isn't Afraid of Virginia Woolf?', translated from the Hindi by Harish Trivedi, in *Indian Literature*, 154 (March–April 1993), pp.49–57.

Recently that famous movie 'Who's Afraid of Virginia Woolf?' came to our town. It came to our town after it had run everywhere else over many years, and it was put on for just one show. But that was quite enough. Considering that good movies depart our town even more unceremoniously than Mirza Ghalib had departed the lane in which his beloved lived, it was quite right that this movie should have been put on for just one show. It did draw a good crowd, looking at which the manager of the cinema hall might have felt that he should have extended it for another show. But then there would have been no crowd for the other show. If all the snobs, intellectuals and fans of Elizabeth Taylor in our town were laid together from end to end, they wouldn't fill more than one cinema hall.

It so happened that the day before the show, a rumour suddenly swept the State Secretariat that a couple of secretaries to the government were going with their families to see 'Virginia Woolf'. It all started when a little official entered the office of a secretary and said, 'Sir, if you have the time, shall I come to your bungalow tomorrow with all the pending files? It's Sunday, but just as you please, sir!' The big boss thought for a while, arm akimbo, and then said, 'No, my dear fellow, no, for we're going to a movie tomorrow. What's its name, you know – yes, 'Who's Afraid of Virginia Woolf?'

It was a moment that admitted of a smile. So the little official smiled a little smile. But just then the big boss grew quite grave. He was trying to decide which pose to strike. Keeping in mind the high official responsibility he bore on his shoulders, he could adopt either of two strategies. He could confess that after all he too was a human being and liked to relax once in a while. Or he could pretend that though he himself had long outgrown the puerility of movie-going, he had been prevailed upon and had no choice. He said, 'It's my daughter, you know – she simply insists that I must take her.' He shrugged his shoulders, 'Well, if I must, I must.' After a pause, he looked the little official in the eye and said, 'It's a really good movie, you know.'

The little official, who had the vestiges of a smile still sticking to his face, panicked. He bowed his head and said, 'Yes sir, so I've heard sir. I did hear it's a very good movie.'

'Yes, it has that famous actress, what's her name, Elizabeth Taylor, and the hero – he's a very famous actor too. Ah, the name slips me just for the moment,' the big boss said, and looked interrogatively at the little official.

The little official bowed his head again and smoothed his hair as if trying to jog his memory. Then, a little shame-facedly, he said, 'I'll find out and let you know, sir.'

Without saying a word the big boss reached out for the local English newspaper from a nearby rack, quickly glanced at the advertisements on the back page, and said, 'Richard Burton, yes, Richard Burton.'

'Yes sir, Richard Burton,' said the little official, still abashed, as if the big boss's not knowing the actor's name was all his fault.

On returning from the big boss's office to his own desk, the little official at once phoned Gupta. 'So what're you doing?'

'Swatting flies, that's what.'

'Are you coming to this movie tomorrow – 'Who's Afraid of Virginia Woolf?'

'Who's afraid of what?'

'Virginia Woolf.'

'Trust the bastards to come up with a name like that! No, no, count me out. The missus is fasting tomorrow, *karva chauth* you know, so I'd better hang around at home and help out.'

'Oh, come on feller, everyone's going!'

'Who's everyone?'

'Our boss's going, with the family.'

'Really!' Gupta now softened. 'Is it really a good movie, then?'

In reply, Gupta got to hear the names of Elizabeth Taylor and Richard Burton. That for him settled it. He didn't want to lag behind in any race which his colleagues in the Secretariat were also running. He told Trivedi. Trivedi told Sharma. Sharma shared an office with Das-Gupta through whom Jauhari came to know and also Agashe. In no time each nook and cranny of the Secretariat was abuzz. 'Who's Afraid of Virginia Woolf. Who's Afraid of Virginia Woolf. The big boss is going with his family. Who's Afraid of Virginia Woolf. Elizabeth Taylor, Elizabeth Taylor! Everyone else's going too. Who's Afraid of Virginia Woolf. With family.'

The news filtered down to the offices of the heads of the various departments that everyone in the Secretariat was talking of some English film to be shown tomorrow. Next to know were the deputy directors and the assistant directors. Even the district officers from the mofussil who happened to be in the state capital on some official business or the other decided to join in what all the bigwigs were doing. In the evening it was the topic of conversation in the drawing rooms of numerous official bungalows. By ten in the evening the senior police officers of the city were apprised of the fact that all the top officers of the state were going to see such and such a film at such and such a cinema hall. They let fly some curses, 'Damn it, even on a bloody Sunday then, one'll have to get into the bloody uniform!' It was decided to go for proper security arrangements. Four constables, one sub-inspector and two highly experienced traffic policemen were detailed to report at the cinema hall at nine o'clock, an hour before the show began. They clicked their heels and answered 'Yessir!'

The officers began to arrive. One by one their cars crawled through the gates of the cinema hall. Some came on two-wheelers and some cadging lifts in other people's cars. On sighting the car of the Home Secretary the sub-inspector of police, who'd been swigging a complimentary Coca-Cola in the manager's office, left the bottle half finished and came rushing out. Some lecturers in English got off a bus, bought two-rupee tickets and were about to go in when they saw the deputy secretary in charge of college matters driving in and they stopped. Apprehensive of being transferred out at any moment to colleges at the back of the beyond, these lecturers would have loved to butter up this official on a relaxed and congenial Sunday morning such as this, except that the deputy secretary with his wife made straight for the Commissioner who was standing by himself smoking a cheroot. The lecturers began to talk to some students who had come to see Elizabeth Taylor.

Gradually the crowd grew thicker. Hands were shaken. Wives of officers, all made up and decked up, pulled the streaming ends of their saris round and did *namaste* to each other. The queue lengthened before the counter selling the most expensive tickets, for the balcony. The two district officers who had come to the state capital on some official business were wearing buttoned up jackets and trousers too wide at the turn-ups, and were doubling over bowing despite their protruding paunches. It was for them a divine moment when all the bigwigs were be found together in one place in a relaxed mood, and they could have the opportunity to *salaam* each and everyone. Some of the officers were truly in a relaxed mood but by no means all. On the whole the atmosphere was quite serious and grave. When the Commissioner suddenly laughed out loud at something a secretary had said, it gave everyone a start. Hardly anyone else had been laughing at all. When the two American girls from the Peace Corps began talking to the Director of Agriculture with particular animation and intimacy, they drew the attention of several of the younger officers. When the car of the big boss arrived and he got out with his wife, son and two daughters, everyone stopped talking and looked at them. He went round noticing everyone, shaking hands with some and merely smiling at others, and said, 'When all of us are here to see this movie, it must surely be a good movie.'

A smile lit up all the assembled faces.

The big boss had spent all his life sitting in dark air-conditioned offices. The ten o'clock sun was for him too much to bear. He looked at his watch and said to the Commissioner, 'We still have a few minutes. Why don't we go in and sit in the hall.'

This was the signal for everyone to go in. Some hastily put out their cigarettes and went in, for there was no point in staying out now that the bigwigs had gone in. The queue at the ticket window was still as long because people were still arriving. But now everyone was in a hurry. They all wanted good seats, which couldn't be had, for they were all numbered. On taking their seats everyone looked around to survey the others. Those who had pretty girls sitting in front or behind were talking loudly to each other and laughing at nothing at all. They believed the girls might be impressed by all this. Which probably they were, for they were silly girls all, whose thoughts were of their own dress and appearance, and who had come solely to ogle at Richard Burton and to pick up cute little mannerisms from Elizabeth Taylor.

The movie started. Martha and George are walking slowly back from the party. They enter their home. The first close-up of Elizabeth Taylor comes up on the screen.

'That's Virginia Woolf', Mr Pant the under-secretary whispered to his fat wife.

'Looks no virgin to me!' she said.

'Oh, it's her name, Virginia Woolf. What's that got to do with being a virgin?'

'Then why can't the bitch call herself Mrs Woolf? Why must she call herself a virgin-ia when she isn't one?'

'All right, that's enough,' said Mr Pant, staring hard at Virginia Woolf on the screen.

Meanwhile the wife of the director Ramkaran Jain leaned towards her husband and said, 'To me this play seems quite like *Psycho*.'

'No, it isn't like *Psycho* at all. This is a comedy.'

'But if there's going to be any murder and bloodshed, just warn me before-hand. I'll go out.' She began telling Mrs Gupta sitting next to her how after seeing *Psycho* she hadn't been able to sleep all night.

Mr Moetay is a humorous man. Sitting with Anandaswami and Bansidhar in a little group of their own, he said, 'Say what you like, but this Elizabeth Taylor looks a right old hag now.'

'Yeah, she isn't what she was once,' responded Bansidhar, with the anguish of an old roué.

'O what a stunner she was then!'

'Ai-hai!'

Just then Mehta, the deputy secretary, laughed loudly at something Martha said to George. Mehta had toured Europe twice and once been to America. He could follow English. If he had laughed, it must surely have been at something funny. On hearing him laugh some others laughed too. Some felt sorry at having missed some entertaining dialogue. They pricked up their ears and tried to catch what followed. But soon they tired of the strain.

Of the silly girls all sitting in a row one said to another, 'Oooh, Burton looks so handsome doesn't he!'

'He may to you but he doesn't to me.'

'Oh dear, just look!' the first girl said to a third. 'She says Burton doesn't look handsome to her.'

'Hai!' said she in wonder. 'Does Burton really not look handsome to you?'

'She said Burton looks handsome to her so I said he may to her but doesn't to me.'

'That's not what I said. I just said Burton looks handsome.'

'Same thing, isn't it?'

'How's it the same? I never said Burton looks handsome just to me. He looks handsome to everybody.'

'But the one who looks handsome to this one here is Shashadhar!'

'Shut up!' she said and pinched her.

'Ooi!'

Mr Pai of the Collegiate Branch turned round and gave a severe look to these girls sitting behind him, who were making such a din that he wasn't able to follow the movie. In return the girls stared back at Mr Pai and made a face. Mr Pai turned and looked at the screen. The girls fell silent. The girls were all quiet now but Mr Pai was still not able to follow the movie. Of all the assistants in the Secretariat he was regarded as one of the best at drafting letters and reports in English; even the Chief Secretary hardly ever altered a comma.

It was quite a situation. The movie was in English but none of them could follow the thread of the story. They were all in their way modern. They had all despised their local language and wooed English and with its help fashioned themselves into what they were. But they couldn't follow the movie. Nor could they have walked out. So there they sat looking at each other. Only a tiny proportion of the audience was actually able to follow the plot. All the rest were sitting around hoping that Burton would kiss Taylor again and again. But he wasn't kissing her at all. He wasn't divorcing her, and he wasn't shooting at her. Nothing at all was happening which they had hoped might happen. The movie went its own way mocking at their Sunday best of coloured bush-shirts and narrow trousers. They were all watching the movie. Their big boss was watching it and so were they. Just then a college student got up, thrust his hands in his pockets and leisurely walked out. At this everyone laughed. By laughing they showed that the boy wasn't able to follow the movie while they were.

In the interval they all got up and came out. They drank Coca-Cola and shook hands again. They were all talking in English and sounding very intelligent. Their pronunciation had at once improved. They shrugged their shoulders and waved their hands and spoke fine phrases. To shake off the inferiority complex generated by their not being able to follow the film, they talked and laughed very loudly. One could have been proud of them. Smart, intelligent and sharp, they looked so good with their pretty and modern wives.

As the tension in the movie mounted they grew increasingly appreciative of the acting abilities of Elizabeth Taylor. They were impressed by sheer histrionics – and never mind the words. They watched and waited for the movie to end.

The movie ended. They rose. Their faces glowed. They got up with the contentment of having watched a good film. They didn't look as if they hadn't followed a thing. They were happy. They had got just what they wanted. They came out walking slowly and gallantly giving precedence to each others' wives. As soon as they came out they were galvanized into action. The hour of lunch approached. To delay lunch was against modern manners as well as against notions of acting like a saheb. They climbed into their cars and honked at each other for right of way. The cinema hall precincts soon emptied. The two touring officials from the districts came out last and made for a *poori-sabzi* restaurant.

'This worked out very well, didn't it. We could see everyone. We had *darshan* [were in the gracious presence] of all the big officers at once. And we got some news too.'

'What news?'

Exchanging the latest rumours of transfers in the Secretariat they entered the eating place.

On Monday morning the little official entered the office of the big boss with some files tucked under his arm, said 'Good morning', and asked, 'And how did you like yesterday's movie, sir?'

The big boss remained grave for a while. He considered what to say. He then shrugged his shoulders and answered in English. 'It was a nice movie, of course.'

At lunch the little official told Agashe that the big boss had liked the movie. He had said that it was a nice movie.

In the afternoon everyone could be heard praising 'Who's Afraid of Virginia Woolf?'

'So, how was the movie yesterday?'

And the answer would come, 'It was a nice movie.'

By evening all those who hadn't been able to go to the movie felt very sorry that they had missed something whose praises were being sung by all.

That night Mrs Gupta said to her husband. 'That English film was a ten rupee note down the drain. We should have gone and seen *Padosan* instead or some other Hindi film.'

'But what to do. Everyone else was going, weren't they, so we went too.' He paused for a moment, and then muttered, 'Who is Afraid of Virginia Woolf, indeed! I'll tell you who's afraid of Virginia Woolf. Everyone, damn it, everyone's afraid of Virginia Woolf. But none of the bastards dare bleat, do they!' And he laughed loud and long.

11.3   FROM KALI-KATHA: VIA BYPASS

Alka Saraogi

Source: Alka Saraogi, *Kali-katha: Via Bypass*, Panchkula: Aadhar Prakashan, 1998, pp.109, 192–9, 205–06.

[Extracts from a novel, translated from the Hindi by Harish Trivedi for this collection.]

In the shade of freedom: a post-chapter

Kishore Babu has lived three lives in one. He had led one kind of life till the country won Independence, when he was twenty-two. Then began his second life – a life of full fifty years. This second life did not bear the slightest reflection of the first. Now, in his new third life after his heart bypass, he looks on these later lives as if they were new births. In a way, one could say these fifty years of his life have been rather like the fifty years of the sovereign democratic state of India, which haven't retained even a vestige or sediment, even the slightest lingering flavour, of our fight for freedom.

*   *   *   *

Hum laye hain toofan se kiśhti nikal ke
Is desh ko rakhna mere bachchon samhal ke

[We have steered the ship of nation home through a tempest.
Our children! it's up to you now to look after it]

On the morning before the 15th of August 1997, the fiftieth anniversary of Independence, Kishore Babu heard this old film-song playing on a neighbour's radio. He felt a surge of emotion at these words. His eyes grew moist: truly, how people had suffered to bring about Independence. What courage filled people's hearts then. In those days he often felt he would think himself blessed if he could even touch the feet of those who had laid down their lives for the nation. How proud he was to be a friend of Amolak and Shantanu – both fierce patriots in their own ways, with one worshipping Gandhi and the other Subhas Chandra Bose. And how he reproached himself for being quite useless – and with reason, for wasn't he the grandson of Kedarnath ... who had hated the British, and especially the policeman Taggart.

Only yesterday when reading a book on the history of Calcutta had he found out that the office of the secret police in those days was in Elysium Row, now called Lord Sinha Road. That was where Taggart sat. So he walked to Lord Sinha Road yesterday, following Taggart's trail. He found that the SB, the Special Branch, still had its office in a cul-de-sac off Lord Sinha Road. To examine the old police building closely he walked right up to it. In front of the building in the deserted lane stood a constable with a rifle. He gave the constable a good look and the constable gave him a look too. Kishore Babu moved on. Returning from the dead-end he gave the constable a quick furtive glance. He still stood there facing Lord Sinha Road, just as he had when Kishore Babu had first seen him.

Does his rifle actually have bullets, he wondered. Having come away a few more steps he turned round to look and found the policeman looking at him. He promptly moved on. Having reached Lord Sinha Road, he looked back for a long time at the policeman while he wrestled with a series of questions. If his rifle has bullets in it, what are they for, and if not, why does he stand there with this useless gun? Whyever should he have any bullets in it? Whom would he want to shoot? But then, a gun is not a piece of decoration either. Kishore Babu grew agitated with all these thoughts. Has a policeman with a gun stood here right from the time of Taggart? In those days, of course, there was the apprehension that someone might have come along wanting to shoot Taggart. But is there some officer even now who fears that he might be shot, and has therefore posted this policeman here with that gun?

Kishore Babu stopped and had a cup of tea at a little stall at the corner of Lord Sinha Road. Then he went back and re-entered the lane and stared at the policeman once again as he passed him. The policeman looked at him too, but Kishore Babu could make out that he hadn't recognized him as the man who had passed that way an hour ago. Suddenly it struck Kishore Babu that though he'd been watching this man for over an hour he hadn't found him yawning even once. Doesn't he get bored or tired standing here all day? How can that be? After all, he too belongs to mankind. And just then, Kishore Babu began to panic.

It occurred to him that if he went into that lane for a third time and if the rifle of the policeman had a bullet in it, he would surely shoot him. After all, he must do something to relieve his boredom. For entering the lane repeatedly under suspicious circumstances he would surely shoot him. He recalled many newspaper reports to the effect that a policeman had shot another policeman or himself or his wife. Kishore Babu was now quite convinced that all those shootings had taken place because someone wanted to relieve his boredom. Somewhat perplexed, he returned home.

Back at home, Kishore Babu sat down to watch on Pakistan TV their Independence Day celebrations. For flag, instead of *jhanda* he heard the word *parcham* being used, an Urdu word which had since fallen into disuse in India, and this awakened a host of memories. He had first learnt the meaning of *parcham* through the famous line of the Urdu poet Majaz: *'Tu is anchal se ik parcham bana leti to achchha tha'* ('My love, how much better would it be if you made a flag out of the front of your sari'). What a line, on reading which one's heart swelled fit to burst. He asked the departed soul of his friend Amolak, who had these days become his constant companion, 'Remember listening in those days to speeches by the nationalist Muslim leaders such as Saifuddin Kichlew, Syed Badaruzzaman, Syed Nausher Ali and many others? How handsome were the Kashmiris among them! Such heroes they looked.'

Kishore Babu detected an ironical smile on the face of his son at his watching the Pakistani celebrations, and was very annoyed. 'What can these people know, Amolak, of our common heritage, of our mutual intimacy? All they know is how to brand someone as an enemy.' He thought of giving a stern lecture to his son on the subject but then thought better of it, for that would involve having to say many words. Let it go. What will these people understand of *parcham*? He himself remembered even now a dream he once had in which he'd been running holding the tricolour in his hand, traversing numerous streams and rivers and ravines until he was ready to drop. Just then Amolak had appeared beside him, taken over the flag and wiped the sweat from his brow.

Kishore Babu noticed his son was greatly excited today for some reason. Time and again he would dial the same number. At last, he had to ask him, 'What is it? Is something the matter?' Kishore Babu knew that many jute mills hadn't paid up. No one in business these days seemed to follow any rules. No one wanted to pay up. Some took as long as a year or two to cough up what they owed. In some jute mills the workers had been on prolonged strike. Altogether, he knew, business was in bad shape.

'Meghna Jute Mill's placed its order with us for raw material, hasn't it?' Kishore Babu asked his son. The son was gratified to see that Kishore Babu had after so long shown some interest in the family business.

'Wish they had, Papa. Their *sales department* has *rejected* our *sample*. Their agent wants a big kick-back,' the English words stood out. 'We have of course a *fixed* rate *per cent* as a kick-back for each mill. But this man isn't happy with that – the shrewd and greedy fellow. He says other companies are offering him so much more. Says he won't accept a rupee less than twenty "Gandhis". What can we do?'

Kishore Babu was so acutely embarrassed he wished the earth would part and he sink into it. What would Amolak think to hear of all this bribery? And to hear a five-hundred rupee note called a 'Gandhi', because it had the Mahatma's portrait on it! How this son of his had disgraced him. 'Listen, let me tell you what to do. From now on, you are not paying a single paisa to any sales manager of any mill. Let those buy from us who will – and if they won't let them not. And reduce your price as much as you can, by saving on all the kick-backs.'

Kishore Babu's son just stared at him in utter disbelief. Then he looked away and began contemplating the back of his own hand, the rings studded with a different auspicious stone on each finger. Gone out of his mind, hasn't he. He's showing me the surest way to ruin, that's what. Actually, he's not to blame; it's his Saturn in an inauspicious house. Nor would he wear a ring made out of the shoe of a black horse to ward off the evil, even after so much pleading. But better not say anything today. Best to toe his line for now, the son thought.

'Who were you talking to on the phone just now?' Kishore Babu asked.

'I can't tell you, because I want to give you a *surprise* tomorrow, on the fifteenth of August,' his son answered.

A *surprise* – for him? Kishore Babu wondered. Never before had his son done anything like this. Well, all right, let him carry on in his own way. Just as well I withdrew from the business. Good for me and good for him. Now, I can sit back and watch and reflect on what I should have learnt over the last fifty years. Well, never mind. It's never too late to learn, though. Kishore Babu was pleased at what his son had said. After all, he had to take over sooner or later. He was the only son, and born after so much trouble, too. Just then Kishore Babu remembered he'd been saying something on the phone about three colours.

Very well, then, he could guess now what the *surprise* was going to be. But let him not say anything yet. His heart filled with pride. His son, that is, the great-grandson of the famous patriot Kedarnath-ji, will tomorrow on the fiftieth anniversary of Independence present his father with a tricolour flag. How wonderful! And how busily was he arranging for the flag, phoning God knows whom time and again. How wrong he was to blame this generation for not knowing what *parcham* meant. One must admit that this generation knew very well how to express any sentiments it had for anyone. Look at how many flower-shops had mushroomed all over Calcutta, almost on every street in certain neighbourhoods. When he had come home after his heart bypass operation, everyone in the family had brought or sent him flowers. How moved he had been to see all those flowers. And now the tricolour flag – what a wonderful way of saying it.

What a golden day it was fifty years ago. Truly, a sun of gold had risen on India's horizon that day. He had hired a taxi and taken his mother and his widowed sister-in-law and his own newly married wife Saroj for a drive around. As he bought a tricolour flag and fixed it on the bonnet of the taxi his heart had swelled with enormous pride. Gandhiji himself was in Calcutta at the time. They had all gone to Beliaghata to have a glimpse of him, for Saroj had been very keen to have his *darshan*. He had thought that if he chanced to see Amolak there, he would hug him to his bosom and wash off all the bitterness which had arisen like a wall between them following the communal riots of the previous year. On the roads all along, Hindus and Muslims were embracing each other and all were delighted at the coming of Independence. Slogans of 'Let Hindus and Muslims Unite', *'Jai Hind'*, *'Inqalab Zindabad'* and *'Vande Mataram'* [32] resounded through the city. Along with Gandhiji, the Muslim League leader Suhrawardy had also kept a fast that day. All day Gandhi had sat and spun his wheel.

He could see it all replayed before his eyes like a film. And yes, he had also taken Saroj to show her the Well of Death, in which a stuntman on a motor-cycle went riding up and down and round and round a circular cage. Saroj was a mere child then, just fifteen years old. When people crammed tight into lorries would pass them on the road shouting *'Jai Hind'*, she too would give a cry of joy. Some lorries carried bands playing the anthem of the Azad Hind Fauj: *'Kadam kadam barhaye ja ...'*. [33] She too would begin to hum the tune. At the stroke of midnight, temple bells had rung out everywhere and conches were blown as on auspicious occasions. Was there a soul anywhere that night who wasn't awake and not crying with joy at the country becoming independent! The following morning at eight, to the thunder of seventeen guns being fired, the tricolour had been raised at Fort William. He had held Saroj to his bosom at that moment. All over the city the poor were being fed, in celebration. Amongst the people holding up huge portraits of Mahatma Gandhi and of Subhas Chandra Bose while they danced on the streets, Kishore Babu constantly looked for Amolak and Shantanu. Just then someone passing on the street told them that the gates of the Governor's House had been flung open and the crowd had swept on to the grounds. When they themselves happened to sight an Englishman on the street, both Saroj and his sister-in-law had shouted *'Jai Hind'* at him. He too had laughed and waved back. What a day that was! It was as if a sea of goodwill and cordiality and joy had surged all over Calcutta.

Fifty years on, Kishore Babu is listening to *'Ham layen hain toofan se kishti nikal ke'*, and agreeing that while it had been up to his generation to look after the country then, it was up to his children's generation to do so now. Oh yes, today his son was going to give him a *surprise*. Kishore Babu quickly went and had a little wash and came and sat down in the middle room.

[32] 'Victory to India', 'Long Live the Revolution' and 'I Salute the Mother[land]'

[33] The Indian Liberation Army; 'Let's go marching step in step ...'

Whenever his son came in, that's where he'd find him seated, all ready for him. And where would he put up the flag? On top of the house, of course, so that every passer-by should see it. Suddenly his son came along laughing and bowed down and touched his feet. Kishore Babu was amazed; he hadn't known his son had such deep regard for old values. Truly, he himself in his vanity had been wilfully blind to everything around him. That his son should touch his feet on the occasion of the fiftieth anniversary of Independence was nothing less than the eighth wonder of the world. He blessed him from his heart, 'May you always be happy, may you flourish and prosper.'

His son still laughing presented his closed fist to him, 'Your *surprise.*'

What? Kishore Babu felt a little shocked. Was it such a tiny flag that a fist could hold it? Where would he fly such a flag? Well, he could perhaps just pin it on his shirt then. He smiled again.

'What's in it?' he asked. If he doesn't enact being surprised by the *surprise*, how will his son enjoy it? How strict has he always been with his son – rather like a sergeant-major. He's never played such games with him before. And if he's changed now it's because of the constant presence with him of Amolak.

Kishore Babu softly prised open his son's closed fist. He saw a key in it and was quite taken aback. 'And what's this?' he found himself asking.

'*Freedom,*' his son laughed and said.

'*Freedom?*' Kishore Babu felt very upset. If a mere key could have got us freedom, where was the need for so many people to lay down their lives. He strongly objected to such cheap play with a word like that. Everyone's gone mad in this age of advertising and of using words any which way, for that seems to be the only trick left to create a sensation. An interviewer asks Sunil Gavaskar, 'How do you write with such *flair*?' and Sunil Gavaskar pulls out of his pocket a pen made by a company named Flair and says, 'Because I write with a Flair pen.' His son was now talking to him at the same level. He kept quiet.

'Don't you get it, Papa? This is the key to a Freedom Ford. Come, let me show you,' and he dragged him out to the verandah.

Kishore Babu saw parked in the drive-way a shining new green-coloured Ford car. He nearly fainted. He now recalled that he had read in the newspapers a few weeks ago that the Ford car manufacturing company planned on the occasion of the fiftieth anniversary of Independence to sell four hundred cars especially painted so that together they made up the three colours of the national flag. These would have all kinds of fancy fittings and would be sold at a heavy discount. He remembered that the suspicion had arisen in his mind even then that Ford cars were probably not selling very well. There was fierce competition in the market between different manufacturers, and each was up to some gimmick or the other.

But where on earth had his son found the money? Kishore Babu knew only too well how the family business was doing. There was no way he could have got hold of so much spare cash. In fact, there was even some danger that their factory might have to be shut down. The finished product they sold wasn't paid for for months to come, while the raw materials they bought had to be paid for in advance. There was a terrible cash crunch. They were barely keeping afloat – and now such extravagance.

Without saying anything to his son or even giving him a look, Kishore Babu left the verandah, returned to his room and lay down on his bed. The son followed him, closed the door from inside and stood before him. He was trembling, as Kishore Babu could see. No, he would not shout at him. For what would shouting achieve? How much Amolak's constant company has changed him. Each one of us on this earth is responsible for his own actions and their fruit, for his karma, whether good or bad. All he would do is ask his son two questions. That's all. The first would be: where did you find the money? And the second: why did you have to do it now? Just those two questions. He would not utter a word more.

'Where did you find the money for the car?'

'Papa, I didn't have to go and ask anyone, Papa. They offer one hundred per cent finance now. We'll just pay it off in instalments,' the son rapidly explained to Kishore Babu in a soft but assured tone.

'So you have bartered away your future; you have spent today what you will earn tomorrow.' Kishore Babu had resolved not to say anything, but it was the Amolak seated within him who spoke up.

'Everyone does that, Papa. Even the *government* takes out a *loan* for any big *project*,' the son muttered back.

Amolak couldn't hold himself back yet again. 'Yes it does. And then takes a loan again to pay off the old loan. It takes out a fresh loan of five thousand crore rupees out of which four thousand crore goes to service old loans. If you are unable to pay off the instalments, will you go out looking for another loan to help you do so? And then for another loan to pay off the second one?'

Kishore Babu's son stood silent for a moment. Then, slightly raising his voice, he said: 'Papa, do you have any idea what kind of a world you are living in? You've been cursing me for buying one little car, as if I had bought it just so I could go bankrupt. You don't know what people get up to these days. They float a bogus company and rake in crores of rupees by selling shares. They never set up any factory but manage to get a loan of crores of rupees from the government for doing so. You remember the scandal concerning C.R. Bhansali – well, he was the one who'd helped my friend in Bombay wangle a government loan of two hundred and fifty crores. What are you trying to tell me? That I have committed some terrible sin by buying one measly car costing just six lakhs on instalments?'

Kishore Babu should now have asked his second question. Before that, however, he wanted to tell his son something. 'Do you remember the name of your grandfather?' he asked. The son could see that a string of similar absurd and mad questions would now follow. There was no way of escaping them though.

'Yes, Bhuramal-ji,' said the son, grumpily.

'And the name of his father?'

'Don't know.'

'Let me tell you, then – Kedarnath-ji. And his father's name was Ramvilas-ji. And his father's was Ghamandilal-ji.'

Kishore Babu's son interrupted him to say, 'And what shall I do with this genealogical tree? Had any of these ancestors of mine come to ruin by buying a Ford car?'

Kishore Babu said, 'No. But none of them had ever taken a single paisa on loan except to put into business. I want to explain to you that if we Marwaris have accumulated so much money it's precisely because we never borrowed any money to splash out on our own enjoyment. We never tried to do anyone out of any wealth they had. If a father died in debt, the son repaid in full. And if he could not, the grandson did. Bit by little bit we saved and accumulated. My father kept a strict account of even the match-sticks we used up.'

Kishore Babu's son feared that he would now have to listen to some great tale of miserliness associated with each of his forebears. He said, 'And that's why we Marwaris have such a terrible reputation. It's not for nothing we are called the Jews of India. And let me tell you, Papa, one may have lived in quiet contentment in times gone by but one can't do so any more. Did they have half as many things to buy then? Did they have TV through which to find out how many things there are to buy? Even if one wanted to, one simply can't live on in the past.'

Kishore Babu did not need to ask his second question. The son seemed about to answer it anyhow. 'You spend hours reading every little bit of the newspaper. Just look at the kind of reasons for which people keep killing themselves. Some girl poisons herself because her father couldn't afford to buy for her the kind of *ghaghra-choli* which Madhuri Dixit was seen wearing in her latest film. And do you even notice what's going on all around you? My friend Arun's wife committed suicide just the other day because he hadn't taken her out to dinner at the Taj Bengal to celebrate their wedding anniversary. And nearer home, we all know about our sister-in-law Kanta. Because my cousin couldn't pay for new furniture and a new set of jewellery for her, she took poison just the day before the festival of Diwali. Two of my own sisters are married to husbands who have swank cars. Why should I not wish to have one? Would you like what happened to my cousin to happen to me too?' Kishore Babu's son choked as he said this.

Kishore Babu was shocked out of his mind. 'You mean, your wife ...?' He couldn't say any more.

The son said, 'Now, let's not go into all that.'

Kishore Babu pulled the sheet right over his head.

* * * *

Kishore Babu's wife came to him at ten o'clock at night to begin once again her practice of reading aloud to him from the scripture *Bhagavat-katha*. She must try and calm him down somehow. The car wasn't going to go away now, and if the father and the son stopped speaking to each other, she would certainly feel stifled even if they did not. Some hour and a half into the reading, they came to the episode of the Jada Bharat, the sage who had turned himself insensate.

Remembering how he had been beguiled into the trap of *maya*, or illusion, in his last two births, Bharat decided in his next life to remain utterly insensate. He would not speak with anyone. He lived as if he were a madman. If asked to do something, he would do exactly the opposite. Asked to guard the ripening crop in a field, he called out to passing birds to come and eat it up. For the reason, as he put it to himself, that if he let on how wise he really was, he would only get caught up in the affairs of the world. Someone would honour him, and that would feed his vanity. Someone else would insult him, and that would hurt his pride. It was best therefore to live like a madman. No one expects anything of a madman and no one minds what he does. Someone who isn't mad must watch all the time what the effect will be of anything he says. But a madman can do just what he pleases. He has no one to fear and nothing to beware of. That was how the Insensate Bharat grew to be the healthiest, happiest man in the world.

Kishore Babu's wife suddenly stopped reading, and Kishore Babu wondered why. He tried to think of what she might be thinking. For the first time in all her nightly readings he had come across a character in the *Bhagavat* about whom he wanted to know some more. By stopping, his wife had caused a void.

Kishore Babu was surprised to see his wife closing the book and putting it away. What was the matter? Why was she so restless? His son and daughter-in-law were away, having gone out for a drive in the new car with some of their friends.

'There's a special session of Parliament today at midnight. Let's watch it. It's gone half past eleven. Some of our best artistes will sing patriotic songs.' She switched on the TV.

On TV, so as duly to impress upon the viewers the significance of the occasion, a young woman was speaking half in English and half in Hindi in a voice histrionically overwhelmed with emotion as if she herself were on the verge of tears. Kishore Babu found her antics to work up the sentiments of the viewers so obscene that he averted his eyes. But he did not say anything. He had really taken a fancy to the idea of the Insensate Bharat. Now he would not say anything even to Amolak. He would not say anything to anyone. No one would have the least notion what was going on in his mind.

Trying to make conversation, Kishore Babu's wife now told him that their youngest daughter had said to her that Parliament tonight was going to copy an idea from her own life. 'On her eighteenth birthday, do you remember, her brother-in-law had sent her eighteen bouquets, one of which was as tall as she herself – five feet two. Now one of the biggest soft drink companies in the world is going to advertise itself by installing a fifty-foot tall brass bottle in Parliament House. Everyone will be given a drink out of it and then the bottle will be preserved with suitable com-memoration. Just imagine how much money they must have spent on a fifty-foot tall bottle – one foot for each year, you know.'

As he listened to all this, Kishore Babu saw Lata Mangeshkar appear on the screen somewhat fussily clearing her throat before beginning to sing. At once, something snapped in his head. Perhaps the soul of Amolak had decided now to leave his body. He felt as if Amolak was preparing to go to Parliament House with a big rod in his hand to break up the whole show.

He tried to stop Amolak. 'No, Amolak, don't leave me alone. And listen, Amolak, how can you forget that you are a disciple of Gandhi? How can you do anything violent? Amolak, listen to me.' But Amolak went off, leaving him all alone. Whereupon Kishore Babu with one blow of his fist smashed the TV screen. His hand began to bleed and his wife began to shout hysterically, 'Help! Let's call someone to exorcise him! O Deity of Mehndipur! I'll offer you a huge heap of sweets if Amolak's ghost can be driven out of my husband.'

Kishore Babu doesn't know what really happened. He doesn't even know whom to ask if he actually smashed the TV or not. Is there anyone who will speak with him? He is alone in the world, all all alone. His right hand hurts, but then it's possible he's imagining the hurt. That something did go snap in his head is all he remembers. Why did Amolak leave him? Afterwards, the same doctor was brought in whom he had hoped never to see again. He's probably giving him sleeping tablets, so that Kishore Babu may not ask him any more awkward questions to which he doesn't know the answer, foreign-trained though he is. But the doctor doesn't know that the Insensate Bharat will not ask any questions of anyone, so he has nothing to fear from him. Kishore Babu pulled up his sheet right over his head and repeated silently to himself a couplet from a medieval saint:

The whole world is happy; it eats and sleeps.
Only Kabir is unhappy; he wakes and weeps.

ACKNOWLEDGEMENTS

Grateful acknowledgement is made to the following sources for permission to reproduce material:

Figures

Figures 1.1 and 1.2: Reproduced from Kulke, H. and Rothermund, D. (1998) *A History of India*, 3rd edition, Routledge.

Text

pp.174–83: Jones, W. (trans.) (1984) *The Works of Sir William Jones*, Garland Publishing Inc.; *pp.184–91:* Vinayak Krishna Gokak (ed.) (1992) *The Golden Treasury of Indo-Anglian Poetry*, Sahitya Akademi, Delhi; *pp.225–9:* Taylor, P.J.O. (ed.) (1996) *A Companion to the 'Indian Mutiny' of 1857*, Oxford University Press, Delhi; *pp.240–44:* Tagore, R. (1924) *Gora*, Macmillan India Ltd, by permission of Visva-Bharati; *pp.256–9:* Yeats, W.B. (1989) *Letters to the New Island*, Bornstein, G. and Witemeyer, H. (eds) Macmillan, by permission of A.P. Watt Ltd on behalf of Michael and Anne Yeats; *pp.259–62:* Yeats, W.B. (1961) *Essays and Introductions*, Macmillan, by permission of A.P. Watt Ltd on behalf of Michael and Anne Yeats; *pp.263–7:* Yeats, W.B. (1981) 'Introduction' in *Gitanjali – Song Offerings*, by Rabindranath Tagore, Macmillan India Ltd, by permission of Visva-Bharati; *p.267:* Tagore, R. (1981) *Gitanjali – Song Offerings*, Macmillan India Ltd, by permission of Visva-Bharati; *pp.268–78:* Tagore, R. (1995) *Nationalism*, Macmillan India Ltd, by permission of Visva-Bharati; *pp.278–85:* Vallathol Narayana Menon (1978) *Selected Poems*, Shri C. Achuthakurup; *pp.286–8:* Copyright © School of Oriental and African Studies 1962. Reprinted from *The Evolution of India and Pakistan 1858–1947: Selected Documents*, ed. by C.H. Philips, H.L. Singh, and B.N. Pandey (1962) by permission of Oxford University Press; *pp.294–9:* Thompson, E. (1908) *The Reconstruction of India*, Faber & Faber Limited; *pp.300–09:* Mukherjee, R. (ed.) (1993) *The Penguin Gandhi Reader.* Penguin Books India (P) Ltd. © Navajivan Trust 1993; *pp.310–14:* Premchand (1921), 'Vichitra Holi', *Mansarovar III*. Published by Hans Prakashan, 1988. Translated for this collection by Harish Trivedi; *pp.314–16:* Premchand (1924) *Rangabhumi*. Published by Hind Pocket Books, 1988. Translated for this collection by Harish Trivedi; *pp.317–21:* Norman, D. (ed.) (1965) *Nehru: The First Sixty Years*, vol.2. Bodley Head. By kind permission of The Random House Group Ltd./HarperCollins. © Copyright 1965 by Indira Nehru Gandhi; *pp.322–9:* Antherjanam, L. (1969) 'Childhood Memories', *Cast Me Out If You Will*'. Stree Books. © 1988 of the Malayalam text by N. Mohanan. © 1988 of this English translation by Gita Krishnankutty; *pp.329–36:* Antharjanam, L. (1994) 'A Leaf in the Storm', translated from the Malayalam by Narayan Chandran; *pp.336–45:* Sahni, B. (1994) 'The Train Has Reached Amritsar', translated from the Hindi by Alok Bhalla; *pp.345–50:* Vatsayan, S.H. ('Ajneya') (1994) 'Getting Even', translated from the

Hindi by Alok Rai, in Bhalla, A. (ed.). *Stories about the Partition of India.* HarperCollins Publishers India Pty Ltd. © Alok Bhalla; *pp.351–6:* Manto, S.H. (1987) 'Toba Tek Singh', *Kingdom's End and Other Stories.* Verso. Translated from the Urdu by Khalid Hasan. © Verso 1987 All Rights Reserved; *pp.357–60:* Weston, C. (1948) 'Be Still, She Sleeps', *There and Then.* HarperCollins Publishers; *pp.360–66:* Bond, R. (1994) 'The Man Who Was Kipling' and 'The Last Time I Saw Delhi', *The Best of Ruskin Bond.* Penguin Books India Pty Ltd. © Ruskin Bond; *pp.366–72:* Stoppard, T. (1995) *Indian Ink,* Faber and Faber. Excerpt from Act One of *Indian Ink* by Tom Stoppard. Copyright © 1995 by Tom Stoppard. Reprinted by permission of Faber and Faber, Inc., an affiliate of Farrar, Straus and Giroux, LLC; *pp.373–7:* Kamaleshwar (1998) 'George Pancham ki Nak', *George Pancham ki Nak.* Rajpal & Sons. Translated for this collection by Harish Trivedi; *pp.378–84:* Joshi, S. (1993) 'Who Isn't Afraid of Virginia Woolf?', *Indian Literature; pp.384–93:* Saraogi, A. (1998) 'In the Shade of Freedom', *Kali-katha: Via Bypass.* Aadhar Prakashan. Translated for this collection by Harish Trivedi.

Every effort has been made to trace all the copyright owners, but if any has been inadvertently overlooked, the publishers will be pleased to make the necessary arrangements at the first opportunity.

INDEX

Page numbers in bold are page ranges of numbered related texts